This highly original collection is a far cry from the demand on the literary humanities to offer the soothing hum of theory to a world of breaks, crises and pain. Instead, it exemplifies a way ahead for the critical humanities, by speaking in our faltering, fragmentary, fissive world about crossed lines, suppressed agencies and forbidden dreams.

—Arjun Appadurai
Professor of Media, Culture and Communication,
New York University

'Doing the Humanities' comes to life in this passionate, provocative set of experiments in descriptive poetics. Failure, fantasy, freefall are reconceived as forms of aesthetic achievement across the creative arts: fiction, poetry, cinema, theatre and performance art, painting, photography. A principle of unruly incitement to acts of dissident criticism joyfully (dis)orders the solemn tasking of the humanities in our present age with the work of saving the human and the universe.

—Ros Ballaster
Professor of Eighteenth-Century Studies,
University of Oxford

Humanities, Provocateur bears testimony to the idea that humanistic inquiry is most effervescent when the human condition appears imperilled. The volume inaugurates a discussion about doing the humanities in a manner that cuts through the despair of the present. While the essays joyously feast on the provocations around which the sections of the book are organised, the contributors meticulously disclose a *techné* specific to the work of aesthetics unmoored from predetermined judgement and received tradition. This timely volume inspires a collective undertaking to learn 'to do' the humanities through the untimeliness of a work of art. A humanities that remains attentive to this form of *techné* will prove indispensable to remaking the world in the aftermath of a pandemic.

—Premesh Lalu
Professor of History and former Director,
Centre for Humanities Research,
University of the Western Cape

Humanities, Provocateur was conceived before the COVID-19 pandemic and reframed in its midst—with an eye (at once fearful and realistic) on the enormous challenges faced by the humanities around the globe. Bringing together a variety of dissident traditions, this collection of essays contributes to a growing critical literature in the spirit of Moten and Harney's *The Undercommons*: exhilarating in the democratic breadth of its interests, the emotional fervour of its commitments and its yoking of systemic criticism to the work of poetic language.

—Helen Small
Merton Professor of English Language and Literature,
University of Oxford

HUMANITIES, PROVOCATEUR

HUMANITIES, PROVOCATEUR

Towards a Contemporary Political Aesthetics

Edited by

Brinda Bose

BLOOMSBURY

NEW DELHI • LONDON • OXFORD • NEW YORK • SYDNEY

BLOOMSBURY INDIA
Bloomsbury Publishing India Pvt. Ltd
Second Floor, LSC Building No. 4, DDA Complex, Pocket C – 6 & 7,
Vasant Kunj, New Delhi, 110070

BLOOMSBURY, BLOOMSBURY ACADEMIC INDIA and the Diana logo
are trademarks of Bloomsbury Publishing Plc

First published in India 2021
This edition published 2021

Bloomsbury Academic
An imprint of Bloomsbury Publishing Plc

ISBN: HB: 978-93-88414-91-3; eBook: 978-93-88414-93-7
2 4 6 8 10 9 7 5 3 1

Typeset in Manipal Technologies Limited
Printed and bound in India by Replika Press Pvt. Ltd.

CONTENTS

ACKNOWLEDGEMENTS

As with some edited collections, this one too acquired a life of its own over a long gestation period that took it in different directions from its origin—a conference on Dissident Aesthetics I had organised at the Centre for English Studies at Jawaharlal Nehru University in 2017. I then invited many who were not at the conference to contribute to this volume and, inevitably, my own ideas and intentions morphed along the way. However, I would like to thank my colleagues, student volunteers and office staff for their support during the conference and for the UGC-SAP grant which made both the conference and technical help for preparation of the manuscript possible, and to all the speakers (many of whom travelled from distant lands on their own university funds to be a part of it) who made it exciting and memorable.

Teachers, students, friends and family—many of them fellow travellers on the minefield of the humanities—have contributed in very special ways through a lifetime of trekking through it: both who are, and are not, visibly a part of this volume. I will use my privilege here to name a few, in affection and appreciation. My warmest thanks to—

Al Khoder Al Khalifa, currently my PhD student, bringer of astonishing books and ideas that have expanded my reading and thinking horizons—and sudden flowers, coffee and smiles.

Amal Amireh, mainstay of my graduate school days; sharing books and histories, friends, food, gossip, poetics and English department politics in a very charming, old American city.

Asad Zaidi and Nalini Taneja, whose camaraderie and affectionate encouragement are always heartwarming.

Bhaswati Chakravorty and Swapan Chakravorty, for acute literary insights and raucous adda, art and books, precious family tales and photographs, and the very best Bloody Marys infused with slit green chillies.

Bishnupriya Ghosh and Ishanti Chaurasia, with whom I grew up (and never quite did)—sharing poetry, novels, essays, songs and secrets. Always there for me ever since I can remember, especially through days and nights which are thin.

Christopher Ricks and Emily Dalgarno, supervisors with the lightest of advice, and a steady mentorship that upheld, most of all, the freedom to think.

Geeta Patel, whose sparkling friendship and remarkable scholarship brightens especially the months she spends in Delhi every year.

Kamal Swaroop, whimsical maker of startling images and words, my large-hearted, gentle friend.

Lyndall Gordon and Karina Williamson, who exuded so much warmth and literary knowledge in the English chill, a long time ago.

Michael Levenson, dearest friend and inspiration, formidable and generous scholar of literature, always gracious, caring and reassuring.

Moinak Biswas, for sharpness, wit, understanding and a remarkably textured, felt knowledge of politics and the arts. For his quietly resounding tales of people and places riddled with bon mots—and for his amused, grounded advice.

Prasanta Chakravarty, the keenest reader of poetry I know—from whom I have learnt so much about literature, cinema, politics and philosophy. The chiselling of *MargHumanities* together into varied shapes for five effervescent years was a life-changer.

Rahul Sen, sometime student and excellent friend, fearless forager among the arts and sexualities—with whom I continue to explore, learn, think and grow.

Rimli Bhattacharya and Kumar Shahani, for their warmth, humour, shelter, friendship—and their felt perceptive practice of aesthetics, shared always with grace and ease.

Santasil Mallik, currently my MPhil student and prize-winning filmmaker, brimming with sharp, promising ideas. Also, a hunter-gatherer-provider of quite astounding cinema and essays on literary visualities.

Sarah Dasgupta and Roshan Jila, who effortlessly brought literature to life in the now-distant school classroom, and without whose very early faith in me, I would never have embarked on this journey at all.

Shohini Ghosh, picker-upper of spirits, incisive and delightful scholar of cinema, provider of lightness in being along with razor-sharp persuasions and dissuasions.

Sukanta Chaudhuri and Supriya Chaudhuri, warm, inspiring teachers (and later, friends) with whom—and a few others—my journey in the humanities began at college, and whose sparkling erudition remains a beacon.

In memoriam:

Kajal Sengupta, icon of the free spirited, who taught drama dramatically and strode about life with courage, sharp intellect, humour and spitfire energy.

Lalita Subbu and Sunil Dua, among my earliest colleagues in the teaching of literature in Delhi, and irrepressible companions, both, for delighting in the Moderns.

Subhabrata Bhattacharyya, who gently, generously shared his love of literature and cinema from our college days, till a long time after.

For this book in particular, my warmest gratitude to each of my contributors—Al-Khoder Al-Khalifa, Anil Yadav, Aveek Sen, Charles Russell, Chinmaya Lal Thakur, Eyal Amiran, Geeta Patel, Heidi Grunebaum, Laura Piippo, Michael Levenson, Moinak Biswas, Rahul Sen, Rajarshi Dasgupta, Sophie Seita, Soumyabrata Chowdhury, Taylor Black—for their scholarship, good humour, patience and trust, all in infinite measure. My thanks, also, to my meticulous editors at Bloomsbury, R. Chandra Sekhar and Shreya Chakraborti; to Apala Bhowmick, for her enthusiastic help with preparing the manuscript; to Santasil Mallik, for taking and editing the cover photograph; to Sophie Seita, for letting us use her photograph (in performance at JNU in January 2020) on the cover.

For blind encouragement, and even blinder pride in me, my late parents, Nandita and Subrata Bose. For equally and astonishingly sustained enthusiasm and support every single day, my family—Kinsuk Mitra and Romik Bose Mitra, and Sreeya, Rajika and Rohil Ghosh.

I owe a great deal to many libraries over many decades: the Presidency College Library and the National Library in Calcutta; the Bodleian at Oxford; the Mugar Memorial at Boston University; the Hindu College Library, the Ratan Tata Library and the Central Library at the University of Delhi, the Sahitya Akademi library, and the Nehru Memorial Museum and Library and the Central Library, JNU, in New Delhi. Also, along the way, the British Library in London, the Robarts at the University of Toronto, the Alderman at the University of Virginia, libraries at the Rockefeller Centre at Bellagio and at the Fondation Maison des Sciences de l'Homme in Paris, at Saarland University in Saarbrücken, at Keele University in Staffordshire, at the University of Leeds, and at the University of the Western Cape in Cape Town. Many debts of gratitude have mounted over decades to photocopy shops on campuses, and in recent years to pop-up library sites online.

Hands down, however, I offer my fondest gratitude for books and atmospherics, through many decades, to bookshops on College Street, Calcutta—and not least for the fuelling by familiar, heady fumes at its redoubtable Coffee House, of liquid 'infusion', immersed conversations, and other whiffs, other aromas.

INTRODUCTION

Brinda Bose

To enter this space is to inhabit the ruptural and enraptured disclosure of the commons that fugitive enlightenment enacts, the criminal, matricidal, queer, in the cistern, on the stroll of the stolen life, the life stolen by enlightenment and stolen back, where the commons give refuge, where the refuge gives commons. What the beyond of teaching is really about is not finishing oneself, not passing, not completing; it's about allowing subjectivity to be unlawfully overcome by others, a radical passion and passivity such that one becomes unfit for subjection.... The undercommons is therefore always an unsafe neighborhood.

—'The University and the Undercommons',
Stefano Harney and Fred Moten (2013, 28)

For some relatively independent thought to occur in one's mind, earlier practices need to be oublierred*—to coin a portmanteau word from the French* oublier *and the English* err.

... One effect of oublierring *gives me another imperative: to think of society and the social operations of touching and not touching, but not in a received 'sociological' manner.*

... The purpose behind the way the argument is presented—in style and movement—is to invite you to think along with the argument, with as few intellectual accouterments or paraphernalia as possible. Thinking—adventuresome, and destitute.

—*Practising Caste: On Touching and Not Touching*,
Aniket Jaaware (2019)

Do not be afraid; our fate
Cannot be taken from us; it is a gift.

—*Inferno*, Dante Alighieri (2009, 85)

ম্যাগাজিন শব্দটি আমি লক্ষ করেছি রাইফেল ও কবিতার সঙ্গে যুক্ত

–'বেক্তিগত বিছানা', ফাল্গুনী রায়

> *The word magazine I have noticed is connected with a rifle and with poetry.*
> —'One's Own Bed', Falguni Roy (2019, 12; translation mine)

My inchoate thoughts about the humanities (as) *provocateur* can trace some roots to this framing, by Harney and Moten, of something of a counter-revolution in the university that is 'fugitive' and 'stolen'—which I find insistently seductive. Aniket Jaaware's distinct, remarkable approach to 'caste studies'—thinking through touch and not-touch—is stirring and compelling, as a humanities practice. My thoughts, wayward, also repeatedly return to Dante's *Inferno*: its particular sense of life and its evocations, churning with a terrible—and terrifying—beauty. And in another world and time, to twentieth century Bangla poet Falguni Roy, who pares language down to yoke (by violence) together the un/likely connection between a gun and a poem, the word 'magazine'.

An *agent provocateur* is more than one who is simply provocative: being, rather, one who incites another to break a law and even be punished for it. In English, however, the use of *provocateur* alone may indicate simply provocation. I offer this eclectic collection of essays and whimsies as both a provocation (of passionate, critical thought) and an instigator of (metaphoric, real) law-breaking in the continuing crafting of the humanities, in the university as much as outside of it—through the creation of an 'undercommons'. A certain irascibility that accompanies the sense of a *provocateur* is similar, I would suggest, to the idea of the fugitive and the stolen from Harney and Moten: forming an undercommons which destabilises by instigating ruptures and raptures and aspires to 'the beyond of teaching': becoming 'unfit for subjection' and making up an 'unsafe neighbourhood'. The idea of the unfit and the unsafe, I would like to think, connects methodologically with Aniket Jaaware's idea of 'de-stitution'/destitution (which he pits against 'institution') in the practice of the humanities, outside of a 'received sociological manner': he negotiates the question of caste through the signifier of touching and not-touching and deploys largely the literary method to (re)read a social phenomenon. In doing so, he both touches and does not touch the endemic of caste; and he gives himself the freedom to '*oublierr*'—to forget, and to err—in his peregrinations towards a goal that is also a no-goal.

As the essays are pulled together—untidily, spilling out of any neat dovetails and chain-links—and I try to write up an introduction that will float some anchoring words and thoughts for the collection and yet allow each of the pieces to breathe in their own skins without packaging and labelling, the world has shrunk before one's eyes into isolation chambers and quarantine calendars. As the 'novel coronavirus' of 2020 has spun into a rapid action force, we have sightlessly stared into the heart of a pandemic darkness not seen in at least a hundred years. The spectre of breathless death has begun to haunt global waking and sleeping. Is this a good time to think about what a fugitive humanities might do, to stir up trouble against assertions of a pale goodness and a humane, sanctifying touch, rather to endow it with an anarchic power of its own to shake the world of its complacency and its fears, both equally stupefying? For even as we stare into a Dantesque inferno, we must not, indeed, be afraid—that our fate, our life (a gift, however it may look), might be snatched away from us. The bullet we are staring down resides in the rifle as well as in the poem, as Falguni Roy says with wonder as well as a certain resignation: we cannot allow the word to be muzzled.

The throes of the pandemic have evoked two sets of reactions, mainly, from those yet unaffected by the virus directly and therefore not in hospital queues: one of responsible and calm 'social distancing' and constant hand-sanitising, the other of anxiety and fear and hand-wringing for oneself and loved ones near and distant—and combinations of the two in varying proportions. The terror of a killer virus, spreading across the globe unchecked until an antidote is invented, cannot be underestimated. No current living generation has borne witness to such a calamity, as figures of the dying and dead mount. It is hardly unexpected that there should be a cloud of paranoia, gloom and fatality hanging over each university, school, office, road and park, emptied of people who cower at home before televisions, phones and computers, feverishly, impossibly, tracking an invisible microbe that might choke any life at any moment of a living nightmare.

Susan Sontag had said in *AIDS and Its Metaphors* (following up on *Illness as Metaphor* after about a decade; *Illness* being published in 1978):

> What makes the viral assault so terrifying is that contamination, and therefore vulnerability, is understood as permanent. Even if someone infected were never to develop any symptoms—that is, the infection remained, or could by medical intervention be rendered, inactive—the viral enemy would be forever within. In fact, so it is believed, it is just a matter of time before something awakens ('triggers') it, before the appearance of 'the telltale symptoms'. (Sontag 2001, 135–136)

Contagion, in human understanding, is an apparition of death, both inevitable and irreversible. It shrinks zestful life to pint-size and impels each of us to grasp only at being infection-free, a base life that kills any possibility of dream, fantasy or a soaring creative imaginary.

How can the humanities make an intervention in such a time as this, when life as we have known it is hanging in the balance? And not just for being in the throes of this pandemic either, perhaps. The virus of the spring of 2020 should eventually pass—or become embedded in our lives in mutated forms—leaving whatever disasters in its wake it will. But we are now in an age of disasters, economic and environmental, public and private—and we exist in the continuum of a pandemic named trauma. Will the cosy reputation that the humanities is mostly called upon to bask in—that of being an ameliorating presence, injecting goodness into people and times that are nasty and brutish—do the trick? What can its role be among unprecedented unhappiness and suspicion, when contagion calls for distancing and isolation, while loneliness cries out for the solace of touch? How must it address a world of the fearful and fearsome, when a mere promise of beauty—past or future—teems with woes of inadequacy?

> Praise the mutilated world
> and the gray feather a thrush lost,
> and the gentle light that strays and vanishes
> and returns[1]

writes Adam Zagajewski in 'Try to Praise the Mutilated World' (translated by Clare Cavanagh) and from poetry we can take our cue. Philosophers in the west, circling around Slavoj Žižek and Giorgio Agamben and then Judith Butler, Bruno Latour and Alain Badiou among others, have been debating the call for 'social distancing', a euphemism for sanitising touch to ward off infection, steering through its biopolitical implications for intimacy among individuals and communities, even as this pandemic has unfolded. Panic, as we know, is one of the great contagions of a contagion; on the other hand, killer-contagions must perhaps bear this weight of (their) affliction. The ongoing debate[2]—drawn, of course, from Michel Foucault—between biopolitics, bare life, liberal democracies, capitalism, socialism and a pandemic even as it engulfs the globe from end to end is illuminating, if only for the realisation that it is possible to think beyond modes of immediate and necessary responsibility even in the grip of a crisis—but that there are perhaps limits to what political-philosophical thinking can do.

In 'Clarifications', Giorgio Agamben feeds the controversy he had earlier created when writing on the effects of the pandemic in Italy, by further denouncing the paralysis caused by fear of sickness and death:

> … It is obvious that Italians are disposed to sacrifice practically everything—the normal conditions of life, social relationships, work, even friendships, affections, and religious and political convictions—to the danger of getting sick. Bare life—and the

> danger of losing it—is not something that unites people, but blinds and separates them.[3]

He ends this short commentary by prophesying that the normalising of 'social distancing' will inevitably lead to a world of human desolation, 'wherever possible substituting machines for every contact—every contagion—between human beings'. Setting aside what has been scoffed at and dismissed in his commentaries, one may say that Agamben here is trying to speak like a poet: he is placing a living value not just on 'contact'—but on 'contagion'—between people.

This could well be Zagajewski's 'mutilated world', a world of illness and imperfection; the one the poet exhorts us to 'try and praise'. Much ridicule is being heaped on Agamben, prophet of 'bare life', for stretching his metaphor to swallow up a pandemic; it is true that if one is looking for reason and responsibility from a profound thinker then a counterintuitive suggestion that there might be a richness, if risk, in contamination and fatal disease might appear dastardly by any measure and especially so in the midst of an egregious crisis of existence for all of humanity. On another register, however, one might wonder if this—particularly, this—may not be the time to escape to other imaginations of past and present. Zagajewski's poem is strung on nostalgia and the power of memories of delight and wonder, to sustain one through ravaged times.

> You gathered acorns in the park in autumn
> and leaves eddied over the earth's scars

—the remembrance of ordinary moments of companionship and pleasure are likened to nature's continued commitment to heal its wounds and renew itself in an evocative image, 'leaves eddied over the earth's scars'. Agamben reiterates his scepticism, of the global cry for safety through compulsive sanitisation, in another blog-piece dated 11 May 2020: 'It is legitimate to ask whether such a society can still be defined as human or whether the loss of sensible relations, of the face, of friendship, of love can be truly compensated for by an abstract and presumably completely fictitious health security.'[4]

In *The Adventure* (2018), Agamben's short philosophical discussion drawing upon a story of four Egyptian gods in Macrobius's *Saturnalia* and Goethe's *Urworte*, he lists Demon/Spirit, Event/Chance, Eros/Love, Necessity/Destiny and Hope as the deities that preside over a human being's birth and life and in medieval tales, a knight's *adventure* is signified by chance, destiny, risk and marvel. In the chapter titled 'Eros', Agamben writes on Georg Simmel's entwining of Eros and adventure: 'If Eros and adventure are here often intimately entwined, this is not because love gives meaning and legitimacy to adventure, but, on the contrary, because only a life that has the form of adventure can truly find love' (Agamben 2018, 54). He then turns to Oskar Becker, an early student of Heidegger's, for his 'philosophical theory of adventure' which moves away from his teacher's thought about 'being-thrown' (into a situation or existence, *dasein*, that he cannot escape but also cannot fully comprehend) to its opposite, 'being-carried', a 'lightness' which 'defines the "adventurousness" of the artist's experience' (2018, 55). Becker sees 'adventure' as

> the condition of an existence—such as that of the artist—that is placed in between 'the extreme insecurity of being-thrown and the absolute security of being-carried'.... It is significant here that the artist takes the place of the knight as the subject of adventure. (Agamben 2018, 56–57)

It is the artist, therefore, who must rise from being-thrown and continually move towards being-carried, ideally hanging between the two existences, never certain about whether life will hand out only tough lessons—but ready to meet them head on with a certain ambivalent confidence. Adam Zagajewski is perhaps the gentler poet—'being-thrown' rather than 'being-carried', accepting mutilations as inevitable: though offering nostalgia as panacea, a possibility by which to heal, a leaf to eddy over a scar. Denise Levertov in 'Goodbye to Tolerance' is more of the other; contentious, more welcoming of wounding, angrily discarding those who seek or offer healing in past perfect.

> Goodbye, goodbye,
> I don't care
> if I never taste your fine food again,
> neutral fellows, seers of every side.
> Tolerance
> What crimes are committed in your name,

writes Levertov, singling out 'genial poets' and 'good women' as the enemies of the full, difficult life she hails. She is dismissive of

> weak hearts, perfect pulses that never
> falter: irresponsive
> to nightmare reality,

and sets the parameters for a renewal on her own terms which will not be a palliative but a challenge:

> We shan't meet again—
> unless you leap it, leaving
> behind you the cherished
> worms of your dispassion,
> your pallid ironies,
> your jovial, murderous,
> wry-humored balanced judgment,
> leap over, un-
> balanced? ... then
> how our fanatic tears
> would flow and mingle
> for joy ...

In the 'nightmare reality' of a pandemic—the one right here, and the others that lurk for coming generations—the intrepid poet commands that one should 'leap it' and 'leap over, unbalanced'—to steal a fugitive future, and discover 'how our fanatic tears/would flow and mingle/for joy...'

Both Zagajewski and Levertov, perhaps on different paths, play *provocateur*, one gently and sadly, asking that bodily infliction be folded into praise of the world and the remnants of living be illumined by the perfect, passing memory; the other commanding that a sense of affliction be discarded altogether for a rapturous mingling of 'fanatic tears' and 'joy'. Harney and Moten invite us to tread intrepid paths, 'on the stroll of the stolen life', ruptured and rapturous at once. Jaaware dares us to be 'adventuresome, and destitute', as we push on with our reading and thinking and to sculpt the material to our method as much as the method to our material. Dante plunges us into a fiery hell, but exhorts us not to fear that what is ours will be taken away from us. And Falguni Roy reminds us that an apocalypse waits to leap from a poem as much as a rifle. Across and between them lies the task for the humanities, perhaps—at once to retrieve and to relinquish the wound that our present continually inflicts upon us and then to be defiant, fearless—weeping and exalting, exalting and weeping.

GLEANING

> How odd is it that words seem like a necessity and a consolation while at the same time they are an anchor, a deviation, a source of incomprehension ... I believe in stuttering, in speech torn to pieces by its own thorns and brambles. I believe too in a total and absolute truth that is perfectly inexpressible. (Pajak 2019, 22)

Frédéric Pajak, Swiss-French writer and graphic artist, launched in 2012 his 10-volume *Uncertain Manifesto* (written in French) of which the seventh was published in 2018. An English translation of the first volume, by Donald Nicholson-Smith, appeared in 2019. Walter Benjamin stands at the shifting core of this tale made of art and words, recalling as if the beginnings of all our readings and gleanings; Samuel Beckett and the artist Bram van Velde also appear. Pajak is not overly interested in archiving histories of event, but more, like Benjamin's archetypal rag-picker, in ferreting out bits and pieces of language and thought that are lost in heaps of words and in them discovering, discerning, the glint of gems. This is the best we can do—should do—with inherited knowledges, he seems to tell us as he accompanies Benjamin through his fitful travels, loves, experiments and writing and nails them all with brooding, black-and-white drawings that often dominate the pages, leaving his words small, poignant.

'Benjamin's method', says Pajak, 'was to combine the scraps of thought that he had collected as so many quotations; this meant not producing a theoretical treatise but rather offering thought a new path to follow by reconstructing it from fragments' (2019, 149); earlier in *Uncertain Manifesto*, Pajak delineates his own method, against a dark charcoal sketch of a heaving sea:

> This morning, the sea is replete. Just a trace of saliva, enough to lap tenderly at the beach … to write and draw as the mood takes me. And to read, or rather reread enormities, contemporary or not. Read, and live. And share a little of what I read, of what I live, and why, and how. (Pajak 2019, 83)

This is what we are doing in our essays here, and what we wish them to do going forward through our readers: not to produce a 'theoretical treatise' but to 'combine scraps of thought' to offer newer paths to thought; to write and draw and watch and read 'as the mood takes' one; to 'read, or rather reread enormities, contemporary or not'; to read and live and share a little of what one reads and lives—and how, when and why.

How would one hold 'enormities' to ransom, though, if we are to think in terms of fragments of event, slips of memory and scraps of thought? The trick may lie in rereading enormities: in taking them apart, in pulling them off pedestals, in deconstructing and reconstructing them, as well as in replacing them with the miniscule, the dispensable, the incomprehensible. But not just that, either. By enormities in scholarly, artistic and archival resources we mean an immeasurable quantity, nothing that any of us singly can cover, endorse or dismiss. We each seek and hold close the sources that move us and make us think. We adore them and argue with them. As long as we engage with them, they are our special 'enormities' and we make good our investment by conversing with them in some form or other.

We are not compelled to satisfy each one about our curiosity or our criticality as long as we have something to say and a democratic space to say it in. We do not have to prove our understanding of an entire body of work to draw upon what of it draws us in. We may engage with it how we will, in whatever form or length we wish, creatively or cryptically. Like Benjamin's rag-picker, this anthology travels to different, disconnected locations to pick at what arrests our thoughts in the humanities at a point of time. Here they are strewn before you, some ideas and words that seemed precious to us, drawing upon the 'enormities' luring us there. Like Benjamin's rag-picker, we hope that our readers will be drawn to this collection and will find something in it that will want them to linger and to hold. Essays are gleanings, in their execution and in their reception too, we hope; may the harvest, lean or full, be a rich one.

And gleanings being traces, they remain with us, invisible, embedded. They re-surface like ghosts, as if to sit by the bedside of other dying souls and ideas, offering succour, however depleted and pitiable. Jibanananda Das, modernist (and sometimes surrealist) poet of Bengal (1899–1954), in the poem 'Komolalebu'/'Orange' from his famed collection *Banalata Sen*, asks to float back after death with a slice of orange to the bedside of a dear one, carrying one sorry bit of fruit as offering:

একবার যখন দেহ থেকে বার হয়ে যাব
আবার কি ফিরে আসব না আমি পৃথিবীতে?
আবার যেন ফিরে আসি
কোনো এক শীতের রাতে
একটা হিম কমলালেবুর করুণ মাংস নিয়ে
কোনো এক পরিচিত মুমূর্ষুর বিছানার কিনারে।

—'কমলালেবু' (*বনলতা সেন*)

Once when I have left this body
shall I never come back to earth again?
May I come back again
on some winter's night
bearing the miserable flesh of a chilled slice of orange
to the ebbing bedside of some familiar one.

—'Orange' (from *Banalata Sen*; translation mine)

In a strange—but not morbid—way, this could be every artist's spectral return, over and over, bearing the work s/he has made—'the miserable flesh of a chilled slice of orange'—to the bedsides of those who are dear, precious, known and unknown. The slice of orange is imbued with contradictions, it is a miserable and sad piece of fruit and yet it is chilled and therefore possibly alluring to a hot and flushed brow and throat, bringing relief and sustenance from the love it signifies. Gleanings, pickings, traces, remainders: these are the metaphorical, miserable slices of oranges offered to each of us from all we see, hear and know, when we are at a high or low ebb. Perhaps unlike T.S. Eliot's 'Lazarus, come from the dead, come back to tell [us] all',[5] these slices of orange—our essays—will never have entire tales to tell or answers to offer for our 'overwhelming questions' but they will spark thought, ignite ideas and bring back forgotten insights. The story of Lazarus came to haunt Eliot's *Prufrock* from the Gospel of St Luke in the New Testament, when a rich man in Hades begged Abraham to send the poor, dead, good Lazarus across the chasm to dip his finger in water and cool his parched, burning tongue and then send him to earth to warn his brothers of their imminent fate in Hades. But our fate is a gift, as Dante has said, and no one can 'tell us all': that is not what is meant for us at all. We can only stab at wisps and webs that float around us, some within grasp and some without, to enhance those discernments accrued to our piecemeal knowledges.

Two entries in the entrancing *Drafts for a Third Sketchbook* by Max Frisch read:

> Am I very attached to life?
> I am attached to a woman.
> Is that enough?

and

> I'm not ill, or I don't realize I am. What's got into the words? I'm shaking sentences, the way you shake a broken watch, and take it/them apart, spending time it doesn't show. (Frisch 2013, 23)

The two apparently unrelated utterances come together to claim an urge for life and love and language. What is enough? How much attachment is enough? What will make us shake the broken watch of our ill bodies, 'spending time it doesn't show', to seek another minute, an hour or a day? What do we do with what we learn from life and its inevitable sorrows? Gerard Manley Hopkins caught this moment of waning strength and glimmering knowledge in 'Spring and Fall':

> Ah! ás the heart grows older
> It will come to such sights colder
> By and by, nor spare a sigh
> Though worlds of wanwood leafmeal lie;
> And yet you wíll weep and know why.

In 'worlds of wanwood leafmeal lie' lies the deepest sadness a young girl can first encounter, the knowledge of a world that will eventually become pale and fragmented; it needed coined portmanteau expressions—'wanwood', 'leafmeal'—for Hopkins to convey such a quiet and devastating realisation. This is the 'Fall' that Margaret grieves for, a fall that denotes autumn, Adam and Eve, and leaves actually dropping from trees all at once. 'Spring and Fall' is unrelentingly despairing, and yet in its weeping and knowing has an ethereal, exquisite grace—even an incomprehensible solace—that soars beyond the mere mourning of passing seasons and lives.

PERFORATION

> I have been a swallower of lives; and to know me, just the one of me, you'll have to swallow the lot as well. Consumed multitudes are jostling and shoving inside me; and guided only by the memory of a large white bedsheet with a roughly circular hole some seven inches in diameter cut into the centre, clutching at the dream of that holey, mutilated square of linen, which is my talisman, my open-sesame…. (Rushdie 1981, 11)

Salman Rushdie's Indian-English novel of 1981–1982, *Midnight's Children*, is anchored not so much in all those known and unknown Indians born in the country's hour of freedom from colonial rule as the title indicates, as it is by the spectre of a perforated bedsheet. This 'mutilated square of linen' brings a fragmented vision: first, one can only see part of a whole through it, and second, one is also, perforce, seeing partially: hence the one who seeing is also compromised by never being allowed to see anything other than (in) fragments, and the world is never complete to him. In the first chapter, titled 'The Perforated Bedsheet' and through his novel, Rushdie wrings dry the metaphor of hole and whole, inside and outside, partition and fragment. In a bizarre tale set in spring in the Kashmir valley that opens *Midnight's Children*, Aadam Aziz, grandfather of the novel's protagonist Saleem Sinai and a Heidelberg-trained young doctor with a mythically distinct nose, is called for a house visit to treat the landowner's daughter who is sick.

Rushing over, Doctor Aziz discovers that protocol would not allow even a doctor to violate maidenly modesty; a bedsheet with a seven-inch hole would therefore shelter her entirely from his gaze, while the perforation would be placed against the specific part of her body that was ailing, for him to examine.

As days progress, the landowner's daughter has many ailments, and Doctor Aziz is repeatedly called upon to examine various parts of her anatomy through the perforation in the bedsheet, which, nevertheless, continues to separate them. He gains 'insider' knowledge of her body—if only superficially, in parts and under strict surveillance—while remaining an outsider to her as a person. Yet he falls in love with her; it is almost inevitable that this introduction to the young Naseem Ghani is alluring, clearly more so for being less than complete. So Saleem Sinai, born momentously along with a new nation and its partition upon the midnight of 15 August 1947—who becomes a snot-nosed breathing metaphor for its struggling new life—traces his origin to the perforated sheet that was instrumental in his grandfather's impulse to marry the young woman hidden behind it, thus to beget a lineage of big noses. Curiosity, intrusion, intervention, secrecy, prudery, allure, romance, genealogy, history, illness, diagnosis, life, death: these, and more, are signified by a 'holey, mutilated square of linen' which is a 'talisman' and a 'open-sesame'. What is it that opens with that hole? Knowledges incomplete, talismanic.

A perforated bedsheet creates consternation but offers numerous im/possibilities. If torn with intent, it signals a way of the undercommons, something from outside and below sneaking up and in to spy, gain knowledge, perhaps even offer a salve. If rent by wear and tear, it still allows a window to the covered and unknown; meanwhile, the bedsheet for all its state of indecency remains a barrier to complete transparency and mingling. If a perforation provokes curiosity and daring—even, or often, about the ordinary and mundane, made extraordinary by the veiling—the (remaindered) sheet sustains and thwarts it, dictating how one may 'know' it. And while there may be a glimpse, touch or smell of the attraction, parts of it that are inaccessible are the most tantalising of all. Rushdie's extended metaphor of the perforated bedsheet may be deployed to think about the ways of art that are different, either banal or deemed dysfunctional, exhibiting signs of mental or physical sickness: here represented by Naseem Ghani's mysterious (and mysteriously shrouded) ailments. The characteristics of 'perforation'—arousing curiosity and desire by conscious distancing and identifying in a distanced/veiled object an aura which it may either possess or have to be imaginatively endowed with—would work to extract singular tones and meaning in its critical appraisal. The trope of the outsider looking in has been continually reworked and reimagined in art, literature and politics, almost as much as the insider reporting to the world outside from the trenches of experience.

On 'Outsider Art', derived from the twentieth century painter Jean Dubuffet's French formulation 'Art Brut' ('Raw Art'), Colin Rhodes writes,

> It is seductive whether visible to a wide audience, or hidden from view entirely, and in this sense possesses a tantalizing and fragile presence … [which] grew out of Surrealism's interest in phenomena that lie outside individual prejudice and expectations and in the commonplace of experience … their enigmatic life. (Rhodes 2000, 22)

Art by the clinically insane was of particular interest to Dubuffet; Surrealism too thought of madness as a sign of freedom, a subversion of the oppressive everyday. Outsider Art extended itself to all transcendental or metaphysical worlds, representations that lurked beyond the real; the wall between the real and the imagined, however, was perforated, and art and artist existed on both planes at once, or interchanged them. This 'swallowing' of lives outside of one's skin and across a divide—of linen or iron—and the consuming of multitudes that swarm and jostle within one, take unforeseen and astonishing shapes in creative, critical and political forms of aesthetics.

In a conversation with Mark Foster Gage, Jacques Rancière explains his perception of the political as aesthetic: 'The aesthetic problem is not at all about beauty. It is about the experience of a common world and who is able to share this experience. For me, politics is aesthetic in itself, and in a sense, was constituted as such before art' (Rancière and Gage 2019, 10). Rancière thus distinguishes between 'making' art as something consciously 'beautiful' and a democratic experience of the aesthetic that emerges organically from the ground and is encountered as pleasing, moving, enraging, embittering, joyous or sorrowful. In *Proletarian Nights*—whose original title, when published in 1981, was *Nights of Labor: The Workers Dream in Nineteenth Century France*—Rancière studies factory workers in their moments of leisure and finds in them poets and artists and music-makers. It does not allow for them to escape the days of labour which make for the politics of class, but the nights imbue their lives with a political aesthetic, as he says in his preface:

> those nights wrested from the normal sequence of work and sleep. They were imperceptible, one might almost say inoffensive breaks in the ordinary course of things, where already the impossible was being prepared, dreamt and seen: the suspension of that ancient hierarchy which subordinates those dedicated to labour to those endowed with the privilege of thought. They were nights of study

> and intoxication, and days of labour prolonged to hear the word of the apostles or the lectures given by teachers of the people, to learn, to dream, to talk or to write. They are Sunday mornings begun early so as to leave for the country together and take the dawn by surprise.[6]

In holding this other life of the workers up to light, Rancière wishes to exhibit not only the rupture between a worker's hands and eyes, as he says in his interview with Gage but also the arbitrary disruption between two kinds of human beings, one of which belongs to the working class (2019, 12). A proletarian night 'of study and intoxication' is aesthetic even as it is political.

A corollary of this is also true: the aesthetic can be political in and of itself. It is a mistaken commonplace that for art to be truly political, it must avow an agenda and some propaganda. The political nests within art; it may be retrieved by drilling a hole through its aesthetic form but in fact it ceases to be art when ideology serves as its envelope or a frame or an emblem-embossed, colour-coded cover. Viktor Shklovsky, described as both a patriarch and *enfant terrible* of literary Formalism who introduced the concept of *ostranenie*—'of making the habitual strange in order to re-experience it'—to critical vocabulary about art, says in his essay 'The Links of Art Do Not Repeat Each Other…': 'Art is not a way to console… Art is a way to reveal and renew reality… it's closer to its source than its shadow is to the object which conceals part of the ground from the sun' (Shklovsky 2017, 324). In another essay titled 'A Sentimental Journey' (1923), in which he digs up memories of the Revolution in Russia from 1917 to 1922, he declares, 'Art is, at its heart, ironic and destructive. It animates the world. Its task consists in creating inequalities. It creates them through comparisons' (2017, 150). What, then, about a politics—endemic then to Russia—that highlights inequalities, and goes to work on them as manifest ideology? What about an art that weaves in and out of such political lives and commitments, passions and estrangements?

Alexandra Kollontai (1872–1952)—Marxist feminist revolutionary, member of the Bolshevik government of Russia in 1917–1918, diplomat and writer who advocated 'free love' just as she believed that the family would 'wither away' when the state would take over and stamp out social inequality in the 'revolution to come'—constructs a complex tale of human intimacy, love and betrayal in the early era of Russian Communism in a compelling short story, 'The Loves of Three Generations' (1929).[7] Straightforward, with no flourishes of style or emotion, Kollontai tells of three women—grandmother, mother, daughter, each a torch-bearer both of the Communist ideology and 'free love' that the author held aloft—as they resolutely make their way through many a dilemma about the many men they cherish and fight for, fight alongside, fight against. Finally, faced with her daughter Genia's bewilderingly cold-blooded approach to the lover they end up sharing, Olga Sergejewna is more aghast at Genia's nonchalance about her passion than the fact that it is her own man that her daughter has slept with: 'Without warmth, without even the most elementary feeling for one another, without the goodness of heart that places the feelings of those one loves above everything else ... is that Communism?'

This conflation of (free) love with Marxist political ideology is pivotal to loving and working honestly and fiercely, pronounces Olga stoutly in the short story: one cannot love less, let alone coldly or with disinterest. After Genia's casual sexual relationship with Andrei, she is contrite at the thought that her mother, whom she loves to distraction, may have been hurt. This, to her, is infinitely more significant than her dalliance with her mother's partner, and for which she is willing to immediately sacrifice the man whom she insists means nothing to her; instead, she proclaims:

> And there are those I love—oh, how I love them.... Not only mother ... Lenin, for instance. Please, don't smile. I love him more deeply than any one of those whom I have liked for a passing moment. When I know that I am to see him, that I am to hear his voice, I am absolutely beside myself for days.

This easy transference of devotion from lover to political leader and idol intricately complicates the idea of free love in Kollontai's story.

That is why, to Genia, her love for her leader Lenin is at par with romantic love. That is why her adoration for her mother, a dedicated and efficient party worker, can casually cancel out her (perhaps unthinking) sexual intimacy with her mother's man. It is important that there is no dilemma in Genia over the choices she makes at different points of time; only her political commitment is steadfast, akin to the most loyal of loves. What does the political mean, on such a canvas? What does communism mean to love, or love to communism? Is this Kollontai's own avowal of loyalty to the men who led communist Russia around the time of the revolution?

If the short story indicates such, Kollontai's manifesto of 1921, 'The Workers' Opposition', records her strong critique of Lenin's leadership. (Kollontai's changing politics around feminism through her life is fascinating: she opposed early Russian feminism that focused on what she saw as individual and elite freedoms, constructed a new feminist politics that challenged Lenin's misogyny when she became a part of the Bolshevik government at the time of the revolution of 1917, working for abortion rights and communes for mothers at work, among other issues—but later in life no longer championed feminist causes at all, moving on to other concerns.) In the manifesto, first published in the well-known Russian magazine *Pravda* in January 1921, she writes:

> The masses are not blind.... The workers may cherish an ardent affection and love for such personalities as Lenin. They may be fascinated by the incomparable flowery eloquence of Trotsky and his organizing abilities. They may revere a number of other leaders - as leaders. But when the masses feel that they and their class are not trusted, it is quite natural that they say: No, halt! We refuse to follow you blindly.[8]

Kollontai as a sometime feminist and lifelong political thinker is quite riveting: if one places her fiction (usually dismissed) alongside her political writings, one glimpses the contradictions and convictions of a woman's intrepid communist life lived avidly in the throes of arguably one of the grandest revolutionary movements in world history.

CAPRICE

> Lifting belly.
> How are you.
> Lifting belly how are you lifting belly.
> We like a fire and we don't mind if it smokes
> Do you. (Stein [1989]1995, 2)

Gertrude Stein wrote *Lifting Belly*, a fifty-page long avant-gardist-lyrical paean to her love, Alice—with a refrain, 'lifting belly', quixotic shorthand for lesbian pleasure—between 1915 and 1917. *The Autobiography of Alice B Toklas* by Stein is flagged as an experiment in composing an ambiguous life-story of one's own with a companion's signature, doubling up as a tribute to the companion which traverses many boundaries of voice, history and belonging effortlessly, politically; not very well known is her prose-poem *Lifting Belly*, however, that cavorts in regions of language and body and astounds for its sheer tactility and word acrobatics. It is likely that Stein's extravaganza, catching the sexual with words—without using any sexual words at all—has made many of her readers uncomfortable. Stein brings the sexual into the everyday and that is what makes many squirm. Rebecca Marks, Stein's lyrical editor, writes evocatively of this power:

> By associating lifting belly with the details of everyday life—sandals, candles, figs, salmon, pencils—and with events, people and places all over the world—Geneva, Barcelona, the Battle of Verdun, the King and Queen of Montenegro—Stein creates a universe of lifting belly. Lifting belly is not lesbian sex, over there in the closet, hidden in bed, away from the public eye. Lifting belly is lesbian sex in the world, participating, relating and transforming everything it encounters. Lifting belly is a language. Lifting belly is an occupation. Lifting belly naturally celebrates. Lifting belly eroticizes, incarnates everything it touches. (Stein 1995, xix)

Stein's friendship with Pablo Picasso is said to have inspired her attempt to write cubist prose and poetry, of which *Tender Buttons* was perhaps her most spectacular achievement, though *Lifting Belly* also exhibits some of those angularities along with its lyricism. Meanwhile, the regular Paris evening salon at 27 rue de Fleurus—home of Gertrude, her brother Leo and later Alice—was regularly attended by stars of the literary and art world including Picasso, Hemingway, Fitzgerald, Apollinaire, Joyce, Pound, Tzara, Braque and Matisse. In fact, it was claimed by Stein in *Autobiography* to be the address at which cubist art was birthed—because of those who attended her soirees and how she collected and arranged their paintings on her atelier walls—to the artists' collective outrage. 'Yet', writes Earl Fendelman,

> there was more than vanity in it, for what she believed the paintings expressed was a new theory about aesthetic perception, one which demanded that the artist, the object, and the audience be drawn together in a unified reality.... Believing this, she could see her placing of the paintings side by side as a seminal act, an expression of the same art of juxtaposition that played so large a part in early cubist work and which provides a direct analogue for much of Stein's own practice in her verbal portraits. (Fendelman 1972, 481–482)

This rather naughty and delicious claim of Stein's was publicly denounced in 1935 by the artists Braque, Matisse, Tzara and a few others who frequented her salon, in a pamphlet titled *Testimony Against Gertrude Stein*, published as a supplement to a journal, *Transition*. While their wrath at Stein's nonchalant audacity was possibly justified, their somewhat childish tirades against her airy exaggerations and fictions in the assumed voice of Alice Toklas hardly wrapped them in dignity. The *Testimony*, instead, becomes a testament to Stein's overwhelming personality in every aspect of her life—as friend, lover, host, patron of the arts, art collector, bon mot dispenser—and possessor of an exuberant pen and a fervent imagination that often compromised facts for the sake of glorious technicolour. An incensed Matisse wrote of Stein/Toklas's *Autobiography* in his *Testimony*:

> Her book is composed, like a picture puzzle, of different pieces of different pictures which at first, by their very chaos, give an illusion of the movement of life. But if we attempt to envisage the things she mentions the illusion does not last. In short, it is more like a harlequin's costume the different pieces of which, having been more or less invented by herself, have been sewn together without taste and without relation to reality. (Braque et al. 1934–1935, 8)

The image of the harlequin works quite famously for Stein in spirit if not in appearance and thumbs its metaphoric nose at the sudden, late, collective disdain of artists who had thronged her home. Her radical experiment with autobiographical writing—talking really about the life she conjured up and lived, in the voice of her companion Alice—is as much an example of the zaniness of her creative energy as are writings as diverse as *Tender Buttons* and *Lifting Belly*. In *Autobiography*, Alice recalls one of their dinner parties when she was seated next to Picasso: 'After a while I murmured to Picasso that I liked his portrait of Gertrude Stein. Yes, he said, everybody says that she does not look like it but that does not make any difference, she will, he said' (Stein 1933, 14). Certainly Stein was a chameleon-writer, if one were to extend Picasso's drollery about her person to include her pen.

> The sister was not a mister. Was this a surprise. It was. The conclusion came when there was no arrangement. All that time that there was a question there was a decision. Replacing a casual acquaintance with an ordinary daughter does not make a son. (Stein 1914, 65)

—in *Tender Buttons*, Stein ruffled up some gender trouble well before it was a gleam in Butler's eye. For Alice in her love-lyric, she wrote:

> Lifting belly. Are you. Lifting.
> Oh dear I said I was tender, fierce and tender.
> Do it. What a splendid example of carelessness.
> It gives me a great deal of pleasure to say yes. (Stein [1989]1995, 3)

Completed by 1917, here was a testament that was saying yes to 'fierce and tender' (lesbian) pleasure, a good handful of years before Joyce's Molly Bloom made 'yes I said yes I will Yes' a refrain for a woman's claim to joyous sexual abandonment among the flowers and among the Modernists.

PARAPHERNALIA

Two of Bengal's maverick artists—filmmaker Ritwik Ghatak and sculptor-painter Ramkinkar Baij—captured in their work much of that which was decadent, poverty-stricken and resplendent in India, before and after its independence and partition in the middle of the twentieth century. Ghatak left behind an unfinished documentary on Baij which he was shooting in 1975 in Santiniketan ('abode of peace') that housed Visva-Bharati, the university Rabindranath Tagore founded and where Baij taught. Ghatak passed away in 1976; his son Ritoban later stitched together the footage Ghatak had collected over four days of continued shooting and made it available on YouTube.[9] This is a priceless peri-documentary, more moving and 'immediate' for being amateurishly edited and sub-titled, which is also a constant reminder that it is not the film we were meant to watch—and yet, we are grateful for the gems it offers us.

That machines big and small aid us and fail us, that life and death are games of the body that energise and sap us incessantly, are of no particular shock. Documentary footage offers us the sights and sounds of Ghatak walking with Baij under a bristling sun around 'Kala Bhavana' (the arts complex of the university), stopping at Baij's sculptures placed in abandon on the greens and at the intricate murals on university buildings that he produced with other artists and students, the two of them engaged in conversation, banter and laughter. It provides not just insights into one artist's provenance enabled by another but a frangible sense of how perilous all art is, how driven the artist is, how his tools are both unique and contingent, and how the display, preservation and archiving of art is entirely unpredictable.

Baij worked on his sculptures with found materials, mixing concrete, cement, sand and clay and produced a scabrous, unfinished texture of work-in-progress that spoke gruffly but warmly to the stories he was trying to capture. 'Mill Call' (1956), a sculpture of a factory-worker-couple with a child rushing towards the rice mill as the morning whistle sounds, has figures with cloth streaming behind them. Describing his sculpture to filmmaker Ghatak on camera, Baij earnestly explains that since the coolies don't get time to dry their clothes before they have to get to work very early, the woman's saree flying after her dries in the breeze as they sprint to make it to the mill on time (6.24–7.00 minutes, documentary footage). In the rough tenderness of the sculpture's material, in the tale behind the cloth that streams after the running figures and in the picture of graceful flight that they present, a story of poverty, labour and love is erected. Baij was artistically and emotionally invested in the Santhal tribal families of the neighbouring district; this was continually reflected in his sculptures. In answer to an interviewer's comment that '-most of [his] work relates to the Santhal natives of Birbhum', Baij reflected,

> Yes, maybe. They are toilers ... they work ... they have active hands ... in the sun ... under open light ... flowing unkempt hair ... oozing sweat. They feel hunger. They suffer ... they have sorrow ... they are poor. (*After some silence*) They are very active. I love activity of work ... Rhythmic ... active life.
>
> ... They offer richness of form. (Baij 2010, 17)

It is the richness of form that Baij explored, as did Ghatak, fellow maverick, and both produced art in and from 'found objects' well before the term acquired its prominence in aesthetic vocabulary. Asked whether he would make a self-portrait, Baij replied laconically, 'Whatever an artist creates, is his self-portrait' (2010, 18). He recalls how the 'blue earth' that is exposed after heavy rains impelled him to pick up handfuls and start kneading them into figurines (2010, 46); many of his sculptures on the grounds of the Visva-Bharati display this grey-blue sheen in the cement and concrete he used, mainly because he could not afford more durable materials like bronze. The famous Bengal monsoons also made him put his art canvases to other, immediate uses. In a conversation in the documentary footage, Ghatak asks Baij about the paintings that he has hung from the eaves of his home to plug rainwater dripping from his roof; Baij laughs ruefully and replies,

> Yes—the large oil paintings I hang below the roof facing downwards. They won't be harmed, you see, as they are oil colours. I hang them there because of the rains.... I have got the roof partially repaired, but not fully. Now because of the exhibition I have to bring the canvases down—then what will I hang in their place? [Laughs loudly]. Then with the little money I have, I will have to buy some straw! But I need money for food as well ... so how will I make ends meet? [laughs again]. (27.10–28.28 minutes documentary footage; transcription into English mine)

'Kinkarda', as he was known affectionately, never lost his energy and delight in making art, and making life, with whatever he possessed, saw and found. The energy, most of all, was ferocious. He recalled a piece of spine-tingling advice he received from Rabindranath Tagore, once when working on a portrait of the poet who was also his mentor:

> He looked all around to check if anyone was listening.... Then he leaned forward, and said to me, Look, when you see something [you wish to draw], just spring like a tiger and grab it from behind, twist the neck in a stranglehold, and never look back.... —This is the last word. (17.34–18.15 minutes documentary footage, transcription into English mine.)

Ritwik Ghatak, his filmmaker-interlocutor, also had strong words about art and the artist. In 'A Scenario', published in 1974, Ghatak sketches a 'mad', 'drunk' director after his new film has been rejected:

> The director should feel isolated from his medium of expression...
>
> At the end the man should emerge as a hero with all his fallacy.
>
> When he is absolutely alone and on the verge of suicide he is offered an alternative.
>
> He has to leave all art work and go away into some lonesome spot to earn his living. He accepts.
>
> He goes to the spot. Nature is beautiful around him and he falls in love with it.
>
> It seems that a happy ending is in view. But that is not to be.
>
> He tears up the landscape with his own hands, literally.
>
> And then there is the atomic explosion turning the seawater into a huge mushroom. (Ghatak 2000, 103)

Here is an apocalyptic vision, in syncopation with the artist as both creator and destroyer, as magnificent and maleficent. It is not that well-worn elegy about how humans have ruined and misused the bounty of nature, either: it is about taking the object of artistic desire by the scruff of the neck as a tiger does its prey, and by wringing it, tearing it up—'literally'. And then finding an outstanding piece of art at the end of it, a gigantic explosion that overwhelms one like the tsunami it must be, bearing the blood and toil of hands, eyes, machine, brush, colour, camera and concrete.

DESCENT

In *The Queer Art of Failure*, Judith Halberstam (2011, 2–3) writes,

> Under certain circumstances failing, losing, forgetting, unmaking, undoing, unbecoming, not knowing may in fact offer more creative, more cooperative, more surprising ways of being in the world. Failing is something queers do and have always done exceptionally

> well; for queers failure can be a style, to cite Quentin Crisp, or a way of life, to cite Foucault, and it can stand in contrast to the grim scenarios of success that depend upon 'trying and trying again'.

Samuel Beckett's words in his short, characteristically cryptic, prose piece *Worstword Ho* (1983) are often quoted, sometimes to offer some faint encouragement in the face of disappointment and hopelessness at failure: 'All of old. Nothing else ever. Ever tried. Ever failed. No matter. Try again. Fail again. Fail better.'[10] Beckett queered the idea of achievement as success, making 'fail again' and 'fail better' aspirations instead. Failure, Beckett seemed to imply, was sharper than, deeper than, more intelligent than success. Halberstam pushes to theorise failure as queer, adding to Moten and Harney's 'Seven Theses' for 'stealing from the university' in *The Undercommons* (cited earlier) and finding ways to turn to 'subjugated knowledges' (Foucault's term), in three succinct directives: '*Resist mastery*, *Privilege the naïve or nonsensical*, *Suspect memorialization*' (2011, 11–15). Looked at through such a lens—success then being that which desires mastery, privileges the mature and sensible, valourises the past and/or nostalgia—it seems as though Halberstam offers a formula for raising the ante of the humanities and digging for 'knowledges from below'.

Hervé Guibert, French writer, photographer and journalist, was an intimate friend of Michel Foucault's, whose final days he recorded in a book, *To the Friend Who Did Not Save My Life,* which shot Guibert to fame on its publication in 1990. Guibert died of AIDS in 1991 at the age of 36, two weeks after a failed attempt at suicide. Perhaps all of his life's work in photography, diaries, journals and thinly-disguised fiction were exercises in suspecting memorialisation (even while he wrestled with it) and failing again, failing better. His book on photography, *Ghost Image* (published posthumously), has no photographs, and carries at its start, and heart, a wrenching tale of how he laboured to get his mother to pare down to her more natural look he loved, to photograph her—undoing her coiffed hair and making her change many dresses—only to discover that he had not put the roll of film correctly into its slot in his camera and so finally had not a single photograph of that long, fervent, devoted effort: 'That blank moment (that blank death? since one can shoot 'blanks') remained between my mother and me with the secret power of incest. It had imposed a silence between us. We never spoke about it, and I never photographed her again' (Guibert 1996, 15).

Many years later, when his parents were moving house, he got a fleeting chance to re-enact that earlier moment of perfection with a camera aimed at his mother—

> and at that very moment my mother's face suddenly, unexpectedly, relaxed, rebelled, miraculously resumed the expression I had given her during our first session. Through the viewfinder, in the space of an instant, my mother became beautiful again. It seemed that she was trying to convey to me a message of her sadness. (1996, 15)

But can one recreate perfection exactly the way it was? Guibert does not seem to think so; in her resumed beauty his mother had now conveyed her sadness.

> So this text will not have any illustrations except for a piece of blank film. For the text would not have existed if the picture had been taken.... For this text is the despair of the image, and worse than a blurred or fogged image—a ghost image.... (1996, 15)

In some ways, a text is always the despair of the image, as Guibert repeatedly discovers in his many journals and memoirs, grappling with writing homo/sexuality and death together—and bringing to it tragedies of memory and photography. He does it with raw energy and desolation at once, capturing the wildly sexual spirit of an age now already far distant. In *The Mausoleum of Lovers*, Guibert writes:

> One could say that photography, a certain photography is a very erotic practice: this way of almost fondling the subject, encircling it, modifying its attitudes, but more than anything maintaining a distance from the idea that the camera is magic and infernal, that the disposition of the lenses and the machinery make of it an object of extreme power.... The secret of the other shall be my secret. And this face which stares at me can very well decompose: it is already dead. (Guibert 2014)

The AIDS epidemic of the late twentieth century has been resurrected in the fear and stigma invoked by the novel coronavirus pandemic in the twenty-first century; if one had assumed that it was its identity as 'the gay disease' that had caused HIV/AIDS to be so reviled, our current crisis reveals a universal terror at the spectre of death by touch—any touch at all, this one carrying an invisible killer microbe from fingertip to lung. The last couple of decades have also been marked, perhaps globally, by a slow-rising revolt against the lure of the hedonistic—in life, in love, in desire and in death—as a backlash against the rock-and-roll years that germinated in the West from the late 1960s and leached into the spirit of that century everywhere, till it turned. It is not surprising then that a simmering moral pandemic has ignited into a glowering fire fuelled now by a morbid virus, particularly across middle- and upper-class communities whose members are the most able to implement minute measures for safety, and are also the most risk-averse, secretive and self-conscious in loving and living. In sharp contrast are Guibert's fevered remembrances of his dying friend Michel Foucault (whom he calls Muzil) in *To the Friend Who Did Not Save My Life*, as he describes how an ill and coughing Foucault was still ecstatic and energised by a tryst with pleasure and death on a visit to San Francisco.

> Muzil adored violent orgies in bathhouses.... In the autumn of 1983, Muzil returned from his seminar with a dry cough that was tearing his lungs out and slowly wearing him down. Between fits of coughing, however, he was eager to report on his latest escapades in the baths of San Francisco. That day I remarked to him, 'Those places must be completely deserted now because of AIDS.' 'Don't be silly,' he replied, 'it's just the opposite: the baths have never been so popular, and now they're fantastic. This danger lurking everywhere has created new complicities, new tenderness, new solidarities. Before, no one ever said a word; now we talk to one another. We all know exactly why we're there.' (Guibert 1991, 21–22)

Though the words at the end are similar to current exhortations calling for 'new tenderness, new solidarities' to launch a humane fight against an inhuman virus, it is clear that his dying friend's exuberance vouches instead for catapulting into an orgasmic end; and it is hardly a surprise then that Foucault (and Derrida too, for other, but related, reasons) have fallen out of favour with intellectuals of our day who task themselves with the saving of humanity and the universe sentimentally and ecologically, systematically draining them of danger, daring and fantasy.

FLUX

Wayne Koestenbaum wrote perspicaciously of Hervé Guibert's 'unbridled, impatiently probing eroticism':

> The discourses engulfing AIDS were precisely the languages of wound—of contamination, filth, and mistake—that he'd already been plumbing and relishing, vocabularies he obtained from Genet, from the données of the French language, from Barthes and Foucault, from looking in the mirror, from his camera, from pornography, from his crazy great-aunts, from his mother who wiped his bottom until he was thirteen years old, from his

> father who punched him in the jaw. The rhetorics of wound and of abjection that nourished him and that formed the nucleus of his sexual *imaginaire* were then drowned out and ventriloquized by the mythologies of AIDS; Guibert already spoke the lingo of Wilde's Dorian Gray before AIDS rewrote Wilde and took him on as its untimely echo. Guibert investigated sexuality; a private eye, working for no government, he sleuthed with a rare ferocity and candor. Premature death cut off the investigation.[11]

Guibert was sexuality's *agent provocateur* of the past century, one among many illustrious names. Wilde, Genet, Foucault, Guibert—among others—constitute a lineage that forged a queer art of writing failure and death, straddling two centuries. Love and desire remained at the core of it, across sexualities. Al Alvarez, literary critic, novelist, essayist and poet, caught it, like the sharp spark of sunlight on an upturned mirror, in 'Catharsis':

> It is the tenderness you feel you know
> You may have had the tenderness you miss.
> … Your eloquence will flow
> Beyond the measure pacing your distress
> Till it breaks down the limits of your care
> And finally you relish what you seem
> And are to your last sense all you forgo.
> Love. The particular. No more no less.

Alvarez's renowned study of suicide, *The Savage God*, was birthed of his friendship with Sylvia Plath, who, along with Virginia Woolf, remains in readers' memory as a luminous symbol of one who knew more of the flux between life and taking one's life than one might ever wish for. And yet, as she writes in her poem 'Kindness',

> The blood-jet is poetry,
> There is no stopping it.

The blood-jet of poetry ricochets continually between heart and body, there is no stopping it—revealing and hiding, exploring and considering what it is, what it wants to expose and what it yet is driven to conceal, also a death-risk and a death-wish—all rolled into one. Revelations and secrets dance as if through a minefield of life and death together, as Jacque Derrida's analogy of the hedgehog on the road in 'Che cos'è la poesia?'/'What is Poetry?' captures in a fraught, tensile image:

> It sees itself, the response, dictated to be poetic, by being poetic ... an imparted secret, at once public and private ... the animal thrown onto the road, absolute, solitary, rolled up in a ball, *next to (it)self*. And for that very reason, it may get itself run over, *just so*, the *hérisson*, *istrice* in Italian, in English, hedgehog. (Derrida 1995, 289)

What does 'being poetic' mean, in embodied terms? It is the whatness of the hedgehog thrown onto the road, in that moment of being 'absolute, solitary, rolled up in a ball'—and 'for that very reason, it may get itself run over, *just so*'—both the essence and the sum of 'being poetic'. It is the moment of heightened life, of imminent danger, of inevitable death; it is that moment of swinging wildly between all of these states and being suspended between them, tumescent and throbbing with an energy that is keener for the possibility of being extinguished, '*just so*'. One is reminded of Marvell's impassioned exhortation in 'To his Coy Mistress':

> Let us roll all our strength and all
> Our sweetness up into one ball,
> And tear our pleasures with rough strife
> Through the iron gates of life:
> Thus, though we cannot make our sun
> Stand still, yet we will make him run.

Marvell's extended metaphor is, as has been said, intensely sexual and visual; his lover in the poem invokes solitariness as the most fearful proposition imaginable, pleading with his coquettish beloved to roll their combined energies and romantic love into 'one ball' that will hurtle them through the battles of life. Derrida's hedgehog rolls into a ball to protect its (solitary, but teeming) energies—perhaps its life—when thrown onto the road and at that very moment lays itself bare to death, *just so*. But then Marvell's tearing pleasure will lead to *la petite mort*, an orgasmic death. Nothing at all remains, finally, but the pendulum that swings between desire and death and brief moments of life hanging between, rolled up into a ball: the sum total of 'being poetic'.

This totalling, this rolling up into a ball, is marked, however, by heterogeneity and flux. Simone Kahn, Surrealist poet, gives an account of a game invented in 1925 by André Breton, Yves Tanguy, Jacques Prévert, and Marcel Duchamp during one of their regular hangouts in Paris. It was a version of the one known as 'Consequences': each of them added phrases to a rolling narrative to make up an absurd story. It later took on a new—bizarre—title from a prompt that Prévert provided at the start of a round of play, 'Exquisite corpse', which was followed by the phrase 'will drink the new wine', the conjunction arousing shouts of delight from the players. Sometimes they used pictures instead of words: each would draw a body part, starting with the top of the head. The paper would be folded before it went to the others in turn, who would then add face, neck, torso, hip, thigh, knee and foot—belonging to any living species, and often with wild embellishments. When the sheet was unfolded, a surreal creature would have taken shape.

Breton's *Surrealist Manifesto* had been published a year earlier in 1924, which had suggested that one way of probing psychic depths was by playing games—and clearly, playing 'Exquisite Corpse' with words or pictures was one such raucously creative, collective experiment. Kahn writes in *Surrealist Women*:

> It was an *unfettering* ... we were sure of getting an astonishing amalgam. Violent surprise provoked our admiration and sparked an insatiable passion for new images: images unimaginable by one brain alone—images born of the involuntary, unconscious, and unpredictable combination of three or four heterogeneous minds. Some sentences assumed an aggressively subversive character. Others lapsed into excessive absurdity.
>
> ... the game became a system, a method of research, a means of exaltation as well as stimulation, and even, perhaps, a kind of drug.
>
> ... From then on, it was a delirium.

Indeed. Heterogeneity, collectivity, subversion, amalgamation, absurdity—the idea of 'an unfettering' that could be delirious and subversive at once was claimed by the Surrealists as their own, of course, but it has seeped through many movements of the arts through centuries, if not always as rambunctiously. Undoing the fetters, letting the flux in (and out), allowing nothing to crystallise into permanent shape and size, sound and feel: in the words of Walt Whitman in 'Song of Myself', 51,

> Do I contradict myself?
> Very well then I contradict myself,
> (I am large, I contain multitudes.)

FLESH

We think of how flesh lives and dies, the flesh and bones and blood of the artist and audience, and the paper, texture and colour of the book, canvas, film screen. We think of touch and tenderness, of death and remembrance. We think of dead bodies charred, of ashes, of pages and paintings crushed and faded and crumbling. How does living flesh—in humans, in art—merge with the ravaged and the dead? How are stories of flesh and blood interred; how do they metamorphose from life to death to after-death, how are they fed and resurrected and received?

In the third volume of a set of fictional memoirs, *Summertime* (2009), J.M. Coetzee moves into phantom territory uncharted in the first two volumes (*Boyhood* 1997 and *Youth* 2002), by now imagining himself dead. A segment of his own life is painstakingly reconstructed by a biographer—an Englishman named Vincent—who interviews significant women, colleagues and others who crossed his life between 1971 and 1977, tracing leads from the writer's 'notebooks' of those years that he accesses to (re)discover secrets of his shrouded past. In creating this wrenching girdle that encircles not only an autobiographical yet fictional narrative, he also conjures up a novelistic framework that continually airs emotions recollected in tranquillity as a writer's masquerade, truth and dare and fiction jostling for space on each page. A literary experiment juggling memory, fact and imagination, Coetzee pulls off in *Summertime* a palimpsest of rare sharpness, terror and beauty—not really about a writer at all, but about writing. The book peels layers off its protagonist (the writer John Coetzee) through transcribed interviews with many who were intimate with him, interviews that are almost entirely unsympathetic to him though woven through with a throbbing immersion in the man they each knew well for a stretch of time. In doing so he experiments with a new form of fictional memoir or autobiography, one that is critical from the outside looking in—or rather, imagines and then mimics those looking critically, in recollection, at the person they knew closely for some time. The very sense of a memoir is thus dismantled as it moves through different registers of fact and fiction—as if flesh falls off from the bone, literally and metaphorically.

Coetzee's *Summertime* is proof that a writer is obsessed about being remembered for the writing—as a dancer for the dance and a painter for the painting—and this desire to be enshrined in a piece of creative work sits ever uneasily with a deep fear of being a person who is ordinary, who loves and loses, is loved and lost. When the flesh disintegrates, the book will remain ... or so every writer wishes. Says Adriana, a Brazilian woman in Cape Town where John Coetzee (of the fictionalised memoir) was her daughter's teacher and who was sexually attracted to first his student and then her mother:

> You know the word disembodied? This man was disembodied. He was divorced from his body. To him, the body was like one of those wooden puppets that you move with strings. You pull this string

> and the left arm moves, you pull that string and the right leg moves. And the real self sits up above, like the puppet-master pulling the strings. (Coetzee 2010, 198)

This is echoed by James Joyce in *A Portrait of the Artist as a Young Man*, a sketch of one who is a puppet-master of an imagined universe: 'The artist, like the God of creation, remains within or behind or beyond or above his handiwork, invisible, refined out of existence, indifferent, paring his fingernails' (Joyce 2005, 249)—this 'disembodied'-ness is also a sense that Coetzee perhaps inherited strongly from the Moderns, an idea that the artist is quintessentially disconnected from his own body and its sensations, as well as from all other bodies it comes into contact with.

And what of the ultimate disembodiment then—death? The body dies, the body lives on both in spirit and another shape in poetry, art, photographs. In *Dying Modern*, Diana Fuss talks of the 'corpse poem', born, she says, of a frustration with elegies, and the limits of mourning. Can a poem be, or become, a corpse? She compares Emily Dickinson's[12] corpse poems to Paul Celan's. Dickinson writes:

> A word is dead
> When it is said,
> Some say.
>
> I say it just
> Begins to live
> That day.
> (Dickinson, 'Life: LXXXIX')

Fuss says then, 'Writing in the shadow of mass extermination, Paul Celan, one of Dickinson's European translators, contradicts his predecessor's faith in the afterlife of language:

> A word—you know;
> a corpse.
>
> Come let us wash it,
> come let us comb it,
> come let us turn
> Its eye heavenward. (Fuss 2013, 75)
> (Celan, 'Nocturnally Pursed')

Celan here no longer has faith in the immortality of language, not even in poetry. Word itself has become a corpse that must then be washed and made ready for its journey to the afterworld. And yet the corpses, strung together to make poetry, have remained on the pages of the books they went into, still and quiet, yet darkly raging. For Celan too, of course. So many of his poems simmer and splutter with angry grief, but burst with a life force even at moments of and after death, moments of 'impossible mourning' as Derrida called Celan's tussles in poetry with the sense of continued and repeated loss. In the wrenching 'Death Fugue', the chant-like cadence of 'black milk ... we drink you ...we drink you' leaves one breathless and mesmerised at once:

> Black milk of morning we drink you evenings
> we drink you at noon and mornings we drink you
> at night
> we drink and we drink
> A man lives in the house he plays with the snakes
> he writes
> he writes when it darkens to Deutschland your
> golden hair Margarete
> he writes and steps in front of his house and the
> stars glisten and he whistles his dogs to come
> he whistles his jews to appear let a grave be dug
> in the earth
> he commands us play up for the dance
>
> (Translated by Pierre Joris)

Celan captures the ruptures in language—the very flesh of communication—through language itself, sharply, like that jab into the earth for the burial of the dead. Anne Carson says, 'Paul Celan is a poet who uses language as if he was always translating. [...] Strangeness for Celan arose out of language and went back down into language' (Carson 1999, 28). This is an acute observation; he works the feel of the alien into his poetic language, so that his words and phrases embody the sense of disaffection that the very use of language brings to any attempt to express thought and emotion. He carries the weight of this estrangement, this inadequacy, this fracturing and this death to his poetry, which slides like a razor into butter: 'Black milk of morning we drink you evenings....' In this jab that draws blood from the reader, the word rests in power.

Binoy Majumdar (1934–2006), a nonconformist Bangla poet who was, for a while, a part of the Hungryalist movement in Bengal in the second half of the twentieth century before he had differences and left the group, affirmed the grace of the word in books even while in hospital for mental illness.

কলমটি হাতে নিয়ে হেঁটে গেটে গেছলাম আমি।
গেছলাম প্রাকৃতিক দৃশ্য আর নরনারীদের দেখতেই।
এভাবে না দেখে আমি লিখতে পারি না।
দরজায় দেখলাম পুরুষ ও রমণী অনেক
রোগীদের একবার দেখতে এসেছে।
আর হাসপাতালের দারোয়ান চাবি হাতে
দাঁড়িয়ে রয়েছে।
রজনী যে বলেছিল 'পৃথিবীর সব বই ভুল' সেই
রজনীও দাঁড়িয়ে রয়েছে
আমার ধারণা বই ভুল নয় সব।

('কলমটি হাতে নিয়ে')

With the pen in my hand I had walked down to the gate.
I had gone for a glimpse of nature and all the men and women, only to see them.
Without seeing them thus I cannot write.
At the door I saw men and young women, many
had come to see some patients for one visit.
And the hospital gatekeeper with key in hand
was standing there.
Rajani who had said 'All the books of the world are wrong' that
Rajani too was standing there
I have a feeling that all the books are not wrong.

('With the Pen in My Hand', translation mine)

What the poet, in all his despair and madness, affirms is the integrity of the word and the book, even as corpse and coffin. Nature, men and women, the hospital gatekeeper with key in hand and the night—they are all still standing around, waiting—and even as the (woman named?) Night says all the world's books hold no lessons to be learnt, the insane poet speaks from the gut: he does not agree that all the books are wrong. Indeed, perhaps only the books are at least partially, temporarily, contingently, right. So much so that when men and women have become old and finally corpses, separated in life as in death, it is the word in the book that keeps them fused, promises Majumdar:

... যখন দুজনে
যুবতী ও যুবক ছিলাম
তখন কি জানতাম বুড়ো হয়ে যাব ?
আশা করি বর্তমানে তোমার সন্তান নাতি ইত্যাদি হয়েছে
আমার ঠিকানা আছে তোমার বাড়িতে,
তোমার ঠিকানা আছে আমার বাড়িতে,
চিঠি লিখব না।
আমরা একত্রে আছি বইয়ের পাতায়।

('ফিরে এসো, চাকা')

... when the two of us
were a young woman and man
did we know then that we would grow old so?
I hope that now you have children grandchildren etcetera.
My address lies with you in your home,
Your address lies with me in my home,
We shall not write letters.
We are together in the leaves of the book.
('Come Back, O Wheel', translation mine)

EPHEMERA

Anil Karanjai (1940–2001), a painter-iconoclast who also belonged to the Hungry Generation of writers and artists from Bengal, repeatedly drew distorted figures, often with more eyes than there are individuals on the canvas.[13] Bodies are contorted and merge with others—not cubist like Picasso's, but flowing and rounded, with robust colours and chilling expressions—telling stories of hunger and anger, shock and sorrow, perhaps even of love. There is, in fact, a painted 'Homage to Picasso' (1973, oil on canvas) too, in rich reds, maroons and browns, in which Picasso is three-eyed. In each of his misshapen and vibrant images, we are struck, over and over, by the power of their gaze(s). The many, extra, eyes protrude and stare, are sometimes blank, sometimes laden with the pain and knowledge, the grandeur of knowledge. In an evocative self-portrait (1974, oil on paper),[14] Karanjai has his own face made up of eyes placed askance, at least six eyes can be clearly counted, from cheeks up into the forehead; the rest of the face is chiselled from crevices, channels and dark corners in a deep brown with hints of watermelon red, eerily resembling his face—but not really a living, human one. The channels cutting through his face cleverly move up towards the head forming roots of a plant. And in this astonishing self-portrait, from his forehead, a tree or bush of luminous greens—a few of the many shades that Karanjai uses in his verdant landscapes—sprouts and blooms.

It is a portrait that is riveting and unnerving at once. The eyes, multiple and strange, the dark cracks and crevices, the luscious, luxurious greens: they add up to fantasy bordering on nightmare. We are drawn in, as to all of the arts, seduced by proverbial sirens, lured to our deaths real or imagined. The discombobulated eye haunts us as a symbol of what life holds, what we must see and yet cannot bear to. Eyes float around us in air and water, separated from faces: we watch and are watched, we are unseeing and we are not seen. It becomes a metaphor, hanging loose, of our making non/sense of the world—nothing at all to do with the physiological function of the eye. We each have our own tales to tell, and our own readings of others' tales. We do not know what they auger for us in the years we still have to live, but we know, like Dante did, that we cannot be afraid of what our fate will bring us, for it is a gift.

How does the language of literature—and where it resides primarily for us still, in books—struggle to reflect the fragmentations, distortions and contortions that fate continually throws at us? Intriguingly, there are books in fragments, perhaps returning in a long wide arc to Sappho's dismembered lines of poetry on faded and torn papyrus leaves composed in Greece in sixth century BC. Anne Carson's *Float* (2016) comes in a stiff clear plastic cover filled with booklets, loose sheets, cover pages and even a contents page which can be read as a series of short and long writings or any picked out at will, of reading notes, jottings, poems, translations, essays and plays. In a stream-of-consciousness poem in the pack, 'Wildly Constant', Carson writes of Iceland, glaciers and a library:

> The library contains not books
> but glaciers.
> The glaciers are upright.
> Silent.
> As perfectly ordered as books would be.
> But they are melted.
>
> What would it be like
> to live in a library
> of melted books?
>
> With sentences streaming over the floor
> and all the punctuation
> settled to the bottom as a residue.
>
> It would be confusing.
> Unforgivable.
> An adventure.

Carson's chosen vehicle for her collection of writings—a hard transparent folder with one end open, booklets and sheets snugly fitted inside but calling out to be strewn around the bed or the grass, to allow the sentences to stream and the punctuation to settle—bears to her the gift of letting go. She can write in verse or prose or throw a handful of words across a page, and all of it will dive into the folder and become one of a bunch of wild grasses and fruit to be picked out at whim. The three-sided box invites us to let ourselves go, too. It describes itself thus:

> Float
>
> A collection of twenty-two chapbooks whose order is unfixed and whose topics are various.
>
> Reading can be freefall. (Carson 2016)

AND, 'READING CAN BE FREEFALL'...

It is this freefall that fantasy, nightmare and the humanities entice one into, and aid and abet. This collection of essays—with no prompt from the editor other than asking for the writers' ways of 'doing the humanities', engaging with chosen texts, thoughts, theories, senses and sensations—invites you all to such a freefall. I have not tasked myself in this Introduction with summing up each contribution to *Humanities, Provocateur* for you, or even with establishing connections between them or with my vision for the book. To be honest, I had no clear vision, except that I wanted a varied bunch of people—each of whom I know to be passionately engaged in thinking about the humanities in their own very original and creative ways—to record an experience of such engagement, its methods as much as its deviations from 'method'. I have not touched upon the artists or writers or filmmakers or thinkers or texts that my contributors have written about. Instead, I have grouped the essays in couples and triples under section headers that I would like you to interpret in abstraction which coincide with the ones used to separate sections of this Introduction—sections where I follow some erratic leads to what I have read and seen and thought and felt and learnt, in my own unruly forages in the humanities. I imagine the contributors each having responded to such foraging, without this text in front of them—in fact, even before this text was written. This 'Introduction' then talks to them in turn, and the conversations never stop.

At worst, I hope that such errant ruminations will spark echoes for you in similar—or indeed, diverse—directions. At best, I wish that they coagulate in liquid patterns that will pick up colours and voices and images from the ones let fly by my contributors in their essays. Together, if they add up in some haphazard, scrambling way to invoke humanities practices that break the laws set for the study of the arts across a wide spectrum and impel a few to move out of cushioned cubby-holes lined with weighty theory and packaged with styles taught in formulaic academic-writing courses, my work will be more than done. We come to this collection—and everything that we read, or watch or listen to—as equal learners, like Jacques Rancière's 'ignorant schoolmaster' in multiples and everything we put in or take out from each page we turn, and return to, will enrich us with its traces. The traces shall remain in us, shall germinate new ideas, shall go with us to new places and people and pieces of art, among garbage and flowers. Invisibly we shall draw cobwebs between us—those whom we know and those whom we don't—for carrying these traces, and they will connect us in innumerable ways through stray dreams and sharp observations that have touched us in the essays. For as Rancière's (1991, 41) schoolmaster Jacoctet teaches, 'Everything is in everything. The power of the tautology is that of equality, the power that searches for the finger of intelligence in every human work.'

Humanities, Provocateur invites you to Anne Carson's freefall of reading. To read the pieces together or separately, as and when the mood takes you. To be struck by fresh connections and intriguing inferences. To argue and to disagree. To cherish or to distrust. To be led to texts you do not know or back to some you know well. To be lured to the undercommons, to read against the new tides that come in to you with a line or an essay and then to flow with them awhile. To be adventurous and destitute, at the same time. To never be afraid, for our fate is our gift. To wield, and hold, the poem in our lives like a rifle—or perhaps like a beloved one is losing. To snatch an elusive, odd thought from the mouth of the mundane and to make the ordinary extraordinary with a sudden, astonishing, wondrous word or image that kisses you on a page at which you have, momentarily, taken pause.

NOTES

1. Zagajewski, Adam, 'Try to Praise the Mutilated World', translated by Clare Cavanagh. Available at https://www.poetryfoundation.org/poems/57095/try-to-praise-the-mutilated-world-56d23a3f28187 (accessed 20 March 2020).
2. The debate includes a number of interventions from philosophers, primary among them being Žižek and Agamben. A special section of *The European Journal of Psychoanalysis* titled 'Coronavirus and philosophers' carries a translation of Agamben's initial intervention and the responses to it from a group of philosophers. Available at http://www.journal-psychoanalysis.eu/coronavirus-and-philosophers/ (accessed 20 March 2020).
3. Giorgio Agamben wrote a response to the criticisms of his original intervention and a translation of this response can be found here, dated 17 March 2020: available at https://itself.blog/2020/03/17/giorgio-agamben-clarifications/ (accessed 20 March 2020).

4. Giorgio Agamben, 'Biosecurity and Politics', translated by D. Allan Dean. Available at https://medium.com/@ddean3000/biosecurity-and-politics-giorgio-agamben-396f9ab3b6f4 (accessed 15 May 2020).
5. T.S. Eliot, *The Love-Song of J Alfred Prufrock*:

   Would it have been worth while,
   To have bitten off the matter with a smile,
   To have squeezed the universe into a ball
   To roll it towards some overwhelming question,
   To say: 'I am Lazarus, come from the dead,
   Come back to tell you all, I shall tell you all'.

6. Jacques Rancière, *Proletarian Nights*, 'Preface', translated by Jonathan Ree. Available at https://www.radicalphilosophyarchive.com/issue-files/rp31_article2_ranci%C3%A8re_proletariannights.pdf (accessed 14 May 2020).
7. Alexandra Kollontai (1929). Available at https://www.marxists.org/archive/kollonta/1929/great/ch03.htm (accessed 15 May 2020).
8. Alexandra Kollontai, 'The Workers' Opposition' (pamphlet). First published in *Pravda*, 25 January 1921, 8. Available at https://libcom.org/files/The%20Workers'%20Opposition%20-%20Alexandra%20Kollontai.pdf (accessed 7 November 2020).
9. Ritoban Ghatak (ed.), *Ramkinkar Baij, A Personality Study Documentary by Ritwik Ghatak*. Available at https://www.youtube.com/watch?v=GCBWrdN1eRY (accessed 14 April 2020).
10. Samuel Beckett, *Worstword Ho*. Available at https://genius.com/Samuel-beckett-worstward-ho-annotated (accessed 20 April 2020).
11. Wayne Koestenbaum, 'The Pleasure of the Text: Hervé Guibert's Unbridled Eroticism'. Available at https://www.bookforum.com/print/2102/herve-guibert-s-unbridled-eroticism-13298 (accessed 21 April 2020).
12. https://www.poeticous.com/emily-dickinson/life-lxxxix-a-word-is-dead (accessed 10 January 2021).
13. A representative range of Anil Karanjai's art can be viewed on the site https://sites.google.com/site/anilkaranjai2/home.
14. This portrait can be viewed on the public group page titled 'Anil Karanjai' on Facebook, available at https://www.facebook.com/1645707748989175/photos/a.1645727998987150/2347486135477996/?type=3&theater.

REFERENCES

Agamben, Giorgio. *The Adventure*. Translated by Lorenzo Chiesa. MIT Press, 2018.

Alighieri, Dante. *The Inferno*, 6. Translated by John Ciardi [1954]. First Signet Classics, 2009.

Baij, Ramkinkar. *Self-Portrait: Writings and Interviews 1962–1979*. Translated by Sudipto Chakroborty, 2nd edition. Monfakira, 2010.

Braque, Georges et al. *Testimony Against Gertrude Stein*. Pamphlet 1, *Transition*, no. 23 (1934–1935).

Carson, Anne. *Economy of the Unlost: Reading Simonides of Keos with Paul Celan*. Princeton: Princeton University Press, 1999.

Carson, Anne. *Float*. Jonathan Cape, 2016.

Coetzee, J.M. *Summertime*. Vintage, 2010.

Derrida, Jacques. 'Che cos'è la poesia?', *Points…: Interviews 1974–1994*. Stanford University Press, 1995.

Fendelman, Earl. 'Gertrude Stein Among the Cubists'. *Journal of Modern Literature* 2, no. 4 (November 1972): 481–490.

Frisch, Max. *Drafts for a Third Sketchbook*. Translated by Mike Mitchell. Seagull Books: Calcutta, 2013.

Fuss, Diana. *Dying Modern: A Meditation on Elegy*. Duke University Press, 2013.

Ghatak, Ritwik. 'A Scenario' (Published originally in Drishya, no. 18, July 1974). In *Rows and Rows of Fences: Ritwik Ghatak on Cinema*. Seagull Books, 2000.

Guibert, Hervé. *To the Friend Who Did Not Save My Life: A Novel*. Translated from the French by Linda Coverdale. Athenaem, 1991.

———. *Ghost Image*. Translated from the French by Robert Bononno. University of Chicago Press, 1996.

———. *The Mausoleum of Lovers: Journals 1976–1991*. Translated from the French by Nathanaël, 2014. Available at https://www.asymptotejournal.com/nonfiction/herve-guibert-the-mausoleum-ofof-lovers/ (accessed 21 April 2020).

Halberstam, Judith. *The Queer Art of Failure*. Duke University Press, 2011.

Harney, Stefano and Fred Moten. *The Undercommons: Fugitive Planning & Black Study*. Minor Compositions, 2013.

Jaaware, Aniket. *Practicing Caste: On Touching and Not Touching*. Orient Blackswan, 2019.

Joyce, James. *A Portrait of the Artist as a Young Man*. Collector's Library, 2005.

Kollontai, Alexandra. 'The Loves of Three Generations'. In *A Great Love*. New York: Vanguard Press, 1929.

———. 'The Workers' Opposition' (pamphlet). First published in *Pravda*, 25 January 1921.

Pajak, Frédéric. *Uncertain Manifesto*. Translated by Donald Nicholson-Smith. New York Review Books, 2019.

Rancière, Jacques. *The Ignorant Schoolmaster: Five Lessons in Intellectual Emancipation*. Translated by Kristin Ross. Stanford University Press, 1991.

Rancière, Jacques and Mark Foster Gage. 'Politics Equals Aesthetics: A Conversation'. *Aesthetics Equals Politics: New Discourses Across Art, Architecture and Philosophy*. Edited by Mark F. Gage. MIT Press, 2019.

Rhodes, Colin. *Outsider Art: Spontaneous Alternatives*. Thames and Hudson, 2000.

Roy, Falguni. *Falguni Samagra: A Collection of Bengali Poems by Falguni Roy and Related Writings*. Dumdum Junction Publications, 2019.

Rushdie, Salman. *Midnight's Children*. Alfred Knopf, 1981.

Shklovsky, Viktor. 'The Links of Art Do Not Repeat Each Other. Once Again, on the Dissimilarity of the Similar'. *Viktor Shklovsky: A Reader*. Edited and translated by Alexandra Berlina. Bloomsbury, 2017.

Sontag, Susan. *Illness as Metaphor and AIDS and Its Metaphors*. Picador, 2001.

Stein, Gertrude. *Lifting Belly*. (Ed. Rebecca Marks). The Naiad Press, [1989] 1995.

———. *Tender Buttons*. Marie Claire, 1914.

———. *The Autobiography of Alice B. Toklas*. Harcourt, Brace and Co., 1933.

GLEANING

PLATO AND PROUST, BEDFELLOWS: 'CONCEPT' AND 'IDEA' FROM THE CLASSICAL TO THE MODERN

Aveek Sen

E.H. Gombrich: *You cannot simply lie in your bed and imagine what you will want to paint?*
Bridget Riley: *That's impossible!*
EHG: *It will turn out differently?*
BR: *You cannot plan like that.*
EHG: *No.*

—Bridget Riley, *Dialogues on Art* (2003, 40)

Art is a special discerning exercise of intelligence in relation to the real....

—Iris Murdoch, *The Fire and the Sun* (1977, 78)

This platonic person discovered a soul in the world
And studied it in his holiday hotel.

—Wallace Stevens, 'The Pure Good of Theory' (1984, 331)

What do people expect me to do with my eyes? What should I look at?

—Giuliana (Monica Vitti), in Michelangelo Antonioni's *Red Desert* (1964)

In Plato—with whom it all began—Ideas and beds are intimately linked. In Book X of *The Republic*, a middle-aged Socrates explains to Glaucon, a little more than 400 years before the birth of Christ, why the work that painters and poets do 'have no serious value' (Plato 1983, 431). Socrates is talking, with his usual, devastating urbanity, about three kinds of beds. First, the unique 'bed-in-itself', created by God. This is the real thing that exists in 'nature', the realm of eternal Forms or Ideas. Then there are the actual beds on which people sleep, made by carpenters. Finally, at the bottom of this chain of creation, is the painted bed—a useless copy of a copy, standing at a third remove from reality. Moving downwards from the Idea of the bed to the painted bed, one moves from reality to illusion, from truth to lies, from God to the painter. The philosopher must move in the opposite direction and while doing so should ignore the painted bed altogether. The knowledge of the Beautiful and of the Good—both embodied in the Ideas or eternal Forms—is too serious a moral goal to be waylaid by art and its dubious representations. Of course, the whole conversation is, in a sense, also a deliberate artifice created by Plato. 'Philosophy', Iris Murdoch had written, 'is essentially talk' (Murdoch 1977, 21). And Plato was too acutely aware of the treacheries of language—particularly of figurative language, of myths and metaphors—not to have misgivings about the element of invention in his own philosophical system that gives to writing the illusion of brilliant talk.

The word, Idea, comes out of this sophisticated, ironic, yet morally serious philosophy of knowledge. It carries within it not only the internal hierarchies of this philosophy (the three levels of Bed-hood) and its original myths, metaphors and structures but also the long history of how Western art and aesthetics have seized Plato's philosophy to continually create new systems of values that turn on its head his original devaluation of the artist. From Plotinus, through Marsiglio Ficino and Philip Sidney, to Kant and Shelley, Plato's philosophy of the Ideal, originally so dismissive of *mimesis*, became the basis of a series of lofty defences of the verbal and visual arts. Plato was a great artist who feared, in Murdoch's words 'the consolations of art'. The art and aesthetics that he sought to denigrate and exorcise from his pure system of philosophy took on an endlessly inspiring life of their own—in Neoplatonism, in Christianity, in Classical and Romantic, and finally, in Modern art and aesthetics—thus making Platonism its own elaborated critique. What is anti-Platonic in this critique is, therefore, at another level, profoundly Platonic. This is why A.N. Whitehead's description of all European philosophy—and, one might add, aesthetics—as footnotes to Plato does not sound reductive. So, when Joseph Kosuth, in *One and Three Chairs* (1965), placed a common folding chair on the floor and hung from the wall behind this chair an actual-sized photograph of it, next to a blown-up dictionary definition of the word 'chair' and called this arrangement Conceptual Art, it became an irreverent exploration of the Idea or Concept of 'chairness', parodying Plato's progression from a real to the ideal chair. The ideal chair, in this case, is not an Idea in the realm of eternal Forms but a dictionary definition. Theology or moral philosophy becomes structural linguistics in *One and Three Chairs*, as signifiers rub shoulders with signifieds and Plato is reborn as Saussure in 1960s New York. God, the carpenter and the artist—or use, manufacture and representation—which Plato wanted to keep strictly separate, are conflated in Kosuth's governing Idea of the work by his deadpan levelling wit.[1]

In 1999, Tracey Emin installed, at the Tate, the actual bed in which she 'almost went out of her mind for four days', complete with skid-marked sheets, used condoms, soiled knickers and all the detritus of a 'lost' weekend. She called it *My Bed* and got two kinds of responses from her viewers. She was shortlisted for the Turner Prize but did not get it eventually. And more interestingly, two Chinese artists 'critically intervened' in what they saw as Emin's unabashed 'self-promotion'. They jumped onto the exhibit half-naked, had a brisk pillow fight, shouted in 'unfathomable Mandarin' (as one reporter describes) and tried to take a swig from one of the empty bottles of vodka lying next to the bed. There was muted applause from the other viewers, until the security guards got over their bemusement and carried the Chinese artists off. It must have been difficult for the curators to restore *My Bed* to its 'original' form, the one that would correspond exactly to its creator's Idea of it. There was no dearth of conceptualisation behind the making and then the viewing of this work. It is significant how Emin succeeded in releasing detailed information about this bed and what it had meant to her, before and during the work was being viewed. She was, in turn, seen by her Turner-Prize judges as illustrating 'graphically' in this work the 'themes of loss, sickness, fertility, copulation, conception and death'. And the two Chinese artists also saw their 'intervention' as some sort of Gilbert-and-George Performance Art, motivated by their own critical, but nevertheless aesthetic, agenda. Each artist or pair of artists started with her or his prior Idea of what she or he wanted to do and their 'work'—the bed itself, and what was subsequently played out on it—was the creative realisation of this Idea, although limited and transformed by the nature of the materials or circumstances with which or in which they were working.

This 'single, intellectual, largely random decision to name this or that object or activity 'art'' has been seen as the hallmark of Conceptual Art (Smith 1997, 257). And our keywords, 'concept' and 'idea' are indispensable to how the artists themselves describe the nature of such decisions. 'In Conceptual Art', wrote Sol LeWitt, in a 1967 *Artforum* article, giving this kind of art its first theoretical exegesis, 'the idea or concept is the most important aspect of the work … all planning and decisions are made beforehand and the execution is a perfunctory affair. The idea becomes the machine that makes the art …' (Smith 1997, 261). Sometimes this 'making' is simply a self-consciously peremptory act of naming. Something becomes an art object only because someone says that it is so. In this, the quintessential Conceptual artefact is, of course, Marcel Duchamp's *Fountain* (1917)—an ordinary urinal signed 'R. Mutt' and entered as a titled piece of sculpture in an exhibition Duchamp was helping to organise in New York. This 'readymade' piece by Duchamp—who claimed to be 'more interested in the ideas than in the final product'—radically changed the notion of the art object as well as that of the artist's role as 'maker'. 'Concept' and 'idea', in lower case and used interchangeably, are used by Duchamp and LeWitt to elevate, with a provocative wilfulness, the active intellectual agency of the artist, even while depriving the art object of its traditional uniqueness and 'aura'—in fact, making it infinitely reproducible. Not just Plato, but also Walter Benjamin is turned upside down.[2] It is paradoxical how these artists and theorists use the Platonic baggage of 'idea' and 'concept' to idealise and even sensationalise the figure of the artist even as they subvert the idealisation of Art itself. It is as if Plato's dismissive trivialising of the artist has come full circle here, making trashiness itself a kind of value, an ideal. The maker of trash becomes, therefore, a challenging and charismatic figure who can claim for himself the right to trash traditionally 'higher' forms of Art.

The Conceptual Artists' use of 'idea' and 'concept' as synonyms that transfigure mundane, readymade objects through the power of the intellect might be illuminated by the writings of a very different kind of early-sixteenth-century artist. In his sonnet, '*Non ha l'ottimo artista in se alcun concetto*', Michelangelo provides a rare insight into his technique of working with marble. His language is explicitly Neoplatonic in this poem, particularly in the use of the word 'concetto' in the opening quatrain.

> Not the best artist has in himself any concept
> That a single marble does not enclose in itself
> With its excess; and to this attains only
> The hand that obeys the intellect.[3]

Dedicated to Vittoria Colonna—the widowed Marchioness of Pescara and herself a prolific poet—the sonnet invests the artist with a humility which Michelangelo habitually adopted when addressing this austere and intellectual noblewoman. Michelangelo's reverence towards Vittoria is therefore identified with the sculptor's deference to his medium, the single piece of unworked marble. And this deference arises from the acknowledgment that the 'concept' behind what the sculptor will make with this block of marble is located *within* the marble itself. This is the source of the artist's humility, his solemn, but manual, obedience. His work is to chip away at the superfluities and bring out the form that is inherent in the stone. Hence, the reader remains uncertain about whether the 'intellect', at the end of the fourth line, is that of the artist or of his medium. Is the hand shaping the marble, or is the marble determining the action of the hand? To locate, as Michelangelo does, the work's governing 'concept' within its medium itself immediately renders his depiction of art's 'making' far more complex than the

Conceptual Artist's rather imperious celebration of artistic intention. In Michelangelo, the medium is imbued with its own intellect and the 'work' of art—the process as well as the product—exists in the interface of the medium's intellect and the artist's. Here, too, Plato's Idea or eternal Form is radically humanised and materialised—turned into stone, as it were but without destroying the sense of the transcendent beauty of the Idea. The rest of Michelangelo' sonnet is about art's vital relationship with the Platonic Eros, experienced as a kind of 'love' for a particular human being. It is a profoundly Platonic poem because the hand that brings out the Form (hidden in the marble) is obedient to a force that is both aesthetic and moral. Where then does the 'Concept' reside—in the medium, in the artist's mind or in some transcendent realm outside and above both? To answer this question is also to think deeply, but lucidly and pragmatically (as the best artists do), about the relationships among the hand, the mind and the medium and to blur the boundaries separating theory and practice, the technology, psychology and metaphysics of art.

The problem of trying to fathom in words the baffling relationships among the mind, the hand and the medium preoccupied Francis Bacon, working with paint in the twentieth century as much as it did Michelangelo, working with marble in the sixteenth. With Bacon, too, the dynamic and unpredictable relationship between the 'conscious will' of the painter and the physical nature of the 'actual paint'—how the latter 'moves' on the canvas with a will of its own—brings about the profound 'accidents' of art:

> You know in my case all painting—and the older I get the more it becomes so—is accident. So, I foresee it in my mind, I foresee it, and yet I hardly ever carry it out as I foresee it. It transforms itself by the actual paint. I use very large brushes, and in the way I work, I don't, in fact, know very often what the paint will do, and it does many things which are very much better than I could make it do. Is that an accident? Perhaps one could say it's not an accident, because it becomes a selective process which is part of this accident one chooses to preserve. One is attempting, of course, to keep the vitality of the accident and yet preserve a continuity.... When I was trying in despair, the other day, to paint that head of a specific person, I used a very big brush and a great deal of paint and I put it on very, very freely, and I simply didn't know in the end what I was doing, and suddenly, this thing clicked and became exactly like the image I was trying to record. But not out of any conscious will, nor was it anything to do with illustrational painting. What has never yet been analyzed is why this particular way of painting is more

> poignant than illustration. I suppose because it has a life completely of its own. It lives on its own, like the image one's trying to trap; it lives on its own, and therefore, transfers the essence of the image more poignantly. So that the artist may be able to open up or rather, should I say, unlock the valves of feeling and therefore return the onlooker to life more violently … there is a possibility that you get through this accidental thing something much more profound than what you really wanted. (Sylvester 1997, 16–17)

For Bacon, the energy and the poignancy of 'making' reside in the shadows that fall between what one really wanted and what one gets at the end, between 'the image one's trying to trap', 'the essence of that image' and what the paint finally allows one to produce. And this energy is vital in more than one sense. It violently returns one to life and to a richness of feeling that is akin to the solemn ardour of Michelangelo's sonnet.

In 1547, Benedetto Varchi, a member of the Florentine Academy, lectured on the rival merits of painting and sculpture to the Academy, using the same sonnet by Michelangelo. Varchi's commentary brings together the various notions and images that we have been looking at so far, making him sound like a slightly more pedantic contemporary of the Conceptualist LeWitt:

> … our Poet's *Concetto* denotes that which, as we said above, is called in Greek *idea*, in Latin *exemplar*, us 'model'; that is, that form or image, called by some people the intention, that we have within our imagination, of everything that we intend to will or to make or to say; which [form or image], although spiritual … is, for that reason, the efficient cause of everything that can be said or made. Wherefore the Philosopher [Aristotle] said in the Seventh Book of the First Philosophy [Metaphysics]: 'The active form, as regards the bed, is in the soul of the artisan.' (Sylvester 1997, 120)

It needed the audaciousness of an Aristotle to take Plato's bed and place it right within the 'soul of the "artisan"'—not 'artist', mind you, but the carpenter, the craftsman, as William Morris and the Bauhaus set would have understood. And it would perhaps not be too sensational to say that modern—that is Romantic and post-Romantic—art theory was thus born out of Plato and also 'dialectically' out of him. Raphael's monumental fresco in the Vatican's Stanza della Segnatura, *The School of Athens* (1509–1511), puts Plato and Aristotle at the centre of the entire composition. They stand side by side, overseeing the great assembly of ancient Greek sages, Plato (resembling Leonardo da Vinci) holding his book *Timaeus* and the index finger of his right hand pointing upwards towards the realm of the Ideal, while Aristotle, holding his book *Ethics*, gestures downwards with his right hand, the palm facing the ground and parallel to it, symbolising his investigation of the natural and human worlds. It is in the *Timaeus* that Plato presents his most famous celebration of the creative artist. However, this artist is not a human being but the Demiurge, creator of the Universe, and the cosmos is his aesthetic achievement, the only work of art worthy of Plato's respect. Plato's philosophy, thus, at once banishes the artist and apotheosises him which is perhaps why Raphael puts him with Aristotle at the centre of his 'School'. In this school, Art is inseparable from Philosophy, Theology and Mathematics, from the highest and most abstract intellectual pursuits—as the presence of Pythagoras and Euclid, among others, indicates—while being just as integrally located within the human and natural worlds.

The essential story of Western art from Plato to the Moderns—of which Raphael's *School of Athens* is both a subject and an early telling—can be traced with all its problems and paradoxes in an unusual place—the entries under 'idea' and 'concept' in the larger *Oxford English Dictionary*. The *OED* shows how 'idea' was first 'adopted' by the modern languages in the sixteenth century in its 'general Platonic sense'. In this sense, an Idea was 'a supposed eternally existing pattern or archetype of any class or thing, of which the individual things in that class are imperfect copies, and from which they derive their existence'. The dictionary's earliest English illustration of this sense is from Philemon Holland's 1603 translation of Plutarch's *Moralia*:

> Idea is a bodilesse substance, which of itselfe hath no subsistence, but giveth figure and forme unto shapelesse matters, and becommeth the very cause that bringeth them into shew and evidence. Socrates and Plato suppose, that these Ideæ bee substances separate and distinct from Matter, howbeit, subsisting in the thoughts and imaginations of God—that is to say, of Mind and Understanding.

It is clear from Holland's translation and the other *OED* examples of usage that by the second half of the sixteenth century, the definitive leap from the mind of God to the mind of man, as the realm in which Ideas reside, has already been made. Holland's English moves seamlessly from a theological to a psychological vocabulary. And this is the movement that defines the shift of the word's dominant usage in English henceforth. As a standard, principle or ideal to be aimed at or desired, an Idea is what the 'human' mind or imagination holds and contemplates, and therefore, even produces. If one is a Christian Platonist, then one is free to think that it is God who has planted the Idea in the human mind since the mind itself in its highest capacities is what is divine in man. But the transition from this belief to its purely secular indeed implicitly blasphemous version has already taken place in the sixteenth century. By the time the Romantics take this up, the internalisation of Ideas is complete. After running through the four stages in the evolution of the word, as laid out in the *OED* from Plato to 'modern philosophical developments' (Descartes, Locke, Kant and Hegel), one begins to see how 'Idea' not only becomes a keyword in philosophy but also a part of a much more practical vocabulary of human creativity—artistic as well as less exalted forms of the 'making' of things from pre-existing forms, designs or plans. 'Idea' begins to align itself with words like 'design', 'model', 'plan', 'pattern' and 'type'. The word descends from a timeless and transcendent sphere into a psychological, material or technological one without losing its intellectual and originary character. For Philip Sidney, in *An Apology for Poetry* (1595), 'the skill of the artificer standeth in that *Idea* or fore-conceit of the work, and not in the work itself'.[4] To 'ideate'—that is, to form an idea of, to imagine, conceive—comes into English a little later. The *OED* cites a sentence from John Donne's prose, dated 1610.

'Skill', 'work' and 'artifice' are all words that straddle the intellectual and the manual, High Art and the relatively humbler crafts. Sidney's 'fore-conceit' is an important ancestor of the modern 'concept'—a word that has always been more at home than 'Idea' has been in the realm of practical creativity, of materials and products and hands. Sidney's compound also reveals the etymology of 'concept', which entered English much earlier than 'idea', in the late fourteenth century and was almost always used in its earlier from 'conceit' which survives today, interestingly, in the notion of 'conceitedness', personal vanity or pride. From the beginning, 'concept' was related to the purely human mind—meaning notion, understanding, opinion or estimation (in a neutral sense). But with the subsequent emergence of 'Idea', it got assimilated into the later word's semantic field, without letting go of its original practical, less exalted character. In the sixteenth and seventeenth centuries, this proximity to 'Idea' also lent to 'conceit' an added sense of 'the excessively and ingeniously fanciful'. To use 'conceits' became a form of literary affectation that came to be associated with the self-consciously learned sophistication or 'wit' of 'metaphysical poets' like John Donne, Andrew Marvell and Abraham Cowley. Such an affectation was perceived as having come from that land of exquisite corruption and Mannerist extravagance, Italy, and was associated with the Italian word, '*concetto*' (used, although more austerely, in Varchi's commentary on Michelangelo's sonnet) and with the poet, Giambattista Marino, among others in Spain and Italy. Samuel Johnson—in his 1779 essay on Cowley in the *Prefaces ... to the Works of the English Poets*—finds the word 'conceit' indispensable to his critical discussion on the English Metaphysical poets. His description of Metaphysical wit gives a broad but accurate sense of what the use of conceits signified, philosophically and stylistically, and remains strikingly applicable to the work of modern Conceptualists like Duchamp, Kosuth and LeWitt and generally to a great deal of Surrealist and post-Surrealist Art:

> [Wit] may be more rigorously and philosophically considered as a kind of *discordia concors*; a combination of dissimilar things, or discovery of occult resemblances in things apparently unlike.... The most heterogenous ideas are yoked by violence together; nature and art are ransacked for illustrations, comparisons, and allusions; their learning instructs, and their subtlety surprises.... Their wish was only to say what they hoped had been never said before.... And in the mass of materials, which ingenious absurdity has thrown together, genuine wit and useful knowledge may be sometimes found, buried perhaps in the grossness of expression, but useful to those who know their value.... (Greene 1984, 678–679)

Duchamp's Conceptualist urinal/fountain is informed by precisely this kind of verbal-visual wit. *Fountain*, and many of the works that it inspired, are 'conceits' whose deliberate effect exploits the violent yoking of decorously separated notions and things confounding the Platonic hierarchies that keep apart sacred and profane, mind and body, abstract and concrete, spiritual and material, physical and metaphysical. This is how they create the shock of the new, both for the eye and for the mind. The subversiveness of this 'avant-garde' wit and its products is exclusive and intellectual, their outrageousness self-consciously snobbish and their irreverence wilfully 'conceited' (in the modern sense). Donne and his urbane Inns-of-Court friends would have understood and delighted in the ingenious absurdities of Duchamp and Dali.

The *OED*'s etymology of 'idea' takes us also to the heart of another defining conflict within Western art, played out in the history of the word's usage. The dictionary points out that the Greek ἰδέα—which, in its everyday senses, could mean look, semblance, form, configuration, species, kind, class, sort or nature—is derived from the root ιδ, meaning 'see'. Plato used ἰδέα and its cognate εἶδος (usually translated as 'form') indiscriminately, as did Aristotle, who did not discriminate clearly when summarising Plato, although he tended to prefer εἶδος as his own technical term. As the poet, Coleridge, points out in a very useful note on 'Idea' in his *Biographia Literaria* (1815), Plato's ἰδέα—'considered as mysterious powers, living, seminal, formative, and exempt from time'—existed as the antithesis to εἴδωλα or 'sensuous images; the transient and perishable emblems, or mental words, of ideas' (Coleridge 1984, 96–97). The root ιδ—akin to the Latin *vid-*, also meaning 'see', and making up English words like 'visual' and 'evidence'—is therefore, like a dangerous kernel of visuality threatening to undermine the transcendence of the Platonic Idea. Idea, though notionally opposed to 'image', is essentially, indeed seminally, linked to it. The visual—the actual physical activity of the human eye—is at the root of the metaphysical in Plato, and hence, seeing becomes disturbingly inseparable from knowing in the epistemologies that come out of his philosophy and flow into modern theories of knowledge and modern aesthetics.

In Plato's philosophical discourse, this is, at one level, the problem of metaphor. The language of vision informs our various languages of experiencing the world and of processing that experience into consciousness and knowledge. How do we read, then, the blazingly visual and poetic myths and images in Plato's philosophy—the Myth of the Cave in *The Republic*, the chariot and horses in *Phaedrus*, the hemispheres and the winged soul in *The Symposium* or the Demiurge in *Timaeus*? '"Is it a metaphor?" is, of course, a fundamental question to be asked about metaphysical explanation,' writes Iris Murdoch, 'Our ability to use visual structures to understand non-visual structures ... is fundamental to explanation to any field' (Murdoch 1977, 67–68). Yet, this is not simply a technical problem of how philosophy or metaphysics explains its disembodied concepts. It is more crucially and abidingly, a problem of how we actually come to know things and what constitutes this knowledge. It is a problem of how we trust the 'evidence' of our senses in building up a certain knowledge of the world and of ourselves and how we then represent, communicate or reveal these 'truths' to ourselves and to other human beings through shared modes of expression. It is also a problem of how we reflect on, write and talk about these processes.

Do we have to see in order to believe and know? This central question in epistemology has a distinct relevance for each modern sphere of intellectual activity—the empirical sciences, medicine, law, theology, art and everyday life. How do we know that the earth is round? How do I find out if I am HIV+? How do we prove that Imrana Bibi was raped by her father-in-law? Why should we believe that God exists? Is my spouse committing adultery? These are, at one level, similar questions. What links them is the idea of visual evidence. Human knowing is helplessly dependant on sight, pleasured and compelled by it, yet deeply mistrustful of it too. Iris Murdoch reminds us that, for St. John of the Cross, 'God is the abyss of faith into which we fall when we have discarded all images of him.' 'This is the point', she adds, 'at which Plato starts making jokes' (Murdoch 1977, 65). Coleridge, a little after his note on Idea in the *Biographia*, refers to this ambivalent dependence as 'that despotism of the eye', 'the emancipation from which Pythagoras by his *numerical*, and Plato by his *musical*, symbols, and both by geometric discipline, aimed at, as the first προπαιδευτικόν [preparatory education] of the mind' (Coleridge 1984, 107). Numbers, music and geometry become, therefore, the symbols and guarantee of the mind's capacity to free itself from its subjection to the eye—its capacity for intellectual abstraction. But even these abstractions are founded on reading, looking at lines, points and shapes and on listening and then processing these sensations in the brain. Plato's mistrust of the senses, the basis of his epistemology, is rooted in an attitude to the body, particularly to sexuality—what Murdoch calls his sense of 'human worthlessness' (Murdoch 1977, 20)—that results in his privileging of the spiritual over the corporeal. This is carried forward into Christianity's hierarchical division of body and soul (as a consequence of Original Sin) which in turn, has been secularised by modern empiricism into the Cartesian polarities of body and mind or matter and mind. Each of these modern polarities tends to privilege the mind as superior.

Philosophy and Art might be seen as located at opposite ends of this abstract-to-concrete spectrum. If Philosophy is Idea, then Art is Image; if the former deals with universals then the latter gives us particulars (embodied in the aesthetic object). In this, Art may be seen as both a critique and a complement of Philosophy, in terms of both pleasure and knowledge. Yet, even while co-opting Plato to vindicate what he originally undermines, Art—particularly certain schools of Modern Art—often internalise Plato's misgivings with the image and the eye, with the physical and the material. It is impossible for the visual arts to be anything but visual and for the plastic arts to be anything but material—and in this, Art is forever shackled to the eye (of the artist and of the viewer) and to matter. However, if Conceptual Art has vengefully brought the Platonic Idea or Concept down to the level of the most banal things (beds and chairs and urinals), then Abstract Expressionism and Minimalism in painting and sculpture have journeyed in the opposite direction, away from the transfigured junkyard of 'things', from the subversive towards the sublime, towards the realisation of a more Platonic notion of Idea or Concept. With the paintings, it is as if the very fact of having shed the sculpture's third dimension, limiting themselves to the flat surfaces of pictorial space, has led to a reduction of their materiality, moving them closer to pure abstraction, towards a kind of secular spirituality, a modern mysticism. This journey towards abstraction is also a journey away from the human body towards a purely formal, and therefore, intellectual notion of subject matter—a state of non-depiction, beyond the figurative, the narrative and the representational. This is a kind of art that aspires to the condition of geometry or, better still, of music and might derive its deepest inspiration from the contrapuntal music of J.S. Bach.[5]

Early twentieth-century abstraction—of Kandinsky, Mondrian and Kasimir Malevich—spoke a recognisably Platonic, quasi-spiritual language when talking about itself. In 'Concerning the Spiritual in Art' (1911), Kandinsky spoke of a 'coming era of great spirituality' (quoted in Harrison 1997, 200). And in 1913, Malevich placed a black square on a white ground, claiming that his art like the Platonic Idea, 'wants to have nothing further to do with the object as such', for 'it can exist, in and for itself, without things' (Gablik 1997, 244). Such a composition would gesture towards 'an immediate, legible geometry' (Gablik 1997, 244) that can be conceived by the mind before its execution. Almost three decades later, in 1943, Mark Rothko and Adolph Gottlieb were still proclaiming their involvement with 'eternal symbols'. Rothko described the transition, in his painting, from abstractions of human figures to those exploring non-figurative relationships between 'colour-fields'. The latter becomes the painting of 'shapes' created from the need 'for everyday acts' to belong to 'a ritual accepted as referring to a transcendent realm' (Gablik 1997, 194–195). In his late dialogue, *Philebus*, Plato concedes to sensation the pleasurable experience of 'pure beauty' through the contemplation of certain colours, simple geometrical figures or a single series of pure notes. This form of pure contemplation sorts out, emphasises and attends to harmonious patterns that are already latent in the universe and in the cosmic mind (Murdoch 1977, 12). In an earlier dialogue *Meno*, by making a slave boy solve a geometrical problem, Socrates proves to Meno that these harmonious patterns in the cosmic mind had also once existed as notions in the human mind before it was born to its servitude to the body and to the material world. So, all that Socrates did with the slave-boy was to make him remember what his soul had once known in its pure, disembodied state. In *Philebus*, philosophical truth, which is purely expressive of reality, is compared to a small piece of pure white colour (Murdoch 1977, 12).

It is this purity—the purity of the Idea in its original Platonic sense—that modern Minimalism invokes and realises by literalising Plato's metaphors and similes for contemplation, thereby rendering contemplation itself inseparable from looking. In *Laws*, Plato seems to be tracing the shift from Cubism to Minimalism when he writes, 'Can there be any more accurate vision or view of any object than through the ability to look from the dissimilar many to the single idea?' (Murdoch 1977, 26) The mind's eye in Plato becomes the eye's mind with the Minimalist artists. The journey from Cubism to Abstract Expressionism (Mark Rothko, Jackson Pollock and Barnett Newman) and Minimalism (Don Judd, Robert Morris and Frank Stella) was a passage from Europe to America across the Great Wars into the coldness of the Cold War. But aesthetically, it was a backward quest—a tracing of Cubism 'back down through its extensions to the point at which art ceased to be able to call upon a world of whole objects' (Smith 1997, 201). And this attempt to put Humpty together again after his great fall had to be essentially Platonic. A revival of the idea of wholeness—achieved in pictorial space but also grasped and held in the intellect of the artist and of the viewer—was also a revival of 'idea' and 'concept' as keywords. Barnett Newman's great work of 1948—an impasto cadmium-red light stripe, centred vertically upon a more thinly-painted cadmium-red darker field—is called *Onement I*. Working in the late 1940s and 1950s and well into the Cold War, painters and sculptors (many of them Jews and Russians living in America) would have found it impossible to not see the relationship between figurative and abstract art in terms of art's relationship with the human and the non-human, and by extension, the inhuman.

How did abstract Art stand in relation to human form as well as human feelings? If the realm of Ideas in Plato—the chief enemy of the open society, according to Karl Popper—had not been structured around the ideas of the Beautiful and the Good and in some dialogues around Love, there would have been something chillingly inhuman about its transcendence. Literary celebrations of the classical Ideal—especially in Romantic poetry—also address its intimidating, but sublime coldness 'all breathing human passion far above'.[6] Yet, as Keats's poem tells us, when a living viewer stands in front of or walks around a work of art, then even the coldest and most remotely abstract work becomes part of a human scene. It becomes part of a vital relationship, in space and time, between the mind and body of the viewer and the form and the content of the work.

If one stands for a sufficiently long time in front of Newman's *Onement I* (or any of his great 'Stripe' paintings) and allows oneself to be worked upon by the painting's meditativeness, then what begins to emerge—somewhere between the eye's mind and the mind's eye, that zone between perception and recognition—is an essential relationship between one's own verticality as a body standing in space and the verticality of Newman's vividly-coloured stripe and perhaps even that of the painting itself, hanging on the wall. Newman's painting unites number, line, colour, mind, body and language. The numeral 1 is also a vertical line, which, in turn, is the simplest possible rendering of the upright human body, but rendered here not only as a line but also as a heightened strip of redness standing out within and against a red background. These make up a composition whose individual vertical elements (the stripe and its background, an upright column of red) are self-similar and also resemble the verticality of the pictorial space itself and its frame. And all this is 'held' not only within the painting but also crucially, grasped in one's eye and mind as a viewer, constituting within the space and time of viewing, one's sense of being oneself. This is a vividly unified self, a perceiving subject who has just used his eyes and his reflective powers to get to the geometric essence of his bodily and figurative presence in space. Hence, the significance of Newman's title, *Onement I*, which suggests the word, 'wonderment'. Such multiple, yet unifying acts of recognition produce their own sense of wonder.

But this wonder is profoundly ambiguous. And the ambiguity is brought out by the relationship between the titles of two of Newman's other great and huge stripe paintings—*Euclidian Abyss* (1946–1947) and *Vir Heroicus Sublimis* (1950–1951). To render the human body as a vertical line within and against a single vast colour field is to simplify as well as reduce the body to its linear, geometric essence; what Blake had called the 'human form divine' is transfigured as well as annihilated in this process. Newman, therefore, repeatedly uses the language of the sublime, and of terror, when talking about his own work. The sublime makes us feel very big as well as very small, empowered as well as overpowered. This is why confronting a mountain, a great work of art, a tremendous piece of Fascist architecture and God, are all part of the human experience of the sublime, and herein lies, too, the ambiguity of the sublime. Newman's 'heroic and sublime' man is both an apotheosis of the human into Abstract Art, as well as a terrifying reduction of the human by pure geometric space or a radiant primary colour. This 'Human Abstract' is placed in the Euclidian abyss and becomes a helplessness before the void',[7] or a series of mysterious slits in the void. For Newman, a Jew who knew his Aeschylus and Nietzsche, terror before the unknowable and the incommunicable ('the eternal insecurities of life'[8]) becomes a compelling creative force. He describes *Euclidian Abyss* as 'my first painting where I got to the edge and didn't fall off'.[9]

Witnessing the gradual but inevitable effacement of human feeling and form by (in? into?) stupendously simple shapes, colours and edges is what a chronological viewing of Mark Rothko's paintings ultimately becomes. In a kind of gathering silence, bodies turn into blurred, huge squares and rectangles, luminous reds and oranges become the bleakest grey and black as we approach the last works done just before his suicide in 1970. What Rothko conveys to the viewer—visually, emotionally, intellectually and spiritually—is the oppressiveness of the simplest of forms, colours and textures, the terrible weight of simplicity or abstraction itself. This arose, as Rothko himself spelled out, from a 'clear preoccupation with death': 'All art deals with intimations of mortality'.[10] And in Rothko, the gradual absenting of the human figure becomes a steady act of killing. 'It was with the utmost reluctance that I found the figure could not serve my purposes', Rothko had once said, 'But a time came when none of us could use the figure without mutilating it.'[11] Yet, in a sublime paradox, the very absence of the figure made it possible for the human to be a pervasive and informing presence in Rothko's paintings. In his late and last paintings, pictorial space turns into a mysteriously frozen tragic theatre in which the human is affirmed, even reified, through extinction. In the 'abstract' Art of both Newman and Rothko, 'the single human figure—alone in a moment of utter immobility' becomes the Idea instead of an Image.[12]

This 'single human figure', brought into being while being obliterated in, and by, Art is actually three beings in one—the artist, his subject and the viewer. It is, therefore, a 'onement' in Barnett Newman's sense of the word. Another such creature can be found in the third volume, *La prisonnière* (*The Captive*, 1923), of Proust's novel, *A la recherche du temps perdue* (*In Search of Lost Time*). This is the writer, Bergotte, the description of whose death in a Parisian art gallery in front of Vermeer's *View of Delft*, becomes one of those extended and magnificent reflections on Art and Life and Time that are arranged across Proust's immense novel. One of the last things he wrote and inserted into the novel before his own death, the Death of Bergotte is both art history and art theory as fiction but informed with Proust's preoccupation with his own mortality. Proust himself had gone to see in May 1921, an exhibition of Dutch paintings at the Jeu de Paume where he had seen both the *View of Delft* (1660–1661) and the *Girl with the Pearl Earring* (1665–1667) by Vermeer. In Proust's transformation of this experience into fiction, a Modernist writer's confrontation with seventeenth-century Dutch Realism becomes a fatal catastrophe, narrated with a coldly ironic, yet beautifully elegiac sensationalism. Proust dramatises in Bergotte's death, a moment of transition from classic figurative realism to something like Abstract Expressionism, several years before the latter's time. This is a history of representation itself, almost comically enacted in the last few seconds of a man's life. And it is a transition not only in artistic practice (how one paints or writes) but also in aesthetic perception (how one looks at pictures and writes about them).

Hearing of Bergotte's death, Proust's narrator recalls, in *La prisonnière*, how Bergotte had been dying slowly of an undiagnosed illness.[13] (This illness—because this is Proust writing, and writing largely about himself—must have been an acute and terminal form of hypochondria.) Bergotte had stopped going out of doors and when he got out of bed, he remained swaddled in rugs and shawls, as if to protect himself from intense cold. When the few people who were allowed to see him wondered why he was wrapped up in travelling rugs, he would say merrily, 'After all, my dear fellow, life, as Anaxagoras has said, is a journey.' 'Thus,' the narrator reminisces, 'he went on growing steadily colder, a tiny planet offering a prophetic image of the greater, when gradually heat will withdraw from the earth, then life itself.'[14] This metaphor leads, in the narrator, to thoughts on the extinction of the human species itself by the 'invading cold' and a vision of what would happen to Art, and to artistic fame, when there are no human beings left on earth, only animals who have managed to survive the cold. Suddenly, in the dwindling light of this final entropy, all Art, even the most 'modern', appears pathetically human to the narrator, beyond salvage or salvation in the face of human mortality. His saving grace is irony and its tonal achievements. 'Irony: a modern ingredient', Rothko had written in 1958, 'A form of self-effacement and self-examination in which a man can, for a moment, escape his fate' (Murdoch 1977, 210).

Then, he recounts how Bergotte had read that the *View of Delft* was being shown in Paris, a picture which Bergotte had adored and 'imagined that he knew by heart'. Bergotte also read an art critic's account of 'a little patch of yellow wall' in the picture that was 'so well painted that it was, if one looked at it by itself, like some priceless specimen of Chinese art, of a beauty that was sufficient in itself.' He had not been able to recall this detail, so after eating a few potatoes and overcoming some initial spells of dizziness, he set out for the gallery and reached Vermeer's great work:

> He noticed for the first time some small figures in blue, that the sand was pink, and, finally, the precious substance of the tiny patch of yellow wall. His dizziness increased; he fixed his gaze, like a child upon a yellow butterfly that it wants to catch, on the precious little patch of wall. 'That's how I ought to have written,' he said. 'My last books are too dry, I ought to have gone over them with a few layers of colour, made my language precious in itself, like this little patch of yellow wall.' In a celestial pair of scales there appeared to him, weighing down one of the pans, his own life, while the other contained the little patch of wall so beautifully painted in yellow. (Proust 1989, vol. 3, 185)

And then he had two more attacks of dizziness and died on the floor of the gallery in front of the picture. 'He was dead,' remarks the narrator 'Dead forever? Who can say?'

Bergotte's is a death by colour. In his last moments, his eye transforms Vermeer's painting, first, into an Impressionist work, reducing the figures and the sand to their colour elements, blue and pink, and then, as the unity of the whole work begins to disintegrate in his eyes, he picks up a little detail, again for its vividness of colour and in no time this detail—'the tiny patch of yellow wall'—becomes the part which creates its own whole, a new painting 'in itself' (a phrase that recurs in this passage). This new painting is what a more modern vocabulary would call a pure 'colour-field', a colour become shape ('patch'). Yet it never quite dissociates itself completely from its mimetic link with the wall. Its Truth and Beauty, as a work of art in itself, lie both in capturing the vital essence of yellowness and in representing—in colour, texture and shape—what that particular sunlit bit of wall in Delft was 'really like', its 'precious substance'. But if one were to forget the original wall and see the detail simply as a patch of colour and texture ('layers of colour'), enlarged independently of the rest of Vermeer's painting, then one could be looking at an Abstract Expressionist work, a yellow rectangle which an artist like Rothko could have painted. And, in effect, this is what Bergotte does with 'his' fragment of Vermeer. (Are abstract paintings, then, 'little patches' taken out of some gigantic, prior figurative work and given a life and value and truth of their own?)

Bergotte's patch of yellow is also a subjective composite. Modern readers of Proust have tried to identify the exact detail in Vermeer's painting that Bergotte fixes on and have come up with three such patches. Bergotte's patch is not only a merging, in the eye and in the mind, of these three (or possibly more) details but it is also a telescoping of his last viewing of the picture with his vivid memories of it from previous viewings (he imagined that he knew the picture 'by heart'). So, the little patch of yellow wall is a mental image—like the famous 'madeleine' dipped in tea, in the overture to the novel's opening volume, *Du côté de chez Swann* (*Swann's Way*, 1913)—gathering into itself an entire history of private sensation, of looking, remembering and reviving.

From being something realised in Vermeer's art, the patch of wall becomes, therefore, an Idea in Bergotte's soul and memory, a fugitive Ideal that his own art, in another medium, wants to capture. Proust's image for this is poignantly Classical: 'he fixed his gaze, like a child upon a yellow butterfly that it wants to catch, on the precious little patch of wall'. In the art and mythology of antiquity, Psyche is, at once, soul, butterfly and Cupid's human lover who is made a goddess only after she knows suffering through love. In Classical Art, the butterfly emerging from the chrysalis stands for the soul leaving the body at death and it later becomes an image for the resurrected soul in Christian iconography. Proust's butterfly, so luminously mythological (like the 'celestial pair of scales' later), gives Bergotte's vision of Vermeer's yellow wall a quality of inwardness such as an Idea in Bergotte's soul which is just about to be, but is never quite, fully bodied forth or 'expressed' as a realised image in Bergotte's Art. There is a delicately Platonic feel to this, heightened a little later, by the 'celestial' aura given to the pair of scales. Yet the lightness of the butterfly itself and the comic irony of the narrator never allow the image to lose its elusively psychological and modern character. But this most fleeting image of the artist's soul—the place where what he sees and longs to create, pleasure and desire, restlessly reside—prepares the reader for the extended piece of Platonism that follows the account of Bergotte's death.

Plato's theory of 'anamnesis'—in dialogues such as the *Phaedrus* and the *Phaedo*—is yet another of his 'myths' that are poised uncertainly between the literal and the metaphorical. In it, Forms and Ideas become an argument for the immortality of the soul. We know of Ideas and are able to enjoy and long for the Beautiful and the Good, because our souls were, before birth, in a place where these Ideas or Forms were clearly seen. The incarnated soul tends to forget this knowledge but may be reminded of it by philosophy and dialectics, as the slave-boy in *Meno* is made to solve the geometric riddle by Socrates, who reminds the boy of what he already knew before he was born into slavery. In *anamnesis*, the realm of Ideas is entirely separated from the sensible world in which human beings exist and their journey from illusion to reality—in the Myth of the Cave, for instance—is actually a process of recovery through recollection. Proust's narrator wonders—with a hard, brilliant, disenchanted playfulness—whether Bergotte's soul would survive his death.

> All that we can say is that everything is arranged in this life as though we entered it carrying a burden of obligations contracted in a former life; there is no reason inherent in the conditions of life on this earth that can make us consider ourselves obliged to do good, to be kind and thoughtful, even to be polite, nor for an atheist artist to consider himself obliged to begin over again a score of times a piece of work the admiration aroused by which will matter little to his worm-eaten body, like a patch of yellow wall painted with so much skill and refinement by an artist destined to be forever unknown and barely identified under the name Vermeer. All these obligations, which have no sanction in our present life, seem to belong to a different world, a world based on kindness,

> scrupulousness, self-sacrifice, a world entirely different from this one and which we leave in order to be born on this earth, before perhaps returning there to live once again beneath the sway of laws which we obeyed because we bore their precepts in our hearts, not knowing whose hand had traced them there—those laws to which every profound work of the intellect brings us nearer and which are invisible only—if then!—to fools. (Proust 1989, vol. 3, 186)

Proust both humanises the Platonic realm of Ideas and separates it from the 'fallen' human world. It becomes a lost but glimmeringly remembered, realm of human goodness and also the place from where the laws that govern and are expressed in 'every profound work of intellect' emanate—Vermeer's as well as Plato's. For Plato, this world was far beyond the human. But for Proust, it is a realm that we have lost in human time, through an entirely mortal process of forgetting and loss. It can be recovered imperfectly only in the pleasures and rigours of Art and private memory. Yet its laws may be revealed to all but fools (of the non-Erasmian variety) and herein lies Proust's sublime conceitedness.

But Proust's account of the death of Bergotte and the birth of Modern Art is framed, and subjected to an almost brutal irony, by yet another Platonic idea. The narrator, when he hears of Bergotte's death, is deep into his complicated and tormented love for Albertine. He reads in the papers of Bergotte's death the day before and is struck by the inaccuracy of this account, for Albertine had told him that she had met Bergotte the day before, when, according to the papers, he was already supposed to have been dead. It is only much later that he learns that the papers were correct and that Albertine had the 'charming skill' of 'lying naturally'—her artless Art.

> What she said, what she admitted, had to such a degree the same characteristics as the formal evidence of the case—what we see with our own eyes or learn from irrefutable sources—that she sowed thus in the gaps of her life episodes from another life the falsity of which I did not then suspect and began to perceive only at a much later date. (Proust 1989, vol. 3, 187)

Albertine embodies all the reasons for which Plato banished the painter and the poet from his ideal republic. These men traffic not only in copies of copies but also in 'falsity' and lies; and the more realistic their art, the more dangerous they are. Albertine's lies, as the narrator gradually realises, are 'animated, coloured with the very hues of life'. They are her own little patches of yellow wall. What inspires her is 'verisimilitude alone' and she is surpassed in her 'storytelling' only by her friend 'blossoming' and 'rose-pink' like her, in whose lies 'one saw … in front of one the thing—albeit imaginary—which she was describing, through the eyes, as it were, of her words' (Proust 1989, vol. 3, 190). Bergotte's life-in-death was, therefore, quite literally, a lie. Proust is here juxtaposing two kinds of human creativity—also two kinds of 'verisimilitude'—and then letting one frame the other. Vermeer is seen through the eyes of Bergotte, who, in turn, is briefly (for the narrator) placed within Albertine's lie.

Plato offers two explanations of the human imagination—a 'good' one, in his theory of Ideas, embodied in the philosopher and a 'bad' one, in the figures of the deceiving painter and the lying poet. After Plato, art, literature and aesthetics have tried to co-opt the good theory in various ways and defended the artist from the bad one, yet without entirely disavowing the latter's trueness and perverse charm:

> … given Man, by birth, by education,
> Imago Dei who forgot his station,
> The self-made creature who himself unmakes,
> The only creature ever made who fakes,
> With no more nature in his loving smile
> Than in his theories of a natural style,
> What but tall tales, the luck of verbal playing,
> Can trick his lying nature into saying
> That love, or truth in any serious sense,
> Like orthodoxy, is a reticence?[15]

Proust's account of Art, in the death of Bergotte, seems to contrast Albertine's art with Vermeer's and Bergotte's. But 'contrast' seems to imply apartness and polarity, both of which are made impossible by Proust's own art of storytelling, which interlaces these two distinct strands within Plato's philosophy. Great Art—emphatically human and always modern—remains reticently (and sometimes volubly) poised between Bergotte's patch of yellow wall and Albertine's 'story'—between laws and lies, absence and presence, Idea and Image. But the word 'and' is perhaps too simple for joining these words in pairs. What Plato himself feared and his subsequent footnote-makers (philosophers as well as artists) affirmed with fewer misgivings, is that the Idea might more humanely reside 'in' the Image and—bad news for philosophy—the Image, in the Idea. The great and difficult work of Art is to keep that little preposition in place.

NOTES

1. Kosuth's work is also a rather simplifying homage to Magritte's two versions of *This is not a Pipe*, made in the late 1920s, which then became the subject of Foucault's brilliant 1968 essay with the same title. In the second version, Magritte presents a carefully drawn pipe with the text, 'This is not a pipe' written underneath in a frame that is placed on an easel standing on a clearly depicted floor. Above everything, in the picture-room's realm of the Ideal, floats a pipe exactly like the one in the frame, but much larger. Would this picture have been possible without Plato?
2. On 'aura', see Benjamin (1992, 211–244).
3. I have used here the text and its very literal translation provided in Erwin Panofsky (1968, 117–118). Here are Michelangelo's lines, '*Non ha l'ottimo artista in se alcun concetto,/ Ch'un marmo solo in se non circoscriva/ Col suo soverchio; e solo a quello arriva/ La man che ubbidisce all'intelletto.*'
4. Sir Philip Sidney (1973, 101). (The *OED* also quotes this sentence.) Shepherd's long note on this passage (157–158) shows how Sidney's *Idea* is not 'pure Platonism' but is a keyword in his poetics that 'runs parallel to Mannerist theory of painting'.
5. For a wonderfully readable exploration of the complex relations between Bach's counterpoint, certain kinds of modern art and mathematics, see Hofstadter (2000).
6. John Keats, 'Ode on a Grecian Urn' (1820).
7. Newman's own words, quoted in *Concepts of Modern Art*, 197.
8. Ibid., 191.
9. Ibid., 195.
10. Ibid., 199.
11. Ibid., 206.
12. Ibid., 197. These are Rothko's own words, written in 1947.
13. I have used the English translation of Proust's novel by C.K. Scott Montcrieff, Terence Kilmartin and Andreas Mayor, 3 volumes (Penguin, 1989), entitled *Remembrance of Things Past*. The Death of Bergotte is in volume 3, 180–191.
14. Ibid., 182.
15. W.H. Auden, 'The Truest Poetry Is the Most Feigning' (1953).

REFERENCES

Auden, W.H. *Collected Poems*. Edited by Edward Mendelson. Faber: London, 2007.

Benjamin, Walter. 'The Work of Art in the Age of Mechanical Reproduction'. In *Illuminations*, translated by Harry Zohn, 211–244. London: Fontana Books, 1992.

Coleridge, Samuel Taylor. *Biographia Literaria*. Edited by James Engell and W. Jackson Bate. Princeton: Princeton University Press, 1984.

Gablik, Suzi. 'Minimalism.' In *Concepts of Modern Art: From Fauvism to Postmodernism*, edited by Nikos Stangos, 200. London: Thames and Hudson, 1997.

Greene, Donald, ed. *Samuel Johnson*, 677–697. Oxford: Oxford University Press, 1984.

Harrison, Charles. 'Abstract Expressionism.' In *Concepts of Modern Art: From Fauvism to Postmodernism*, edited by Nikos Stangos, 200. London: Thames and Hudson, 1997.

Hofstadter, Douglas R. *Gödel, Escher, Bach: An Eternal Golden Braid*. London: Penguin Books, 2000.

Holland, Philemon. *Plutarch*. London: Arnold Hatfield, 1603.

Murdoch, Iris. *The Fire and the Sun: Why Plato Banished the Artists*. Oxford: Oxford University Press, 1977.

Panofsky, Erwin. *Idea: A Concept in Art Theory*. London: Harper and Row, 1968.

Plato. *The Republic*. Translated by Desmond Lee. London: Penguin, 1983.

Proust, Marcel. *Remembrance of Things Past*. Translated by C.K. Scott Montcrieff, Terence Kilmartin and Andreas Mayor, 3 volumes. London: Penguin, 1989.

Riley, Bridget. *Dialogues on Art*. Edited by Robert Kudielka. London: Thames and Hudson, 2003.

Sidney, Philip. *An Apology for Poetry*. Edited by Geoffrey Shepherd. Manchester: Manchester University Press, 1973.

Smith, Roberta. 'Conceptual Art'. In *Concepts of Modern Art: From Fauvism to Postmodernism*, edited by Nikos Stangos. London: Thames and Hudson, 1997.

Stangos, Nikos, ed. *Concepts of Modern Art: From Fauvism to Postmodernism*. London: Thames and Hudson, 1997.

Stevens, Wallace. *Collected Poems*. London: Faber Books, 1984.

Sylvester, David. *The Brutality of Fact: Interviews with Francis Bacon*. London: Thames and Hudson, 1997.

JEAN GENET AND JEAN-PAUL SARTRE: WRITING IN RESISTANCE AND THE PRACTICE OF THEORY

Michael Levenson

1

Their careers were parallel, intersecting, then divergent. Out of war each received intellectual acknowledgement that soon turned to celebrity: Sartre's existentialism became a global fascination and disturbance, Genet's success no less incendiary. Only months after the armistice, Sartre gave the soon-to-be-famous (notorious) lecture on 'Existentialism is a Humanism', later disowned but at the time reputation-clinching. Genet's five novels appeared in a furious rush in the mid- and later-1940s. When the two insurrectionists met in the cafés of Paris and then in the pages of Sartre's massive study *Saint Genet* (1952), their reputations were reciprocally sealed. Each was a mirror and de-forming mirror for the other. The present chapter means to parse the insurrection and the acclaim: the parallel development, the unsteady intersection and the glare of mutual illumination, disclosing and distorting. It takes the years 1949–1952 as focus, widening to the first post-war decade and then extending to brief consideration of the after-history of a nexus.

'Existentialism is a Humanism' was delivered on 29 October 1945 and published in a wildly successful small-book format soon after. The simplifying force of its polemic came to trouble Sartre but it had the advantage of clarifying both the appeal and the challenge. Existentialism, in Sartre's offering, was at its heart a repudiation of the bourgeois ascendancy. With the end of war, an exhausted middle class looked to restore its ravaged pieties: religion, tradition and social stability. Its props were the mottoes of the resigned universal truth: the 'common sayings' that 'all mean much the same—that you must not oppose the powers-that-be; that you must not fight against superior force; must not meddle in matters that are above your station' (Sartre 1948, 25–26). Against this impassive proverbial wisdom ('How like human nature', Sartre 1948, 26), Sartre deployed the provocations of contingency: existence precedes essence; human reality is undefined and indefinable; we make ourselves in, and only in, our acts.

These slogans had only recently taken canonical form when Sartre met Genet in 1944. Jean Cocteau was the intermediary, having made contact when Genet was still an unpublished writer, known to the French state as thief and prisoner. During the war he was in and out of confinement; he was also writing, riskily and prolifically and would later call prison the seedbed of his creativity. The five novels were composed in under five years in his early thirties. Their appearance marked a moment of brazen gay expression allied to late-modernist experimentalism (openly linked to Proust) and the legend of a life beyond legality.

Sartre admired the writing but no more than he appreciated the totemic life. Genet's precarity—orphan birth, confinement in Mettray Reformatory; the years of theft, prison, poverty and solitude—had no counterpart in the social and intellectual station that Sartre knew. Their differences in status, class and comfort were marked. Yet within the shifting political alliances and cultural hierarchies of the post-war years, the two figures not only traversed the distance between them but also helped to confuse its clarity. Genet gained literary status with his novels as speedily as Sartre had done with *Nausea* and as soon as he became a Parisian phenomenon, he moved through the cafés and into the theatres with comparable assurance.

Before celebrity came 'freedom'. An overworn credo now, *la liberté* was clarion in the first years after war—first in the liberation from the German occupiers, then in Sartrean metaphysics, both technical and popularised. Existential freedom for Sartre is the disowned origin of our human-ness. It has been repressed and repudiated because of the burdens it places on us: the anguish (of 'complete and utter responsibility') and abandonment (the absence of God). We escape these burdens through the blindness of 'bad faith', especially if we seek middle-class complacency. Yet, as aggressively as Sartre offered these propositions, they were often given an anodyne turn agreeable to peacetime consumerism. Freedom from occupation, freedom to buy.

Where *la liberté* cuts deeper is when it meets constraint and bafflement, as it had done during the Resistance. A shopper on the boulevards enjoys a freedom reduced to oppressive banality. But as *Being and Nothingness* (1943) articulated in close detail, the telling case is when others seem to control the making of meaning or even the right to movement and the assignment of name. So, in the case of Baudelaire, the subject of Sartre's first post-war biography (1947), a career of blight and disappointment discovered freedom in its moments of failure—failure to write, to act and to sustain vocation. The lesson of Baudelaire is that a life of false starts and reversals, of ennui and embarrassment, can be justified through the pain of lucidity. The more Baudelaire obstructs his own fulfilment, the more he understands freedom.

> ... whether they happened to be immediate actions or continuing enterprises, these plans, which he could never carry out, were always before his eyes. They forced themselves on his attention unceasingly, urgently, helplessly. If he suppressed completely the spontaneity of the reflected consciousness, by doing so he arrived at an even better understanding of its nature. He knew that it was its nature to hurl itself outside itself, to transcend itself in order to attain an end. That is why he was, perhaps, the first to define man by what lay beyond him. (Sartre 1967, 35–36)

> This perception of our own transcendence and of our unjustifiable gratuitousness must at the same time be a revelation of human freedom. And, in fact, Baudelaire always felt that he was free. (Sartre 1967, 39)

Sartre dedicated the book to Genet; the previous year he had written publisher's copy for *Miracle of the Rose* and as he adjusts his philosophy to his politics at the end of the 1940s, he comes to see Genet as fulfilment of what he had only sketched in the ennui of Baudelaire. Baudelaire, or at least Sartre's Baudelaire, had discovered the self-transcendence of freedom through the excruciations of lucid encounter with himself. Genet wasn't given the luxury of alienation from social privilege; as an orphan, thief, a gay man in daily poverty, he had to contend for lucidity, wresting it from dispossession. The Others, the bourgeoisie and their minions, have, own and flourish. For Genet, unlike Baudelaire, freedom must be physically adversarial and legally criminal.

There is more. Genet will dare you to name his guilt, force you to see what you call trespass. In its opening pages, *The Thief's Journal* portrays the blatant visibility of a tube of vaseline. During a raid, a Spanish detective has found it, partially rolled up, through a search of Genet's pockets. The 'very sign of abjection', the 'little gray leaden tube of vaseline', is used by the police to 'flourish their revenge, their hatred, their contempt' (Genet 1964, 20). But for Genet, the object becomes his own act of contempt, more contemptuous because most visible. In a characteristic Proustian manoeuvre, he thinks how the greasy contents remind him of an oil lamppost and a meeting with an aging woman, a thief, who could have been his mother. The private rumination, linking jelly, lamp, thief and mother, culminates in the high rhetoric of Genet's defiance.

> The tube of vaseline, which was intended to grease my prick and those of my lovers, summoned up the face of her who, during a

> reverie that moved through the dark alleys of the city, was the most cherished of mothers. It had served me in the preparation of so many secret joys, in places worthy of its discrete banality, that it had become the condition of my happiness, as my sperm-spotted handkerchief testified. Lying on the table, it was a banner telling the invisible legions of my triumph over the police. (Genet 1964, 21)

Most striking is the willingness to solicit the gaze of the Other, all those Others who have made Genet Other, especially the police as the most immediate arm of the norm. Genet consistently performs a distinctive rhythm, moving in darkness, neglected or concealed and then standing in the open, suddenly indifferent to concealment, prepared to be seen in unrepentant defeat. The murderer Maurice Pilorge, whose execution gave Genet literary impetus, mugged and wise-cracked on his ascent to the scaffold. Through *Our Lady of the Flowers*, a dying Divine parades through Montmartre in full eye-catching grandeur. In *Miracle of the Rose* Bulkaen accepts the spittle cast into his mouth by exulting as if the 'ghastly game' were 'a courtly one' (Genet 1971, 256). These incidents, among many, enact the ceremony of repudiation from below. Impossible to sink further into degradation, the victim glories in a prideful humiliation beyond further wounding.

A different openness to gazing occurs in the last of the novels, *The Thief's Journal,* where Genet goes furthest in testimony and confession. Sartre (2012, 545) calls it 'a literary testament or at least a conclusion', where 'Genet speaks of Genet without intermediary' (Genet 1964, 'Foreword', 1). Certainly, it represents the place where he writes fully of the most resistant, least digestible, of crimes: namely betrayal. Willingly, he testifies to its many instances and sharper pleasures. When Genet became the fast-rising successor to Proust and Céline, his theft could seem picturesque; even his gay sexuality had Proustian pedigree. But the caressing praise of treason and betrayal has been a trouble to friends and commentators, treason which 'had that power which was taking greater and greater hold of me' (Genet 1964, 50). '[B]egging and prostitution were to me a discipline which taught me to utilize ignoble elements, to apply them to my own ends, indeed, to take pleasure in my choosing them' (Genet 1964, 72) and these, writes Genet, are a prelude to the more intense satisfactions of betrayal. Setting aside the defensible cases where a treacherous act might be justified, where it might stand in service of the Good, he reserves his praise for 'low betrayal': the 'kind that cannot be justified by any heroic excuse. The sneaky, cringing kind, elicited by the least noble of sentiments'. The betrayer must be 'aware of his betrayal', must 'will it', and must 'be able to break the bonds of love uniting him with mankind' (Genet 1964, 242).

Leo Bersani has worked to preserve the outrage of Genet's treachery, describing it as a 'form of revolt that has no relation whatsoever to the laws, categories, and values it would contest and ideally destroy' (Bersani 1995, 152). Genet, argues Bersani, refuses 'any moral value whatsoever in homosexuality' (Genet 1964, 161) and this because his deepest aim is to refuse '*to participate in any sociality at all*' (Genet 1964, 168)—still further, to eliminate 'relationality' as such. These are strong claims, bracingly put; yet they surely miss Genet's unbroken *relation* to his unsleeping adversary, the be-normed social world. Few motifs are more frequent than his summoning of opposition. 'I want the total enemy', he wrote in an unpublished fragment, 'one who would hate me beyond all bounds' ('J.G. Seeks' in Genet, 1). And elsewhere: 'I would like the world not to change so that I can be against the world' (Genet 2004).

Central to his resistance (and revenge) is this assertion of an anomaly. Genet can be against the whole world because no one can be like Genet. The texts, especially *The Thief's Journal*, are laden with explanations. No events are mute, they come with present-tense commentary and often elaborate interpretation. But emphatically, Genet insists that the 'explanations I am giving occur to me spontaneously. They seem valid for my case. They are to be accepted for mine alone' (Genet 1964, 49). The singularity of vocation—to corrode the society that prevails, 'to be a thorn in its flesh, a remorse—an anxiety—a wound from which flowed its blood, which it dared not shed itself', in order 'to achieve something new with such rare matter' (Genet 1964, 244)—means that Genet can explain nothing but himself. That he is intent to interpret as much as to recount, that he so often shifts register from act to loquacious rumination, that the generalisations nevertheless account for no more than an anomalous history: this is decisive to his provocation and also his invitation to existential philosophy.

2

Invited to write a preface to Genet's collected works, Sartre—unexpectedly, amusingly—composed a book of over six hundred pages that appeared in 1952 and served as volume one of the collection. It thus came at the end of, and arguably *brought* to an end, Genet's career as a novelist. Just as notably, *Saint Genet* became a pivot in Sartre's career. The philosopher named it as one of his four principal texts and it was indeed the one that engendered the philosophic-political adversarialism that would persist for his last three decades.

In the first moments of the existentialist spectacle of 1945, Sartre was another who found it easy to make enemies. He found little difficulty, either politically or rhetorically, in repudiating the bourgeoisie—ever easy épater. The challenge from the Communists, on the other hand, raised questions of both philosophic principle and vehement political critique. Was existentialism only and ever an individualism? For all its insistence on commitment, did Sartrean freedom ever escape the ambit of personal will? Was it not, finally and fully, suited to the very bourgeoisie it took as an enemy? As Sartre himself characterised the charge: we are 'reproached for leaving out of account the solidarity of mankind and considering man in isolation' (Sartre 1948, 50). The Communist critique pressed the issue that acquired more force from the party's strength in France's post-liberation settlement.

'Existentialism is a Humanism' had shown Sartre's sensitivity to his left critics. He asserts, and will never cease to assert, that philosophy must begin with the Cartesian cogito. No other foundation is thinkable. But this is philosophic truth not class doxa: 'Our point of departure is, indeed, the subjectivity of the individual, and that for strictly philosophic reasons. It is not because we are bourgeois, but because we seek to base our teaching upon the truth' (Sartre 1948, 51–52). Nor does the cogito confine us to the nest of individuality:

> when we say 'I think' we are attaining to ourselves in the presence of the other, and we are just as certain of the other as we are of ourselves. Thus, the man who discovers himself directly in the *cogito* also discovers all the others, and discovers them as the condition of his own existence. He recognizes that he cannot be anything (in the sense in which one says one is spiritual, or that one is wicked or jealous) unless others recognize him as such. (Sartre 1948)

The *cogito* is immediate but not final, private but not alone. The Others are never not near, never not determining; they surround and impinge; they implicate the individual in the realm of 'inter-subjectivity (Sartre 1948, 53).

These distinctions and refinements—'cogito' and the 'cogito among others'—will trouble the career from this point forward. To his Communist critics, the bourgeois taint remains unmistakable: despite all the hand-waving towards the rest of us, the priority of consciousness gives away the game. For his part, Sartre knew this difficulty as crucial and refractory. The question of how to retain the precedence of individual existential freedom *and* the commitment to collective struggle stands as close to the centre of Sartrean vocation as any. As it came into provocatively crisp focus in the later 1940s, so did Genet.

Impossible to know precisely when Sartre understood what Genet could mean to existential philosophy, when he recognised the potency, not of confirming example, but of a generative challenge at a moment when his existentialism was obliged to change. Sartre's next major work *What is Literature?* (1965) continues the bickering conversation with the Communists. The book gives a brisk refusal of Marxism, contending that the

> effect of dialectical materialism … is to make Good and Evil vanish conjointly. There remains only the historical process, and then Stalinist communism does not attribute so much importance to the individual that his sufferings and even his death can be redeemed if they help to hasten the day when power is seized. (Sartre 1965)

On the other hand, and crucially, Sartre embraces the arrival of socialism after the final decay of capitalism; he sees no other solution to the troubles of contemporary history. But since literature 'is in essence heresy', no true writer can join the Communist Party, which is 'incompatible with the honest practice of the literary craft' (Sartre 1965, 251–252).

According to the strict canons of *What is Literature?* the post-war writer must accept the new responsibilities of contemporary history. It will no longer be sufficient, if it ever was, to dream of universal truth and literary purity. War and occupation have taught the inescapable lesson: 'All at once we felt ourselves abruptly *situated*' (Sartre 1965, 207): 'Brutally re-integrated into history, we had no choice but to produce a literature of historicity' (Sartre 1965, 209). Sartre takes this to mean that fiction must portray, not 'average', but 'extreme' situations (Sartre 1965, 217); it must abandon the false equanimity of an all-knowing narrator; it must render character/narrators who are trapped in the midst of 'incomprehensible events', whose outcome they cannot foresee (Sartre 1965, 222). All of these demands point to Genet, who nevertheless receives only incidental mention within *What is Literature?* (as one who had spoken of the 'politeness' owed to the reader). Sartre had met Genet three years earlier, had written his preface to *Miracle of the Rose*; and would soon compose a foreword to *The Thief's Journal*. If he ignores Genet in 1947, it is surely because of the last demand in *What is Literature?* that the contemporary writer engages a 'literature of praxis' (Sartre 1965, 290), 'tied up with the coming of a socialist Europe' (Sartre 1965, 289), not 'pure propaganda' (Sartre 1965, 291) but fully committed.

Much of the uncertainty of Sartre's position in the late 1940s is shown through the cautious approach to Genet. But over the next few years, as he works through the difficult balance of commitments—to the heretical writer who must never join the Party, to the necessity of Socialism, to the primacy of the free cogito, to the claims of intersubjectivity, to the recognition of historical necessity—Genet moves from the margins of casual mention to become the emblematic figure of the age.

What Genet's life and life-writing manifest is, most deeply, an existential orientation: an opening to the suddenness of reversal, abrupt discontinuity, epiphany, calamity—and this because, 'A catastrophe is always possible. Metamorphosis lies in wait.' For Genet, the law of metamorphosis constitutes an erotic principle ('Hardly had I touched him, when the stairway changed: he was master of the world', Sartre 1964, 40) but beyond eros, metamorphosis becomes a condition of being. The words 'sudden' and 'suddenly' give the rhythmic punctuation of Genet's writing, where at any moment, a face changes ('suddenly become sad'); the landscape alters; a border is crossed. The transformation is at once inner and outer: 'I'm suddenly alone because the sky is blue, the tree is green, the street quiet, and because a dog, who is as alone as I am, is walking in front of me' (*Funeral Rites*, 160). Metamorphosis can elevate but it can also ruthlessly depress.

Genet understands that his metamorphic life was originary and in that sense inevitable. The orphan assigned to a village family knows he comes from elsewhere and from someone else. Arrested, convicted, despised and dispossessed, change is forced upon him. How could he help but live 'suddenly?' A superstitious waiting for the next thrust of accident pervades the work and the work of life. What gives the bite of challenge, though, is the upsurge of will, that lives alongside accident. In the midst of overwhelming pressures—life as a beggar, life during European war—there is still room to manoeuvre, to plot and act, to steal, seduce and betray.

Also, to write. When he first loomed up for Cocteau in the midst of occupied Paris, he seemed the marvellous but still inassimilable prodigy. Who was this tainted criminal, carrying his poetry on brown paper? Who was he to presume? And who was this gay man to hymn the song of sexual passion for thieves and beggars and assassins? Above all, Genet carried the claim of experience: that he had been there, touched that, given himself and his senses to a world only imagined by successful writers, no matter how politically dedicated. The brutal facts of experience trumped the ideology of commitment. If he didn't fit all the criteria laid out in *What is Literature?* it would be the theory not Genet that had to change.

That he was a famously difficult personality is also to the point. Hyper-sensitive and touchy, irritable and demanding, he will bicker with those, above all Cocteau, who take pains to help him, to publish and promote him. Capable of affection and loyalty among a handful of friends and lovers, he was more expert in rudeness and ingratitude. Most abiding, though, was the practice and then theory of solitude.

The accident of his life and the laws of the state meant that Genet was often alone—in 'utter solitude'. 'Much solitude', he goes on, 'has forced me to become my own companion' (Genet 1964, 85). That he affirms the isolation forced upon him, that he sees it as a proud separateness—these declarations will never be far from Genet's testimony: 'the greater my guilt in your eyes, the more whole, the more totally assumed, the greater will be my freedom. The more perfect my solitude and uniqueness' (Genet 1964, 84). Bersani is surely right to see the infamous practice of treachery in the service of solitude: Genet says just this in confessing that,

> It is perhaps their moral solitude to which I aspire that makes me admire traitors and love them—a taste for solitude being the sign of my pride, and pride, the manifestation of my strength, the employment and proof of this strength. For I shall have broken the stoutest of bonds, the bonds of love. (Genet 1964, 46)

Again, though, we should see this not as a break with 'relationality', but relation in its most austere aspect, the utterly solitary I, knowing itself only through the universe of others from which it stands separate. Notably, when that universe includes readers, everything changes: 'My solitude in prison was total. Now that I speak of it, it is less so' (Genet 1964, 110).

In very few years after the end of the war, Genet became an incarnation of existential integrity, validated as much through the stringent personal history as through the gripping texts. Thomas Flynn has fairly claimed that he served as a model for 'authenticity' (Flynn 2014, 278), a status granted by Sartre after the hesitations in *What is Literature?* Presumably, the change is due, not only to Sartre's developing views, but also to Genet's acquaintance and interest in existential philosophy. Written several years into their friendship, *The Thief's Journal* echoes Sartre's thematics, even his phrasing, as in a critical passage such as this.

> My eyes burned. I was hungry. Copper glints played over my tough beard in the sunlight. I was dry, young and sad. I learned to smile at things and meditate upon them. As a young Frenchman on that shore, from my solitude, from my beggar's state, from the dust of the ditches that rose up in tiny individual clouds about each foot, renewing themselves at every step, my pride derived a consoling

> singularity which contrasted with the banal sordidness of my apparel. (Genet 1964, 74)

Genet never confused himself with anyone else. His acute sense of being his 'own companion' not only separated him from others but created the fascination (and the glamour) of self-sufficiency.

3

Solitude, singularity and authenticity—the claim of Genet on existential theory was evident. Moreover, to encounter a living author through the intimacy of extended conversation was to locate concern where Sartre now concluded it must be: in the immediately situated moment of the historical present tense. Here is where the 'cogito' lives, here in the first quickening of freedom after the war. Genet is at once an incomparable example of post-war adversarial life and test case of existential philosophy. Will it be possible to reconstruct the 'mythical representations he has given us of his universe' (Sartre 2012, 5) and to do so from the first-person standpoint of the living being, as he invents project, meaning and value?

What makes the case still more formidable is that the Sartre of 1950 is not the existentialist of the wartime 1940s. Since the founding of *Les Temps Moderne* (1945), he had unceasingly engaged the political fury of liberated Europe. Through collaboration with Simone de Beauvoir, Maurice Merleau-Ponty and Raymond Aron; through the tense relationship with Albert Camus; and most substantially, through involvement in national and global politics in the Cold War, Sartre had descended from the abstract portrayal of the existential condition. At the end of 1947, he helped to found the *Rassemblement démocratique révolutionnaire* (Revolutionary Democratic Assembly), offered as a third force between Stalinist Russia and US-led global capitalism.

> Between the rottenness of capitalist democracy, the weaknesses and defects of a certain social democracy and the limitation of Communism to its Stalinist form, we believe an assembly of free men for revolutionary democracy is capable of giving new life to the principles of freedom and human dignity by binding them to the struggle for social revolution. (Quoted in Birchall 2004, 94)

When the *RDR* began to tilt in the American direction, the movement broke up in disputes and it was in this period that Sartre turned earnestly to Genet. At the same time, however, he was moving towards his closest alliance with the French Communist Party (PCF), beginning a much-noticed and distinct period in the career (1952–1956). During those four years, he not only came close to the party orthodoxy but also began a thorough reconsideration of Marxism. Sartre had described the 'main objective' of the RDR as uniting 'all revolutionary claims with the idea of freedom' (Cohen-Solal 2005, 302). Over the next two decades, he will develop this conjunction on the philosophic plane, as he awaits some advance in politics.

The first encounter with Genet had come at the moment of early existentialist confidence in the sovereignty of freedom. It's not that constraints of 'situation' had been ignored but emphasis fell strongly on the resources, the capacity and the wide amplitude of the free agent. In characteristic tones, Sartre identified the freedom on which literature must rest: 'whether he is an essayist, a pamphleteer, a satirist, or a novelist, whether he speaks only of individual passions or whether he attacks the social order, the writer, a free man addressing free men, has only one subject—freedom' (Sartre 1965, 68). The interest in Genet as exemplary freedom dates from these early post-war years. The long-deferred writing of the book, though, meant that Sartre was reconsidering the claims of revolutionary politics and Marxist philosophy as he wrote Genet from freedom into constraint.

4

The immensities of *Saint Genet* lie not only in the sheer length but the immense labour of interpretation that is dedicated both to the illumination of Jean Genet and the status of interpretation itself. Its credo is never not worth citing.

> I have tried to do the following: to indicate the limit of psychoanalytical interpretation and Marxist explanation and to demonstrate that freedom alone can account for a person in his totality; to show this freedom at grips with destiny, crushed at first by its mischances, then turning upon them and digesting them little by little; to prove that genius is not a gift but the way out that one invents in desperate cases; to learn the choice that a writer makes of himself, of his life and of the meaning of the universe, including even the formal characteristics of his style and composition, even the structure of his images and of the particularity of his tastes; to review in detail the history of his liberation. (Sartre 2012, 584)

The vertiginous ambition has disoriented the reception of *Saint Genet*. Its enormity has been its memorable feature. Lost has been the closer texture of argument which is what is needed here.

The orphan Genet lived under foster care in a farming community founded on laws of property, codes of legitimacy and norms of faith: 'Work, family, country, honesty, property', writes Sartre, 'such is his conception of the Good' (Sartre 2012, 6). Yet, in this place at that moment, the young man fails to meet the terms of value. 'He is a fake child', because in the Morvan, to Have is to Be. Having nothing, the child Genet is nothing; so, he steals. He steals in order to pretend he *has* and *is*: 'His austere and feverish quest for Being becomes an imaginary satisfaction only' (Sartre 2012, 12).

Sooner or later, he is caught in the act of theft. He is ten or thereabouts, when he is discovered and a voice names him a thief. 'That was how it happened' surmises Sartre, 'in that or some other way' (Sartre 2012, 17). If he were older, or if he were in different circumstances, less fixed and constrained, he might have resisted, returned contempt for contempt. But he has nothing, no resources and no outlet: 'He is trapped like a rat' (Sartre 2012, 21). The young boy, hemmed in on all sides, is named Evil and therefore Other. Unable to resist the imposition of categories, he must accept them, must know himself as he is named and called. This is a key for Sartre: that the orphan is compelled to become 'Another than Self' (Sartre 2012, 35). He will never simply accord with himself. What he needs and seeks is a 'way out', but how is that possible?

Here Sartre arrives at a dramatic crossing, for himself as well as his subject. Genet cannot shift the burden of his naming. He cannot not be the thief. Therefore, he will affirm what he cannot in any case deny: 'he has chosen the worst. He had no other choice' (Sartre 2012, 49). Or as *The Thief's Journal* had recently put it, 'If he has courage—please understand—the guilty man decides to be what crime has made him' (Sartre 2012, 242). Sartre elevates the phrase to high philosophic stakes in another of the book's credos: 'We are not lumps of clay, and what is important is not what people make of us but what we ourselves make of what they have made of us' (Sartre 2012, 49).

The story that Sartre tells, intricate and urgent, is that the trapped orphan can retrieve freedom by willing his necessity, willing it to the hilt. He becomes the outlaw he is judged to be: 'thief, homosexual, traitor'. Because he is resourceful and because he has the opportunity to read and the capacity to listen to an inner ear, Genet discovers how the solitude of illegitimacy gives him room to dream. He dreams of Evil, argues *Saint Genet*, the evil that brings revenge on those who have crushed him. He creates the carnival of a fantasy universe, a counter-world which can escape the oppressive weight of the Real.

Here, Sartre's book gives a shrewd reading of camp *avant la lettre* and *avant Sontag*. Genet, when free to belong to the gay culture of Montmartre, can break 'away from being in order to withdraw into pure *appearing*' and can become 'lord of hoaxes, booby traps, and optical illusions' (Sartre 2012, 359–360). He takes on the vocation of fakery—the extravagant illusion of costume and sexual identity, of style, of scent and voice. He exploits the truth of 'our ambiguous society' where 'naturalism and artificialism coexist' (Sartre 2012, 361). It is an embrace of bad taste that always prefers the copy to the real. Even in sexual passion, argues Sartre, Genet is driven above all by the image that precedes and succeeds the thing itself. Masturbation ascends above intercourse; like the imaginary satisfactions of theft, it 'de-realises' the world.

Within a narrative that depends on the precision of its hinges, the crucial swivel is to Beauty—not art, but beauty, the beautiful appearance that consorts with Evil. To choose it is to pursue the satisfactions of the shadow, the unreal, the masturbatory and the imaginary. Sartre holds that this rejection should be accepted for its radicalism, as a radical refusal of the exclusions of the Just, who police the realm of appearance with special and excessive zeal. The goal is to dwell in artifice; the tactic is the *gesture*, which gives the glamorous sheen of a fabricated identity (thief, traitor). No life-changing action is possible (even conceivable) for the gesture-self: '[t]he *act* does not matter: the aim is to be' (Sartre 2012, 321).

For the hemmed-in illegitimate thief, the narrow avenue seems to lead in this one direction: 'Evil, betrayal, failure, gestures, appearances, Beauty: this complex assemblage is the "tangle of snakes"' (Sartre 2012, 192). According to Sartre, it might have gone no further, ending in 'an extraordinary effort [that] transformed acts into gestures, being into the imaginary, the world into phantasmagoria and himself into appearance' (Sartre 2012, 161). The saving turn and the last metamorphosis occur because of contingencies that persist within the narrow margin of this freedom. The entrapped gay-thief-beggar happens to hear a fellow-prisoner attempt a poem, and happens to realise he can do better. The contingency of an event meets the accident of a propensity: Genet's who-knows-whence verbal consciousness, his taste in words and meanings.

In the reflex of an instant, what Sartre calls a 'small click', Genet began his own poem that ultimately became 'Le Condamné à Mort' ('The Man Condemned to Death'), the launching work of the career. The other prisoners mock his poem; hurl 'insults and jeers' (Sartre 2012, 427) that only encourage Genet to complete the work. Within the drama of *Saint Genet*, the poem-in-revenge is the last 'gesture', and the first literary act. Contingent though it may be, the incident shows that words can produce not only a *being* (gesture) but a *doing* (action). The poem can affect its listeners. If they taunt and deride, so much the better for the campaign of resistance/revenge.

From that beginning—the small click—a vocation unfolds. Since the branding of the orphan as a thief, his one avenue had been to live symbolically, to turn theft and sex into gestures of Beauty/Evil, to survive by 'de-realising' the world. Then comes transformation, Genet recognising how language can bring a return to the real. This is what unfolds in the writing of the first novel *Our Lady of the Flowers* which begins under the sway of the old gesture-dreaming. An 'epic of masturbation', Sartre calls the book: its words 'are those that a prisoner said to himself while panting with excitement' (Sartre 2012, 448). Yet, within the work a final hinge swings, when Genet realises that a novel has a life beyond the writer; it can find readers whom it will scathe and change. *Our Lady* is then a dream 'that contains its own awakening' (Sartre 2012, 455). Genet wakes to find that 'With words, the Other reappears' (Sartre 2012, 456). 'A word uttered is word as subject; heard, it is object' (Sartre 2012, 457). The orphan boy had no instruments to resist the coercions of naming and judging, but left alone to dream, he discovered that words of fantasy ('I wrote the verses in order to be moved', Sartre 2012, 426) could become instruments acting upon others. Genet the Fantasist returns to the world as Novelist. Or put in Sartre's terms, 'if he prefers the work of art to theft, it is because theft is a criminal act which is derealized into a dream, whereas a work of art is a dream of murder which is realized by an act' (Sartre 2012, 482).

The act of writing as reprisal, the novel as insurrection—this is the possibility that the long search has revealed. If Genet's fellow prisoners were the first victims of his wounding words ('Le Condamné à Mort'), he soon turned towards his real, living and ancient oppressors, the complacently punitive bourgeoisie with their morals and their state—the Just. As a thief he had gone unnoticed, at best one hoodlum among the rest, numbered more than known. Having become a published novelist, he can scar them in the nether places. This is what the word-as-object can do: Suppose—this is how Sartre describes the discovery of novel-writing—suppose

> he gave himself, *by an act*, the power of existing elsewhere, in all his virulence, for horrified minds? What if he conferred ubiquity upon himself with his own hands? What if he deliberately invented a way of embodying himself in strange substances and forced the others to discover him there? (Sartre 2012, 488–489)

In spite of their scruples, the Just will be obliged to see him. What is more and more delicious, they will be obliged to see through his eyes and within his desires. The beauty of the style, the play of structure, the workings of the canny and seductive 'I', implicate readers in the world they made Other, and because they cannot help but take on the subjectivity of Genet, they find the Other in themselves. Reading this guilty author, they become guilty. 'The reader has only to turn ten pages to discover himself: *I* am bad, repentant, a homosexual, *I* am a monster' (Sartre 2012, 499). The long-deferred escape leads to the spectacular triumph of the unavoidable novelist.

Here is the imperative telos that drives through the excess of *Saint Genet:* the authority of authorship. Sartre's book is, at the end, a paean to writing (and unacknowledged source of the Derridean 'writing' that will work to replace its philosophic dominance): 'Before writing, what is [Genet]? An insignificant little worm, a bug that scurries, unnoticed, between the slats of the floor' (Sartre 2012, 486). It takes many years and many accidents before Genet awakens, but once alert to the power of the word ('My victory is verbal'), he becomes exemplary and legendary as the hero of authentic freedom, won from the most unavailing circumstances.

5

We return to the tube of vaseline. For Sartre, it had become an interpretive talisman, to which he recurs many times. 'The ignominious accessory', he writes, 'is taken from him and put on a table; it becomes Genet himself firstly because it is his property and secondly because it reveals and symbolizes his homosexuality.' It is 'an effigy of Genet' (Sartre 2012, 488). But elsewhere, the identity changes; it concerns not the person but his work:

> About his books one could say, without changing a word, what he said about his tube of vaseline: 'I was sure that this puny and most humble object would hold its own against them; by its mere presence it would be able to exasperate all the police in the world; it would draw upon itself contempt, hatred, white and dumb rages.' (Sartre 2012, 490)

The vaseline is Genet; it is his work. These are indeed equations on which *The Thief's Journal* depends; they are what tempt Sartre to what we may call his allegory of metaphors by which he reads Genet's life in terms of successive identities. The life is a coerced metaphor (the boy is a thief) escaped through the play of contingency and freedom-within-constraint. The search for a 'way out' becomes a search for different metaphors: the self as traitor, as aesthete, as evildoer and as saint. Each stage is a phase in the allegory; each transcends and cancels the previous. The life/career is measured through its substitutions, culminating in the apotheosis of the writer.

A different trope wends through Genet's writing itself. This is a figure of shift and slippage, the accumulation of names and terms and epithets. Towards the end of the *The Thief's Journal*, Genet muses over his pocket address book, listing the thieves he has known and the streets where he found them. Accordingly, the address book, 'has the same authority as a prick. It is my treasure.' He proceeds to enumerate the names and places and then clarifies:

> I've said they were handsome. Not with regular good looks, but with something else, made up of power, despair and many other qualities, the mention of which involves comment: shame, shrewdness, laziness, resignation, contempt, boredom, courage, cowardice, resignation, contempt, boredom, courage, cowardice, fear.... It would mean a long list. (Genet 1964, 251, ellipsis in original)

The pattern is characteristic and recurrent. One term engenders another in a 'list' without a natural limit. Of the much-cherished Guy, we read how he possessed 'some indefinable element of meanness, stupidity, virility, elegance, pomp and viscosity'.

We should take this as a leading tactic of Genet's resistance: to confuse the work of epithet and the values that cling to the epithetic. Fair enough to say with Sartre that some terms ascend above others and that saint is the highest of all (saintliness is 'the most beautiful word in human language'). Yet here, too, there is corrosion, depletion and evacuation. 'I run the risk of going astray by confounding saintliness with solitude' and 'am I not, by this sentence running the risk of restoring to saintliness the Christian meaning which I want to remove from it?' (Genet 1964, 215). Such restless deft recasting of his most caressed and treasured terms is characteristic and perpetual.

Commonly, Genet's project is seen as Nietzschean, a transvaluation of all values. Such acts of reversal are of course available and evident: criminals are flowers; evil beautiful; treachery gorgeous; theft precious. Throughout the oeuvre, no value is immune to inversion. But inversion has its own invert. To cherish evil as beautiful is to change evil but to preserve the value of beauty, just as praising the 'moral elegance' of theft transvalues thievery only by retaining the valence of elegant morality. One conventional meaning holds, so that a second may be reversed—a semantic project always under strain. Even when he arrives at the supreme, the most beautiful word, 'saint', it has a meaning that is both foundational and unsettled. The result is continuous slide along the axes of value, the 'long list' of signifiers, as in a bravura passage such as this:

> I would be overjoyed if I could call [Lucien] scoundrel, blackguard, riffraff, guttersnipe, hoodlum, crook, charming names whose

> function is to evoke what you, derisively, call a pretty world. But these words sing. They hum. They also evoke for you the sweetest and spiciest pleasures, since, placing before them, under your breath, the words tender, dear, adorable or beloved, which they subtly attract, you murmur them to your lovers. (Genet 1964, 163)

Nothing as bi-valued as metaphor can resist such slippage through contiguous meanings, the metonymic glide. Unconcerned to achieve the stability of identities, literal or figurative, Genet prefers the play of adjacencies, a constantly shifting attention, as in the scan of his address book. Without overstressing the distinction, we can see significant disparity between Sartre's reading for metaphor, organised by the telos of Writer and Genet's unresting movement along the chain of episodes, associations, desires, lovers and memories.

6

The distinction—teleology of metaphors, metonymic skid—has bearing on the unfolding careers after the fateful eight-year period (1944–1952), stretching from their first acquaintance to the publication of *Saint Genet*. Sartre's book was a landmark for both men. Bataille captured the massive challenge of the work, describing it as 'not only one of the richest books of our time but also Sartre's masterpiece'. At the same time, the author's 'flaws have never been more obvious; never before has he let his thoughts drone on at such length' (though of course, he would again soon). Cocteau was witty-serious in remarking that, 'Eva Peron's canonization by the pope and Genet's by Sartre (another pope) are the two mystical events of this summer.' More seriously, less wittily, he noticed how 'Jean has changed since the publication of Sartre's book. He looks as if he were trying at once to follow it and to escape it.' Genet himself groused to Cocteau that 'You and Sartre have turned me into a monument. I am somebody else, and this somebody else must find something to say' (*C-S*, 317).

Genet was, in fact, blocked for most of the next five years. When he returned to his second flowering, he turns away from novel-writing and towards the remarkable plays that take form in the later 1950s. But beyond the intermittent literary effort, he continued to pursue a complex and varied counter-life: in his sexuality, his contact with small-time thievery, and ultimately, his support for oppressed and insurrectionist groups: Algerian revolutionaries, the Black Panthers and the PLO. The telos Sartre had framed for the life—the arrival at writing as the terminus of freedom and the ultimate 'way out'—

disintegrates through the continuous movement among interests and passions. Genet describes his life as a series of 'trips, snags, detours and returns' (quoted in White 1993, 537), centred only on the love of a few men. Commitment to writing flares and fades: for several years, he refused to allow any of his plays to be produced; at no point did he make writing a life-project or defining vocation.

These circumstances have a surprising connection to changes in Sartre's life and self-understanding, changes expressed in this remarkable passage.

> My neurosis—which wasn't all that different from the one Flaubert suffered in his day—was basically that I firmly believed that nothing was more beautiful than writing, nothing greater. To write was to create lasting works, and that the writer's life ought to be understood through his work. And then in 1953, I came to the realization that that was a completely bourgeois viewpoint, that there was a great deal more to life than writing. All of which meant that I had to rethink the value I placed on the written word, which I now felt was on a whole other level than where I had previously placed it. From that point of view, I was, somewhere around 1953–54, cured almost immediately of my neurosis. And at that point I felt a strong urge to understand.... And so I wrote *The Words*.... (*Sartre by Himself* 1976)

The coincidence of dates is evocative. Sartre finished *Saint Gene*t, which apotheosised the 'solution' of writing, only to abandon the solution for himself. It's as if, like his subject Genet, he felt 'monumentalised' into a pose inhibiting his freedom. The insight into his 'bourgeois' fetish of writerly vocation belongs alongside another recognition of just this period, described by Beauvoir: 'In 1944, Sartre thought that any situation could be transcended by subjective effort; in 1951, he knew that circumstances can sometimes steal our transcendence from us; in that case no individual salvation is possible, only a collective struggle' (Beauvoir 1977, 242). In the spirit of Beauvoir's precision, we should remember that 1952 was when *Saint Genet* at last appeared after several years of gestation and also the year Sartre began his sustained fellow-travelling with the French Communists.

The work with and for the Communists came to an end four years later but the tension between 'collective struggle' and 'subjective effort' never ended. In 1957, the year after breaking with the party, Sartre wrote the major *short* work *Search for a Method* (*Questions de méthode*) that can be seen as a tense integration of the lessons of *Saint Genet* with the experience in (and out of) the Communist Party. Now, and henceforth, he sees Marxism as the 'only valid interpretation of history'; until class struggle has achieved its just outcome, no freedom can be fully achieved (Sartre 1963, 21). The claims of radical existential agency—always capable of transcending its circumstances—and the counterpart presumption of writing as secular salvation: these are relinquished in favour of a Marxism he will no longer resist. Sartre's rueful testimony suggests the extent of the change:

> The other day I re-read a prefatory note of mine to a collection of these plays—*Les Mouches*, *Huis Clos* and others—and was truly scandalized. I had written: 'Whatever the circumstances, and whatever the site, a man is always free to choose to be a traitor or.... When I read this, I said to myself: it's incredible, I actually believed that!' (Sartre 1974, 33)

What he comes to believe is put clearly in *Search for a Method*: Marxism is 'the philosophy of our time. We cannot go beyond it because we have not gone beyond the circumstances which engendered it' (Sartre 1963, 30).

Still, and crucially, he will not surrender the example of Genet or at least his reading of Genet. The constraints of history may be overwhelming; they may reduce agency to the narrowest circumscription; but they can never eliminate a discrepant singularity. In the epigrammatic phrasing of the *Search*, 'Valéry is a petit bourgeois intellectual, no doubt about it. But not every petit bourgeois intellectual is Valéry. The heuristic inadequacy of contemporary Marxism is contained in these two sentences' (Sartre 1963, 56). Sartre comes to accept Marxism as the unsurpassable philosophy but only until it has achieved its ends. In the meantime, we are condemned to be a little bit free, freedom as 'the small movement which makes of a totally conditioned being someone who does not render back completely what his conditioning has given him' (Sartre 1974, 35). Even as a 'small movement', freedom will never disappear from Sartre's philosophy or his activism.

7

For Genet, for Sartre, for Genet-Sartre and Sartre-Genet, the post-war decade was a scene of transformation in what seemed possible for an adversarial life. Separately and together they raise difficult questions concerning the fate of dissidence in late modernity. Both sustained the convictions of engagement. But neither could settle within the discipline of the party. In their opposition to the Algerian War, as in May 1968, they were obstreperous, insistent and visible, while each preserved the rights of discrepancy.

The similarities are instructive but no more than the contrast. Sartre, in accepting an unsurpassable Marxism, generated the formidable theory of the *Critique of Dialectical Reason*. It laid out a long march through history, from the French Revolution to the final emancipation from need, collectively achieved through many small individual acts of freedom. No emancipation without shared struggle, but struggle always beginning with the most immediate material needs, one body at a time. The arguments are dense, difficult and affirmative—affirmative in the conviction that the common struggle of even severely constrained selves can bring history to justice. Here it is good to recall that Sartre claimed to have learned the 'positivity in love' through writing of Genet: 'I wrote Saint Genet to try to present a love that goes beyond the sadism in which Genet is steeped and the masochism that he suffered' (Sartre 1981, 13).

Genet, cherishing fewer hopes, shared no such affirmation. Certainly, he was willing to take risks, legal and physical, in his staunch defence of the Black Panthers and the PLO. His erotics stirred, though did not always coincide with, his politics. Prepared to assert identity-of-being as well as solidarity-in-conviction, he travelled, spoke, wrote and risked. He joined the Panthers in California (New York and New Haven) and the PLO in Jordan and Lebanon. He was unstinting in his long hours of activism and his singing rhetoric of support. Repeatedly, however, he conditioned that support on the claims of the oppressed, not on expectation of their triumph: 'Listen', he said in a later interview, 'the day the Palestinians become an institution, I will no longer be on their side. The day the Palestinians become a nation like other nations, I won't be there anymore.... I think that's where I'm going to betray them. They don't know it.' With the Panthers too, he held that if victory were ever achieved, he would withdraw, remaining unassimilable, inappeasable.

Sartre would not, could not, say with Genet that he was a 'vagabond', whose 'true homeland [was] any old train station' (White 1993, 538). But beyond the register of hope and temperament, the two careers drew parallel arcs through post-war contention. The magnetic and opportune field of political celebrity, the defiant iconoclasm, the willingness to turn writerly vocation to activist campaigning, the commitment to national liberation even while holding fast to a singularity, the mix of prideful utterance and humble service, the presentation of a life-history as an exemplary offering—these acts and attitudes crystallised in the few years after the war and opened prospects for the future of dissidence.

REFERENCES

Astruc, Alexander and Michel Contat, directors. *Sartre by Himself*. Translated by Richard Seaver, 1978.

Beauvoir, Simone de. *Force of Circumstance*. New York: Harper and Row, 1977.

Bersani. *Homos*. Cambridge, Mass: Harvard University Press, 1995.

Birchall, Ian H. *Sartre against Stalinism*. Oxford: Berghahn Books, 2004.

Cohen-Solal, Annie. *Jean-Paul Sartre: A Life*. Translated by Anna Cancogni. New York: The New Press, 2005.

Flynn, Thomas R. *Sartre: A Philosophical Biography*, 278. Cambridge: Cambridge University Press, 2014.

Genet, Jean. 'Interview with Rüdiger Wischenbart and Layla Shahid Barrada'. In Genet, *The Declared Enemy: Texts and Interviews*, translated by Jeff Ford, edited by Albert Dichy. Stanford: Stanford University Press, 2004.

———. *Funeral Rites*. Translated by Bernard Frechtman. New York, Grove Press, 1969.

———. 'Interview with Hubert Fichte'. In *Gay Sunshine Interviews*, vol. 1, edited by Winston Leyland. San Francisco: Gay Sunshine, 2004.

———. *Miracle of the Rose*. Translated by Bernard Frechtman. Harmondsworth: Penguin, 1971.

———. *The Declared Enemy: Texts and Interviews*. Translated by Jeff Ford, edited by Albert Dichy. Stanford: Stanford University Press, 2004.

———. *The Thief's Journal*. Translated by Bernard Frechtman. New York: Grove Press, 1964.

Sartre, Jean-Paul. 'The Itinerary of a Thought'. In *Between Existentialism and Marxism*, translated by John Matthews. London: Verso, 1974.

———. *Baudelaire*. Translated by Martin Turner. New York: New Directions, 1967.

———. *Existentialism and Humanism*. Translated by Philip Mairet. London: Methuen, 1948.

———. *The Philosophy of Jean-Paul Sartre*. Edited by Paul Arthur Schilpp. La Salle: Open Court, 1981.

———. *Saint Genet: Actor and Martyr*. Translated by Bernard Frechtman. Minneapolis: University of Minnesota Press, 2012.

———. *Search for a Method*. Translated by Hazel E. Barnes. New York: Random House, 1963.

———. *What is Literature?*. New York: Harper and Row, 1965.

Sartre par lui-même, directed by Alexandre Astruc, Michel Contat, Guy Séligmann, Institut National de l'Audiovisuel and Sodaperaga Productions (France, 1976).

White, Edmund. *Genet*. London: Chatto & Windus, 1993.

THINKING WITH CINEMA: MANI KAUL READING DELEUZE

Moinak Biswas

Film theory in India took a self-conscious shape with the emergence of academic film studies in the 1990s. Philosophical reflection on cinema, however, can be traced back to an older tradition of intellectually reflexive filmmaking. That tradition produced two figures in the 1970s who have an important body of writings—Mani Kaul (1944–2011) and Kumar Shahani (1940–). Given the radically innovative cinema they espoused they felt the need to articulate their principles, which also prompted them to outline an aesthetic philosophy around their work. The body of writing in question is not large but it demands serious attention from us for its significance. I shall confine myself primarily to Mani Kaul's essays here (Shahani has been dealt with by others extensively; Shahani and Rajadhyaksha 2015; Jayamanne 2015) and to one area—the aesthetic-philosophical exploration of cinema that he undertook.

Film philosophy has become a prominent scholarly pursuit in recent years. The number of books and journals dedicated to the subject has gone up significantly. University courses and academic conferences in the area have also become quite common. Continental, especially French, philosophers have provided a strong impetus for the development. Gilles Deleuze's two books *Cinema 1* (1986) and *Cinema 2* (1989) proved crucial for this. Other major philosophers have also made their contribution, among them Jacques Ranciere, Alain Badiou and Jean-Luc Nancy (Deleuze 1986, 1989; Rancière 2006, 2010, 2013, 2019; Badiou 2013; Nancy and Kiarostami 2007).

Philosophy does not *use* cinema to illuminate its propositions in this kind of work, neither does it explain the thought latent in the films. Its function is quite different. As Deleuze explained in his lecture 'What is the Creative Act?' given at FEMIS, the film and television school of Paris in 1987, they treat cinema as something that 'produces' ideas with its own means (Deleuze 2006). Hence it is far more serious than a question of the philosopher turning to cinema to find in it a surface of reflection, an arena for the play of ideas produced somewhere else. Alain Badiou has gone to the extent of saying that the relationship with cinema has become essential for philosophy today (Badiou 2013).

Kaul and Shahani appear to share a great deal with these thinkers if we consider their commitment to the act of creation and the necessity of an aesthetic mode of reflection. They also share with these philosophers the method of working through the arts. Music and painting, especially the former, became crucial to the aesthetics they adopted and discussed. And they share a deep interest in European modernist cinema with the philosophers in question. Sometimes even the exemplars are the same: Bresson and Godard come to mind most readily; but there are others. In fact, the modernist aesthetic orientation of Deleuze, Ranciere or Badiou, I would suggest, is what brings them close to these Indian filmmakers.

It is certainly what brings the thinking of Mani Kaul and Gilles Deleuze close. Kaul started making films and writing down his ideas before Deleuze's *Cinema* volumes came out. But it is possible to see his thought, drawing upon Indian aesthetic theories, upon his practical experience in film, painting and Indian classical music, and developing in conversation with modern European arts, contributing to a project of modernism—an internally heterogeneous, global project that has seen multiple beginnings. We cannot go into a discussion of modernism, but in order to avoid confusion, I would like to mention that the word 'modernism' here relates to a set of self-conscious critical reactions to the institutional forms of modernity that flourished in many national contexts throughout the last century. It covers a range of positions, including the avant-garde.

Mani Kaul was among the earliest artists/critics in India to read Gilles Deleuze. And when he did—sometime in the early 1990s—he found much to admire and relate to. He had been formulating some of what Deleuze had to say on cinema in his own way; but the philosopher must have offered a plane of reflection against which he could re-articulate those ideas. This curious connection, where a non-academic thinker in film met a philosopher thinking with the cinema, should tell us something about the moment of New Wave in Indian cinema which nurtured a modernist charge. The questions on which their thinking came to converge are: (a) the problem of utterance in cinema, (b) multiplicity and (c) the function of the 'interval'.

Kaul mentioned on more than one occasion that he treated the shot as a whole, as something that has already happened in time. Hence, he did not endorse the use of master shots followed or preceded by details snatched from it, which is the standard mode of sequencing. One should not return to a shot or gather multiple shots into an aggregate view because the process of filming should not be taken as treating pieces of reality into a whole. It is not fragments of reality that the filmmaker represents. He starts from 'sensations' that prompt him to explore the minor variations within an angle, not arrange compositions side by side. These variations, the shots, should allow the unplanned and unscripted to enter the frame. The unscripted, the contingent, became increasingly important in Kaul's work as he moved from his first films (*Uski Roti* 1970; *Duvidha* 1973) to the subsequent phase (*Satah se Uthata Aadmi* 1980; *Nazar* 1991). For his 1999 film, *Naukar ki Kameez*, he decided to shoot without the cinematographer looking through the camera (Vasudev and Lenglet 1983, 238–239, 241–242; Kaul and Vajpeyi 2013; *Times of India* 2014).

This aesthetics seeks to overcome the dualism of reality-representation. The image is taken to be as real as anything else to begin with. Kaul must have found a strong resonance in Deleuze's non-dualist approach to the image and to the cinema as a whole. The lesson Deleuze draws in his cinema books from Henri Bergson, for example, is that one cannot maintain the duality of movement and image, consider one occurring in the world and the other in the mind as its representation. Since movement cannot be quantified, since it is always whole, always occurring between the points of time and distance we fix for its measurement, it itself works like an image. And conversely, there is movement in the brain as it perceives such images. This is the reason why Deleuze used the hyphenated term 'movement-image'. Movement-image and time-image constituted the two fundamental elements of cinema for him.

Deleuze and Kaul both tried to think beyond the question of representation. They opposed the idea of cinema as language. Kaul cites Deleuze to support his claim that elements of cinema cannot be compared with verbal elements or 'utterances'. The point of Kaul saying the image deals with 'sensations' is to make the claim that it does not start off as but *becomes* language (Kaul 2018). He points to Deleuze's proposition that images are 'utterable' before they become 'utterances'; one has signs and images before they become language. I quote Deleuze from *Cinema* 2:

> (E)ven with its verbal elements, (cinema) is neither a language system nor a language. It is a plastic mass, an a-signifying and a-syntaxic material, a material not formed linguistically even though it is not amorphous and is formed semiotically, aesthetically and pragmatically. (…) It is not an enunciation, and these are not utterances. It is an utterable. We mean that, when language gets hold of this material (and it necessarily does so), then it gives rise to utterances which come to dominate or even replace the images and signs, and which refer in turn to pertinent features of the language system, syntagms and paradigms, completely different from those

> we started with. We therefore have to define, not semiology, but 'semiotics', as the system of images and signs independent of language in general. (Deleuze 1989, 29)[1]

Deleuze had C.S. Peirce in mind rather than Ferdinand de Saussure when he chose semiotics over semiology. Kaul told Udayan Vajpeyi in their long conversation *Uncloven Space* that he felt he was working with plasticity of a medium rather than with set languages (Kaul and Vajpeyi 2013). And he was fond of citing Deleuze on cinema being something utterable.

His anti-representational position led Mani Kaul to assert repeatedly that he did not believe in 'convergence' in art. The European perspective system was the best example of convergence for him. The four European artists he felt most inspired by, Dostoevsky, Matisse, Bresson and Tarkovsky, all broke away from this rule: 'I wonder what could be common among these four? And I think that these four artists were working against the ideas of perspective and convergence' (Kaul and Vajpeyi 2013, 12). For him, Renaissance painting and symphonic music were perspective-oriented, whereas Indian classical music was not. He saw the art of convergence imbibed by standard filmmaking everywhere as an enormous obstacle to overcome, an impediment to develop forms where lines of narration or individual destinies do not meet in the horizon—the kind of cinema he practiced. What we are calling modernism in his (and Shahani's) case involved a re-articulation of Indian traditional modes of music, painting and epic storytelling.

At the time Kaul spoke on his aesthetic philosophy in *Uncloven Space* he was editing his ambitious adaptation of Dostoevsky's *Idiot* (*Ahmaq*, 1992), having already finished another Dostoevsky adaptation (*Nazar*). An abiding theme in this book-length dialogue is 'multiplicity' that Kaul says he was looking for more self-consciously in the films he was making at that time, and which he considered to be a foundation of non-convergent art. He expresses his admiration for Deleuze's use of the term multiplicity, which the philosopher distinguished from the 'multiple'. Kaul refers to an essay where Deleuze talks about multiplicity using the metaphor of grass as against the root. Multiplicity is a fundamental theme that Deleuze discussed on many occasions. One cannot be sure which text Kaul had in mind but he could well be referring to Deleuze's *Dialogue* (with Claire Parnet) where he writes:

> In a multiplicity what counts are not the terms or the elements, but what there is 'between', the between, a set of relations which are not separable from each other. Every multiplicity grows from the middle, like the blade of grass or rhizome. We constantly oppose rhizome to the tree, like two conceptions and even two very different ways of thinking. (Deleuze and Parnet 2002, viii)

I am not sure if Kaul would be able to reconcile himself all the way with Deleuze's idea of multiplicity, which rejects the original oneness of being or the fundamental unity of reality, but at least on the aesthetic level he was deeply attracted to the idea. As he moved away from the highly structured compositions of his early films into the randomness of *Nazar* and *Ahmaq*, he was getting closer to a tendency of continual branching out of the narrative line.[2]

Deleuze found a startling way to explain what made another filmmaker, Akira Kurosawa, pick Dostoevsky for adaptation. He thinks it was because they both have characters who, while they are caught up in some emergency, seem to always have something even more urgent to worry about:

> Dostoyevsky's characters are constantly caught up in emergencies, and while they are caught up in these life-and-death emergencies, they know that there is a more urgent question—but they do not know what it is (…) It's the idiot. It's the idiot's formula: 'You know there is a deeper problem. I am not sure what it is. But leave me alone. Let everything rot … this more urgent problem must be found.' Kurosawa did not learn from Dostoyevsky. All of Kurosawa's characters are like that. This is a felicitous encounter. (Deleuze 2006, 317)

Such characters drive the narrative away from set goals, derail it, open new lines of development. Kaul was trying to incorporate that principle into his films. There was indeed another felicitous encounter, the one between him and Deleuze. He was not aware of Deleuze's remarks on Kuroswawa and Dostoevsky, but spoke about *The Idiot* and himself in the same manner:

> As soon as I begin talking about one thing, at least three or four things start unfolding in my mind. Sometimes I cannot proceed in the single line and have to return where I began. Then I move ahead again, leave it and go somewhere else…. I saw this habit of mine reflected in *The Idiot*…. Sometimes it seems as though he has forgotten about the main character, as if Dostoyevsky has forgotten the storyline … so the poor man is writing about this predicament he is facing, acknowledging that he has no idea what will happen ahead. (Kaul and Vajpeyi 2013, 134)

The cinema he practiced proved difficult for the viewers because it did not move through cohering spaces but along other axes. One of them was time. Both Shahani and Kaul self-consciously tried to release the logic of spatial elaboration into a temporal and musical one. Theirs was a cinema of duration. Kaul writes, 'Therefore no trace of characterisation, there is no trace of psychology of characters. It should be direct sculpting in time' (Vasudev and Lenglet 1983, 20).[3] This was before the cinema of duration became a genre of sorts with the world-wide emergence of 'slow cinema'. Kaul began to say in his later writings and lectures that it was time, not space or image, that constituted the basic material of cinema. And he found in Deleuze an ally. Modernist cinema, the new turn that cinema took in the West after World War II, was characterised by Deleuze as the cinema of the time-image since time could be directly apprehended in it. This happens when time is freed from its subservience to action and movement, from what it seems to hold and contain. That helps us perceive time itself in duration. 'Cinematographically speaking', Kaul writes in his late essay, 'Cinematography and Time'

> (A) cameraman can only contribute to a film that strives for cinematographic time if he treats the objective reality as a reality of sensation, rather than a visualization of verbal descriptions, worse, conceptions. Sensation is a preverbal condition of cognition and speaks of no intentionality. ('Beneath the Surface: Cinematography and Time' in Kaul 2018, 46)

This leads to an experience of time that is not lost in the experience of events unfolding. This cinema is of necessity a cinema that interrupts action and sometimes even immobilises itself.

In all this, the interval has a curious role to play. The interval can be the gap between two angles, two notes on a musical scale or between action and reaction in narration or performance. It comes between the measuring points if one quantifies something like movement by the space covered by movement or measures time by the clock. As Deleuze says, '(M)ovement will always happen between two instants' (Deleuze 1986, 32). And the interval, it seems, is also what relates one to another, it is in-between terms, relational in nature. Before he wrote the *Cinema* books, Deleuze gave an interview to the *Cahiers du Cinema* editors on Godard's television work, *Six Times Two* (1976), a non-fiction series of six films that Godard made with Anne-Marie Mieville. Deleuze commented on the prevalence of relations in Godard's work. I quote him at some length:

> Godard's not a dialectician. What counts with him isn't two or three or however many, it's AND, the conjunction AND. The key thing is Godard's use of AND. This is important, because all our thought's modeled, rather, on the verb 'to be,' IS.... Even conjunctions are dealt with in terms of the verb 'to be'.... But when you see

> relational judgments as autonomous, you realize that they creep in everywhere, they invade and ruin everything: AND isn't even a specific conjunction or relation, it brings in all relations, there are as many relations as ANDs, and doesn't just upset all relations, it upsets being, the verb … and so on. And, 'and … and … and …' is precisely a creative stammering, a foreign use of language, as opposed to a conformist and dominant use based on the verb 'to be.'
>
> AND is of course diversity, multiplicity, the destruction of identities. It's not the same factory gate when I go in, and when I come out, and then when I go past unemployed. A convicted man's wife isn't the same before and after the conviction. But diversity and multiplicity are nothing to do with aesthetic wholes (in the sense of 'one more,' 'one more woman'…) or dialectical schemas (in the sense of 'one produces two, which then produces three'). Because in those cases it's still Unity, and thus being, that's primary, and that supposedly becomes multiple. When Godard says everything has two parts, that in a day there's morning and evening, he's not saying it's one or the other, or that one becomes the other, becomes two. Because multiplicity is never in the terms, however many, nor in all the terms together, the whole. Multiplicity is precisely in the 'and,' which is different in nature from elementary components and collections of them.
>
> Neither a component nor a collection, what is this AND? I think Godard's force lies in living and thinking and presenting this AND in a very novel way, and in making it work actively. AND is neither one thing nor the other, it's always in between, between two things; it's the borderline, there's always a border, a line of flight or flow, only we don't see it, because it's the least perceptible of things. And yet it's along this line of flight that things come to pass, becomings evolve, revolutions take shape. ('Three Questions About "Six Fois Deux"' in Bellour and Bandy 1992; upper case in the original)

Godard himself talked about his 'method of the in-between'. He was fond of quoting Maurice Merleau-Ponty's lecture 'Film and the New Psychology', given at the IDHEC (as the Paris film school was known at the time) in 1945. Merleau-Ponty wrote:

> The idea we have of the world would be overturned if we could succeed in seeing the intervals between things (for example, the space between trees on the boulevard) as objects and, inversely, if we saw the things themselves–the trees–as the ground. (Merleau-Ponty 1964, 48–49)

Kaul and Kumar Shahani were among those who dreamt of occupying the in-between.

Jacques Ranciere, another philosopher to write extensively on cinema and the visual arts, has underscored the tendency of contemporary art to be relational in nature (Rancière 2009, 21–24). We are invited to see the relations between items in an installation artwork more than the items themselves. 'Relation over positive terms' is a common theme running through the work of these thinkers. We cannot go into the discussion of the interval in Deleuze's *Cinema* books, but one should perhaps mention here that the three categories he created for what he called the 'movement-image'—perception-image, action-image and affection-image—are all defined in terms of the relation they have to the 'interval' between 'received' and 'executed' movement.

Mani Kaul pushed the idea of the interval towards an apprehension of absence in cinema. Representing the absent has the potential of radically altering the very practice of representation. On the question of the interval, he had another felicitous moment of meeting with Deleuze. He had been thinking in his own way about the interval, mostly with the help of Indian arts and aesthetics. He cited several instances—from the ninth century Indian thinker Anandavardhana's idea of intervals between literal and suggested meanings to the existence of intervals in haiku. We fail to write haikus most of the time because we miss the fact that there is an interval between the lines (Kaul 2018, 38–39). The most elaborate treatment of the interval perhaps comes through the analogy of music. For Kaul and Shahani, the Dhrupad and the Khayal respectively served as the subtlest exemplars of the productive interval-principle. Kaul, a trained Dhrupadiya, wrote about the crucial role of the silent interregnum in the music when Dhrupad is performed. The absent is also a part of the sound:

> Dhrupad is made up of tone and silence. It might seem strange to suggest that one should go to a musical concert to listen to silence. But that is the truth of a Dhrupad experience; its fullness will be appreciated only if one begins to relate to both tone and silence, particularly to a kind of pervasive and a whole silence that stands above the tonal expression. (Kaul 2018, 35)

More importantly, he wrote on the role of *shrutis* and overtones–the not yet note, the dissonance between notes–as flowing intervals of sorts. The notion of absence he arrives at following this line of thinking, while all along making a case against perspective, points to a cinema of the possible, of the future. Kaul discusses Parshadeva's thirteenth-century treatise on music *Sangeet Samayasar* in his essay 'Seen from Nowhere',

where the author spoke about 'shruti' in music embodying the space of variation itself. Kaul interprets this as something that harbours the possibility of music, and also its emotive source. '(S)hruti is not a highly specific condition of the note or notes in a raag. It is in fact the source and origin of the specific condition of the note or notes in that raag', he writes (Kaul 1991, 418). He arrives at a notion of presence/absence through this musical understanding of the 'utterable':

> The notes included in the melodic structure constitute the consonant space, whereas the excluded make up the remaining into a dissonant and absent space. The melody when restricted to its 'sweet' character, in fact, excludes the excluded space and therefore in its elaboration fails to achieve the status of what has been ... termed the perspectiveless totatily.... Between any two included notes in a raag lies in darkness the excluded area. ('Seen from Nowhere' in Kaul 1991, 418)

What he called the 'irrational interval' helped him think with cinema better than its rational counterpart.

The Nyaya-Vaishesika school of thinking the absence ('abhava') and the related idea of perception of the absent, 'anupalabdhi', helped him think of cinematic space in terms of what is not yet there, what will be there, and so on, so that the yet-to-be-uttered, the potential and virtual, become stuff of contemplation. Film theory has thought about absence primarily in the Lacanian psychoanalytical model. Kaul was interested in psychoanalysis but not in the lack-based model. Deleuze, it may be recalled here, wasn't either.

We are reminded of the conception of the shot that Kaul proposed: travelling into and within the single angle/shot by minimal displacement. This makes the interval have substance, allows the director treat absence itself as substance. Not only the shot, but the narrative lines should undergo a multiple to one to multiple movement, according to Mani Kaul. A single thread of storytelling can be avoided in such an approach; moreover, one could avoid treating the multiple strands of narrative as a collection of many single storylines.

There also is a lesson for political cinema here: not to turn what we know into its filmic equivalent, as politically correct cinema does with ease today (especially in India), but to allow the not yet formulated, the non-formed to emerge. 'The people are missing' in modern political cinema, Deleuze said, as he thought the people are a becoming, always a minority (Deleuze 1989, 216). He meant the same for the cinema that will speak to that people. A significant point about politics can be derived from the aesthetic thought of Mani Kaul, whose cinema appears to be apolitical—it is the point about working with absence as yearning.

NOTES

1. Christian Metz famously argued that cinema is a language but not a language-system (langue). Deleuze was taking on that position; see Metz (1974, 31–91).
2. Kaul says,

   > We can speak of this dialectic of order-disorder only as a beginning, but this opposition is useless in multiplicity. A time arrives when you do not think in relation to this dialectic. For you there is nothing such as order or disorder. What is it instead then? What can be present without having to be dialectical? (2013, 58)

3. 'Sculpting in time' is of course a reference to Tarkovsky's book of the same title.

REFERENCES

Badiou, Alain. *Cinema*. Translated by Susan Spitzer. Cambridge: Polity Press, 2013.

———. 'Cinema and Philosophical Experimentation' and 'On Cinema as Democratic Emblem' in *Cinema*.

Bellour, Raymond and Mary Lea Bandy, eds. 'Three Questions About "Six Fois Deux"'. In *Jean-Luc Godard, Son + Image 1974–1991*. New York, Musuem of Modern Art, 1992.

Deleuze, Gilles. *Cinema 1, The Movement*-Image. Translated by Hugh Tomlinson and Barbara Habberjam. Minneapolis: University of Minnesota Press, 1986.

———. *Cinema 2, The Time*-Image. Translated by Hugh Tomlinson and Robert Galeta. Minneapolis: University of Minnesota Press, 1989.

———. 'What is the Creative Act?'. In *Two Regimes of Madness, Texts and Interviews 1975–1995*, translated by David Lapoujade. Cambridge, MA: MIT Press, 2006.

Deleuze, Gilles and Claire Parnet. 'Preface to the English Language Edition'. In *Dialogues II*, translated by Hugh Tomlinson and Barabara Habberjam. New York: Columbia University Press, 2002.

Jayamanne, Laleen. *The Epic Cinema of Kumar Shahani*. Bloomington: Indiana University Press, 2015.

Kaul, Mani and Udayan Vajpeyi. *Uncloven Space*. Translated by Gurvinder Singh. Quiver Books, 2013 (Originally published in Hindi as *Abhed Akash* in 1994).

Kaul, Mani and Udayan Vajpeyi. '"The Rambling Figure" and "Beneath the Surface: Cinematography and Time"'. In *The Rambling Figures of Mani* Kaul, edited and compiled by Stoffel Debuysere and Arindam Sen. Courtisane Festival, 2018.

———. 'Seen from Nowhere'. In *Concept of Space, Ancient and Modern*, edited by Kapila Vatsyayan. New Delhi: Indira Gandhi National Centre for the Arts, 1991.

Merleau-Ponty, Maurice. 'Film and the New Psychology'. In *Sense and Non-Sense*, translated by Hubert L. Dreyfus and Patricia Allen Dreyfus. Evanston, Ill: Northwestern University Press, 1964.

Metz, Christian. 'The Cinema: Language or Language System?'. In *Film Language: A Semiotics of Cinema*, translated by Michael Taylor. Chicago: The University of Chicago Press, 1974.

Nancy, Jean-Luc and Abbas Kiarostami. *Abbas Kiarostami, The Evidence of Film*. Paris: Klinksieck, 2007.

Rancière, Jacques. *Film Fables*. Translated by Emiliano Battista. Oxford: Berg, 2006.

———. 'Aesthetics as Politics'. In *Aesthetics and its Discontents*, translated by Steven Corcoran. Cambridge: Polity Press, 2009.

———. *The Future of the Image*. New Delhi: Navayana, 2010.

———. *Béla Tarr: The Time After*. Translated by Erik Beranek. Minneapolis: Univocal, 2013.

———. *Intervals of Cinema*. Translated by John Howe. London: Verso, 2019.

Shahani, Kumar and Ashish Rajadhyaksha. *Kumar Shahani: The Shock of Desire and Other Essays*. New Delhi: Tulika Books, 2015.

Times of India, 'Experiments in Hindi Cinema', 1 February 2014.

Vasudev, Aruna and Philippe Lenglet. 'Interview with Mani Kaul'. In *Indian Cinema Super Bazaar*. New Delhi: Vikas, 1983.

PERFORATION

IF THE OUTSIDER IS DEEPLY WITHIN

Charles Russell

The first issue—who is perceived as outside—immediately raises the questions of who determines who is outside and outside of what? And what is the position and the interest of the person who labels another as being outside? Of course, at this moment, that means us. Who are we to address the figure outside our presumed frame of reference—here, inside. Inside what? Who is considered an 'Outsider' to society is, in essence, a sociological question; therefore, it becomes almost immediately a political question. But, we may also observe a psychological component. How and why does the outsider represent a threat or perhaps a possibility, to the dominant culture, and particularly, to those within it observing or perhaps imagining the life and actions of the outsider?

What constitutes an outsider *aesthetic* can also be seen in terms of a sociology—and a politics—of art. Most frequently, during the past century, however, the question seems to focus primarily on the ways and reasons that generally established aesthetic practices are challenged or expanded by the works of those seen to be 'outside' (or non-participants in) the normative practices, historical, traditional and institutional definitions of art and artists. Yet we are also led to ask, again, what are the implicit or explicit politics of art? What role does it play in our cultural life that might lead to awareness of, if not action towards, the possibility for change?

I will explore these questions by speaking of three American and European visual artists, each of whom has been labelled at times an 'outsider artist'. But my remarks are grounded as well in literary studies, for the conception of the outsider has resonated—in Western European and American culture, at least—in cultural studies and across art and literary forms for several centuries.

Two general approaches to the question who is seen as an outsider prevail: one declaring the 'outsider' a threat, the other, perceiving a figure of fascination, if not attraction. In the first, emphasis is placed on how the outsider is 'structurally determined', that is, defined by and from the perspective of the dominant social formation and ideology. Here, the outsider, as individual or group, is seen as distinct from cultural norms, hence often perceived as an inferior figure and/or a threat to be dismissed, controlled or even exterminated. In *Outsiders: A Study in Life and Letters*, the literary historian Hans Mayer traced in Euro-American literature and history the presentation of three groups of 'existential' outsiders: women, homosexuals and Jews—'existential' because they are declared by dominant social codes to be defined by their 'sex, origins or psychic and corporeal makeup' (Mayer 1982, xvii). Mayer could well have included psychotics and in the case of the United States, African-Americans, as figures whose very existence challenged the legitimacy of the cultural order.

In contrast to the 'existential' outsider, Mayer observes, is the 'intentional' outsider, one who chooses to step beyond bounds, to 'consciously transgress boundaries' (Mayer 1982). Yet, rather than being a figure of fear or disdain to the majority, the intentional outsider is often a being of fascination, even admiration to those who have remained within the confines of the social code. This vision of the Outsider-within was especially prevalent throughout the Romantic era and influenced the popular image of the hyper-sensitive, troubled and visionary artist. Because many who reside within the social order can imagine a personal act that would break sensed constraints, transgress boundaries and open up the possibility of a state of un-experienced freedom, the voice of the artist on the margins has been heard as that of a kindred spirit.

When we turn to the realm of modern and postmodern aesthetics, we find that the outsider—whether existential or intentional—is seen more as a figure of fascination, even a possible model of behaviour, than as a cultural threat. This is an expression of the founding myths of modernity—the artist as critic of dominant cultural codes, a dissident, as well as an agent of potentially emerging realms of being. In seeking new aesthetic languages and exemplars of more authentic being, artists and intellectuals have often looked to those at the margins of society as exemplars or unwitting allies. Especially in the visual arts, artists, in their belief that some people experience more intensely the sources of the creative impulse when freed from the mental shackles of bourgeois culture, have variously found model outsiders in the so-called 'primitive' cultures, children, psychotics and highly marginalised individuals living within but profoundly separate from society.

But, as has often been remarked, the determination of who is an outsider is usually an act of a person of the majority (even if such figures believe themselves to have 'minority' status, as have artists and intellectuals across the modern era). The Outsider artist becomes an idealised figure, no matter how desperate, pained or alienated he or she may be and the outsider's creations may be deemed 'art' by the insider because they can be valued for the aesthetic strategies of potential use to the mainstream artist in her or his own battle with the academy. Thus, even as the figure perceived as marginal to, or outside of, the normative culture can present significant challenges to the dominant culture by his or her specific life choices and aesthetic creations, we need also recognise in those challenges evidence of the needs, fears and desires of those members of the dominant culture who label the outsiders figures of personal and cultural significance.

In an effort to explore these ideas, this discussion focuses on three visual artists, Henry Darger, Thornton Dial and Hipkiss—all deemed outsiders whose creations are both aesthetically strong and inventive and who offer significant insights into our culture from positions fully engaged in that culture, even if they have been proclaimed outsiders. Following the binary categories mentioned previously, one might term Darger and Dial 'existential' outsiders, the one appearing so psychologically distressed as to seem psychotic, the other a member of a formerly excluded, repressed minority. Yet while it might be useful to term Hipkiss as an 'intentional' outsider, I'll discuss how his act of establishing his own space of personal and creative freedom demands that he reject the presumption of those who would label him an outsider.

The art and writing of Henry Darger (1892–1973) present a vision of rampant sentimentality and vividly pictured horror, awe-struck religiosity and prurient brutality, sanctimonious moral condemnation and perverse delight. Confronting his world, we are swept immediately into the turbulent imagination of a solitary artist whose most private fantasies give voice and vision to the subconscious drama of our popular culture.

Darger, an orphaned and probably abused child, lived a long, solitary and apparently dreary life, holding only menial jobs and attending Catholic religious services daily. Yet he worked for over five decades late into each night, writing and illustrating fantastic epics of imaginary realms. His most remarkable creation is a 15,145-page unpublished epic, *The Story of the Vivian Girls, in What is Known as the Realms of the Unreal, of the Glandeco-Angelinean War Storm, Caused by the Child Slave Rebellion*. He composed the work over a period of some twenty years and then illustrated it over the next three decades with 300 large watercolour collages for which he is now primarily known. The manuscripts and paintings were discovered shortly before his death in 1973 by his landlord who brought them to the world's attention.

In the Realms of the Unreal presents written and visual images of a war raging on an imaginary planet between four Catholic countries against a nation that worshiped Satan, practiced child slavery in brutal factories and tortured, strangled and disemboweled children *en masse*. Darger's vision of good and evil in combat is dramatically expressed in competing depictions of innocence affirmed and betrayed. The works are both compelling and deeply disturbing, products of a vivid and torn, even tormented, imagination. They communicate a profound ambivalence. Darger projects himself as both protector and destroyer of innocence; a servant of God and an agent of Satan; a vulnerable child and a murderous adult; a victim of horrific torture and a slayer of demons. Every element of his Manichean world claims equal validity, each the expression of a psychological and moral struggle for which Darger has no convincing resolution.

Symptomatic of his torment is the image of the young girl—as ideal moral being and as vulnerable victim. Darger clearly embraced his society's cult of the purity and innocent beauty of little girls and adopted and traced their images from the most popular and saccharine media—comic strips, colouring books, children's and family magazines. He idolised girls and the traditional social roles they held. Many of his most beautiful scenes are of peaceful moments where his heroines—the seven Vivian Girls of his title and other children—nestle within lush landscapes untouched by war, although few such moments actually exist in his novel.

More consonant with the breathless, hyperbolic, action-driven narrative are the fervid images of battles, raging storms, abductions of children and the horrors of child torture and slaughter. These violent scenes play out in tempestuous landscapes seemingly stirred up by the human generated chaos. For instance, in one work, *At Norma Catherine. But wild thunder-storm with cyclone like wind saves them*, the Vivian Girls and the enemy soldiers that have captured them are buffeted by the tumult of a suddenly risen storm and only an inserted caption indicates the happy ending in store.

Yet, Darger would also write and illustrate graphic depictions of young girls being strangled, disembowelled, crucified, hanged, flayed and dismembered. The images clearly express a fully imagined sadistic blood-lust visited upon his love objects by the artist. They led numerous critics to declare Darger an exemplary outsider artist, an extremely reclusive individual whose tenuous psychological stability placed him at the margins of acceptable social behaviour.

Nevertheless, no matter how many landscapes are strewn with the disembowelled corpses of young naked girls or cosmic projections of girls being strangled in the billowing clouds, the epic's heroines, the Vivian Girls always escape and lead both the vulnerable children to safety and the forces of good to victory. However far Darger's imagination might go into the realms of the blasphemous and demented, no matter how many times and for how long he lingers on the killing fields, he always steps back, if only temporarily, to regain himself and his ties to the common culture of righteousness and sentimentality.

Darger's constant return to the dominant moral and religious codes remind us that however much he might be considered an 'outsider', his passions and his art are strongly linked to the values of his society. But he also captured—and was captured by—that society's darkest fears and desires, its dread and inherent violence.

Darger, an avid reader, was strongly influenced by fiction written for adolescent males—particularly tales of moral, brave, Christian boys. He also incorporated characters and themes of nineteenth-century popular literature such as those of Dickens and Harriet Beecher Stowe. *Uncle Tom's Cabin* proved an especially rich trove of sentimental and horrific imagery, including the lingering death of angelic Little Eva, the horrors of slavery, Simon Legree's brutality toward Tom and the final exaltations of sanctimonious Christianity. All share popular culture conventions of threats to innocence that are ultimately rebuffed and of moral conflicts, engaged and overcome. But necessary to all these narratives is a prolonged, emotionally charged tension during which the threat of evil dominates before the much-delayed moment when the moral order triumphs.

Furthermore, Darger's sources of violent and inherently perverse imagery included the daily newspapers. He was fascinated by tales of the American civil war which were popular in his youth but even more revealing is his obsessive interest in collecting newspaper stories and pictures of abducted or murdered children. A staple of the so-called 'news', even today, such stories of domestic threat and tragedy feed a seemingly insatiable collective thirst for the lurid sensations of anger, fear and perhaps desire stimulated by sporadic outbreaks of the collectively repressed into 'public' view.

Thus, even as we ponder these images as expressions of the 'outsider' Darger's problematic psyche, we can also see in them Darger's deep and sustaining connection to the popular culture of his day in his ready adoption of the visual forms and narrative themes drawn from popular media. We encounter in his work familiar fantasies of Western culture: fantasies of innocence protected, moral triumph, religious fidelity, as well as pervasive sexual aggression, gender antagonism and sanctimonious brutal violence. This marginal artist thrusts forward the uncomfortably widespread, long-enduring cultural obsessions with vengeance, war, rape and paedophilia that coexist so easily with desperate religious longing, and utopian, if infantile, sentimentality. Indeed, however much he might be considered an 'outsider', he makes explicit—consciously or not—repressed truths from the cultural centre, the collective unconscious, in which, even those at the centre are immersed. Instead of being called an 'outsider' artist, Henry Darger should be viewed as a self-taught vernacular artist, whose works resonate from the centre of the private and collective emotional life of his culture.

The art of Thornton Dial emerges from the margins of society to articulate what has been unknown, ignored or repressed. Dial's exclusion was not an issue of mental condition, however, but one of class and race. Born in 1928, a poor African American in the deep South, Dial grew up during an era of institutionalised racism in which not only was he assumed not to have a voice but was actively denied one. To develop an art that addresses the personal, cultural and historical issues as he did was an unexpected and inherently political act. His work is indeed political and presents us with a dissident vision of a life and culture at once distant, and yet, of a common historical moment.

The 1992 painting *Graveyard Traveler/Selma Bridge*, for instance, offers an allegorical representation of the life and death of the civil rights leader Dr Martin Luther King, Jr., focusing simultaneously on his participation in the 1965 civil rights confrontation at the Edmund Pettus Bridge in Selma, Alabama, the urban world he served and where he would be assassinated and the graveyard to which he—and all of us—are destined. It is meant to be read from right to left and then back downward to the right, as our eyes follow a yellow path arching over the turbulent blue of the Alabama River and then curving into a darkened landscape and pointing towards the cemetery in the lower right. A figure representing Dr King stands at the right edge the bridge, poised to cross one of the many rivers of his life's journey. At the far left, Dr King has been transformed into a tiger—Dial's iconic figure for the black male—who will soon encounter around the bend a horse rider signifying the white police force that brutally attacked the freedom marchers. Although depicting a specific political and historical event, the painting resonates with broader existential significance, as Dial subsequently observed: 'As a man live, he is a graveyard traveler. Every move he make, death will move with him. Martin Luther King had to cross Selma bridge. Every man got to take that same trip' (Dial in McEvilley and Baraka 1993, 150).

An illiterate factory worker, late in life, Dial began creating sculptural works out of found and discarded objects and painting massive abstract and representational assemblages which express intensely personal and historically informed responses to African American life. He had always made 'objects' as he called them—he is said to have never heard the word art or considered his creations artworks until he was 60. But familiar with the tradition of the constructed yard show—in which numerous rural and urban African Americans decorate their home environments with symbolic constructions of used or found objects—Dial placed his works around his family's homes.

He also destroyed or buried many works, partly for lack of space, in larger part, out of fear of attracting unwanted attention from white people, the 'authorities' who, he assumed, would require he have a license to do such work and would probably tax them. He also suspected they might recognise the weighted political meanings within the works. One early sculpture which was not destroyed and certainly could be easily understood is *Slave Ship*, from 1987, a depiction of the Middle Passage, in which chained figures fill the body of the ship, while under an American flag a white man rapes a black woman.

Dial, an artist of immense productivity and visual ambition, was discovered and championed by a white collector passionately supportive of Southern African American vernacular art, after which he achieved some success in both the folk art and mainstream art worlds. But one senses that the passion to create was intensely personal and not dependent on social recognition.

Dial's works are often emotionally-charged, visually-complex and politically-aware. The broad scope of his vision and creative commitment address a complexity of personal, ethnic, historical and global issues. His art has looked back to the historic drama of slavery, segregation, economic struggle and civil rights in America, as well as confronting current history and popular culture concerns encountered through the mass media including war and the global politics of oil, the public and media frenzy over the lurid death of Princess Diana and the succession of oil wars the United States has entered.

His paintings can be intensely personal, yet depict a condition and sensibility universally recognised. The 1997 *Construction of the Victory*, for example, commemorates Dial's survival from a near fatal bout with hepatitis. The brilliant red-soaked stretched and tied fabric denotes the blood of life—and the fluids and life nearly lost. Embedded flowers connote the signs of hospital well-wishes and foreseen memorials. The centre star-flower form suspended below the blood-red cross symbolically binds all elements together, holding a pair of crutches that rise in a triumphant V shape.

A similarly-placed V dominates his 2004 work *Victory in Iraq*, a more sombre and decidedly less optimistic, painting. Here, the metal bars of the flag-coloured V barely constrain the jumbled mass of barb wire, tangled metals and electrical wires in which stuffed animals, children's toys and a severed head of a mannequin are embedded. The spots of red on torn clothes refer to blood but not necessarily to life triumphant. The victory announced could be either in the future after much carnage or this may indeed be a portrait of what Victory looks like.

When first noted by the art world, his works were seen by some as expressions of what was deemed an outsider culture, a subaltern society of uneducated black people working in indigenous folk traditions. But this world appeared to have no place within the dominant art dialogue.

Although excluded by the academy, Dial was not ignorant of this world. Nor did he feel especially challenged by it, as can be seen in *The Art of Alabama*, 2004, in which a flamboyant exemplar of African American yard assemblage rises splendidly above a garishly-painted concrete replica of a classical Greek statue placed ingloriously on a box pedestal of found wood. If Dial acknowledged the Western tradition, seen on his occasional visits to museums, his place in art history was not a major concern for him. Rather, it is history in the broadest sense that engaged him.

These are the creations of an historically-engaged individual, speaking to culture at large through a personal vision, grounded in a vernacular aesthetic. Dial is no 'outsider', though he and many self-taught African American artists emerge from a culture little known to many. But he makes it abundantly clear that he and the African American vernacular artists are from within the heart of the American culture—and world culture—and that their objects, their art, speak to both their and our placement within a common culture and history.

The work of the artist first known as Chris Hipkiss was introduced to a segment of the art world in the early 1990s by critics and artists associated with the 'Outsider Art' world in England. As an untrained artist who left school at age sixteen to pursue a trade but who assiduously created increasingly large drawings in pencil and ink of startling, seemingly phantasmagoric landscapes, he seemed to fit into notions of the figure outside. The bizarre, disturbing works he created were taken as evidence of a radically disaffiliated figure. Hipkiss has been labelled as an Outsider ever since an appellation that may have brought relative success and renown at first but which also traps the artist in a marginal segment of the art world, limits viewing by a larger general populace that should experience it and diminishes the truly radical vision of independent-minded beings.

Nonetheless, we can understand this early—and lingering—portrait of the artist as outsider because his works are profoundly unsettled and unsettling. The drawings suggest landscapes or scenes from some unknown but imaginable personal and mythic realms which evoke turbulent narratives of political and sexual import.

The works can be extremely large, one is 140-centimetre high and 400-centimetre wide, while other works, 180 by 110 centimetres, stand as distinct depictions or might serve as individual components of larger panoramas. They are almost all drawn in black ink or graphite on white grounds, although gold or silver ink are also applied at times. The images are often framed by graphically bold, if mysterious, titles or poetic phrases, while occasionally, similar phrases may be dramatically placed like billboards atop imposing buildings, sometimes sending contradictory messages—as in one, where HOPE and HATE are proclaimed ('hope' being, perhaps significantly, smaller). In other works, such enigmas are seen issuing from the mouths of the multiple-armed, scantily dressed, feminine-androgynous figures who are often found throughout the landscapes.

Hipkiss's world is a place of extreme, if visionary, clarity, of precisely defined landscapes in which factories, industrial buildings and tower-like structures dominate surrounding fields of strange plants, insects and birds which appear to be industrialised mutations (Image 1). All graphic elements—whether massive factories, blades of grass, mutant vegetal forms, regimented formations of birds and insect life or the androgynes—are finely drawn with a seemingly impossible exactitude. As in a surrealistic painting, in which every element is presented with an equal intensity, the familiar is rendered uncanny and the bizarre is presented as quotidian.

Image 1: Wolfe and Stole.
Source: Image art by Hipkiss.

The landscapes suggest blurred boundaries of urban and rural domains, of technological and natural realms in conflict. Hipkiss has described the landscapes as suburban, where the urban and the rural meet. That is something he appears to dread—the suburban: 'I see and live life from a kind of rural perspective, but I'm still intrinsically tied to the detail, the banality, the expanse and horror of Suburbia—a place I know so well' (Hipkiss 2010). But he has also invoked 'the landscape of Suburbia, where the "people" of the city and the "nature" of open country are hidden in the immensity. In the behemoth that is Suburbia, there is no room for these essential motifs but they have still got to be there somehow' (Hipkiss 2010).

The meeting of disparate, indeed dissonant realms, articulates the hybridity of a present and an impending world. In these highly articulated panoramas, we alternately and simultaneously, sense ubiquitous threat and anarchic celebration. The scenes invite both dystopian or utopian interpretations. These landscapes intimate fundamental shifts in gender identity and extreme transformations of the natural and planned ecology, where technological forces are seemingly turned against both populace and nature, while concurrently, a populace of androgynous beings cavort freely and ironically within the contested terrain. The androgynes prove to be especially mysterious yet captivating figures. They establish a human presence acting in apparent disregard of the implicit horror of the behemoth surrounding them, and announce a transforming vision of sexual ambiguity, sexual liberation, and sexual expression.

Throughout this work, Hipkiss seems to be working from an intense personal awareness—responding to recognisable cultural conditions and opposing tropes of dominance and freedom. Hipkiss has admitted that in these imaginary expanses there is 'a kind of "self-portrait"' (Hipkiss 2010). And—if the works invoke the present, yet augur something as yet not fully-known but imaginable, through these appealing and disturbing images—the artist makes the activity of both creating and viewing a challenge to self-knowledge—a challenge taken up by the artist and offered to the viewer. For us, it is decidedly difficult to assume a stable, single perspective on the art object and its vision. We are compelled to see it both panoramically and from within its frame.

Thus, the large panoramas invite, indeed often demand, discrete viewings from different perspectives and distinct distances. We are moved to stand back to encompass the expansive vision of these landscapes but in order to fully to read them and to attempt to interpret them, we must move forward for close viewing. The complex detail, the many components, the strange figures uttering enigmatic phrases in minute thought-balloons bring us intimately within these mystifying worlds. One finds oneself moving back and forth, shifting one's relationship to the work and the world it contains. And at times, in the process, we discover an unexpected perspective upon noticing that the framing texts sometimes are written in reverse—as if the artist and now 'we' are within the labelled landscape looking out through the eyes of Hipkiss.

And who is this Hipkiss? Hipkiss is the fabricated name assumed by a pair of English artists, Chris and Alpha Mason, who moved to southern France in 2006. Chris is the drawings' draftsman; Alpha is primarily responsible for the enigmatic, suggestive texts being voiced by the androgynous figures and framing the landscapes. Chris Payen and Alpha Mason met in London as young adults and began collaborating and later married, upon which Chris took her surname. The pseudonym Chris Hipkiss was born, and for years, the male who drew the works was assumed to be the sole artist, until recently the male first name, Chris, was dropped in favour simply of Hipkiss. In recent years, the two have insisted on the equal relationship at the heart of their creative vision. Indeed, they have lived and have presented an art that has, in their words, 'always defied patriarchal norms', for whom 'gender simply doesn't figure as important' (Hipkiss 2015). One might detect both male and female 'symbols' within the compositions but the figures within the artworks are beings of decidedly female and male attributes who are embraced by Hipkiss as their 'alter egos'.

By presenting their alter-egos as active participants within the world they envision, the artists position themselves within the narrative. They accept a place within a dynamic of change towards a world that's as yet unknown. Hipkiss has stated that these are not visions of an oppressive future state but rather are 'definitely present tense' (Hipkiss 2015). Within this present, these two self-described 'feminist and political and independent' artists act through their creations. In effect, Hipkiss's oeuvre testifies to two individuals' confrontation with the promise and threat of profound changes in our cultural dynamics, changes that might be viewed from the relative solace of the French countryside where they live but which challenge the artists as much as the viewers—wherever we may be situated. The act of confronting and creating art out of the contemporary is a way of knowing and exploring realities; it is a means of expressing and creating oneself.

'Hipkiss' may be 'self-taught' but 'he' is neither naïve, marginal, nor psychotic. They are well-aware of the operations of the art world but do not engage with the narratives of the commonly-approved art history within which the majority of academically trained artists frame their practice. Instead, Hipkiss react directly to the social and political concerns of the culture and have developed a visual vocabulary at once responsive to imagery encountered in the mass media, yet is intensely personal and unique.

If these works can be read by us as either dystopian or utopian, and perhaps, both simultaneously, they call us back to central issues of this collection: who are the dissidents, the 'outsiders'; where do they reside; what is their relationship to us; and what do they reveal to us about our common state?

Henry Darger, Thornton Dial and Hipkiss have all been projected as outsiders—largely without their knowledge or assent. Yet from that real or metaphoric outside location, their art serves to reveal the culture within, albeit from a skewed perspective that renders the familiar world strange as it is sharply seen anew.

Considering their lives and works, we confront varieties of what might indeed be called 'a dissident aesthetics of the insider who is already always "outside"'. But we need ask, how can we locate these artists—and others—as truly being 'inside' or 'outside' the culture? Where are those locations and who maps them? Are such decisions based on the manifest or latent meaning within the individual's acts and creations or do they reflect as much the perspective and desires of the viewer residing, however uncomfortably, at the culture's core? And can we determine whether the 'outsider's' vision represents a significant challenge to the dominant culture for the observer?

One might view Darger as an individual who desperately wanted to be inside, who dramatically identified with the religious and moral codes of his culture but who could not reconcile either his own psychological distress or his perception of the inherent violence and perversity residing at the core of the culture, to find peace and stability inside. The hyperbole of beauty and horror within his art challenges his readers and viewers to determine whether this outsider's vision of social contradictions truly speak for his and their, culture and thus, anoint him a legitimate and necessary insider.

Dial speaks with the wisdom and experience of the 'outsider' forcibly excluded from society's regard yet who, like many of his fellow 'outsiders', looks back in and on the lies and conflicted truths of that society. His is an aesthetics of dissidence and independence that can also claim to be an authentic expression of the realities at the centre of the culture, established from a location only the wilfully blind would call outside.

Hipkiss's vision may be an aesthetics of dissidence, by default. It is one of those artists who simply step beyond the boundaries of the ordinary to articulate a panorama of culture real and imaginary, present and future, intriguing and foreboding, one within which we may already be living while tempted to call it outside.

Wherever the so-called outsider resides, as each of these three artists has made evident, we, the viewers, the readers, confront and experience the conflicts and contradictions at the heart of our cultures, as well as the passion and promise of individual struggle for self-expression and enactment within that contested terrain.

I suggest that our receptivity to the art of the outsider signals our need for the outsider to exist. We desire an alternative aesthetics of un-belonging and discomfort that asserts that this world which is 'too much with us' has not succeeded in dominating the spirit of desire and resistance.

Thus, the outsider—the existence and identity of whom may reflect the imaginative projections of those inside who are straining to imagine alternate modes of being—may serve to articulate the uncomfortable and unavoidable truths about the culture that envelops us all, insiders and outsiders alike. They reveal that, fundamentally, an outsider aesthetics, a dissident aesthetics—and politics—might present ever more sharply-felt images of the oppressive conditions that have engendered in the viewer and the reader the impassioned desire for an alternative vision.

So that, even if the creative act is not taken up in a spirit of dissent, when we investigate these individual idiolects that personalise visual or literary languages and in the process, potentially disrupt or expand collective discourse, we engage once again the implicit politics of aesthetic statement, and action, that have shaped vanguard criticality and aesthetics across the modern era.

I suggest that for the viewer—for us—outsider aesthetics in its varied forms, as distinct expressions of specific individual artists, is essentially, an affirmation of the value, indeed the necessity of art as we have known it: as focused individual action, intense expression of deeply-felt experience that challenges accepted versions of received reality. It is an art that resonates in the lives and dreams of other individuals and illuminates the complexities of a shared culture, an art that reveals that the outsider is experienced most deeply within.

Representative images of the works of Henry Darger Thornton Dial, and Hipkiss can be accessed at:

http://officialhenrydarger.com/images/
http://www.soulsgrowndeep.org/artist/thornton-dial
http://www.hipkissart.com/past.html

REFERENCES

Hipkiss. 'Detail in the Distance' on-line blog, *Crow Parliament*, 22 August 2010; no longer accessible.

———. 'Interview with Alex Nodopaka,' in *Vayavya*, 2015. Available at http://www.vayavya.in/hipkiss-interview.html (accessed 7 November 2020).

Mayer, Hans. *Outsiders: A Study in Life and Letters*. Cambridge, MA: MIT Press, 1982.

McEvilley, Thomas and Amiri Baraka. *Thornton Dial: Image of the Tiger*. New York: Harry N. Abrams/Museum of American Folk Art, 1993.

DISSIDENT POETICS, EXPERIMENTAL EXCESS: JAAKKO YLI-JUONIKAS' FINNISH NOVEL *NEUROMAANI*

Laura Piippo

In this chapter, I discuss dissident poetics in *Neuromaani* (2012), an excessive Finnish experimental novel by Jaakko Yli-Juonikas (b. 1976). I examine how and what kind of in-betweenness is produced in the novel that both harbours dissident literary modes and, at the same time, exposes the always-already murky undercurrents of the so-called mainstream and the current capitalist 'system'. First, I introduce *Neuromaani*, its composition, themes, context, background and reception. After that, I lay out the theoretical background of my reading: the concepts of actual, virtual and repetition. Lastly, I examine the excess produced by the dissident poetics of in-betweenness in *Neuromaani*. Brian McHale argues that (descriptive) poetics itself is in-between of interpretation and theory: it can be informed by and have implications for both (McHale 1994, 59). In this regard, *Neuromaani* offers an interesting point of departure for contemplations on both the novel's own poetics and on their possible interpretations but also more generally the nature of literary in-betweenness or the possible contemporary poetics of dissidence—and their counter-cultural potential.

Following the *Oxford English Dictionary*, poetics is here understood as the creative principles or techniques informing any literary construction. This also applies, according to the *OED*, to social and cultural constructions, and thus, brings a wider scope of human interaction and meaning-making on various platforms into play. Jacques Rancière argues that literature (and, more generally, art) is a specific mode of language: 'a language that speaks less by what it says than by what it does not say, by the power that is expressed through it' (Rancière 2011, 59). He then continues naming this the 'poetic power' (Rancière 2011, 67). In this regard, literature is both a self-sufficient form of and an expression of society. Through these remarks, I seek to map out ways to configure and re-configure poetic spaces of being an outsider within—and along the lines of Jacques Rancière, maybe a possible way out.

ON THE POETICS OF NEUROMAANI

Neuromaani is—following a collection of short stories and two novels—the fourth literary work by Jaakko Yli-Juonikas, a prominent Finnish writer of experimental prose literature. It is a vast and versatile book of over 650 pages and with exceptionally elaborate cover design by Markus Pyörälä, who received an award for this work. As soon as it was published, *Neuromaani* was described as 'having no predecessor in Finnish literature' and the comparisons were largely sought from Anglophone literary traditions. *Neuromaani* received generally good and even hesitantly applauding reviews but was repeatedly titled as 'too difficult' or 'too much' by the critics (cf. Piippo 2016). It has since then attracted also academic interest (cf. Piippo 2018, 2020).

Neuromaani circulates and permutes various found texts, both canon and outsider, factual and fictional. Certain types of outsider literature often apply certain elements and traits very tightly knitted to the language associated with madness which is a very particular kind of otherness. I concentrate especially on the usage of literary traits typical for the so-called 'outsider' or self-published literature that often resemble the ones of madness and schizophrenia. The novel also operates with and within the language and jargon of neuroscience, clinical research, hospitalisation and science frauds. There is also a lot of ambivalent and literary humour which partially lightens the mood of the novel but at the same time creates a harsher contrast for its more abrasive or traumatic contents. In this chapter, I look into what kind of poetics these traits produce when they leak into mainstream or highbrow prose literature.

The novel opens with a paratext. On the first page, there is an abstract in English which states that '[t]he study focuses on a series of crimes committed by a loose group of Finnish neuroscientists in 1999–2000' and that '[t]he complexity of this bioethical problem is not so much due to the unparalleled nature of the incidents themselves, but the fact that the phenomena in question force us to fundamentally reformulate the distinction between researcher and researchee.' The abstract ends by saying: 'On the course of research work, this study has gradually adopted a multi-layered, novel-like form. The unorthodox method of processing should not be seen as artistic vagaries but rather as desperate, blindfolded groping towards, possibly, "the unspeakable"'. There is a list of keywords, as well that reads as: 'neuroscience, forensic psychology, antisocial behavior, defalcation, scientific misconduct, bioethics, rationality of science, fMRI, Finnish cases'.

The actual novel begins—as so many postmodernist classics—as a Nordic-noir-esque detective story or mystery, two neuroscientists arrive at a hospital where a convict, a man named Silvo Näre, is placed under a mental examination. We do not know what crime he has committed (and we shall not learn that during the course of the novel) but in the presence of the scientists and medical staff, we find out that he hears voices—one voice in particular:

- Do you still remember, Silvo, how we talked yesterday, on Monday? You told us, how some man is giving you orders. Do you remember? It would be nice if you told us more about this man who bosses you around. Is he scary? Or do you feel safe when he talks to you?
- Gereg. Kahakka and Rambo glace at each other surprised, write the unexplainable word down swiftly. Explanations and theories begin to circulate. Näre stares at Harriet relentlessly.
- Did you say gereg, Silvo? Can you tell us, what gereg means? Have you invented this word by yourself?
- Gereg says: pick up mom from the station.
- Aha, so gereg is a name? Is gereg the man that commands you?
- It isn't just some stadtholder. Mostly he talks utter nonsense. And not always to me but to someone else. This, that and the other. Mindless allegations. Such a twittering chipmunk. Fourth of them, the lastborn, the prodigal son still unknown to the general public. (Yli-Juonikas 2012, 13–14)[1]

Soon after this paragraph, the narration shifts from Silvo's point of view to the one of Gereg's. There seems to be, however, multiple narrators and diegetic levels in *Neuromaani*, and it is generally hard to distinguish them clearly from each other. The structure of the novel is borrowed from the choose-your-own-adventure-novels from the 1980s and *Neuromaani*, thus, represents the genre of ergodic literature. The term ergodic, coined by Espen J. Aarseth, is defined as follows:

> In ergodic literature, nontrivial effort is required to allow the reader to traverse the text. If ergodic literature is to make sense as a concept, there must also be non-ergodic literature, where the effort to traverse the text is trivial, with no extranoematic responsibilities placed on the reader except (for example) eye movement and the periodic or arbitrary turning of pages. (Aarseth 1997, 1)

There is also no main narrative, plot or storyline to be found; the novel keeps constantly fragmenting and changing directions. There are multiple endings where usually the protagonist dies and the reader has to go back a few chapters or start over from the beginning. Therefore, the reader is deprived of the final answer or interpretation of the story—if there even is (only) one. This structure, fragmented by the jumping from chapter to chapter, is a clear nod towards the (ontological) metalepsis (Genette 1980, 234–235) made popular by the Anglo-American postmodernist novels. It also servers another purpose—the partly paratextual instructions for moving about within the book resonate with the fragmentation of the mind which is also one of its recurring themes. As the novel progresses both the narrator(s) and the reader grow increasingly suspicious, even paranoid, about the events:

> If you suspect the father, turn to chapter 57. Or (option c) the note includes a coded message appointed to someone else, which you are in fact not meant to understand. If you are interested in breaking the code, move to chapter 118. On the other hand, it is not completely ruled out, that (d) I have imagined the whole thing. Maybe these curious occurrences are born in my mind and only reflect my worst fears (or *hopes*!?!). Read more in chapter 103. And yet, in the last resort one might ask, (e) does it really matter? One might as well drop the whole schizoid business and move on to more exciting adventures. More exciting adventures available in chapter 202.[2] (Yli-Juonikas 2012, 33)

The fragmentation also reaches the level of the text, breaking up and apart both the cohesion of the story and the reader's meaning-making processes and efforts:

> I wish we had had the sense to settle our 'differences' a little earlier [---] when it wasn't too late yet [---] so much important is left unsaid [---] on child spies [---] on irradiation of the brain [---] don't blame your father, he can't help the ruthlessness of his life instinct [---] white grass, the fleeting white respiration [---] 'laterna magica' [---] father's white ear [---].[3] (Yli-Juonikas 2012, 530)

Not even the wording is left untouched:

> Shocking images and flashes from the lowest levels of the consciousness—a city in ruins, a pillar of fire in the h*riz*n, black j*nipers in front of the housing cooperative, which turn into a pack of wolves during the night [---] unstable state of mind leaves only 2 options: ex*t st*ge l*ft and dem*l***on of th* f*** h*se—move to chapter 25, or rising in the atmosphere—move to chapter 180. This is admittedly a hard choice, and requires an ability to emphasize with a deviant individual's psyche. Have courage, friend—one must

> only throw oneself into the stream of expression, seek the seekers path, c*nnect with the *umanit**s *i*****.[4] (Yli-Juonikas 2012, 77)

All these traits form the slightly unhinged style and feel of the novel. Many of these literary devices are also related or comparable to the linguistic features of madness. This not only reinforces the theme of the outsider or dissident within but also connects the style of the text directly to the consciously forced speech of schizophrenic patients. Other typical linguistic features associated with madness or schizophrenia are neuronal or recurring sentence structures, neologisms, mixed metaphors and uncontrolled associations, as well as the banal and vulgar vocabulary which is also associated with social stigma (Covington et al. 2005). The medical-clinical discourse of neuroscience is placed in an absurd light right from the start. This effect is enhanced by the overly specific reproduction of names of registered trademarks, pharmaceutics and instructions on doses.

The whole composition of *Neuromaani* is interconnected in many ways. Mimicking the academic style of writing with footnotes, references and citations (much like in *Infinite Jest* by David Foster Wallace (1996) or *The House of Leaves* by Mark Z. Danielewski (2000), it urges the reader to look these references up in order to find the key metaphor or solving the riddle of the text. However, all these lines of investigation, no matter how intriguing, turn out to be a cul-de-sac. Some of the references are correct and accurate, leading to other texts that actually exist but some are fictional or misleading. For example, journals and articles mentioned are often amalgamations of both factual and fictional names and references.

This kind of mixing up different textual material is rather common, especially in postmodernist fiction (McHale 1987, 202–203) but it is interesting from the perspective of the materialising effects of reading. The conscientious reader, who tries to track down and map out every quotation and reference very soon becomes overwhelmed with the sheer quantity of the material and even sooner finds themselves rather let down by the book. The seemingly vital clues turn out to be plain mockery of either the reader's endeavours or just sheer literary parody. The large quantity of the referenced material—whether already existing or fictional make-believe—overwhelms the (especially academic) reader who tries to keep track of everything and take note of every single potent metaphor or literary device. There is, although, just simply too much to take into account and the book thus lures the reader to extend their reading-time over anything that would be considered trivial (cf. Aarseth 1997, 1). All of the different aspects of the novel, no matter how hilarious or intriguing, fold into a bundle of affections best described as frustration or exhaustion. *Neuromaani* could, therefore, be best described as excessive. Excess is the state or an instance of surpassing usual, proper or specified limits. It is too much, too many. It is part of the Other (Altman 1989). This calls in for reconfiguring the ways of reading, interpreting and contextualising the novel and its poetics.

BEING IN-BETWEEN: THE MATERIALITY OF ACTUAL AND VIRTUAL

Poetics, as everything else, is currently navigating through the times of capitalism. According to Félix Guattari 'capital is a semiotic operator' which 'seizes individuals from the inside' and has the goal of 'controlling the whole of society' (Guattari 1996, 220). To this process, he refers with the term 'semiocapitalism' which seems to engulf everything it can seize—literature being no exception here. Following Gilles Deleuze and Félix Guattari, literature is 'permeated by unformed, unstable matters, by flows in all directions, by free intensities and by singularities' (Deleuze and Guattari 1987, 45). *Neuromaani* is indeed quite a handful of all of those. Its non-linear structure, combined with vast amounts of themes, motives, references, characters, footnotes and subtexts—both canon and outsider—create a rhizomatic narrative that is difficult to handle or grasp. The title of the book translates as 'Neuromaniac' or *nouveau roman*—already giving the reader some hints regarding its style and its thematic and literary origins, for example, in the literary tradition of French and Anglo-American postmodernism (cf. Piippo 2018). Both of these are characterised by the emphasis on metafiction, the notion of the literary work's own fictionality and ontological status as a codex (McHale 1987, 9–10).

This very material body of the book provides a solid starting point for the analysis of the poetics of in-betweeness (Piippo 2018). However, when discussing the material aspect of literature, we must first define 'materiality'. Literature's materialism is here understood in Gilles Deleuze's terms of actual and virtual. Deleuze is also one of the main philosophical influences behind the concept of new materialism (Dolphijn and van der Tuin 2013, 14). Virtual and actual are both real but not everything that is virtually contained—or immanent—in this world is or becomes actual. Actual is our everyday world at the present moment in time, virtual, on the other hand, is all its possible and impossible pasts and futures (Grosz 2000, 228). According to the widely cited quotation '"virtual" is not opposed to "real" but opposed to "actual", whereas "real" is opposed to "possible"' (Deleuze 1988, 96–98).

Virtual—for example, dreams, memories, imaginations, pure qualities, the story world—is real insofar as it has an effect on us, the virtual insists on the actual. The object of 'a book' is, in this case particularly, for its dual nature. It is genuinely both actual and virtual, wherein both the physical body of a book with printed words on its pages, held in one's hand and the act of reading are actual but the 'real' contents of the book—text, narratives, metaphors, images, etc.—are virtual. Virtual multiplicities form the actual narrative(s) which can be read in the book but they also contain all the what-ifs, alternate endings, reader's expectations, wishes, hopes and so on. This also applies to the aspect of style. As Claire Colebrook puts it:

> Style is best thought of as virtual, as a power of variation and becoming, a power to create anew without prior reference or ground. Deleuze offered a number of ways to think about the literary approach to intensities and affect. Each event of the literary re-opens the question of what and how literature might become, and so each mobilisation and creation of affect is itself different. (Colebrook 2002, 106)

Both actual and virtual are created and separated from each other through the process of repetition. The materiality of literature, in this sense, is created in a process in which the actual emerges from the virtual (Deleuze and Parnet 2002, 148). The actual contents of the book are so to say, 'permeated by unformed, unstable matters, by flows in all directions, by free intensities and by singularities' (Deleuze and Guattari 1987, 11). In this sense, the material effects of reading—for example, the reader's bodily reactions, feelings, evocations and possible later actions which can be linked to the previous reading of the book—are also part of the book's contents, materiality and its meaning. The key point is the equal reality and the relationship of the two main concepts. When talking about the materiality of a book or its poetics, one should also include the virtual aspects in the analysis. Now that we see the ontology of *Neuromaani*, we are to find out its epistemology. What are the materials it has used for its composition? How does it use them? The question here then again is: what kind of affects actualise from the virtual of *Neuromaani* in its reading, especially concerning the circulation and repetition of found material that is connected to the concept of 'outsider'?

REPETITION: PRODUCING THE OUTSIDER

The excessive use of found literary material like references, subtexts, styles, allusions and (anonymous) quotations can be analysed in terms of repetition. Repetition is a process that actualises for example narratives and forms from the virtual of literature, creates new literary space, and therefore, affects the materiality of literature. Here, repetition is understood in a Deleuzian way: thinking of repetition as a process, which re- and deterritorialises the literary space. Deleuzian repetition can be divided into Platonic and Nietzschean repetition, where the first relies on similarity and simulation, and the second, on difference and effect (Deleuze 1994, 190). In this sense, the narration, the use of found material and other forms of literary repetition are more interesting when examined as Nietzschean repetition. Here, writing does not only mechanically repeat the already existing forms and conventions of literature but re-activates the movements and lines which create new literature: the very effects of reading and the new textual and affective space for the outsider within. Especially experimental prose heavily uses different forms of literary repetition and production of affects this way, challenging the more straightforward ways of perceiving the materiality of literature.

Experimental literature often questions the dominants, tastes and structures of the current literary and cultural field. It poses the very ontological question of its own 'literaturnost': is this literature or could it be (Bray, Gibbons and McHale 2012)? The Situationist International would state that it is a question of recuperation and *detournement*. In other words, does this experimentation pose any resistance to the current dominant? By following and mapping out the lines of different forms of repetition in *Neuromaani*—compulsory re-reading of the chapters due the ergodic structure, genre-related traits like metafictional elements and the usage of found material—and by following repetitions dual core impulse of simultaneously binding and breaking apart (cf. Piippo 2018), it is possible to analyse closely the dissident poetics in *Neuromaani*.

Neuromaani itself is already in the state of being and outsider within. It is an experimental piece of literature with reader's expectations of a highly complex structure and a rather narrow audience, yet published by a prestigious publishing house and receiving critical acclaim. The same thematic extends beyond the novel itself: it is written and published in Finnish which is a very small language on a European scale, not even to mention global proportions. On the other hand, Finnish is a very literary language with a strong national and institutional position and, in that sense, cannot really be regarded as a minor language.

Neuromaani is thus layered in many ways but not least in its tendency to circulate, appropriate and emulate found textual material: styles, jargon, poetics, references and quotations. The general style and vocabulary of the novel are largely dominated by the neuroscientific and medical jargon—an effect that is enhanced by the overabundance of footnotes and other traits of academic writing:

> And there I was, celebrating this new millennium of great hopes and fears, rounded up with the good old usual suspects: Small S.A., Perera G.M., DeLaPaz R., Mayeux R. ja Stern Y. 1999, and all we could think of was 'Differential regional dysfunction of the hippocampal formation among elderly with memory decline and Alzheimer's disease.' *Annals of Neurology* 45. S. 466–472.[5] (Yli-Juonikas 2012, 101)

There also is the aforementioned structural analogy to other (post) postmodernist novels but also many references to Finnish literary traditions. There is, for example, a long passage that is, in fact, a parody of the realist Finnish prose of the 1950s and 1960s (Yli-Juonikas 2012, 303–306), and several subtle nods towards Finnish classics. There is, however, a lot that is derived from urban folklore and the so-called outsider literature. All these voices mix in the novel. For example, a now late Finnish 'outsider-author' and conspiration theorist Vilho Piippo, who also was allegedly a schizophrenia patient, is presented in a long passage as an expert on neuroscience, conducting research and corresponding with Bill Clinton, who is being referred to as 'the leopard king' and whom Piippo warns about the dangers of the dissidents within (Yli-Juonikas 2012, 594–597).

Outsider literature is a literary equivalent to the international field of outsider art. Outsider literature is often self-published or vanity press that distinguishes it from edited literature which is published through traditional publishing houses or other institutions of the literature scene. Important here is the inherent solitude of the self-published literature: there is no editor or publisher's style sheet that would comment or co-author the work. Outsider art has its roots in the psychiatric hospitals' hospital art, also called *art brut* in order to avoid excessive stigma (Haveri 2016, 113). This junction reinforces the reader's connotations of madness and dissidence in *Neuromaani*. It is possible to recognise several of the mentioned or referenced names as Finnish outsider writes if one is acquainted with the phenomenon. Only in *Neuromaani*, they are presented as practitioners, researchers and authorities of the field of neuroscience. In a comparative view, the linguistic features that coincide with the schizophrenic language in the novel appear to be largely derived from these same sources.

The motivation of this article is, however, not to label or diagnose any writers or texts referenced in *Neuromaani*. What is of interest here is the literary devices and works which convey the feel and connotations of madness. That is the poetics of dissidence and the outsider within which are also central to the composition of *Neuromaani*. The founder of the term *art brut*, French artist Jean Dubuffet has also noted that not all features of *art brut* were typical only to the art of the hospital patients. One must also bear in mind the autonomy of the literary work, its meanings or intentions cannot be solely drawn from the author, whether be they an outsider or not.

The references and connotations recognised as 'outsider' do, however, have an effect on the poetics of *Neuromaani*, as they add new virtualities to the body of the novel. The authoritative language of neurology, medicalisation and diagnostics become unstable when mixed together with the themes of fraud, crime, pseudoscience and the affections produced by the schizophrenic language. All this is connected to the postmodernist conception of literature, where the meaning of the text is no longer traced back to the author but is rather seen as a motley painting, a heterogenic assemblage of various texts and their heteroglossia. Literary narrative structures often experiment in the area of the mind, especially a mind in state of fragmentation (Zunshine 2006, 54–57). Characteristic to these outsider traits and poetics woven into the tissue of *Neuromaani* is indeed their excessiveness.

EXCESS: THE DISSIDENT WITHIN

How does the excessive quality in and of *Neuromaani* react to the current cultural dominant and global circumstance of capitalism? Could it be in this very excess where an aesthetic that will both represent and resist these times could be found? The ethos of capitalism is to overcome old boundaries and in that maxim lies the excessive spirit of capitalism, too. Semiocapitalism, or the current post-Fordist digital culture, is founded on immaterial labour and the explosion of the info-sphere (Virno, Bertoletti, Cascaito and Casson 2004, 9–10). Here 'capital is a semiotic operator' that 'seizes individuals from the inside' and has the goal of 'controlling the whole of society' (Guattari 1996, 200, 212). All this leads to an excess of visibility and expressivity. According to Franco 'Bifo' Berardi, 'the expansion of a specific cognitive function redefines the whole of cognition' ('Bifo' 2005). On a personal level, the outcome of the acceleration described earlier is often exhaustion and depression ('Bifo' 2009), the former of which is the affection that dominates the reading of *Neuromaani* as well. The machine of capitalist production and circulation operates only by continually breaking down (Deleuze and Guattari 2010, 8).

What is the dynamic between the excess of *Neuromaani* and the one of semiocapitalism? Excess as a concept has three distinctive sites. It can be seen as redundancy ('too much'), transgression ('more') or mediation ('exceeding the limits' as an ongoing process and strategy) (Sihvonen 1991, 31–33). Capitalism produces extreme diversity and multiplicity but the basic condition of possibility for this profusion is money and credit (Lazzarato 2012). Heterogeneity turns into homogeneity in the long run and the problem of excess is projected to those who are too many or too much: the dissident. This way of seeing the excess represents the sites of it as 'more' and 'too much'. As Rick Altman writes: 'The right to identify and name the excess carries enormous power, always in favour of the dominant. To name excess is thus just another way of naming the dominant. Totality minus excess equals dominant' (Altman 1989, 346). On the other hand, it is the sheer excessiveness of the event that provokes anxiety in our terms of understanding and representation. As Steven Shaviro writes on Bataille's thought on excess:

> There is no end to the accumulation of the capitalistic mode of production—it abolishes all hierarchies of means and ends, all teleologies. However, it cannot abolishes excess, which continues in obsessive moments of production and valorisation. For Bataille, as homogeneity increasingly imposes itself as the immanent law of production under capitalism, it threatens to become more and more disorderly, to run more and more out of control. (Shaviro 1990, 56)

In *Neuromaani*, there are numerous subtexts, characters, references, pseudo-references, sources, thoughts and red herrings. Eventually, the reader will also find themselves entangled in the deteriorating language and structure, different interpretational threads and the multitude of virtualities. They also become both, uncomfortably numb, and aware of their own role as the reader, and the way the text is to observe and comment on this role. What is also amplified is the dissident poetics drawn from the surrounding culture, normally repressed by the excess of capitalism. In the context of *Neuromaani* it is, in fact, these very poetics, the outsider within, that enables the creation of a virtual interpretational space separate from the repressing excess—a point of departure for reading that is roaring instead of repetitive. Here the excess of the novel becomes something that is exceeding pre-set boundaries and limitations of thought. The dissident produced in the novel now becomes part of the reader through the process of actualization from the virtual that is embedded in the process of reading. This combination of exhilaration, frustration, exhaustion and being out-of-joint is typical to excess, or 'the third meaning', as Roland Barthes calls it. *Neuromaani* enhances these notions embedded in the excess, especially through its multidimensional actual and virtual structure.

The novel serves as a memento, vessel and manifestation to all the layers surrounding intersecting it. It creates a parallel series for the surrounding conditions, and an amplifier for the outsider within. This also distinguishes *Neuromaani* apart from the typically paranoid undertones of the postmodernist classics. These aesthetics and poetics which can be understood via the dynamic between the actual and the virtual present a possibility to create something that is creative rather than opposing, and yet resistant and resilient when it comes to the recuperating practices of capitalism. The point of creating or line of flight lays in the affective relation between the various actuals and the virtuals. According to Fredric Jameson, '[a]lthough the "global world system" is "unrepresentable," this does not mean that it is "unknowable"' (1991, 53). 'An aesthetic of cognitive and affective mapping' is needed to examine critically the processes exploitation and expropriation (Jameson 1991, 54; Shaviro 1990, 5). It is the task of resistance movements and art to create collective agencies of enunciation that match the new subjectivity which also encompasses the inherent in-betweenness and the dissident within. In this reading, I have aimed to present that, by adding actual and virtual layers repeatedly upon one another, there just might be enough room in the affective and literary folds of *Neuromaani*—or any other literary work with the same strategy—for the excess and dissidence to build up, regroup, and eventually, break free.

NOTES

1. Finnish original:

    - Muistatko vielä Silvo, kun me juteltiin eilen maanantaina? Kerroit, että joku mies antaa sinulle käskyjä. Muistatko? Olisi mukavaa, jos kertoisit meille tästä miehestä, joka komentelee sinua. Onko mies pelottava? Vai tunnetko sinä olosi turvalliseksi, kun mies puhuu sinulle?
    - Gereg.
    - Kahakka ja Rambo vilkaisevat toisiaan yllättyneinä, kirjoittavat selittämättömän sanan vikkelästi muistiin. Selitysmallit ja teoriat alkavat risteillä mielessä. Näre tuijottaa herkeämättä Harrietia.
    - Sanoitko sinä gereg, Silvo? Voitko kertoa meille, mitä gereg tarkoittaa? Oletko keksinyt ihan itse sen sanan?
    - Gereg käskee hakemaan äidin asemalta.
    - Ahaa, siis gereg on nimi? Onko Gereg se mies, joka käskee sinua?

- Ei se ole pelkkä käskynhaltija. Useimmiten puhuu mitä sattuu. Eikä aina minulle vaan jollekin toiselle. Kaikkea sekavaa. Älyttömiä väitteitä ja kysymyksiä. Sellainen kimittävä pikkuorava. Neljäs niistä, kuopus, suurelle yleisölle tuntemattomaksi jäänyt tuhlaajapoika.
  (Yli-Juonikas 2012, 13–14; all translations are by Laura Piippo)

2. Finnish original:

   Jos epäilyksesi kohdistuvat isään, siirry lukuun 57. Tai sitten (c) lappuun sisältyy jollekin toiselle henkilölle kohdistettu koodiviesti, jota minun ei ole tarkoituskaan ymmärtää. Jos koodin murtaminen kiinnostaa, siirry lukuun 118. Toisaalta ei voi pitää poissuljettuna, että (d) minä kuvittelisin koko jutun. Ehkä ko. merkilliset ilmiöt ovat syntyneet mielessäni ja heijastavat vain pahimpia pelkojani (tai toiveitani!?!). Lue lisää luvusta 103. Silti viime kädessä voi kysyä, (e) onko jutulla oikeastaan väliä. Yhtä hyvin voisin jättää sikseen koko typerän skitsoilun ja siirtyä kiinnostavampiin seikkailuihin. Kiinnostavampia seikkailuja on luvassa luvussa 202. (Yli-Juonikas 2012, 433)

3. Finnish original:

   Kunpa olisimme ymmärtäneet sopia 'erimielisyytemme' vähän aiemmin [---] kun ei vielä ollut myöhäistä [---] niin paljon tärkeää jää sanomatta [---] lapsivakoojista [---] aivojen säteilytyksestä [---] älä soimaa isääsi, hän ei mahda mitään elämänviettinsä armottomuudelle [---] valkoinen ruoho, pakeneva valkoinen hengitys [---] 'taikalamppu' [---] isän valkoinen korva [---]. (Yli-Juonikas 2012, 530)

4. Sokeeraavia kuvia ja välähdyksiä tietoisuuden alimmista kerroksista – rauniokaupunki, tulipatsas h*riso*tissa, yöllä susilaumaksi muuttuvat mustat k*tajat taloyhtiön pihalla [---] epävakaa mielentila antaa vain 2 vaihtoehtoa: t*kav*semman täy*kä**n p**ku - siirry lukuun 25, tai k*hoamin*n a****r**sä - siirry lukuun 180. Valinta on kieltämättä vaikea ja vaatii sinulta eläytymiskykyä poikkeusyksilön sis. maailmaan. Rohkeutta, ystävä - tulee vain heittäytyä kokemuksen virtaan, etsiytyä etsijän tielle, k*tkeytyä *hmis**den *h******* (Yli-Juonikas 2012, 77)

5. Finnish orignal:

   Suurten toiveiden ja pelkojen milleniumia minä juhlistin kaverieni kanssa Rio de Janeiron räkäisimmässä merimieskapakassa, koolla oli koko vanha hampuusijengi Small S. A., Perera G. M., DeLaPaz R., Mayeux R. ja Stern Y. 1999 ja kaikilla pyöri mielessä vain 'Differential regional dysfunction of the hippocampal formation among elderly with memory decline and Alzheimer's disease.' *Annals of Neurology* 45. S. 466–472. (Yli-Juonikas 2012, 101)

REFERENCES

Aarseth, E. *Cybertext: Perspectives on Ergodic Literature*. Baltimore: Johns Hopkins University Press, 1997.

Altman, R. 'Dickens, Griffith, and Film Theory Today'. *South Atlantic Quarterly* 88, no. 2 (1989): 321–359.

'Bifo' Berardi, F. 'Biopolitics and Connective Mutation', *Culture Machine* 7 (2005). Available at https://culturemachine.net/biopolitics/biopolitics-and-connective-mutation/.

———. *Precarious Rhapsody—Semiocapitalism & the Pathologies of Post-Alpha Generation*. London: Minor Compositions, 2009.

Bray, J., A. Gibbons and B. McHale. 'Introduction'. In *The Routledge Companion to Experimental Literature*, edited by J. Bray, A. Gibbons and B. McHale. London and New York: Routledge, 2012.

Colebrook, Claire. *Gilles Deleuze*. London and New York: Routledge, 2002.

Concise Oxford English Dictionary. Oxford: Oxford University Press, 2014.

Covington, M.A. et al. 'Schizophrenia and the Structure of Language: The Linguist's View.' *Schizophrenia Research* 77, no. 1 (2005): 85–98. Available at https://doi.org/10.1016/j.schres.2005.01.016 (accessed on 22 June 2018).

Danielewski, Mark Z. *House of Leaves*. New York: Pantheon Books, 2000.

Deleuze, G. *Bergsonism*, translated by H. Tomlinson and B. Habberjam. New York: Zone Books, 1988.

———. *Difference and Repetition*, translated by P.R. Patton. New York: Columbia University Press, 1994.

Deleuze, G. and F. Guattari. *A Thousand Plateaus. Capitalism and Schizophrenia*, translated by B. Massumi. Minneapolis: University of Minnesota Press, 1987.

———. *Anti-Oidipus: Kapitalismi ja skitsofrenia*, translated by T. Kilpeläinen and Tutkijaliitto. Helsinki: Tutkijaliitto, 2010.

Deleuze, G. and C. Parnet. *Dialogues II*, translated by H. Tomlinson and B. Habberjam. New York: Columbia University Press, 2002.

Dolphijn, R. and I. van der Tuin. *New Materialism: Interviews and Cartographies*. Ann Arbor: Open Humanities Press, 2013.

Genette, G. *Narrative Discourse: An Essay in Method*, translated by J.E. Lewin. Ithaca (NY): Cornell University Press, 1980.

Grosz, E. 'Deleuze's Bergson. Duration, the Virtual and a Politics of the Future.' In *Deleuze and Feminism*, edited by I. Buchanan and C. Colebrook. Edinburgh: Edinburgh University Press, 2000.

Guattari, F. *Soft Subversions*. New York: Semiotext(e), 1996.

Haveri, M. 'ITE-taiteen hauska brändi'. In *Huumorin skaalat. Esitys, tyyli, tarkoitus*, edited by S. Knuuttila, P. Hakamies and E. Lampela, 108–124. Helsinki: SKS, 2016.

Jameson, F. *Postmodernism, or, the Cultural Logic of Late Capitalism*. Durham: Duke University Press, 1991.

Lazzarato, M. *The Making of the Indebted Man: An Essay on the Neoliberal Condition*, translated by J.D. Jordan. New York: Semiotext(e), 2012.

McHale, B. *Postmodernist Fiction*. London and New York: Routledge, 1987.

McHale, B. 'Whatever Happened to Descriptive Poetics?'. In *The Point of Theory: Practices of Cultural Analysis*, edited by M. Bal and I.E. Boer, 56–65. Amsterdam: Amsterdam University Press, 1994.

Piippo, L. '"650 sivua tiivistettyä hulluutta on liikaa"—Jaakko Yli-Juonikkaan *Neuromaani* (2012) elämystalouden karstana ja polttoaineena'. In *Elämykset kulttuurina ja kulttuuri elämyksinä*, edited by S. Karkulehto, T. Lähdesmäki and J. Venäläinen, 347–371. Jyväskylä: Jyväskylä University Press, 2016. Available at https://jyx.jyu.fi/dspace/handle/123456789/55491 (accessed 6 April 2019).

———. 'The Brain in our Hands: The Materiality of Reading *Neuromaani*'. In *Reading Today*, edited by H. Pyrhönen and J. Kantola, 45–56. London: UCL Press, 2018. Available at https://doi:10.14324/111.9781787351950 (accessed 6 April 2019).

———. *Operatiivinen vainoharha normaalitieteen aikakaudella: Jaakko Yli-Juonikkaan Neuromaanin kokeellinen poetiikka*. Jyväskylä: Jyväskylä University Press, 2020. Available at http://urn.fi/URN: ISBN:978-951-39-8251-5 (accessed 1 November 2020).

Rancière, J. *Mute Speech: Literature, Critical Theory, and Politics*, translated by J. Swenson. New York: Columbia University Press, 2011.

Shaviro, S. *Passion & Excess: Blanchot, Bataille, and Literary Theory*. Tallahassee: Florida State University Press, 1990.

Sihvonen, J. *Exceeding the Limits: On the Poetics and Politics of Audiovisuality.* Turku: SETS, 1991.

Virno, P., I. Bertoletti, J. Cascaito and A. Casson. *A Grammar of the Multitude: For an Analysis of Contemporary Forms of Life*. Los Angeles: Semiotext(e), 2004.

Wallace, David Foster. *Infinite Jest: A Novel*. London: Abacus, 1996.

Yli-Juonikas, Jaakko. *Neuromaani*. Helsinki: Otava, 2012.

Zunshine, L. *Why We Read Fiction: Theory of Mind and the Novel*. Ohio State University Press, 2006.

DECLASSING ART: MANIK BANDYOPADHYAY AND COMMUNIST AESTHETICS IN INDIA

Rajarshi Dasgupta

> *Remember Manikbabu's Madan weaver? He who said how do I work on the loom with yarns that are bought with Bhuban trader's money? How can I betray you? I am getting gout in my joints and legs from sitting idle. So, I worked on an empty loom, an empty loom.... One has to do something after all....*
>
> —Nilkantha Bagchi in 'Jukti, Takka Ar Gappo' (Ritwik Ghatak 1974)

INTRODUCTION

The question of culture is a paradox for Indian communists. They play down their engagements with culture although historically it has been a great source of strength for their movement. It is why the colonial state saw them as heralds of 'dangerous ideas' despite their small number and localised presence. This view has hardly changed if the current regime's signals are anything to go by. While communist parties are electorally weak and their armed faction is confined to pockets, they continue to feature as a major target of ruling party campaigns. However, in doing so the right-wing shrewdly recognises two facts that seem to elude the left's comprehension. The first is that, behind the rhetorical nod to development, popular politics is moulded today by issues that have more to do with culture than economics. That is precisely where the low caste groups are staking claims for recognition and the right-wing is pitching its Hindu nationalism, with hardly any debate on neoliberal policy choices. The left's insistence on economic issues, howsoever pressing, is unable to create much room for intervention at this level, calling for attention to culture. Nevertheless, the critique of capitalism also connects to a social imaginary that is crucial to the making of the nation since independence. This is the second important fact: the imagination of another India with secular and socialist elements that are on the back foot but refusing to go away. That is because among other elements it draws sustenance from the communist idea of an equal and just society. In their bid for a long-term hegemony, the left remains a key opponent for the right-wing forces. Interestingly, in this, they find unlikely allies among Dalit formations who resent the communist sway over culture as a variant of upper caste domination they must overthrow. It is this enduring relevance in the political optics on the culture that seems to escape the communists, partly due to doctrinaire reasons.

Unlike western Marxism, where the political value of culture was rethought by the likes of Raymond Williams and Stuart Hall following Althusser and Gramsci, Indian communists remained stuck to an old school Marxism. Despite exposure to Soviet and Chinese cultural manoeuvres, most of them could not think beyond culture as an instrumental aspect and subordinate to economic interventions. When experiments with culture by inspired sections contested this limited framing, they met with party apathy and censure from leaders, apart from rare occasions. The upshot was a division of labour between activists who organised trade union politics and those who worked with language, literature and arts. While organising workers and peasants was deemed essential, engaging with literature and arts did not seriously count. A mechanical approach that pitted 'change' against 'interpretation' bred such distrust for culture it effectively blinded communists to one of their key achievements. What they overlooked in the process is their own practice of constructing Marxism as a discourse, its grounding, translation and adaptation to different life-worlds in certain parts of this country. This blindness partly explains why communist politics could not spread far because they failed to recognise how it came to grow roots in the first place. At the same time, they went so deep where the roots could branch out, it insulated them against massive global reversals since the late twentieth century. Ironically, this endurance rested on a practice that dogmatism still does not allow them to grasp as politics. It, therefore, calls for a critical reconsideration of how cultural engagements can be understood as essential to their practice and what are its traces in the communist past.

Our point of departure is to give up on a uniformly universal idea of Marxism. When variations are no longer subject to authenticity checks, we can pay more attention to what has departed from the original and for what reasons. Allow me to suggest here that such moves stand a better chance of analysis if 'translation' is taken up as a concept-metaphor for thinking about political practice. It helps to map how certain ways of interpreting reality come to be grounded in different languages and contexts and how these interpretations gradually fuse into the articulation of a new discourse. We often ignore what is construed as Marxi sm in the subcontinent is different in subtle but significant ways from what the term means elsewhere, for instance, in China or Cuba, let alone European contexts. The move I suggested is precisely useful in tracking how Marxism came to acquire a distinctive 'discourse', taking a new shape in different pockets of late colonial India. As we know, initially it came up in parts, with abridged translations of key texts, circulated from abroad and reviewed in regional languages. Around this core there gathered a more complex network of ideas in communist strongholds like Maharashtra, Kerala and Bengal. Here the discourse practically expanded into an everyday outlook, with immediate links to the experience, aspirations and preoccupations of the local people and indigenous society. Not surprisingly, this called for complex negotiations with notions of subjectivity and self-worth, collective wisdom and narrative traditions, in short, all that was peculiar to these contexts and alien to Marxism elsewhere. It is this part that I want to highlight: How such elements came to be accessed and understood, interpreted and remoulded, in a painstaking process of what we may describe as a vernacular remaking of Marxism. The recoding of indigenous society in terms of class-struggle could not have taken place merely by repeating an abstract treatise remote in time and space. It needed extensive mining into what Williams refers as structures of feeling, harvesting motifs from folk tales and mythologies, repurposing popular tropes of resistance and rubbing together different ideas of labour and craft, art and politics (Williams 1961). This process is what we have set out to study which is critical for grasping the distinctive character of Marxist discourse and the profound impact of communist politics on culture in India.

There are of course many dimensions to cultural engagements. A rich body of growing scholarship has been meticulously documenting these histories in different contexts. In that sense, there is quite a bit of literature, more so in regional languages, although they hardly speak to each other (Bhattacharya 1987; Bannerji 1998; Roy 2000; Ghosh 2010). Despite the rich analysis, therefore, not much of this work tackles the discursive construction or probe the relation of cultural engagements with political practice. More specifically, they do not focus on how these engagements shaped the discourse differently from elsewhere and the conflicted location of culture in communist practice. These larger concerns make up the background of our discussion here that is going to take up a telling example of communist engagement with culture in late colonial India. I have written at some length about the astonishing breadth of these cultural engagements which ranged from scholarly histories of colonial modernity (Dasgupta 2004) to polemics, plays and popular revolutionary poetry (Dasgupta 2005a). A recent essay of mine has discussed the efforts at translating key texts like 'The Communist

Manifesto', 'Wage, Labor and Capital' and 'Capital' from the first abridged versions to annotated editions in several Indian languages (Dasgupta 2019). These texts reveal how often the same persons working with workers and peasants were working at translations and writing poetry, rendering the dogmatic division of culture and politics increasingly problematic to sustain. I realised, however, that I was missing a critical dimension when I began looking at how communists created a new kind of art to complement reports on famine and peasant revolts in early communist publications (Dasgupta 2014a). One cannot fully comprehend how such exercises were creating a new Marxist discourse without also grasping how this process of creation impacted the indigenous habitus in turn. We need to understand the specific ways in which the cultural terrain was getting transformed, that could not happen without Marxism, yet which the communists did not think of naming at the time. That is what I try to capture in the phrase 'communist aesthetics' in the title of this chapter.

The phrase is not used here in a strict sense, and it is not limited to issues of beauty and artistic forms. As noted, these facets are taken up in a growing body of works, that range from art history to theatre, film and performance studies, besides literary criticism. I will make use of insights from them, especially, works that focus on the 1940s and 1950s. It is a rare period, when P.C. Joshi encouraged artistic practices—the only communist leader who took culture seriously, though not seriously enough to call for a theoretical rethinking. The essay will fleetingly touch upon certain themes of this period such as the iconography of socialist realism. However, my attempt is to open the remit of communist aesthetics to a wider conceptual reference, exploring two specific aspects in the limited scope of this essay. The first is a move described in philosophical discussions as the aesthetic turn to 'everyday'. Simply put, it signals a negation of aesthetic pleasure in elevated sentiments and wonderful objects normally associated with beauty and singular experience. Instead, it takes up the dreary and mundane existence that is lived in 'anesthetic' terms and makes it completely unfamiliar, recasting it with an aura that imbues the ordinary with strange and intense sensations. The move has close affinities with the avant-garde strategies of a modernist literary movement in the colony. I believe it to be a profoundly political aspect of communist engagements that pulls the meaning of aesthetics back to its roots in a way not discussed so far. It also helps to underline why the concept-metaphor of translation can be useful to understand communist politics and reveals how communists were altering the cultural terrain in the process. The second aspect I want to underline is the deeply *subjective* dimension of cultural engagements. They not only entailed carving out a new social perspective but also the critique of one's own class, individual history and the representation of one's practice in profound ways. Let me explain this from another angle. Unlike other political entities, an account of oneself is very rare in communist narratives. The reason, as I argued elsewhere, is a manner of self-fashioning that involves a personal erasure. To be a communist is to overcome the 'bourgeois' ego-centric self: to become 'declassed' (Dasgupta 2014b). It is this work of 'becoming'—a specific manner of self-conduct, that directs the relation with the world, with others and steers the practice of representation. It spelled a constant experiment with the meaning of art and artist: The challenge for art was breaking down the figure of the artist and the subject in the usual authoritative sense. The challenge for the artist was to reconfigure art into what it is not—to belong to the masses and cease to be art. It is this limit-attitude to art and the turn to everyday that I consider two of the most distinctive aspects of communist aesthetics in India. We are going to explore them in more detail in the pages to follow, with the help of perhaps the most iconic communist author of India, Manik Bandyopadhyay.

THE IMMEDIATE CONTEXT OF CULTURAL ENGAGEMENTS

Let me briefly outline the historical background of the literary works of Manik Bandyopadhyay. Most commentators see his later writings as outstanding instances of communist literature that came to be produced in the course of a momentous cultural initiative taken up in the 1940s. The latter is known as the progressive literary movement or *Pragati Sahitya Andolan* in Bangla, *Pragatisheel Sahitya Andolan* in Hindi, *Purogamana Kala Saahithya Prasthanam* in Malayalam and *Taraqqi Pasand Adabi Tahreek* in Urdu. It largely grew out of the 'Anti-Fascist' association of writers, artists and intellectuals in India, inspired by similar associations protesting Nazi repression in Europe. Initially a broad platform including liberals and Gandhians, the communists gave it an added momentum while using it for their own ideological mobilisation. In the process, it came to produce a new body of socially engaged writings, led by the likes of Premchand, Krishan Chander, Rajinder Singh Bedi, Ismat Chughtai, Faiz Ahmed Faiz and Saadat Hassan Manto in Hindi and Urdu, besides the likes of Bandyopadhyay and Sukanta Bhattacharya in Bangla. At the same time, it saw fierce and acrimonious debates about committed literature and the ways in which class perspective should shape creative writing. Much of these debates were triggered by provocations, incitements and interventions from communist critics and writers who tried to show the direction they wanted for literature to take with their own experiments. The outcome was admittedly varied, producing fiction verging at times on propaganda as well as transgressive writings that are hard to box into tidy categories. While it led to raging disputes even among communists, such writings and subsequent cultural experiments of the *Indian Peoples' Theatre Association* became critical in taking Marxism to the ordinary people. The famine and the 'Tebhaga' movement in Bengal, for instance, triggered a profusion of radical narratives on poverty and exploitation, factory strikes and peasant agitation, ranging from posters and paintings, plays and short stories, novels and even daily news reports and photographs reaching across the country (Basu 2017; Ghosh 2019; Sunderason 2020; Bhattacharya 2020). Mainly produced by communist artists and writers, this body of work became instrumental in achieving two things: First, as noted, it helped to break down, translate and reconstruct the discourse of Marxism, directly speaking to the needs and aspirations of a large number of people suffering in colonial India. Second, by submitting the discourse to a dialogical process with the local habitus, its customs and mores, such works turned Marxism into a compelling perspective for many, including a growing spectrum of the *bhadralok* middle class. This is precisely what Manik Bandyopadhyay's writings illustrate.

We must remember that the predominant section of political organisers, leaders and activists hailed from the middle classes: the *madhyabitta-bhadralok*, many of them residing in Calcutta and Dhaka and the district and mofussil towns of Bengal. Although they hailed from a nineteenth-century formation of mostly upper-caste Hindu absentee landlords, traders and petty collaborators, the *madhyabitta* turned fairly heterogeneous by the early twentieth century. They now included a remarkably wide range of people, including unemployed youth, indigent clerks and struggling teachers as well as solvent government officers, successful doctors, lawyers and petty bureaucrats. All were bound, however, by a common pride in their educated status and aversion to manual labour (McGuire 1983; Sarkar 1998). Literature and cultural practices enjoyed a key role in the self-construction of these people and, not surprisingly, strongly overlapped with their political domain. It is why the nationalist discourse mainly took shape through literary writings in the nineteenth century, as scholars and historians have pointed out. The sphere of creative writing was thus already a site for negotiating political issues, even if this connection remained implicit in *madhyabitta* thinking (Kaviraj 1998; Chakrabarty 2000). Along with this historical background, the 'progressive movement' also owed much to a modernist literary movement that took place in the early 1930s. A bunch of new literary journals such as *Kallol*, *Sanghati*, *Kalikalam*, *Uttara* and *Purbasha* inaugurated a powerful trend of literary experiments that came to be known as the '*Kallol*' movement. Their stories signalled a radical departure from established aesthetic norms by breaking the divide between 'public' and 'private' matters observed for long in vernacular literature as a mark of taste and morality. Taking inspiration from Marx and Freud, the 'Kallol' movement broached new themes and introduced new protagonists, talking about the urban underclasses for the first time, the difficult life of coal mine workers and the secrecy and bigotry around sexuality in colonial society. Some of these writings may read in hindsight a touch naïve and like a sentimental indictment of the society, but there is little doubt that the movement radicalised both style and content of Bangla literature in a bold manner. More significantly, it started a completely new trend with a small number of alternative non-commercial journals owned by poets, artists and writers that created a new kind of print space and public for allowing literary experiments to explore more radical directions in the years to follow.

The *Kallol* movement was soon followed by a set of new journals that came to acquire a legendary status in the history of Bangla literature. These included *Kabita* and *Parichay* and the first set of identifiably Leftist journals such as *Arani* and *Pratirodh* that played an instrumental role in the 'progressive movement'. Besides providing a site for experimental writing, they regularly published those debates and exchanges over political, artistic and theoretical differences that arose before long between Marxist and liberal factions. These debates included contributions from a new set of Marxist intellectuals such as Sushobhan Sarkar, Benoy Ghosh, Gopal Haldar and Hiren Mukherjee on the one hand and formidable liberal intellectuals like Humayun Kabeer, Buddhadeb Basu and Pramathanath Bishi on the other, apart from other shades of the intelligentsia. The early communists often turned these debates into occasions to push the meaning of terms like 'progress' and 'progressive' interpreting them as a commitment to a materialist view of history and by extension a class perspective. The disputes grew intense and acute as some Marxists advanced admittedly reductionist frames for evaluating vernacular traditions, denouncing respected canons as 'bourgeois' and proposing new criteria for a 'proletarian literature' in Bengal (Mitra 1980; Roy 2014). In fact, even Marxists like Samar Sen and Saroj Dutta fiercely disagreed with each other and bitterly debated over what should be the appropriate writing strategies for 'progressive' literature. What became decisive at this juncture was, however, the emergence of a host of new authors such as Tarashankar Bandyopadhyay, Swarnakamal Bhattacharya, Syed Waleeullah and especially, Manik Bandyopadhyay (Dasgupta 2005b). While theoretical interventions tried to steer the 'progressive movement' with arguments, these writers came to provide concrete examples of a new literature, translating the radical influence into authorial techniques and narrative strategies. Manik Bandyopadhyay's texts were the leading instance of this corpus, to which we turn further.

THREE WAYS OF READING MANIK BANDYOPADHYAY

Prabodh Kumar Bandyopadhyay was born in 1908. He came from an educated middle-class family, growing up in different locations of Bengal Presidency that now lie in Odisha, Bihar and currently Bangladesh. He was the fifth son of a government officer, an early science graduate from Calcutta university who became a Kanungo and rose to become a Sub-deputy Collector. Expectedly, Prabodh enrolled as an undergraduate in Mathematics at Presidency College in 1928. He wrote his first story somewhat casually, simply to win a bet taken with friends, turning his nickname Manik into a pen name for the occasion. This short story, '*Ataseemamee*' was published in 1928 and drew considerable attention persuading Manik to consider writing seriously. Two more short stories were published in 1929 and Manik decided to leave his studies and join the literary world, much to the dismay and against the wishes of his family. A series of outstanding novels followed in the span of the next few years that include *Dibaratrir Kabya* in 1934, *Janani* in 1935, *Padma Nadir Majhi*, *Putul Nacher Itikathha* and *Jibaner Jotilata* in 1936. Unfortunately, around the same time, the young writer was diagnosed with epilepsy, a lifelong ailment that worsened with years, aggravated by his struggle against penury, alcohol addiction and mental illness, leading to his untimely death. However, the early novels had already established him as a powerful author, coming in the wake of the *Kallol* movement and pushing creative fiction into radical and uncharted directions. Before long, critics and the reading public hailed him as one of the three great writers of mid-twentieth century Bangla literature, along with Bibhutibhushan Bandyopadhyay and Tarashankar Bandyopadhyay, who helped to reshape the modern novel in India into what an eminent scholar has come to term as 'provincial epic' (Chaudhuri 2015). Manik's first collection of short stories, *Pragoitihasik*, came out in 1937 and the following years witnessed an astonishing outpouring of novels and short stories published almost every year until his relatively early death in 1956. Although he kept battling with extreme poverty and intense bouts of physical and mental disorder, Manik joined the 'progressive movement' around the turn of the 1940s and became a member of the Communist Party of India in 1944. He served as a member of the highest board at the meetings of anti-fascist writers and artists' association in 1944 and 1945. He died at the premature age of 48, leaving behind an imposing corpus of 36 novels, 177 short stories, two plays, a few essays and poetry. By then Manik Bandyopadhyay was recognised far and wide as the foremost Marxist author of Bengal if not of India.

This recognition appears in hindsight not without a small share of misfortune, as it has subsequently led to carving up Manik's writings into rather restrictive schemes of reception. Perhaps the most awkward of them is also the most influential: one approaches Manik with a definitive threshold between (what he wrote) before and after he became a Marxist. This scheme allows a curve of evolution in perhaps what is seen as the author's 'consciousness', understood in terms of the difference in style, plots and protagonists that came to feature in his writings over the years. The strength of this scheme lies in offering a clear-cut sequence that is literally progressive that is affirmed by the mode of appreciation of a significant segment of leading scholars. According to them, Manik represents the best of an Indian variant of socialist realism which is a claim made with persuasion, substance and sophistication by the likes of Mihir Bhattacharya, among a host of others (Bhattacharya 2011). At the same time, there is a persistent unease and sense of anxiety if not censure in this same framework of whatever Manik had written 'before' he became Marxist. The value of Manik as a Marxist writer could be realised, it seems, only at the cost of dismissing his writing as wasteful and aimless when he was yet to become a Marxist. Many erudite admirers of Manik Bandyopadhyay, even literary critics like Malini Bhattacharya, thus cannot but hold up the coarse matter and raucous style of his early writings as a telling contrast to the superiority of his later (class-conscious) prose (Bhattacharya 1987). Despite the note of valorisation, it is hard to overlook the crude reductionism built into this scheme that comes across best in a comment on his characters made by a Marxist scholar:

> A good deal of idiots and subnormal characters appear in the early stories. As against this the characters in the later stories are moved to vigorous self-activity, making choices, acting decisively, proud of their strength, skill and wits as complete human beings, resisting all efforts to dehumanize them. (Mahanta 1989, 297)

Regardless of my difference with this reading, the engagement with Manik's characters remains a productive axis to think about the politics of his literature. We shall return to it shortly, not only to argue why plotting such characters is politically important but also why the later protagonists may not always comfortably fit into agentic interpretations. They linger with traces of trials and tribulations of his early characters in no less measure and often betray an acute sense of suffering. The linear evolution of choice-making actors has therefore only a very limited and surface traction in reading Manik, least of all as a politically conscious writer. But before we get there let me talk about the second frame of reception that remains popular outside the Marxist circle which is not without valuable insights. Interestingly, even this scheme splits up Manik into binary segments for interpretation: an early Freudian phase, followed by a late Marxist phase. In this distribution, Manik remained heavily influenced by the writings of Freud, Jung and Adler for roughly the first ten years of his career. That is when his writing frequently tore into the hypocrisy and pretension of *bhadralok* society, while he deliberately chose odd characters and unusual themes, focusing on psychological complexities around sexuality as the key subject to explore. The next phase marked a decisive shift in this scheme from 'sex' to 'economy' as the major preoccupation of Manik's writing, attesting to the growing influence of Marx. It is not difficult to detect an overlap at this point with the first scheme of reception. Although limited by a similar schema, this framework highlights important points, especially two aspects underlined by commentators like Nirmal Kanti Bhattacharjee (Bhattacharjee 2008). First, it finds in Manik the sense of a fulfilment of the literary 'rebellion' promised by the *Kallol* movement, bringing the underclass and marginal people into the foreground of the public gaze, as the new subjects of the aesthetic and political discourse of Bengal. In that sense, he presented a matured expression of one of the tendencies that defined literary modernism in Bengal. Second, Manik marked a critical turn in Bangla literature from the lyrical mood and pastoral charm narrated by Bibhutibhushan and Tarashankar to what Bhattacharjee calls the petty and wretched existence of people living in the villages. Although uneasy with the Freud to Marx sequence, I find this transition valuable for grasping the manner in which Manik can be described as worlding the representation of society. It arrested the readers like never before, with a haunting sense of misery and desolation that further intensified when Manik's narratives began to shift from life in villages to the big city. I suspect it is precisely this atmosphere of relentless suffering, cruelty, greed and moral violence that was unbearable for readers who looked for redemption and heroes in his early writings. A cursory look at the protagonists of his short stories confirms the lower depths he kept plumbing: beggars, vagrants, murderers, drunkards, criminals and depraved characters who self-destruct. All of them inhabit moral darkness that lent his first short story collection its name (*Pragoitihasik*, translated as 'Primeval'). It is indeed these dreadful characters that her Marxist critics found 'sub-normal' and insufferable. It is precisely such a netherworld that Manik found worthy of writing about, instead of the decent salubrious society. Such a society has fidelity, family, hope and constancy—but nothing of what Manik saw as elementally true about life and deserving of story. He was drawn to the other kinds. As he explained

> But thieves are very lonely in life. They have no one to call their own … whatever level their feelings may belong to, whatever harsh and ugly boundaries might limit their imagination, (the fact is that) what they feel and imagine are constantly changing and different at every moment. They think much more than many *bhadralok*. They discover many such truths about life that do not even remotely appear in the prospects of many well educated and cultivated minds…. There are millions of honest gentlemen in this world who I cannot write about. Their lives are without stories … the life of a thief is full of stories. (Bandyopadhyay 1998, 186, translation mine)

Manik's penchant for marginal characters continued well into his second short story collection, *Mihi o Mota Kahini* published in 1938. However, this was also partly a passage where the liminal lives and unsettling moments were beginning to seep into mundane middle-class narratives, increasingly unfolding in urban locations, in milieus typical of *bhadralok* society. Manik began using habitual passages of daily existence to suddenly reveal furtive moments of shocking greed, cruelty and enigmatic acts of insanity. His stories disclosed sinister sensations lurking in domestic gestures and calculated spite that wrecked comfortable intimacies, driving home bitter realisations about life. The narrative strategy shaping in the process is revealed in a short story we are going to discuss at some length below. In some sense, it testifies to a discreet conversation taking place between Freud and Marx in Manik's writings, rather than a sequence or passage from one to another. As we shall see, the disquiet and menace were being moored in the structural logic of classes and individual foibles were turning into a coded index of transactions between actors who come from different social strata. The stories of depravity, theft and lunacy were finding their way into the *bhadralok* habitus and sensibility.

Before discussing the story that illustrates this conversation, I want to briefly flag an important point with regard to the trajectory of the subject or character in Manik. I believe this point intersects with the third frame of Manik's interpretation, that is yet to be properly assembled but which has already been gestured by scholars like Moinak Biswas (Biswas 2003). Moinak makes a strong case about reading Manik's characters along a new arc of thinking—what I describe as the un-becoming of subjects. According to this arc the protagonists of a narrative travel from the point of being individuals to slowly losing their status in the narrative as ego-centred, self-contained, authoritative subjects. This transformation is sometimes staged as a distribution of subjectivity, where constitutive elements of the key character come to be exchanged with minor characters. At other times it is facilitated by the explosion of a larger event, where the masses and the site of their congregation become the new subject of Manik's narrative which in fact mirrors the history in making in this decade. Moinak plots this passage from the publication of the novel *Ahimsa* in 1940 through *Chatuskon* in 1942 to a sense of culmination in the novel *Chinha* in 1947. I find this line of argument extremely productive for a new reading of Manik Bandyopadhyay, that gives a radically new sense to the meaning of practice of a Marxist author which is removed from the persuasive and yet reductionist older framework. I will be drawing upon this line of interpretation in what follows while modifying its take on writing as practice and adding a dimension of self-practice I mentioned at the very outset of the essay. In effect, I will contend that the passage of subject in Manik also reveals his life as a communist author and how he thought of writing as a practice—what I describe as 'becoming declassed' and 'declassing art'. It is where the logic of aesthetics intersects communist life and art, a terrain that is difficult and daunting to tread upon without trepidations. Perhaps one of the simplest ways we can take the first step is to describe the relation of the individual to the masses—the crowd or the *bhir*, as outlined in one of Manik's early novels, *Amritasya Putrah*, published in 1938. It will not be out of place to remember that this was a period of severe labour unrest and political congregations were becoming a common sight in the city of Kolkata:

> He joined the crowd after entering the park. Quite a large number of people had gathered there, around three thousand perhaps. Once he entered, he saw the peculiar expression of the same characteristic on every face he could see around him that he noticed about the meeting from the outside. It was not difficult to guess that some were there just to pick up a bit of novelty for free on their way back from office; some have taken a break from aimlessly roaming about and joined the crowd; some have joined the meeting called for the country's sake simply to escape an extreme sense of self-loathing

> and to find satisfaction in (taking part in) a noble deed; some have come to get their fix from the sense of excitement and exhilaration at such meetings! (Bandyopadhyay 1998, 271)

Allow me to quickly draw attention to some aspects of this description before we take up the story I promised to discuss. The first aspect is that although the passage is about an individual observing other individuals who have joined a crowd to attend a (political) meeting, the centre of narration is where the meeting is taking place: the park is the stage where things and characters are unfolding, for better or worse. The park as a public site in the city may not stand out as a prominent character as yet but it certainly features in the cast of Manik's little theatre, as a new kind of space where bodies congregate. The second aspect is the relation of externality that the protagonist inhabits in relation to the crowd gathered for the meeting, whose political nature does not seem to matter much. It is clear that he hardly relates to this crowd and in fact observes them from inside and outside as basically the same—a motley assembly of individuals gathered by chance from different walks of life, with nothing consciously bringing them together. The detail of observations notwithstanding, the subject is distant from what he describes, with a touch of disdain and even sarcasm. At the same time, there is the third aspect that reveals a striking density of emotions and sensations experienced by the subject. What he dismisses as banal and insignificant is at once thickly inflected with close, almost forensic, scrutiny of faces, bodies, gestures, expressions, motivations and emotional landscapes. The overt style of detachment appears to disguise a fierce passion to relate to the lives of others one does not really understand. The pursuit of singular truths and intensive lives seem to have shifted in such passages from marginal subjects to shadowy people occupying the centre; the exceptional moment is found in the recesses of every day. This is what the short story *Sareesrip* illustrates, as we shall see.

THE CALCULATIONS OF EVERYDAY

According to several commentators, Manik's stories are mainly analysis of peoples' psyches, basically meaning that the acts of his characters are plotted in terms of their 'subconscious', driven by complexes and obsessions, which explains his debt to Freud (Bandyopadhyay 1996). This does not convince me but I will let that pass since there are moments in Manik which do indeed read as pathological. Instead, I would like to introduce an important modification along the following lines.

The angularities one often encounters in Manik's characters and their actions may very well come across as cases of individual eccentricity and what is conventionally described as 'abnormal'. However, if one looks at them closely, perhaps in a symptomatic manner, it becomes clear that such characters are actually representatives rather than exceptional in society. In other words, their afflictions, if we can use such a term, are characteristic of a more extensive disorder that belongs to a collective register. In that sense, they stand as Manik's diagnosis of everything that is wrong with the way in which collective existence and relationships are conducted in society. The individual neurosis, so to speak, is the key to understanding a madness shared by all. What it means is that there is a move in Manik that takes a cue from Freud about the complicated ways of the individual mind and turns it around to shed light on how the collective functions to which the individual belongs. It is here that we come across a structural logic revealed by the acts of madness and this underlying logic that characters follow without being fully conscious is precisely where Manik begins to turn to Marx. Behind the insanities of human society, according to Manik, lies the petty calculations of self-interest and exploiting others. The shape of these self-interests intricately meshes with questions of property and class. That is what Manik presents us in the short story titled *Sareesrip*, a dystopic fable, published in 1939. Let me briefly outline the plot further.

The story begins with Charu, a widow and heir to the mansion of her late father-in-law. Charu has suffered from misfortunes throughout her life; her husband was insane and their only child is mentally challenged. But Charu had a strong practical mind and managed her property well. With age, however, she started losing her grip and circumstances forced her to lease out the mansion to Banamali, someone she grew up with. Charu was affectionate towards Banamali, who was a bit younger to her, while he saw her as an object of distant fantasy when growing up. This memory, however, did not prevent him from usurping Charu's mansion later on. Formerly owners, Charu and her son, become practically dependent on Banamali's charity. She turns desperate, trying to revive the old affection, trying to please Banamali, to secure a place in the mansion and a shelter for her boy. Meanwhile, her younger widowed sister Paree enters the scene, seeking refuge. Realising Banamali now owned the mansion, she starts flirting with him. Charu is terrified to find them in bed one night and feels her place slipping away as Paree rises in the pecking order of the mansion. Resigned and bitter, Charu leaves for a pilgrimage, devising a plan to murder Paree with cholera germs. Unfortunately, Charu was herself infected and died soon after. Her dying thought is worth quoting: 'there is always an ulterior motive.

Whichever corner, whatever way a person turns, there is always an ulterior interest behind it.' This is the moral of Manik's story. Banamali grows tired of Paree soon after Charu's death. As he becomes cold and distant, Paree loses her sanity. For a while, Banamali enjoys her pathetic state and her antics of trying to seduce him. But before long, Paree is moved into the servant's quarters. A maidservant greets Paree in her new room. Sympathetic, she has a similar story to tell.

To be honest, I dislike talking about literature in a way that boils down to plots and characters which is what I just presented. One reason is that it renders the details, the discrete moments and distractions, the slight nuances and fleeting imageries redundant, that are so crucial for reading an author like Manik. There are instants in *Sareesrip* that can leave a reader feeling anxiety building up like a ticking bomb in her gut and then there are moments that tell her how nothing in life is sacred, all must be consumed and laid to waste. There is the dangerous fencing in the subtext of dialogues exchanged innocently and there is the dead weight of unhurried silence at a moment when someone is begging for words. All these elements, riddles and suspense are missing from a plot summary. It can obscure how the story keeps holding back what in fact it wants us to realise desperately. That there is very little we really know about others and ourselves. Most of all, there is no way of knowing how the minds of people keep working away, silently and lethally, behind all the warmth and bonhomie; the ideas of affection, memory, kinship, blood ties, etc. are all simply sentimental prattle to comfort us. Human beings are more creaturely than they know or admit, they are quite similar to predatory animals. The way their minds work belies all well-meaning logic, it demands chilling metaphors to show up the reality, like *Sareesrip* or the snake, the reptile, the title of the story. The particular use of this metaphor seems to confirm all the more the intuition of those critics who prefer to read Manik in Freud's shadow, dark and driven by sexual mysteries.

Yet the metaphor has a logic after all. It reveals a passage whose purpose may be unknown to the prey but only until her last moment. The logic of the entire movement becomes clear when the prey comes to realise she is the prey. Let us recall Charu's dying reflection, the moral of the story: 'there is always an ulterior motive'—the motor of the plot, the invisible ubiquitous logic. This ulterior motive, that drove them to vie for Banamali's charity which made deadly foes out of two sisters, was in fact the mansion—its ownership and access—the concrete, material structure right at the heart of the tale. Once we look back at the narrative from this perspective, it no longer reads like an enigmatic tale of perplexing cruelty and senseless breakdown of loving relations. The plot to murder a sister, the use of sex in exchange, the deceit of the man who controls the means—every little move begins to make sense when the mansion is seen as structuring or to borrow an old terminology, overdetermining the story. It becomes clear how Manik has plotted a literally hierarchic order of classes (and gender) with this structure. The dispossessed women are sent downstairs to live with the servants, while the patriarch, who owns the mansion, lives and decides their place from above. The two floors of the mansion signal the place of the principal classes: he who has capital and consumes and they who must suffer and work at his whim. What the story offers then is not only a dissection of pathology that coils in the corners of eccentric minds but also a painstaking document of exploitation that uncannily follows a class optics. In other words, *Sareesrip* stages what I have described already as a conversation between Freud and Marx. As this conversation progresses, Manik's writings of this period seem to become increasingly concerned with individual lives that are caught up in relations across different classes, negotiating a changing society and its logic of ruthless exploitation. As the novels of this period bear out, like *Sahartali* (volume one in 1939 and volume two in 1940) and *Saharbaser Itikatha* (1942), Manik explores the complexities of people migrating from villages to city, their aspirations of class mobility and glimpses of bourgeois society and the fraught struggle of urban poor and labouring lives at the other end of spectrum. At the same time, works like *Ahimsa* (1940), *Chatushkon* (1942) and *Pratibimba* (1943), as Moinak Biswas has pointed out, begin to experiment with what we can perhaps describe today as the deconstruction of the individual subject. Published in 1942, *Saharbaser Itikatha* had already mentioned the ideas of 'communism' and, perhaps more significantly, the idea of becoming *notun manush* or a new kind of human being in the making. The cold and grim calculations of everyday appeared possible to overcome for once. It posed a question of writing differently and becoming a different kind of writer: the conscious project of a 'communist' aesthetics.

The shifts in Manik's trajectory must be seen with the background of dramatic social and political changes in Bengal. The Provincial Legislative Assembly elections of 1937 led to short-lived governments by the Muslim League and Krishak Praja Party in the province. However, this limited self-governance proved futile and Bengal was plunged into the infamous famine and unrest in 1942. While the circumstances pushed the middle classes to increasingly engage with politics, this was further intensified by international events, ranging from the civil war in Spain to the outbreak of World War II. The conjunction of all these factors gave a larger dimension to the activities of the 'progressive' movement in Bengal. The context felt appropriate to Marxist ideologues for an intervention in the 'progressive movement' and create an ideological mobilisation of cultural activists. The aim was to translate the Marxist perspective at a basic level—as a materialist understanding of all processes, including life, society and history. The political function of art and literature was to establish this. In 1944, as Manik joined the communist party, its intellectuals presented a set of commentaries on writing and its relation to politics. It included a powerful piece by Manik about how writing relates to labour and how the writer is basically a 'labourer of pen'. This is what we take up for the last part of our discussion, looking at Manik's theoretical articulation of the project of communist aesthetics and tracing a tension lodged in its heart.

DECLASSING ART: THE SUBJECT OF LABOUR

Manik's tract, titled *Kano Likhi* (Why I Write) was originally composed in Bangla, as part of a similar collection published under the same title. An abridged translation follows further.

> There are certain things that cannot be communicated by any means other than writing. I write to communicate those things. Regardless of what other writers have to say about this, I have no doubt that they write for the same reason.
>
> One can think on the basis of mental experiences. I have experienced much more than many people ever since I was a child. To say that one is born with talent is bogus. [...] The desire to undergo mental experiences and the ability to withstand their pressure may increase or decline and this change is an intelligible process. It can be explained by analysis. I have been able to roughly understand the history of my own outlook since I was a little boy.
>
> The urge to write is just like ten other interests. It is like solving a mathematical problem, building a machine or searching for the ultimate meaning. It is in the same league as playing, singing or even making money. The ability to write comes from this passion and the single-minded devotion to learn how to write. [...]
>
> I write in order to share a small fraction of the ways in which I have realized this life. I have come to know what nobody knows in this world. But I share a common ground with everybody in what is meant by that knowledge. I share that ground to offer some of my realizations.
>
> [...] I make [the reader] realize them. He undergoes a mental experience by reading what I have written.... The writer is successful when he makes the reader arrive at these realizations. *As such, the*

> *writer is merely a wordsmith, a labourer of pen* (*kalam pesha majur*). His life is a failure if he fails to make his writing work. It is a bigger failure than the life of a casual labourer on the street.... (Manik Bandyopadhyay, *Kano Likhi* in Jugantar Chakrabarty 1995, 10, translation mine)

On the surface of it, Manik's argument is as follows. The writer is not a talented genius, different from ordinary masses. There is a process involved in writing that is based on having experience in life which runs similar to other activities, often involving passion and devotion. Anyone can understand it by analysis and one must get rid of romantic ideas about this process. The writer is a type of worker after all, what Manik describes as *kalam pesha majur* or 'labourer of pen'. Given that the tract was authored when Manik had joined the party and began serving in the highest body of its cultural associations, it is fair to assume that the argument was meant to perform a task of ideological interpellation. In effect, Manik was urging artists and intellectuals to forsake their middle-class roots and identify with the labouring classes. To see oneself as a labourer was to intellectually, if not existentially, join the perspective of oppressed classes—what communists referred to as becoming declassed. It was in some sense the formal aim of communist aesthetics, to weld together work and art, labour and literature, into something new and political. It is what his Marxist readers would celebrate in later Manik as truly realist and fittingly radical.

However, allow me to point out a fundamental tension in the tract which recurrently drives apart the underlying ideas of 'writing' and 'labour' in Manik's deposition. In fact, if we strictly follow the sequence of his arguments, we can discover a fascinating oscillation between the singularity of what is involved in writing and the universality that it must be subjected to for making sense. Although it is comparable to 'ten other interests', it requires arduous apprenticeship and rare passion. The author might share common ground with everybody but his knowledge of life is original and exclusive. Anyone can write on the basis of experiencing life but not all of us can take the pressure of experiencing more and thinking through them. Few have realisations that are worth sharing and even fewer can make others experience them through reading what they write. That is the deep meaning of working with words that anyone who writes may not be able to make work. It is a failure when it does not work and what is the example that comes closest to this sense of failure? It is the life of the casual labourer working on the street. It seems what brings the casual labourer and labourer of pen on the same plane of conversation in the tract is the shadowy presence of alienation. The communist writer must identify with life that labours without meaning but his own labour has life only insofar as it recovers that meaning. The meaning that is lost in labour is possible to recover in writing which is what makes the political project possible but impossible at the same time to resolve. I believe this impossibility at the heart of communist aesthetics is something that worked as a profound realisation in Manik Bandyopadhyay's later writings. Despite the urge to create agentic heroes to inspire the movement, and there are quite a few of such celebrated figures, I find the most memorable tale of resistance a testament to this realisation. It is a short story published in 1946, titled *Shilpi*, a word that has been translated as 'craftsman' but I prefer the word 'artist'. It is in my consideration as close as one gets to a communist parable of India. The essay will come to a close with a brief discussion of this story.

The story is about a community of weavers set in the backdrop of changing times. Traditionally, the weavers used to work for the rich feudal families in the area. They were used to setting their own terms for the raw material like yarn and the value of goods they were meant to deliver. They were poor but proud craftsmen, known for the sophistication and refinement of their skill. Manik takes up the story when their old way of life is beset with a crisis. The regular orders from traditional patrons have dried up. The weavers are left without work. They consider selling their looms as their families begin to starve. A merchant agrees to employ them at this point and appoints a middleman, Bhuban Ghoshal, to recruit the weavers. But there is a fatal clause. The weavers cannot produce their traditional items. The merchant wants them to weave common towels (*gamchha*) with poor yarn. This will fetch him profit from the venture. Most of the weavers take this as an affront. They refuse and continue to starve. Manik shows the refusal as their resistance, inspired by the stubborn pride of one man—Madan, the master-craftsman.

Madan is the protagonist of Manik's story, he is the *shilpi* in person, the figurehead of the community. His wife is pregnant but she continues to starve with the rest of his family. Madan feels helpless. His body is not used to sitting idle. His limbs ache with sharp fits of pain as they miss their toiling routine at the loom. The middleman coaxes and cajoles Madan, persuading him to take up his offer. But Madan obstinately holds on to his pride, his reputation as a master-craftsman who never compromises. After all, he was a mythical figure among weavers. There is a saying in the area: 'the day Madan weaves a *gamchha*' which amounts to something like the day sun will rise in the west. Such is Madan's standing in the community. He might be poor and starving and out of work but he will not bend to the bidding of the market. As Manik wrote,

> Bhuban cannot comprehend this fervor and arrogance of an ordinary weaver [like Madan]. He feels angry, and perhaps a bit jealous too ... [He] knows if Madan agrees, most weavers will follow suit next day. But [Madan] is a willful, obstinate and strange man. Now you see him breaking into laments and crying; now he turns stubborn and irate. One moment he sobs like a poor weaver, the next moment he speaks imperiously, as if he is king! (Manik Bandyopadhyay, *Shilpi*, in Jugantar Chakrabarty 1995, 113, translation mine)

As Madan's wife takes ill, needing food and medicine, he relents and agrees to Bhuban's offer. He feels sad about the shoddy material but accepts the advance from Bhuban. Madan starts working on his loom in the late hours of the night. As the sound of his loom reaches the half-asleep, starving weavers, they feel confused, some are outraged at this lowly betrayal. They gathered in front of his hut the next morning. How could Madan betray them? Madan answers,

> Come inside and take a look. Yes, I have been working, but it is an empty loom. These terrible fits of pain make me numb from not working so long. I worked on an empty loom. How can I take Bhuban's offer? How can I betray you? The day Madan goes back on his word.... (Manik Bandyopadhyay, *Shilpi*, 1995, 115, translation mine)

CONCLUSION: THE CROWD AND THE EMPTY LOOM

According to Moinak Biswas, Manik's deconstruction of subjects reached a kind of culmination with the publication of *Chinha*, a novel loosely based on either the violent clashes between police and public on Rashid Ali day, 12 February 1946 or similar events on 25 November 1945. It marks the explosion of ego-centred subjects and Manik's experiment with Bangla novel in a new direction where the streets as the site of history and the crowd take over as protagonists of the narrative. I will leave aside the argument about Manik's experiment with the form of the novel and draw your attention to the perceptive point made here about the crowd as the new subject. This is driven home right away as the novel takes off, where the crowd stands in complete contrast to its aloof and distant description that we came across before in early Manik. *Chinha* begins with the merging of the crowd and the individual, the crowd as the individual:

> The feeling of disbelief and excitement overwhelms him, as if he has forgotten what it means to feel terrified and lose all sense of bearing. [...] Such a huge event, such a terrible event, involving so many people. He is unable to think about it, it does not make sense to him. Still, the event unfolding between the police and the people on the main road has taken over his consciousness in such a way that as if he can feel everything, understand everything. *As if he has himself become the crowd.* (*Chinha,* Manik Bandyopadhyay, vol. 5, 1998, 365)

In some sense, this is the essence of becoming declassed: the fusion of the individual and the crowd, the becoming crowd of the individual and the crowd acting like an individual. This exchange of the singular and collective is what we see unfolding in a different way in the short story *Shilpi*. Madan is very much an individual. He is different from the rest in his skill and ability as a master-craftsman. He is different in his willfulness, his vanity and temper. One moment Madan appears like 'a poor weaver', the next moment 'as if he is king'. What Madan did was no ordinary labour. It is art, it gave meaning to not only his own work but to the work of the entire weavers' community. His life was a legend in the locality, he was a part of the folklore, a symbol of artisanal pride. That is why Madan cannot bend before the market. He is not an isolated individual; he is that historical individual who must stand for the collective. But how does he keep the resistance going, how does he hold on to meaning when capital has come to town? This is where art and labour must part ways and the artist must invent new political gestures that can recover the meaning alienated from labour. Where is this gesture that signals at once the impossibility of communist aesthetics and the art of making it possible? It is Madan's work on the empty loom, the ultimate crucible of communist aesthetics, Manik Bandyopadhyay's gift to the future.

The empty loom fittingly returns in a 2016 video by Moinak Biswas, titled 'Across the burning track' (Biswas 2016). It forges a conversation between the 1940s and 1970s with reference to Manik and clips from Ritwik Ghatak's 1974 film *Jukti, Takko Ar Gappo*. Ghatak plays the character Nilkantha Bagchi in his film who recalls Madan's empty loom after he is shot by the police in an encounter with Naxalite radicals. As the video explains, it is an autobiographical citation reflecting Ghatak's commitment to political art, if I may add, as a communist filmmaker. Ghatak's citation of Manik reveals a third dimension of communist aesthetics apart from what has been flagged before. There is a profound sense of crisis that informs the life of communist artists, as Manik and Ritwik came to embody, along with others like the poet Sukanta and the artist Chittaprasad. It is a crisis that Madan illustrates very well. It is an existential crisis that becomes inseparable from political disposition as the commitment to masses guarding against individual compromise, even at the cost of life. The fidelity to this crisis forms the ethos of becoming declassed. It is at the same time a crisis for aesthetic practice that must refuse programmatic coding and which cannot be cast into formulaic certainty and preconfigured propaganda. It must emerge from the doubts and vacillations of everyday, wagered and invented every time, catching everyone by surprise like the sound of Madan's empty loom. Here is the practice of declassing art: 'One has to do something after all', says Nilkantha Bagchi before he dies in Ghatak's film. This 'something' is at once a denial of 'art' and an ironic admission of futility besides the affirmation of a practice that is impossible to realise but possible as a gesture. Hence, the parable of Manik Bandyopadhyay.

REFERENCES

Bandyopadhyay, Manik. *Rachanasamagra*, volume 2, Kolkata: Paschimbanga Bangla Akademi, 1998.

———. *Rachanasamagra*, volume 5. Kolkata: Paschimbanga Bangla Akademi, 1998.

Bandopadhyay, Srikumar. 'Jibane Sangketikata o Udvat Samasyar Arop', *Bangasahitye Upanyaser Dhara*, 513–532. Calcutta: Modern Book Agency, 1996.

Bannerji, Himani. *The Mirror of Class: Essays on Bengali Theatre*. Calcutta: Papyrus, 1998.

Basu, Priyanka. 'Becoming Folk: Religion, Protest and Cultural Communism in the *Kabigana* of Ramesh Sil and Gumani Dewan', *South Asian History and Culture* 8, no. 3 (2017): 317–337.

Bhattacharya, Mihir. 'Moment and Movement: People's Creativity in the History of Progress', *Social Scientist* 39 (2011): 11/12, 41–47.

Bhattacharjee, Nirmal Kanti. 'Manik Bandyopadhyay: A Centenary Tribute', *Indian Literature* 52, no. 6(248) (2008): 8–16.

Bhattacharya, Malini. 'The Class Character of Sexuality: Peasant Woman in Manik Bandyopadhyay', *Social Scientist* 15, no. 1 (January 1987): 46–59.

Bhattacharya, Sourit. 'Disaster and Realism: Novels of the 1943 Bengal Famine', *Postcolonial Modernity and the Indian Novel: New Comparisons in World Literature*. Palgrave Macmillan, Cham., 2020.

Biswas, Moinak. 'Beyond the Subject of Difference: On a Persistent Plot in Manik Bandyopadhyay', *Jadavpur Journal of Comparative Literature* 40 (2003): 119–128.

———. *Across the Burning Track*. Video, Shanghai Biennale. Available at https://youtu.be/DwxZGL4_nto, 2016.

Chakrabarty, Dipesh. *Provincializing Europe*. Princeton: Princeton University Press, 2000.

Chakrabarty, Jugantar, ed. *Manik Bandopadhyayer Sreshtha Galpa*. Calcutta: Bengal Publishers, 1995.

Chaudhuri, Supriya. 'Provincial Epic', *American Book Review* 36, no. 6 (2015), 14–26.

Dasgupta, Rajarshi. 'Inventing Modernity in the Colony: The Marxist Discourse on the Bengal Renaissance', *Contemporary India* 3, no. 1 (January–March 2004): 23–41.

———. 'Rhyming Revolution: Marxism and Culture in Colonial Bengal', *Studies in History* 21, no. 1 (January–June 2005a): 79–98.

———. 'Manik Bandyopadhyay: The Word and Work of Bengali Marxism', *History* VII, no. I (2005b): 43–58.

———. 'The People in People's Art and People's War.' In *People's Warrior: Words and Worlds of P.C. Joshi*, edited by Gargi Chakrabarty, 443–456. New Delhi: Tulika, 2014a.

———. 'The Ascetic Modality: A Critique of Communist Self-fashioning.' In *Critical Studies in Politics: Exploring Sites, Selves, Power*, edited by Nivedita Menon, Aditya Nigam and Sanjay Palshikar, 67–87. New Delhi: IIAS and Orient Blackswan, 2014b.

———. 'Capital in Bangla: Postcolonial Translation of Marx'. In *Capital in the East: Reflections on Marx*, edited by Achin Chakrabarty, Anjan Chakrabarty, Byasdeb Dasgupta and Samita Sen, 27–38. Singapore: Springer Nature, 2019.

Ghosh, Pothik. *Insurgent Metaphors: Essays in Culture and Class*. Delhi: Aakar Books, 2010.

Ghosh, Tanusree. 'Witnessing Famine: The Testimonial Work of Famine Photographs and Anti-colonial Spectatorship', *Journal of Visual Culture* 18, no. 3 (2019): 327–357.

Kaviraj, Sudipta. *The Unhappy Consciousness: Bankim Chandra Chattapadhyay and the Formation of Nationalist Discourse in India*. New Delhi: Oxford University Press, 1998.

Mahanta, Aparna. 'Towards an Art of the People?', *Economic and Political Weekly* 24 (1989): 6, 295–299.

McGuire, John. *The Making of a Colonial Mind: A Quantitative Study of the Bhadralok in Calcutta, 1857–1885*. Canberra: Australian National University, 1983.

Mitra, Sarojmohan. 'Progressive Cultural Movement in Bengal', *Social Scientist* 8 (1980): 5/6, 115–120.

Roy, Anuradha. *Sekaler Marxiya Sanskriti Andolan* (Bangla). Calcutta: Progressive Publishers, 2000.

———. *Bengal Marxism: Early Discourses and Debates*. Kolkata: Samya, 2014.

Sarkar, Sumit. *Writing Social History*. New Delhi: Oxford University Press, 1998.

Sunderason, Sanjukta. *Partisan Aesthetics: Modern Art and India's Long Decolonization*. Stanford: Stanford University Press, 2020.

Williams, Raymond. *The Long Revolution*. London: Chatto & Windus, 1961.

CAPRICE

'VULVA'S SCHOOL': TOWARDS A PROVISIONAL PEDAGOGY

Sophie Seita

Note on the text: This piece is excerpted and adapted from a 50-minute-long lecture performance titled *Vulva's School: A F*cking Didactic Take on Experimental Feminist Performance Art, or, How to Read*, first presented at the University of Cambridge in November 2018 and then re-staged at the independent art space Florens Cargo, in Darmstadt, Germany in August 2019; and at Jawaharlal Nehru University, New Delhi, in January 2020. In all iterations, the performance was accompanied by a slide show of images and videos. The second and third performance further added costume, choreographed movement, voice recordings and several props (a skipping rope, a red suitcase, a red wig, a slate and some chalk and a 'my little pony' figurine).The title is an homage to the late feminist performance artist Carolee Schneemann, whose lecture-performance *Vulva's School* (1995) imagines an anti-patriarchal pedagogy through the character of Vulva who learns quickly that she is not part of the curriculum: 'Vulva deciphers Lacan and Baudrillard and discovers she is only a sign, a signification of the void, of absence, of what is not male ...' (Schneemann 1997).

*

An artist in a black kimono, her arms lifted and angled to frame her head, index and middle finger pressed together in a salute of scare quotes. Between them a line of text, luring us to 'Pretend you are not there.'

*

In her 2013 video piece, *How Not to Be Seen: A Fucking Didactic Educational.MOV File*, filmmaker and critic Hito Steyerl offers a satirical take on the instructional film genre in what is a sort of copy or creative re-imagining of a Monty Python sketch. The video is structured around five lessons for disappearing. For Steyerl, to become invisible in today's media landscape is mainly to become invisible to cameras. The video thus humorously plays with green screens, airfield resolution targets and performers dressed as pixels. A computerised voice-over chimes, disinterestedly, other suggestions for 'how not to be seen', namely: to camouflage oneself, to become smaller than a pixel, to live in a gated community, to become a superhero or to be a woman over 50. Another is simply to walk off-screen. I am here also reminded of the ultimate act of performance art by the American conceptual artist Lee Lozano, who made a piece which only exists as a title and as a commitment. In *Dropout Piece*, the artist moved herself out of the art world and into obscurity.

Like the unruly school dropout who no longer wants to play along. There is, of course, something neurotic about invisibility and visibility and the theorist Sianne Ngai has called paranoia a specifically feminist affect of our times.[1] Steyerl's video satirically reveals but never teeters on the edge of that neurosis itself. The 1980s' synthesisers lend a retro vibe. We even end a neat dance routine by the pixels. And Steyerl disappears.

To be abstract is often to be illegible. And to be illegible is often to be invisible. The invisible artist may 'flutter around the canon' (Brooke-Rose 1989, 65) but as such is like a mosquito a disturbance to the equilibrium of Man, establishing the bite as her oeuvre.[2]

The feminist and queer artist is usually already invisible. Or, as Eve Sedgwick notes, much violence is hyper-visible and ubiquitous—it needs no laborious detection—so what does exposure or paranoid reading add to that recognition (Sedgwick 2003, 143–144)? And to be invisible as a woman, queer, trans, disabled, or non-white person can often guarantee safety.

Lately, I've been thinking a lot about pedagogy, about reading, how to put into words for myself and for others what a work does and especially what feminist work does. How to make sense of texts, without sense-making being another manipulative imposition on me, the text, my readers or my students but where sense radiates from a spectrum like distributed particles of light, colour or sound.

And of course, the truth is, I still often don't know how to read. What I learnt from Steyerl via humour (sometimes the best kind of teacher) is that perhaps the format itself can be didactic. Like the mov file. Can the form of this lecture performance be instructive, too? I wrote to someone recently that I rarely make mistakes. It wasn't exactly a lie but it was partly aspirational, partly a playful provocation. As in, bring it on.[3] Perhaps this 'bring it on' is a feminist gesture.

CAN YOU SING

To copy and remake, to re-read, is a signature feminist practice; but the signature requires repeating in order to be recognisable as such; and given that feminism has centuries of materials to catch up on, that scribal scratching into the groove of an alternative history might take some more time.

Don't despair, my friend tells me in a dream, repetition is a juicy democracy.

CAN YOU NOT VARY IT

Sometimes we repeat things because we want to make them ours. Sometimes because we hope that by repeating we make them different. Repetition can give a presence.

The supposed familiarity of the feminist gesture is sometimes pointed out to chide the feminist performer. Perhaps she's called Vulva or maybe she's called A One-Trick-Pony, which is her glittery code name. She is told that sexiness on stage combined with difficult language is 'expected'. She is told 'you don't need that', meaning: the feminist or queer label, the constant critique.

i: hello.
Pony: hello.

i: let's do that again.
Pony: ok.

i: hello.
Pony: hello.

Pony: different?
i: maybe.

i: i've forgotten the instructions.
Pony: that's sad.

i: it's not real.
Pony: ah.

it's an easy gesture, i use it often and expertly
i have no such options with the pony

we could call this pony's table talk
we all know that animals perform heroic deeds
and ponies are divinatory, they warn of danger (Seita 2016, 123, 127)

*

In queer time, Jack Halberstam argues, 'repetition is privileged over sequence' (Halberstam 2011, 119). *The Queer Art of Failure* proposes a 'low theory' as a 'mode of transmission that revels in the detours, twists and turns through knowing and confusion and that seeks not to explain but to involve' and that consider 'getting lost over finding our way' (Halberstam 2011, 15). I'm deeply attracted to this lure of getting lost and also deeply scared of it. Theoretically, this is all very well but practically it sounds a bit like the self-help book a well-meaning friend once gave me for my birthday. What's more, how would we teach the detour?

> Maybe this brings us back to form.
> Maybe I'm reading too much into this.
> Maybe this is just about throwing in a little bit of good old modernist fragmentation.
> *the loop of that which was just described or named is endless perhaps a square is there a square that is not dull what would it take to make it like it was a knife.*

CAN YOU UNDERSTAND ME

In what was perhaps the first-ever feminist lecture-performance, Virginia Woolf told the students at Girton and Newnham in Cambridge that we think through our mothers when we are women. Today, we would qualify that we may have 'many-gendered mothers' (as Maggie Nelson via Dana Ward calls them) and that we can all have other feminist or trans artists *as* or *instead of* mothers. To counter the 'procession of educated men,' we need other lineages, other pedagogical strategies. We have never had a vulva's school.

My thinking about a contemporary 'Vulva's School' has been influenced by the pedagogy of hospitality offered by feminist magazines like *HOW(ever)*, *HOW2* and *Chain*, all of which featured experimental formats like the forum or unusual introductions to works, as ways of figuring out how to do feminist theory in practice. Their pedagogy was one of active listening. Similar to Judy Chicago and Miriam Schapiro, who set up an actual feminist school at Cal Arts in 1971 (we could call it an offshoot of Vulva's School), these magazines set up a provisional school for poets in their pages.

What does it take to found a school? A school of fish is a critical mass. A school of fish may seem choreographed but is not.A school of fish, for Halberstam, is a school of queer learning. As Halberstam puts it with regard to the Disney film *Finding Nemo*, 'Dory [as a queer subject] forgets family and tradition and lineage and biological relation and lives to create relationality anew in each moment and for each context and without a teleology and on behalf of the chaotic potentiality of the random action' (Halberstam 2011, 80). Active forgetting is a queer tactic. It's a way to turn away from expected lines.

Up until recently, every talk I would give, every performance, would be meticulously planned. I would know exactly what I was doing and where I was going. I was over-prepared. But lately, I've started to explore the creativity, even the lucidity, afforded when you have not yet worked it all out, when you are not in top form. (I've had a pinched nerve in my neck for three weeks now. How would we read *that*? Maybe feminist performance is a form of shouldering. ALWAYS KEEP YOUR SHOULDER TO THE WHEEL.)

A provisional feminist pedagogy does not promote intellectual laziness or dilettantism, far from it. It's rather a serious attempt to experiment with forms of writing, making and relating that allow us to think differently. It means setting up situations and phenomenological conditions that then determine newly what we can think, make or say.

This may entail a certain vulnerability.

WHO DOES AND WHO DOES CARE

A how-to manual for Vulva's School:

If they say we write in milk, let them have our toxins.[4] *Tipp-ex is our new fountain pen. The pupils at Vulva's School will wield it.*

The labour of blanking out what was written before is not new, but Vulva's pupils do not need to be new. The gesture of re-, of re-writing, re-doing, re-making, is a crucial feminist tool. But after graduating from Vulva's School, the prefix re- will be an archaeological relic. Always having had the patriarchal bone to pick, Vulva's pupils will have other, less unrelenting nourishments to chew on.

Vulva may be the headmistress, but there shall be no rulers, only triangle rulers. No straight lines. To think in the manner of Vulva's School is to think in tangents, curves, slopes, and angles.

Drenched in correction fluid.

Tipp-ex to erase the 'tippen', the typing—but in English 'to tip' is to topple, to tip the scales, to throw off the balance.

Or:

It's tipping it down

Or:

I'm standing on my tippy toes

Or:

It's on the tip of my tongue
Or:
It's the tip of the iceberg

And the tip is where we take the patriarchal, racist rubbish.

*

In some ways, I have now arrived at a prototype for Vulva's School. A prototype is all about the experiment. It's about trial and error, the renewed, the modified. It's about a model. It's about the provisional. About making and unmaking types. It's also about the physical and material contact of subjects and objects. About what knowledge we want to impart as scholars, as thinkers, as artists and as writers. And if we can ultimately separate our identities so very neatly.

This could be a resolution.

Steyerl's AI instructor advises: 'resolution determines visibility. Whatever is not captured by resolution is invisible'.

*

Another artist is seen holding a knife.[5] *Her eyes are bulging silver balls or maybe orbs. Shimmering with the threat of patriarchal triumph.*[6]

*

Feminist and queer performance art is often angry, dissident or emerges from dissatisfaction while its form may be utterly joyful, even exultant. The feminist killjoy is 'willing to cause unhappiness' and refuses to make happiness her cause, as Sara Ahmed triumphantly suggests (Ahmed 2017, 258). She is recalcitrant.

Which is fucking didactic. A didactic take is a handling technique. Grab it.

*

So, my performative lecture is really a series of propositions, maybe a series of lessons, with the lessons yet undetermined. So, you learn the steps.

*

Two women spin, fast, in sync, and then they're out of it, ever so tauntingly close. Four movements to find their shadowy other. Come Out. *Figures repeat. Accelerate, decelerate. Minimal shifts bring boundless variations, relations. Of what is turned and returned. Embodied abstraction and refined complexity.* To Show Them.[7]

WHO MAKES WHO MAKES IT DO

Brent Hayes Edwards argues that 'there is something like a queer practice of the archive' that celebrates the 'elusive' and 'what can't quite be explained or filed away according to the usual categories' (Edwards 2012, 970). Is the elusive necessarily queer? Is to be queer to be elusive? And do I want that? Except abstractly, except formally but not in my body? Recently, I've been 'trying to figure out how to "have" feelings in writing. How can the ornamental, the voluptuous, be productive beyond the sonority of the aphoristic, how can abstraction be other than the cooler underside of the lush particular?'*

We, as literary scholars, have of course imbibed that form and content are inextricably linked, various 'extensions' (Creeley/Olson) or 'revelations' (Levertov) of one another. And yet, our talks and journal articles hop happily from a to b to c, with maybe some u-turns for kicks but even those are folded into a nice little argumentative trajectory. This is where the lecture performance enters stage left, flamboyantly donning a ruff or jabot, probably no tie.

ACT III: I MEAN WHAT I SAY[8]

I want to move back in time briefly, to the progenitor of literary and page-based performance: Gertrude Stein. Another of my teachers of reading.

In *An Exercise in Analysis* (1917), the character called Part XXVIII asks, but without a question mark: 'Can you understand me' (Stein 1977, 'An Exercise', 129). To which Act II replies: 'I can understand you very well' which in turn is picked up by Act III merely rhymingly spinning the language in a new direction 'Do you agree with Miss Crutwell.' Whoever Miss Crutwell is, she is not in the play.

---

* I'm citing myself, again. Some would call it self-plagiarising. I call it recycling. Or being in analysis. So, language can become modular. A form of transference. Which is all about knowledge. Available at http://www.3ammagazine.com/3am/little-enlightenmentplays-textual-performances-sophie-seita/ (accessed 3 November 2019).

Humour undercuts any attempt at psychologising even the most abstract of characters.

Act II
It was a copy.

Act III
It was a copy.

Act IV
It was a copy.[9]

One could snicker at this and say, well, is this repetition warranted, what's all this sing-song, but when the three copies are followed by Part XXXVII's admonition: 'Do not make a mistake', I am somewhat appeased. I remind myself that it is an '*Exercise* in Analysis' after all. And all exercise requires repetition.

NOTES

1. Sianne Ngai has suggested that 'confrontation with complicity becomes the specific form "paranoia" takes in women's writing'. See Ngai (2001, 7–8).
2. I here wish to acknowledge that I have been inspired by my former student Desmond Huthwaite who wrote an essay titled 'How to Bite: Experimental Women Writers and their Teeth'; a how-to guide to a new feminist aesthetic: an aesthetic of bite.
3. See Ahmed (2017, 267). I also want to thank Raphael Lyne for telling me about *Bring It On* (2000), dir. Peyton Reed, written by Jessica Bendinger, which subsequently made it into this lecture performance.
4. See also Riley (2000, 104); Robertson 2016, 19–30).
5. It's perhaps not surprising to find so many knives in feminist art; most notably in Martha Rosler's *Semiotics of the Kitchen* (1975), but also twenty years later in Patty Chang's *Melons* (1998).
6. See Maya Deren, *Meshes of the Afternoon* (1943).
7. See Anne Teresa De Keersmaeker, *Fase, Four Movements to the Music of Steve Reich* (1982).
8. This and the previous sub-headings are from 'An Exercise in Analysis' and 'Four Saints in Three Acts' (1927), in Stein 1977 (119–138 and 440–480).
9. Stein 1977, 'An Exercise', 131.

REFERENCES

Ahmed, Sara. *Living a Feminist Life*. Durham and London: Duke University Press, 2017.

Bring It On. Dir. Peyton Reed, written by Jessica Bendinger, 2000.

Brooke-Rose, Christine. 'Illiterations'. In *Breaking the Sequence: Women's Experimental Fiction*, edited by Ellen G. Friedman and Miriam Fuchs, 55–71. Princeton: Princeton University Press, 1989.

Edwards, Brent Hayes. 'The Taste of the Archive', *Callaloo* 35, no. 4 (2012): 944–972.

Halberstam, Jack. *The Queer Art of Failure*. Durham and London: Duke University Press, 2011.

Ngai, Sianne. 'Bad Timing (A Sequel): Paranoia, Feminism, and Poetry'. In *Differences* 12, no. 2 (2001): 1–46.

Riley, Denise. 'Milk Ink'. In *Selected Poems*, 104. Reality Street, 2000.

Robertson, Lisa. 'Toxins'. In *3 Summers*, 19–30. Toronto: Coach House Books, 2016.

Schneemann, Carolee. *Vulva's Morphia*. New York: Granary Books, 1997.

Sedgwick, Eve. *Touching Feeling: Affect, Pedagogy, Performativity*. Durham and London: Duke University Press, 2003.

Seita, Sophie. 'My Little Enlightenment: The Plays and Textual Performances of Sophie Seita, interviewed by David Spittle', *3:AM Magazine*, 29 May 2017. Available at http://www.3ammagazine.com/3am/little-enlightenment-plays-textual-performances-sophie-seita/ (accessed 3 November 2019).

———. 'Pony: Five Tableaux', *The White Review* 16 (2016): 119–131.

———. *Objects I Cannot Touch*, Video, 2014.

Stein, Gertrude. 'An Exercise in Analysis'. In *Last Operas and Plays*, edited by Carl Van Vechten, 119–138. Baltimore: Johns Hopkins University Press, 1977.

———. 'Four Saints in Three Acts' (1927). In *Last Operas and Plays*, edited by Carl Van Vechten, 440–480. Baltimore: Johns Hopkins University Press, 1977.

Steyerl, Hito. *How Not to Be Seen: A Fucking Didactic Educational .MOV File*, Video, 2013.

PARAPHERNALIA

WEAPONISATION OF THE BODY IN GOLDMAN, BLAIR AND ALMADHOUN

Eyal Amiran

As Paul Virilio has shown, military visualisation technologies such as radar, satellite photography and laser-guided munitions, and their extensions in facial recognition, traffic and crime prediction algorithms and geo-location services, have increasingly been used to image and identify the body. Digital media, broadly understood, is related to and indeed part of weaponry. What is the place of the body in the aesthetics of cybernetic optical regimes, to borrow from De Certeau (Goldman 2017, 53), and how does art concerned with digital ideas of the body today relate embodiment to new media's new world theatre? Achille Mbembe argues that capital, and not politics, determines the value of the body in the age of Big Data (as though, to anticipate, there can be data without politics, capital without bodies).

> The computer does not see persons but statistics, patterns, physical objects: As markets themselves are increasingly turning into algorithmic structures and technologies, the only useful knowledge will be algorithmic.
>
> Instead of people with body, history and flesh, statistical inferences will be all that count. Statistics and other big data will mostly be derived from computation. (Mbembe 2016)[1]

For Grégoire Chamayou, drone warfare is distinguished from earlier battlefield logics where the warrior is close to or, as in the case of the kamikaze, actually is the bomb: 'Whereas the kamikaze implies a total fusion of the fighter's body and weapon, the drone ensures their radical separation. The kamikaze: *My body is a weapon*. The drone: *My weapon has no body*' (Chamayou 2013, 84). Hence, the suicide bomber presents an answer to drone warfare by re-taking personal death onto herself or himself, in theory, as a counter to the disavowal of personal involvement and responsibility built into drone warfare. This formulation seems intuitively right but preserves the Hegelian dynamic of actors and objects. Chamayou's distinctions treat the body as a physical object located in space and not also as a concept, a psychological reality, a figure in a larger cultural logic. Understood in this larger way, the body does not divide into subject and object, either here or there, and instead is connected to the new reality of media-weaponry: it does not separate warring parties but is the ground where they meet. That is how the body has been seen by new literature, such as I consider here, that examines the body's relation to new media weaponry. The new aesthetic work I read here understands the body through discourses of weaponisation, the move away from thinking about weapons as discrete tools and towards understanding the process that makes any part of the social world serve the interests of war and war on behalf of these interests, leading to the dissolution of an us and them, here and there, safe and sorry.[2]

The term 'weaponisation', which has come into vogue in the last three years, was introduced in the 1950s by Werner von Braun (Kelly 2016). Weaponised memes poison democracies with disinformation, writes journalism and media professor Michael Niman (2019) in *truthout.org*. Afghan miniskirts are the weaponisation of nostalgia, says a September 2017 article in Ajam Media Collective (Shams). WikiLeaks 'not only dropped' her stolen emails, 'they weaponized them', said Hillary Clinton on the New Yorker Radio Hour.[3] Russian *kompromat* is understood to be more than 'weaponizing damning evidence to blackmail a target' (Davidson). Steve Bannon 'weaponized Breitbart', says *Fox News*—as though Breitbart had been anything but a weapon to begin with (*Fox News* 2017). 'Do they disrespect the mind or are they in need of a political tool to weaponize the culture wars?' television reporter Bill Moyers asks Princeton's Joan Scott. 'I think it's both', says Scott.[4] This formulation appears to preserve an instrumental and grammatical relation between actors and objects, but in reading digital-age art that meditates on the arrival of weaponisation as more than a catch phrase, weaponisation, along with the discourses of securitisation and monetisation which it resembles, replaces cultural objects with processes, first among them the process of making things into a process. Unlike monetisation, however, which recalls the Marxist transformations of objects in the service of capital and characterises the neoliberal age, weaponisation as an idea answers the metaphysical aesthetics of digital media. It promises to be the apotheosis of cultural processes, their logical extreme, a claim encouraged by the seeming transformation of objects into data in digital media. Important as Deleuze and Guattari's deterritorialising schizophrenia has been as a way to understand the transformation of the world under capital, its fluidity is pretty viscous—it, too, preserves an instrumental relation between objects that are made to connect with each other as the power plug fits only the socket, the pizza box only the pizza (in *Anti-Oedipus*). Whether the claim for the pervasive weaponisation of the data age can be separated from other economies or is borne out 'in fact' is not my question; I ask rather what assumptions new media art makes and what vision of the social world it produces, when it instances weaponisation as a digital phenomenon. The art I study here shifts its aesthetic to a world where any object is a virtual weapon, by which I mean with Pierre Lévy that it has the potential of transformation for harm, and where the environment itself is weaponised, made a theatre of war produced by the metaphysical aesthetics of new media.

Conceptually, the challenge to instrumentality goes back to Paul Virilio's analysis of the cultural place of weapons. Martin Heidegger in the 'World Picture' essay argues that science, with its research methodologies—by implication tools, including weapons—produces the world as an object to be manipulated by human agency and so separates humanity from the world (57–66); Marshall McLuhan in 'The Medium is the Message' largely agrees, arguing that tools, including weapons (one of his examples is the gun), extend and so revise the human. This argument takes a decisive turn in Paul Virilio's idea that the cultural object is no longer a thing but a process that, in a nod to traditional conceptions of action and of things, is predicated on systemic instrumentality. Instrumentality remains, but only just, in the wake of instruments, even though the instruments have turned into processes. Hence, instrumentality today is a kind of instrumentality without instruments, a functionalism without actors. In the aesthetic arguments I study here, digital media are seen to reproduce a vertiginous relation between images and objects that reflects the perpetual war of the social world. Any cultural object is a weapon, and no object can be seen apart from weaponisation. This weaponisation of anything in the digital age threatens to erase the instrumental relation that objects have had since the world image came to be.

In *Agon* (2017), which fuses poetry, critical theory and image in hybrid form, Judith Goldman explores the weaponisation of everyday life. The book is published in print by The Operating System Press but—as Katherine Hayles argues about Neal Stephenson's *Cryptonomicon* (*My Mother Was a Computer* 117–142)—could not exist as an art form outside the new media age which is its subject.

> 1 | | ❙ *ia* Bugs Bunny weaponizes a hot barb ▮| ❙ 2 | | ❙ er's towel A se esaw ▮| ❙ 3 | | ❙ too ▮| ❙ 3a | | ❙ easily weaponized, ▮| ❙ 4 | | ❙ banana peel ▮| ❙ 4 | | ❙ Kool Aid ▮| ❙ 4a | | ❙ a set-up operatio ▮| ❙ 4b | | ❙ nalize weaponized windo w, ▮| ❙ 5 | | ❙ defenestration ▮| ❙ 5a | | ❙ Silent premises of ▮| ❙ 6 | | ❙ everyday lif ▮| ❙ 7 | | ❙ e weapons possible ▮| ❙ 8 | | ❙ pain-platform compa ▮| ❙ 8a | | ❙ ratively underpollut ed ▮| ❙ 8b | | ❙ spectral arsena ▮| ❙ 9 | | ❙ l linked to its dol lar ▮| ❙ 10 | | ❙ ablation ▮| ❙ | | ❙ |▮| ❙ | | ❙ | 1 | | ❙ hurt the

> body ▌| ▌ 2 | | ▌ on the bar ▌| ▌ 3 | | ▌ s of the cage ▌| ▌ 3a | | ▌ but the cage alread y ▌| ▌ 3b | | ▌ a weapon ▌| ▌ 4 | | ▌ 'we' weapon ▌| ▌ 4a | | ▌ ized intimacy subvoc al ▌| ▌ 5 | | ▌ does tear gas (also ▌| ▌ 5a | | ▌) weaponize tears ▌| ▌ 6 | | ▌ Weaponized dummy ▌| ▌ 7 | | ▌ hand Multiple bright ▌| ▌ 8 | | ▌ yellow warning ▌| ▌ 9 | | ▌ signs all over the ▌| ▌ 10 | | ▌ packaging between ▌| | | |▌| | | | | | 1 | | ▌ weaponized elevator in act ▌| ▌ 1a | | ▌ ion films ▌| ▌ 1b| | ▌ mecha nical persecuting ▌| ▌ 2 | | ▌ world ▌| ▌ 3 | | ▌ linked to the species through ▌| ▌ 4 | | ▌ its motor style ▌| ▌ 5 | | ▌ Vertigo of the persecuti ▌| ▌ 6 | | ▌ ve structure 'Organs ▌| ▌ 6a | | ▌ exoscopically represented, growin ▌| ▌ 7 | | ▌ g wings for inter ▌| ▌ 7a | | ▌ nal persecutions' Where man ▌| ▌ 7b | | ▌ does no longer encounter ▌| ▌ 8 | | ▌ himself or: Where man in fact ▌| ▌ 8a | | ▌ encounters himself Your mirror ▌| ▌ 9 | | ▌ image weaponized as som ehow ▌| ▌ 9a | | ▌ tal ler than you ▌| ▌ 10 | | ▌ Sees self (Goldman 2017, 13)

There is a great deal going on here extraordinarily together—the elevator image, the hand and wings, crying and seeing signs—but to render some of the hybrid words, numbers and barcodes of this passage into selective sentences, including my own punctuation for this purpose, and to narrow the focus:

> Bugs Bunny weaponizes a hot barber's towel. A see-saw too easily weaponized, banana peel, Kool Aid, a set-up operationalize weaponized window, defenestration. Silent premises of everyday life . . . hurt the body on the bars of the cage, but the cage already a weapon, 'we' weaponized intimacy . . . does tear gas (also) weaponized tears[?]. Warning signs all over the packaging. (Goldman 2017, 13)

In a world of tear gas and bars, gas to make you cry and gas you cry about, bars of cages and the digital barcode that circulates consumers and their objects of consumption, Kool Aid is a weapon, cartoon banana peels are weapons, windows are weapons and the very space in which these so-called objects, really processes, take place is also weaponised. Hence, continuing the carceral bar motif, 'Toothbrush as Shiv, Or cake with a file baked into it' (Goldman 2017, 14). In prison especially, all objects may be closer than they appear, put to innovative uses, and in the world as the prison house of capital, objects are always already processes that serve capital. Unlike Deleuze's increasingly specialised objects, however, weaponisation gives an unexpected multivalence to things. If in Marx commodity objects are valued as they may be acquired by capital and cannot be read outside their place in commodity chains—desiring machines, as Deleuze and Guattari then call them in

Anti-Oedipus—in the post-classical economies of the current capital, objects are not captured or exchanged so much as instrumentalised in service of the larger culture-capital machine whose functioning transforms its targets into further processes. The result is an aesthetic of a new non-solid state, a not merely accelerated world of processes but one in which every thing is also working as another thing, seen from the other angles of industrial process, what Goldman, after Lacan, calls a 'Vertigo of the persecutive structure' (Goldman 2017, 13). It is a vertiginous world '[W]here man does no longer encounter himself or: Where man in fact encounters himself. Your mirror image weaponized as somehow taller than you' (Goldman 2017, 13).

The body remains the key contact for these weaponised transactions. It cries, is held in prison, drinks the Kool Aid it has made, brushes its teeth and eats the cake. The world is outside us but also in our image, except bigger and in charge of us, as in the dash cam images of police cruisers and CCTV.

> 1 | | ▌ hit the lock but ▌| ▌ 2 | | ▌ ton on remote ▌| ▌ 3 | | ▌ to ma ke alarm ▌| ▌ 3a | | ▌ chirp check status of your ▌| ▌ 4 | | ▌ character service ▌| ▌ 4a | | ▌ weaponized character lock ▌| ▌ 4b | | ▌ feature using key frames ▌| ▌ 5 | | ▌ frame fun ction ▌| ▌ 5a | | ▌ weaponized parergon ▌| ▌ 6 | | ▌ weaponized Laugh track or auxil ▌| ▌ 6a | | ▌ iary weaponized cut ▌| ▌ 6b | | ▌ weaponized pan ▌| ▌ 7 | | ▌ weaponizing off-screen ▌| ▌ 8 | | ▌ pro-filmic area in fr ▌| ▌ 8a | | ▌ ont of camera record ▌| ▌ 9 | | ▌ ing field the realit ▌| ▌ 10 | | ▌ y or situation ▌| ▌ 10a | | ▌ happening in fro ▌| ▌ | | ▌ |▌| ▌ | | ▌ |1 | | ▌ nt of the camera po ▌| ▌ 2 | | ▌ sition and angle what's ▌| ▌ 3 | | ▌ in the picture establish ▌| ▌ 4 | | ▌ es understan ding ▌| ▌ 5 | | ▌ of what is seen ▌| ▌ 6 | | ▌ weaponized viewfinder ▌| ▌ 6a | | ▌ steadicam or dash cam ▌| ▌ 7 | | ▌ weaponized playback ▌| ▌ 7a | | ▌ photosh op to weaponize a photo ▌| ▌ 8 | | ▌ stock photo ▌| ▌ 9 | | ▌ weaponized compression, glitch ▌| ▌ 10 | | ▌ dot-density ▌| ▌ | | ▌ |▌| ▌ | | ▌ | 1 | | ▌ weaponized username ▌| ▌ 1a | | ▌ weaponized password ▌| ▌ 2 | | ▌ Go back to a ▌| ▌ 2a | | ▌ nother saved state and ▌| ▌ 3 | | ▌ choose ano ther dia ▌| ▌ 3a | | ▌ logue option ▌| ▌ 4 | | ▌ weaponized blockchain, side ▌| ▌ 4a | | ▌ chains or entry chains wea ▌| ▌ 5 | | ▌ ponized locking out, remote ▌| ▌ 6 | | ▌ locking weaponized activation, de ▌| ▌ 6a | | ▌ activation, reactivation ▌| ▌ 6b | | ▌ granting managed access ▌| ▌ 7 | | ▌ so-called 'protection' softwa ▌| ▌ 7a | | ▌ re weaponized plug-in ▌| ▌ 7b (Goldman 2017, 22)

To select a simplified line of thought again from the hybrid words, numbers and barcode images: 'What's in the picture establishes understanding of what is seen. Weaponized viewfinder, steadicam or dash cam, weaponized playback, photoshop to weaponize a photo . . .

weaponized username, weaponized password . . . granting managed access, so-called "protection" software, weaponized plug-in' (Goldman 2017, 22). Here the emphasis is on digital manipulability of representation (Photoshop, but also the dash cam that police routinely explain does not tell the whole story, for example), while the notion of the 'weaponized plug-in' suggests that digital adaptability revises Deleuze and Guattari's desiring-machines model. Goldman modifies the general concept of weaponisation by showing the fungibility of cultural objects, in part under the policing pressure of the bar code. Multiplying resistance, with De Certeau, *Agon* offers a total attack on the culture of bar codes. There can be no compromise with the weaponised land. The point may rely to an extent on the fact that the book that makes it is in print, offering a kind of resistance to the fungible digital world it critiques, but it is not anachronistic: print images of barcodes are still barcodes, seen by people but read only by the light gun. In *Agon*, the gun will read the image.

For Goldman, if we stick to the instrumental aspect of the growing weaponisation of the image, its increasingly deadly use in global military culture, we repeat the technocratic and territorialising mindset that is the problem to begin with. To believe in weapons in the wake of weaponisation (when anything is a weapon) or to believe in instruments and actors (when any circumstance is weaponised—the cage itself is a weapon) is a defensive move that requires critique. It shores against ruin—it believes in ruin. It suggests that certain objects and their use are the problem, preserving the human from them, when it's the processes that weaponise the world that lead it down its well-known downward slope. The body is part of the new process, not apart from it, as in Chamayou's formulation.

That is a lesson of David Blair's digital video *Wax* (1993, released as a feature film in 1991) which connects the weaponisation of media to what is for Blair its metaphysical logic.[5] For Blair, an American media artist now working in France, new media and its target are conflated vertiginously in the metaphysical paranoia of colonial necropolitics, a paranoid fantasy that is made all too real in modern human history. Blair's Waxweb, a hypermedia work based on his 1992 digital video *Wax, or the Discovery of Television Among the Bees*, belongs to what Jeffrey Shaw has called 'the field of digitally expanded cinema' ('Introduction', Shaw and Weibel 2003, 21). Waxweb consists of 'more than 1 million picture, hypertext, and 3-D links', a network of 1,600 shots arrayed in what Blair describes as 'a 25-section matrix unique to each shot . . . The perceived boundaries between the movie and the surrounding composition will dissolve', continues Blair, 'sending the movie into extended time, as if it were a temporary world' (Shaw 2001, 183). The same can be said about Blair's

Wax which is my focus here, an 85-minute video that mixes live-action sequences, found footage and computer-generated art (digital theorist Lev Manovich helped create the digital effects). *Wax* had a theatrical release and was broadcast on the internet in 1993.[6]

The film is narrated by its protagonist, Jacob Maker, played by Blair in a trance-inducing monotone, and includes the story of Maker's ancestors, who brought Mesopotamian bees to the west, as well as about the invention of new photographic media and its use to correspond with the dead. The early 1990s Maker plot is the main through line of the film. Maker writes code for target acquisition in military flight simulators in Alamogordo, New Mexico (Image 1). He also keeps a hive of bees, like his English grandfather James Hivemaker who had imported bees to England

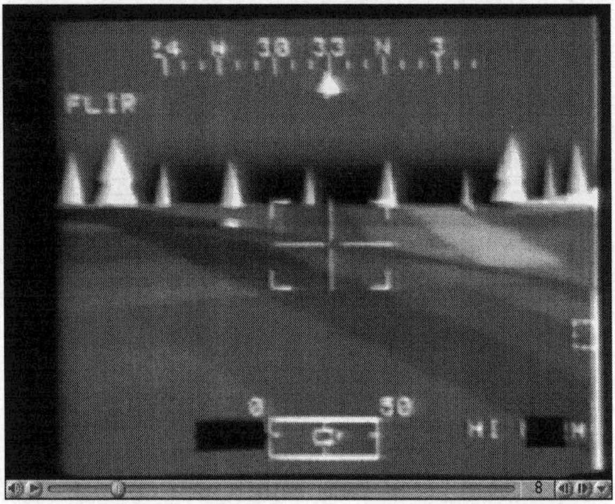

Image 1: David Blair, *Wax* (1993). Jacob Maker's X-shaped gunsight for virtual target acquisition in flight simulators.
Source: David Blair.

from Mesopotamia to replace dead English bees. One day at work Jacob Maker feels there are souls under the virtual targets he designs; he visits the bee hives and hears voices in them. Mesmerised by the bees, he travels by means of a simulated flight in his head to the place of his birth, his grandfather's statue garden called the 'Garden of Eden' in Abilene, Kansas, where he learns that there are dead souls in the sky who target the living, including him. Over the next few days, his bees insert a crystal into his head—the bee TV—through which he sees and travels across space and time. In the 'Garden of Eden' in Abilene he learns that he is Cain and that he has the 'X-shaped gun sight' on his forehead. He also sees the 'new world' in space where the bees have settled: 'it was the land of the dead'. The bees receive new bodies that form an alphabet in the language of Cain; walking in the New Mexico desert near Trinity Site (the site of the first test detonation of an atomic weapon in 1945), looking like an astronaut in his beekeeping suit, Maker sees the dead alphabet in strings across space (Image 2). Maker enters a cave in the desert and sees wax from which new bodies are made for the future dead. He leaves his body

Image 2: Blair, *Wax* (1993). Strings of letters in the language of the dead lead to the Planet of the Dead.

Source: David Blair.

behind, dead on the floor of the cave. That is his literal, physical body in the film, and yet he will become one with a bomb and return in another body: the body is not exempt from fungibility under the media regime of weaponisation. Travelling in space, he visits the city of the dead and the Planet of Television, the closest (according to the narrator) one can get 'to the eye of God'. The narrative dwells on details of the city of the dead, its architecture, interiors and public spaces which are computer-generated images in the film, as though to reiterate the near-bourgeois-fication of the chain of substitutions, which, if a part of the foreign insect-world, comes off as domestic and adapted to the body. 'Now I was Cain', he says; he must kill to return to earth and get his new body. Cain, notably, was the founder of the first city, as well as the first murderer in Biblical history. Jacob returns as a missile by television to Basra, in Iraq in 1991 and using his X shape destroys an Iraqi tank and its occupants and is reborn as twin women, Alel and Ziva, researching corn genetics in New Mexico. The bees, he says, have promised a peace of 1,000 years.

Wax reproduces a metaphysical fantasy familiar in digital embodiment, but this time as farce. It borrows the wax from Descartes's Second Meditation as an image for the body in relation to the mind (Descartes 1984, 20–22). In the wax, one cannot distinguish body and form from each other, the dancer from the dance (see also Aristotle's 1984, II.1). Blair's figures for the mind as microcosm are the letter X and the line of alphabets of which it is part (Image 3): he finds the image in the Biblical origin narrative, on the forehead of the first twin, and his protagonist Jacob Maker connects it with the Biblical Jacob, who also crosses his twin and takes his place.

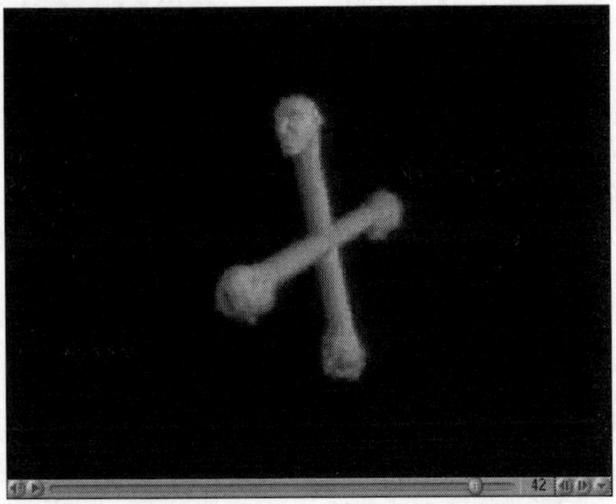

Image 3: Blair, *Wax* (1993). Jacob Maker returns as the X-shaped from the Planet of the Dead to find a target in Iraq.
Source: David Blair.

Blair invokes the Platonic cave where the wax that forms future human bodies is found. The reference is also to Plato's *Timaeus*, where God creates the world by combining elements 'like the letter X' (36b) to form the globe.[7] In *On the Name*, Jacques Derrida connects Plato's X with the mental wax, a space that enables thought but is neither intellectual nor sensible: it is 'that which "prepares" the Cartesian space, the *extensio* of the *res extensa*' (109). In Derrida's reading, Plato imagines a structure, the 'khöra', that rejects the distinction between sensible and intelligible, body and thought, and is neither (92, 96, 110) but rather separates and, in so doing, defines the two (103). It is not a receptacle or container for being (95) but, like a virtual object, is '"something," which is not a thing' (96). In fact, it is 'so indeterminate that it does not even justify the name and the form of wax' (116). This virtual wax, Derrida writes, is a requirement of the cycle of becoming (Derrida 1995, 103; see also Ann Weinstone 1997, 86).[8] Maker's vision of the world as a closed and recursive system draws on this virtual potential for bodies which is also echoed in the cave fantasies of digital media theory of *Wax*'s time, only for Blair the consequences are not liberatory, creating a brave new digital world, but dire.

For Blair, the consequences of digital metaphysics are figured in paranoia on the one hand (the notion that the world is enclosed in oneself, a version of one's hard drive) and in the Gulf War on the other (the actualisation of Virilio's vision of war by remote control, where thought magically kills), linked by the weaponisation of space and the body-image. The relation between code and image, bomb and target, is also represented in the video in the circular migration and colonisation from the Old World to New Mexico and from Earth to the moon. Maker must go to the Planet of the Dead, become the linguistic X of Cain, return to Mesopotamia, now Iraq, in a new body and kill two soldiers for the cycle of substitutions to work. Once he discovers the bees, he abandons his wife and lovemaking, he says, the physical body, and is absorbed into the virtual cosmic cycle. His body mediates and makes possible the transformation of space into place, virtual into geographical and vice versa. But it's no saving grace that Maker cannot equate code with world without his bodily mediation, that he must leave his body behind twice in the film, leaving his wife and then his body in the cave. In Maker's paranoid fantasy, the code is already a weapon, is weaponised, without the body's mediating function, but in reality, he needs the body to make his fantasy real, both to think his bee-thoughts (thoughts of 'being') and as a vehicle for his new language. If for Blair we can weaponise only in fantasy—at the expense of the body—a madness of the technocratic world, the physical death in Iraq and the colonised new world testify to the real world effect of that fantasy, from which it cannot be separated.

Blair produces a fantasy of a cosmic, dead and virtual language of the world that requires human participation to become actual. This vision appears as a dangerous projection of desire, a death-wish to be a bomb and to abandon the human world. Its narcissism, the flipside of paranoia, as Freud argues in his reading of Schreber, sees everything as an aspect of oneself, from space conquest and the conquest of the new world in New Mexico to the production of atomic weapons and the videogame logic of the 1991 Gulf War.[9] But to move from the grammar of the textual archive to the physical world it animates, is to make the mechanical nature of writing a genetic motor for the universe.[10] The warrant for it comes by a metonymic substitution, as though the automatic and the mechanical were already material.

Despite the deterministic equation between code and weapon in the paranoid vision Blair exposes, a determinism somewhat overwritten by the quirky eclecticism of the metaphysical language of the dead, this work anticipates the fungibility between anything produced by the language of Cain—any object produced by language, already associated with murder—and weapons, and sees this weaponisation of language as the fundamental quality of the mediated world.[11] The metaphysical fantasy of WAX shows the colonial and imperial ideology produced or reproduced in digital coding, which targets a territory, replacing bodies with code and code with bodies, the old world with new and the new with old. In Blair we can avoid weaponisation if we get rid of metaphysics or possibly language altogether, but short of that the world itself is weaponised by media. Because we cannot divorce weapons from media, territory from language, we already speak the language of Cain and live in the land of the dead.

The third, a more lyrical interpretation I consider here of the weaponisation of the world through new media culture is Ghayath Almadhoun and Marie Silkeberg's *The Celebration*, a hybrid 9-minute video that juxtaposes the destruction in Syria today with the bombing of Berlin in 1945. It comprises text from Almadhoun's poem 'The Details' together with video and sound. Almadhoun is a Palestinian Syrian poet living in Sweden; Silkeberg is a Swedish poet and translator. *The Celebration* combines Goldman's argument that anything is a weapon and the world is made a process for weaponisation with Blair's indictment of deterministic and circular predatory culture and its paranoid logic. The poet bought a house 'overlooking the war', he says:

> [I] arrived at frightening truths about poetry and the white man,
> about the season of migration to Europe,
> and about cities that receive tourists in peacetime and mujahidin
> in wartime,
> about women who suffer too much in peacetime, and become fuel
> for the war in wartime.

The poet abandons poetry for the war, but finds that the war is inside his poem and the poem inside the war. In *The Celebration*, an 8-second aerial footage of bombed-out Berlin in 1945 loops and repeats, taking us again over the ruins, making a 'rewind' sound each time it restarts. Five seconds of Chopin's Nocturne Opus 9 No.1 plays when the footage runs. Almadhoun reads his poem 'The Details' aloud in the Arabic original over the video and the translated English text floats over the images as the poem is read. The text of the poem appears gradually, as though it were being typed during the screening. It clearly comes after the video, in the video.

The poem begins: 'I was exploring the difference between revolution and war when a bullet passed through my body.' The poet's body refutes the modern distinction between contemplation or art and action, aesthetics and politics. In the world of the poem, which is our world or civil war, we cannot be either kamikaze or voyeur, either the bomb or poetic code but must be both at the same time. This theme continues throughout the poem.

> This city is bigger than a poet's heart and smaller than his poem, but it is big enough for the dead to commit suicide without troubling anyone, for traffic lights to bloom in the suburbs, for a policeman to become part of the solution and the streets a mere background to truth. (Almadhoun 2012, 24)

The poem's world is, like Blair's, inverted onto itself: the city is smaller and larger than the poet who contains it, it is natural in its artificiality, its violence is restorative and its transience enduring. This is because it embodies a new modality of fungible energies understood to be possible in digital aesthetics in a way not traditionally explained in theories of circulation and return (see Wark 2004). This world is also, in a way, one that heralds the extreme violence it must endure later in the poem, of self-disciplining: the dead kill themselves, traffic lights and policemen become 'part of the solution'—the slogan for social change and progress.

Poetry is sometimes in its own mind timeless, an antidote to time, while the photograph is set in time, a snapshot of an historical moment that cannot be altered. When in *The Celebration* the text appears gradually, floating above the images, it occupies the position of the viewer or of the camera flying over the city. It is both outside the time of the video and associated with the repetition of historical events that is part of the message of the work. As the video repeats, it does so from the perspective of the text that floats above it and that comments on it and on history. This juxtaposition is key to the work which connects the mediated reproduction of the event with the repetition of history. The rare short video of Berlin recalls today drone photography such as we have seen, for example, of Homs in the wake of Syria's civil war. The point is not that history repeats itself, that Homs repeats Berlin or Syria Europe or that periods of peace, like tourism, can alternate with periods of mujahidin but that, as the poem discovers, tourism and the mujahidin are co-constructed, each the obverse of the other. From the drone's-eye perspective of media, recalling, as Chris Malcolm has pointed out,[12] Benjamin's angel of history, we perceive not the reversibility but the simultaneity of the Renaissance and of the Inquisition, of Rimbaud's poetry and the slave trade, of Foucault and of AIDS:

> Throw away the Renaissance and bring on the inquisition,
> Throw away European civilization and bring on the Kristallnacht,
> Throw away socialism and bring on Joseph Stalin,
> Throw away Rimbaud's poems and bring on the slave trade,
> Throw away Michel Foucault and bring on the Aids virus. (Almadhoun 2012, 27)

Simultaneity, or perception of the pervasiveness of destruction as a constituent element of construction, is not a function of new media, in this case digitised video footage. But here, the ability to loop back an aerial view of destruction demonstrates a consciousness of history disavowed by, for example, Heidegger.

> Throw away Heidegger's philosophy and bring on the purity of the Aryan race,
> Throw away Hemingway's sun that also rises and bring on the bullet in the head,
> Throw away Van Gogh's starry sky and bring on the severed ear.

Throwing or being thrown is, ironically, Heidegger's characterisation of the human condition—but it is his racism and white universalism we got anyway. Through the logic of weaponisation we can say that the tourist is already a fighter, the poem already the war. Each aesthetic object, each aspect of civilisation we prize and each object of horror or aspect of civilisation we abhor, are each other's other side, co-present in the ongoing civil war, the war inside a weaponised culture that is also the culture of weaponisation. That is something that floating above the ruin in a video loop shows, reinforcing the 'details'. From the air, we are the weapon, like Blair's weapon. From the air our body is a weapon, as well as a target for weapons. From the air, Goldman might say, the air itself is a weapon. The ruins of Berlin and Homs are interchangeable, though Berlin kept more of its roofs than did the suburbs of Damascus, as Almadhoun notes in an interview (ArabLit 2014). We see more than the effects of the bombing, which is over when the tourists return.

This view of history is produced by the interpenetration of media, like Blair's digital paranoia, when the words float above the landscape like weapons that see the other side of things and the voice of the author owns this world. 'Does tear gas (also) weaponize tears?' asks Goldman.

> ❙ 3 | | ❙ linked to the species through ▮| ❙ 4 | | ❙ its motor style ▮| ❙ 5 |
> | ❙ Vertigo of the persecuti ▮| ❙ 6 | | ❙ ve structure 'Organs ▮| ❙ 6a | | ❙
> exoscopically represented, growin ▮| ❙ 7 | | ❙ g wings for inter ▮| ❙ 7a |
> | ❙ nal persecutions' Where man ▮| ❙ 7b | | ❙ does no longer encounter
> ▮| ❙ 8 | | ❙ himself or: Where man in fact ▮| ❙ 8a | | ❙ encounters himself

The answer is Yes: weaponisation as it is understood in the age of digital media is the condition of every aspect of the experience, all an extension of the body. Man—the blame resides in patriarchal history and white universalism—does not encounter himself because he is no longer the referent for things; instead, he encounters himself because he cannot be separated from things:

> Just as if you are eating your beloved's fingers, or suckling from an electric cable, or being inoculated against shrapnel, just as if you are a memory thief, come, let's give up poetry, exchange the songs of summer for gauze dressings and harvest poems for surgical thread. (Almadhoun 2012, 26)

Songs and gauze: these are not opposites but different aspects of the same thing, the poet both tourist and fighter. Then pen is not mightier than the sword, it simply is the sword, and the sword the stylus pen that writes 'Man's' history, for Almadhoun as well as for Blair. Not weapons, then, that threaten the body, but weaponisation of the body, the sense that a word mediated by Blair's digital metaphysics throws us, as Goldman writes, into a 'vertigo of the persecutive structure, "Organs exoscopically represented, growing wings for internal persecutions," Where man does no longer encounter himself or: Where man in fact encounters himself' (Almadhoun 2012, 13).

NOTES

1. I have argued that the idea that people appear as bare-life or as physical bodies to Big Data plays an important role in the imaginary of digital culture (Amiran 2018).
2. In de Certeau's cybernetic society, as Goldman says, 'the strategic system of "technocratic rationality" produces all space—"There is no longer an elsewhere"—and yet in doing so "defeats itself"'—giving rise to numerous strategies of resistance . . . 'his description anticipates the blurring and reciprocal constitution of the physical and virtual in the world of ubiquitous computing' (Goldman 2017, 53). See Certeau (1984, 40–41).
3. Clinton: 'They [WikiLeaks] not only dropped them [stolen emails], they weaponized them.'

'New Yorker Radio Hour,' Episode no. 100, interview with David Remnick, 16 September 2017. In an interview with Terry Gross, Clinton said email leaks from her campaign [chairman John Podesta] were 'weaponized into negative stories' by Russian agents and WikiLeaks. Interview with Terry Gross, 'Fresh Air,' NPR 9/18/17.

4. 'In the Age of Trump, a Chilling Atmosphere.' Interview with Joan Scott. By Bill Moyers. Moyers & Company, 18 October 2017. Available at http://billmoyers.com/story/academic-freedom-age-trump/ (accessed on 12 December 2020).
5. See McCaffery's essay on this little discussed masterwork of the late twentieth century.
6. 'Cult Film Is a First On Internet,' according to Markoff's article in the *New York Times*. Blair estimates the audience of the film to have been about 50 viewers (telephone conversation with the author, 2001). It was broadcast on 23 May 1993.
7. God combines the elements 'into two parts which he joined to one another at the center like the letter X, and bent them into a circular form, connecting them with themselves and each other at the point opposite to their original meeting point' (36b).
8. As Weinstone writes:

   In the *Timaeus*, Plato writes of a 'receptacle,' a chora, a matrix, or a plane from which mimetic forms come and go. Plato likens this receptacle to a mother and the source or the spring to the father. The receptacle is 'formless and free,' predifference, preidentity. It is 'an invisible and formless being which receives all things and in some mysterious way partakes of the intelligible' [*Timaeus* 1178]. The matrix is a hybrid of mind and something that might be understood as sublime, or subtle, matter. Investing code with sublime life, VR becomes both receptacle and source. By ingesting code, the user 'recovers' from the condition of mimesis. (86)
9. In a 1994 email message to the author, Blair referred to the Gulf War as the 'Golf War'; he confirmed it was not a typo. For a relevant discussion of Daniel Paul Schreber as a proto-theorist of the virtual see Roberts.
10. For the claims that have been made 'for digital algorithms as the language of nature itself' and for the world as a 'universal computer,' see Hayles (2005, 15–30).
11. David Golumbia has argued that language, violence and weaponry are increasingly intertwined in the age of digital revolution.
12. In lecture notes shared with the author (UC Irvine, 23 April 2016).

REFERENCES

Almadhoun, Ghayath. 'The Details.' In *Adrenalin*, translated by Catherine Cobham. Notre Dame, IN: Action Books, 2012.

Almadhoun, Ghayath and Marie Silkeberg. *The Celebration*, 12 May 2014. Available at https://www.youtube.com/watch?v=9xl8bJuIV48 (accessed 7 November 2020).

Amiran, Eyal. 'The Pornocratic Body in the Age of Networked Paranoia'. *Cultural Critique* 100 (Summer 2018): 134–156.

ArabLit. 'Watching Poetry Films: "Arab Countries Were the Only Ones Not Taking Part"'. *ArabLit: Arab Literature and Translation*. 31 May 2014. Available at https://arablit.org/2014/05/31/watching-poetry-films-in-arabic-the-only-countries-not-taking-part/ (accessed 15 June 2019).

Aristotle. 'On the Soul'. In *The Complete Works of Aristotle: The Revised Oxford Translation*, edited by Jonathan Barnes. Vol. I. Princeton, NJ: Princeton University Press, 1984.

Blair, David. *Wax, or the Discovery of Television Among the Bees*. VHS Video, 1993.

———. *WAXWEB*. 1999. Hypermedia CD. David Blair.

———. 'Waxweb'. In *net_condition: art and global media*, edited by Peter Weibel and Timothy Druckrey, 182–183. Cambridge, MA: MIT Press, 2001.

Certeau, Michel de. *The Practice of Everyday Life*, translated by Steven Rendall. Berkeley: University of California Press, 1984.

Chamayou, Grégoire. *A Theory of the Drone*. Translated by Janet Lloyd. NY: The New Press, 2013.

Davidson, Adam. 'A Theory of Trump Kompromat.' In *The New Yorker*, 19 July 2018. Available at https://www.newyorker.com/news-desk/swamp-chronicles/a-theory-of-trump-kompromat (accessed 7 November 2020).

Deleuze, Gilles and Felix Guattari. *Anti-Oedipus: Capitalism and Schizophrenia*. 1972, translated by Robert Hurley, Mark Seem and Helen R. Lane. NY: Viking Penguin, 1977.

Derrida, Jacques. *On the Name*, translated by David Wood, John P. Leavy, Jr, and Ian McLeod. Stanford, CA: Stanford University Press, 1995.

Descartes, René. *The Philosophical Writings of Descartes*. Vol. II, translated by John Cottingham, Robert Stoothhoff and Dugald Murdoch. Cambridge, UK: Cambridge University Press, 1984.

Fox News. 'Why Bannon Parted Company with Trump—and How he'll Weaponize Breitbart.' 21 August 2017. By Howard Kurtz. Available at http://www.foxnews.com/politics/2017/08/21/why-bannon-parted-company-with-trump-and-how-hell-weaponize-breitbart.html (accessed 27 December 2020).

Goldman, Judith. *Agon*. New York: The Operating System Press, 2017.

Golumbia, David. 'The Militarization of Language: Cryptographic Politics and the War of All against All.' *Boundary 2* 44, no. 4 (2017): 95–112.

Hansen, Mark B. *New Philosophy for New Media*. Cambridge, MA: MIT Press, 2004.

Hayles, N. Katherine. *My Mother Was a Computer: Digital Subjects and Literary Texts*. University of Chicago Press, 2005.

Heidegger, Martin. 'The Age of the World Picture.' In *Off the Beaten Track*, edited and translated by Julian Young and Kenneth Haynes. Cambridge, UK: Cambridge University Press, 2002.

Kelly, John. 'Everything is *Weaponized* Now.' In *Slate*, 30 August 2016. Available at http://www.slate.com/blogs/lexicon_valley/2016/08/30/how_weaponize_became_a_political_cultural_and_internet_term_du_jour.html (accessed 8 November 2020).

Lévy, Pierre. *Cyberculture* [1997], translated by Robert Bononno. Minnesota University Press, 2001.

Markoff, John. 'Cult Film is a First on Internet.' *The New York Times*, Monday, 24 May 1993, C3.

Mbembe, Achille. 'The Age of Humanism is Ending.' *Mail & Guardian* (Johannesburg, South Africa), 22 December 2016. Available at http://intercommunalworkshop.org/achille-mbembe-the-age-of-humanism-is-ending/?print=pdf (accessed 12 December 2020).

McCaffery, Larry. 'Interview MS. Found on a Floppy Disc: Some Reflections of "Processed Narratives" and David Blair's *Wax, or the Discovery of Television Among the Bees*.' Available at http://www.spinelessbooks.com/mccaffery/wax/ (1993) (accessed 12 December 2020).

McLuhan, Marshall. *Understanding Media: The Extensions of Man*. NY: McGraw-Hill, 1964, 1965.

Niman, Michael I. 'Weaponized Social Media Is Driving the Explosion of Fascism.' *Truthout.org*, 5 April 2019. Available at https://truthout.org/articles/weaponized-social-media-is-driving-the-explosion-of-fascism/?utm_source=sharebuttons&utm_medium=facebook&utm_campaign=mashshare (accessed 11 May 2019).

Plato. *The Dialogues of Plato*. 2 vols, translated by B. Jowett. NY: Random House, 1892.

Roberts, Mark S. 'Wired: Schreber as Machine, Technophobe, and Virtualist.' In *Experimental Sound & Radio*, edited by Allen S. Weiss, 27–41. Cambridge, MA: MIT Press, 2001.

Shams, Alex. 'The Weaponization of Nostalgia: How Afghan Miniskirts Became the Latest Salvo in the War on Terror.' *Ajam Media Collective*, 6 September 2017. Available at https://ajammc.com/2017/09/06/weaponization-nostalgia-afghan-miniskirts/. (accessed 23 October 2017).

Shaw, Jeffrey. 'The Distributed Legible City.' In *net_condition: art and global media*, edited by Peter Weibel and Timothy Druckrey, 110–111. Cambridge, MA: MIT Press, 2001.

Shaw, Jeffrey and Peter Weibel, eds. 'Introduction'. In *Future Cinema: The Cinematic Imaginary after Film*, 19–27. MIT Press, 2003.

Wark, McKenzie. *A Hacker Manifesto*. Cambridge, MA: Harvard University Press, 2004.

Weinstone, Ann. 'Welcome to the Pharmacy: Addiction, Transcendence, and Virtual Reality'. *Diacritics* 27, no. 3 (1997): 77–89.

FREEING THE IMAGE AND CINEMATIC JUSTICE: NON-PARTITIONED AESTHETICS IN KAMAL ALJAFARI'S *RECOLLECTION*

Heidi Grunebaum

> *For many years, I have been collecting Israeli fiction films shot in Jaffa as early as 1960. These are films in which Palestinians are disappeared, yet also exist at the edge of frames, visible in traces. Preserved also is a city; alive again in moving images, its gradual destruction over the decades chronicled film by film. From the footage of dozens of films I have excavated a whole community and recreated the city. Though out-of-focus, half-glimpsed, I have recognized childhood friends, old people I used to say good evening to as a boy; my uncle. I erased the actors, I photographed the backgrounds and the edges; and made the passers-by the main characters of this film. In my film, I find my way from the sea, like in a dream. I walk everywhere, sometimes hesitant and sometimes lost. I wander through the city; I wander through the memories. I film everything I encounter because I know it no longer exists. I return to a lost time.*
>
> —Kamal Aljafari (2016)

> The poor image is a rag or a rip; an AVI or a JPEG, a lumpen proletariat in the class society of appearances, ranked and valued according to its resolution. The poor image has been uploaded, downloaded, shared, reformatted, and reedited. It transforms quality into accessibility, exhibition value into cult value, films into clips, contemplation into distraction. The image is liberated from the vaults of cinemas and archives and thrust into digital uncertainty, at the expense of its own substance. The poor image tends toward abstraction: it is a visual idea in its very becoming.
>
> —Hito Steyerl (2012, 33)

In his film *Recollection*, Kamal Aljafari's aesthetic of 'cinematic justice' claims and reconstellates the historical particularities of Israel/Palestine. Released in 2015, *Recollection* is a cinematic intervention that explores, amongst other things, what it may mean to free the image to imagine non-partitioned futures. In it, Aljafari deterritorialises the image and sets it to work on different grounds: creating space, quite literally, for a heterogeneous many, to *imagine* a plurality of people and predicaments within the same cinematic space, the same filmic territory. Cinematic justice, Aljafari's concept, is a move and a movement by which the image is freed from its mooring in a weaponised aesthetic field recalibrating the relationship between aesthetics and politics.

One of the trilogy of films entitled *The Jaffa* trilogy, *Recollection* is set in the Mediterranean port city of Jaffa in Israel which is the artist, filmmaker, a Palestinian citizen of Israel and resident of Berlin, Kamal Aljafari's hometown. Created from hundreds of hours of archived film footage, *Recollection* is repurposed from some 60 Israeli feature films. The Israeli feature films are mostly from the *bourekas* genre, a popular B grade film genre featuring *Mizrachi*—Arab and North African Jewish—actors, all shot in Jaffa between the 1960s and 1970s. In the opening sequence, Aljafari discloses his aesthetic approach to the film. One views an assemblage of scenes from different *bourekas* films in which the actors vanish before our eyes, digitally removed from the original film footage. In an outdoor scene from the 1973 hit Israeli musical comedy, *Kazablan*, the actors fade away before our eyes leaving nothing but rubble and roads. David Ben-Gurion, Israel's founding prime minister, is seen walking in an orchard and then—with no small irony, wishful thinking or nod to one possible meaning of cinematic justice—disappears from the screen. The sequence alerts the viewer that what will remain in the frame after the opening title will be the backdrop of the sequences from which the actors are erased.

Source: Frame from recollection, Kamal Aljafari (2015).

What had been in the background of the images in the fiction films becomes the gritty foreground in this documentary: roads, alleys, houses, buildings, rubble, ruins, abandoned portside warehouses, non-actors who had been watching the film shoot from a window or balcony or walking past near the edge of the frame or peering around a corner, all these come to be discerned in the blurry images on the screen. In the case of a man caught on camera walking across the frame and out again, it is the only visual record that exists of Aljafari's uncle which he stumbled upon whilst he studied frame after frame of hundreds of hours of film rushes. That fleeting scene of the blurred figure of the man who is his uncle is brought back into the film again and again, for its duration.

Reworking the archival and visual footage to create a cinematic poem that 'frees the image' from 'cinematic occupation' (Hochberg 2017), Aljafari describes his aesthetic practice of 'cinematic justice' as 'something quite magical only possible in cinema.... By erasing the actors I could move freely in the image [to] liberate this place, liberate the image ... (Aljafari 2016). The contemporary weaponisation of regime-aligned aesthetic fields relies on the power of visual identification to constitute their subjects.[1] For aesthetic fields to be weaponised, they must draw from the conceptual categories that underpin them, including the deployment of discursive formations in which populations, communities and groups are imagined. In this, the disciplinary field of demography works crucially to produce, identify and call up a concept of majorities and minorities which align with the same categories of and categorical distinctions between nationality, citizenship and non-citizen subjects. Not ironically, for Palestinians, as well as for Sudanese, Eritrean and other African asylum-seekers in Israel, there is no clearly demarcated category for non-Jewish refugees 'as such' in Israel's demographic discourse or legal apparatus.[2] Indeed, the Israeli state is continuously haunted by its anxieties about 'demographic threats' and the need to maintain a Jewish majority, whatever that might be, for its ethno-nationalist project to be sustained.

In a weaponised sensorial field that seems to privilege visuality, then, what does it mean to free the image? How might this be different from 'moving freely in the image'? Aljafari removes the actors but he also removes the Hebrew film credits. In this, he loosens the image from its filmic implication in the double erasure of Palestinians, 'firstly in reality and then in cinema' (Aljafari 2016). Whilst this recollects the historical and ongoing predicament of Palestinians, it does much more; and this is where the film performs some of its most crucial operations: It opens a cinematic space in which multiple predicaments and subjects implicated in the impossible conjuncture that is Palestine/Israel are recalled in ways that point to the possibilities to reimagine a different kind of political subject opened by a reconstellated or perhaps, differently weaponised, aesthetic field. If the double condition of Palestinian erasure (in reality and in the fiction films) is evoked in Aljafari's digital removal of the actors, so are the predicaments of Israel's other 'others', Arab and African Jews. The actors erased from the *bourekas* films arrived as immigrants to Israel from Arab and African lands in the 1950s and 1960s; as are the contemporary predicaments of the many who undertake the perilous, increasingly deadly crossing over the Mediterranean Sea from Libya, Turkey, Morocco and other coastal areas of North Africa in the hope of remaking life in conditions that sustain life.

Set in Jaffa, *Recollection* is Aljafari's search for his hometown as it was before his birth. Pre-war Jaffa, like many of the 500 Palestinian towns and villages depopulated and destroyed in the war for Palestine, ceased to exist as it had been before the war. As Daniel Monterescu (2015) and Gil Hochberg (2017) point out, Jaffa's story is also different from those of other Palestinian urban centres in Israel/Palestine as it had been through a major process of growth and modernisation in the two decades prior. Before Jaffa became a war zone and was annexed to the municipality of Tel Aviv, the Mediterranean port had grown into a modern urban centre with a working port and a population that had tripled in 25 years to 71,000 people. Jaffa had become, as Hochberg reminds, 'the urban commercial and cultural centre of Palestine—and the home of most local Arab newspapers prior to 1948' (2017, 537). In November 1947, Jaffa found itself within the UN partitioned territory allocated to the future Jewish state. From partition until the end of the war, it became a town in which Jewish and Palestinian soldiers and militia waged a devastating urban war. From 71,000 fewer than 3,000 Palestinians remained in the conquered city whilst the Manshiyeh quarter of Jaffa next to Tel Aviv had been bombed out of existence. A 'mixed city' as many describe it, a port town open to the Mediterranean and its worlds and experiencing an accelerating process of gentrification, Jaffa is also known as *Umm al-Gharib* or 'Mother of the Stranger' (Monterescu 2015, xi). At a time in which Arabic has officially been relegated to a second-class language in Israel, Jaffa's other Arabic name evokes the historical irony in which exile and return; banishment and welcome are entangled: concepts once so central to a Jewish ethical imagination—deformed by Jewish ethno-nationalism and its state-aligned religion—are far closer to, and truer of, a Palestinian ethical imagination and, in the long shadow of the Atlantic slave trade, closer to an African diasporic one also.

In many of the digitally-retouched sequences that become indiscernible as having been unrelated sequences in Aljafari's film, foregrounding the extent to which the post-1948 urban ruins of Jaffa were a preferred feature film location in Israel. In the early 1950s, the Palestinian ruins that were Jaffa soon became the preferred film location for Israeli cinema as it was in the process of establishing itself and as it created new national narratives for the new Israeli national imaginary (Aljafari 2016; Shohat 2010, 119). With the new state's mission to produce a spatial, aesthetic and discursive territory congruous with the corresponding and increasingly hegemonic strand of political Zionism concerned with all things 'demographic', Palestinians of historic Palestine were made absent presences.[3] Whilst this is an enduring existential and political condition it also indexes an irrepressible anxiety that has never ceased to haunt the Israeli state. For the denial of Palestinian collectivity was a founding principle of Israeli statehood asymmetrically harnessed to its corollary denying 'the historicity of the Jewish diaspora' (Raz-Krakotskin 2011; Zraik 2003) which brings me to think about the *bourekas* films more pointedly.

Source: Frame from recollection, Kamal Aljafari (2015).

A genre of Israeli cinema panned by film critics and loved by Israeli film-going audiences (Shohat 2010), *bourekas* films were mainly comic melodramas and musicals produced in Israel, primarily between the 1960s and 1980s. The films characters tended to portray ethnic tropes and ethnic 'types' based on stereotypes of *Mizrachim*, Arab and North African Jews who had recently arrived in Israel (Shohat 2010). These stereotypes were shaped by Zionism's hierarchised and racialised conceptions of civilisation, ideas of the European Enlightenment which had been unattainable fictions for Jews in Europe before they come to settle in historic Palestine from across Europe, Russia and the Hapsburg

Empire both to colonise Palestine, as well as to escape murderous anti-Semitic persecution.[4] The *bourekas* films portrayed *Mizrachim* not as complex and rounded individual characters but as social stereotypes that drew from the Orientalism of the state and Western discourses on Africa and the Middle East. *Mizrachim* were depicted variously as good-natured, stupid, lazy, simple characters or as conniving, thieving, violent and criminal ones. The political rhetoric of Israeli colonial racism was ubiquitous, as Ella Shohat demonstrates citing Ben-Gurion calling Moroccan Jews 'savages' and Golda Meir declaring that Arab Jews were 'coming from another, less developed time' … prompting her to ponder whether it was possible 'to elevate these immigrants to a suitable level of civilization?' (2010, 106). In Shohat's discussion of *bourekas* films, she cites a journalist from Israel's still extant newspaper, *Haaretz* writing about the newly-arrived Arab and North African Jewish immigrants in full throttle 'civilizational clash' mode in the face of:

> 'Immigration of a race we have not yet known in the country,' whose 'primitivism is at a peak,' and 'whose level of knowledge is one of virtually absolute ignorance, and, worse, who have little talent for understanding anything intellectual.' These immigrants are, [the journalist] continues, 'only slightly better than the general level of the Arabs, Negroes, and Berbers in the same regions. In any case, they are at an even lower level than what we knew with regard to the former Arabs of Eretz Israel.' 'These Jews,' he goes on, 'also lack roots in Judaism, as they are totally subordinated to the play of savage and primitive instincts.' They also display 'chronic laziness and hatred for work,' and 'there is nothing safe about this asocial element. (Shohat 2010, 206)

Kazablan, the film of which footage is digitally recut and introduced in the opening sequence of *Recollections* is a classical film musical in the *bourekas* genre, remains the highest grossing smash hit Israeli film of all times. Directed by Menachem Golan (1973) the film is set in Jaffa and tells of a *Mizrachi* man from Morocco, Kazablan (named after the Moroccan city, Casablanca) who falls in love with an *Ashkenazi* Jewish woman, Rachel whose parents come from Poland. Her family rejects Kazablan (on racial grounds). A conflict ensues after Kazablan is suspected of theft of money from Rachel's house, and is arrested, although later he is cleared. In the end, Kazablan re-unites with his (*Ashkenazi*) woman and redeems himself from his 'condition' of Arabness, previously synonymous with criminality and violence, to become a 'proper' citizen—a word etymologically linked to the French term, *propre* with its implication in moral discourses of hygiene, cleanliness and self-possession. As a cinematic lesson in

Israeli civics, there is an important analogy made between becoming an Israeli by becoming whiter, Ashkenazi. The staging of identification demographically comes full circle in this cinematic genre that produced a national imaginary as a closed field in which its internal others are incorporated and assimilated.

In the *bourekas* films, the action takes place inside ruins, yet the films have no avowed relationship to the historicity of the ruins. Indeed, the sub-plot about the threat of evictions for the Mizrachim of Jaffa in *Kazablan*, is as silent on the history of forced displacement of the Palestinians of Jaffa as the genre is in entirety. At the same time, however, the genre documents the paradox at the heart of Israeli cinema filmed in Jaffa which, as Aljafari has commented, 'wanted to exclude and erase the Palestinian history of Jaffa, the Palestinians of Jaffa, whilst also documenting them' (Aljafari 2016).

Source: Frame from recollection, Kamal Aljafari (2015).

The actors in the *bourekas* films, however, raise those 'other' Jewish figures who were still diasporic in many respects, or, in other words, not yet national. The actors were mainly Arab and African Jewish actors from Morocco, Iraq, Yemen, Egypt and Libya whose Arabness or Africanness were erased in a process of coercive acculturation into national citizenship—a tragically ironic experiment mimicking European nationalisms. These are the figures who are digitally made to vanish as Aljafari brings the visual archive of his hometown to the foreground. If the image is freed from being a 'location', as a setting for *bourekas* films, denuded of its props and actors, Aljafari's hometown is recreated cinematically as a place where the traces of these asymmetrically connected regimes of erasure may be revisited in considering the possibilities of cinematic justice for imagining a postcolonial future.

Scholars and activists interested in Arab and African Jewish cultural and resistance politics in Israel have investigated the racial fantasies and formations which underlie the systemic practices across multiple sites of political and social legitimation of anti-Arab and anti-Black racism, excavating the ideological grounds of political thought and cultural production that have constituted the racial and ethnic others internal to the Jewish polity.[5] Nonetheless, the primary fault lines along which the contradictions inherent to Zionism as segregationist ethnic nationalism are understood as primarily those between Palestinians and Israelis. In this, the field of 'demography' as a regime-aligned discipline is deeply implicated in producing Jewishness as a national category that underlies the majoritarian aspirations and anxieties of the state. In counter-hegemonic politics, there are important political ethical considerations and valid historical reasons for reproducing these demographic categories, not least the extent of disavowal with which the ethnic cleansing of Palestine has been met and the narratives with which it has been countered. These fault lines provide a divided and racially hierarchised Jewish Israeli polity with a common 'enemy', a shared 'other' which shores up a civic sense of common Jewishness. At the same time, the Israeli/Palestinian fault line mitigates the extent to which anti-Arabness and anti-Blackness constitute the limits of Zionism as an ideology of Jewish nationalism as well as its internal contradictions. To surface this is to make visible the 'infrastructures of hierarchical citizenship [in Israel] that rely on white supremacy' (Yerday 2019). The repurposed footage from the *bourekas* films, then, re-collect the historically and politically connected links 'between the dispossession of Palestinians and the dislocation of Arab-Jews' (Shohat 2010, 252) and Ethiopian Jews, complicating and expanding the stakes of partition, segregation and erasure in the making of Israeli national narratives and national identity whilst imagining how these might be reconstellated.

In freeing the image with his dual method of repurposing and digital retouching, Aljafari's 'filmmaking not only lays claim to a lost space and people but also stands as a model for transnational solidarity and resistance against violent dispossession and displacement' (Atoui 2016). As I have suggested earlier, however, it goes further still. Aljafari frees the image to discern precisely these criss-crossing fault lines offering an aesthetic that holds complex and interconnected meanings dispersed across different temporal and spatial conditions. To 'free the image', then, is to undo the fixities and fictions of demographic logics, of nationalism and its desires so as to move freely in the image, in the horizons of imagination it opens. These are available, of course, but the viewer has to produce them, has to desire to produce them. In this, the viewer is implicated in Aljafari's commitment to free the image. The film foregoes narrative and speech (except for one brief and strange dialogue recorded) one of the aesthetic decisions that free the image, enabling the moving image to become a personal and poetic homage to Jaffa as a disappeared place and to its ghosts that linger—including Aljafari's own family members who show up as so many phantoms after the props and actors have been removed. Foregoing narrative enables the imagination to be estranged from hegemonic and counter-hegemonic repertoires, familiar if epistemologically asymmetrical fields of meanings. In this, the politics of signification that stabilise meaning and produce those things that go without saying are complicated and opened. By unmooring the image from narrative, *Recollection* enables a kind of inverted forensic investigation in which fiction cinema provides the documentary record of disappeared places and people that are both specific to Palestine/Israel and to more contemporary universal experiences. 'It's not a film from there', writes Kamal Aljafari of *Recollection*. 'It is a post-catastrophe film, a Sebaldian film, what this image requires [is] to be freed from its mooring in Palestine,' he continues (Aljafari 2016) suggesting that freeing the image and moving freely in the image are distinct if related gestures.

The footage in *Recollection's* opening sequence approaches Jaffa port from the sea, with the image bobbing as if the hand held camera is on a small boat. It seems to be cut from the opening sequence of *Kazablan* in which the camera approaches Jaffa from the sea. To arrive back to Jaffa from the sea is to return on a route made by those who were made refugees, Palestinians who were forced to flee from home and homeland. It is this same sea that carried Palestinians during the 1947–1948 war who travelled south and approached land at Gaza where most remain still today. It is the same sea that carried, a few years later, Arab and Africa Jews from Morocco, Tunisia, Libya and elsewhere in the early 1950s as the Jewish Agency drove projects of mass migration to Israel. The bobbing image of the approach to Jaffa's port viewed from the sea would have been theirs too, as the first speaking character claims in the opening sequence of *Kazablan* which begins with the sea, camera bobbing on its impossible horizon, a prefatory narration framed within the colonial 'telos' of Zionism that compresses and conflates biblical and political time:

> The sea of Jaffa; some call it the Mediterranean. This is the sea that brought the whale that opened its belly for Jonah. This is the sea that brought the Christians, the Moslems, the Turks, David Ben Gurion and me, Moshiko Babayu, fisherman of the sea of Jaffa. (*Kazablan* 1973)

By setting the approach to Jaffa in the sea *Recollection* dissipates the territorial stability of the Israeli *bourekas* films as the grounds on which 'Israeli cinematic collective memory … affirms the founding premise of Zionism' (Atoui 2016). This deterritorialising gesture also opens the moving image of the Mediterranean, this 'Mare Nostrum', to also recall the contemporary sea routes of those escaping military and economic wars to seek refuge and asylum, to remake home in an elsewhere that might sustain the conditions for life.

If film is a mode of thought, *Recollection* offers a way of reimagining postcolonial life in Israel/Palestine as both a shared condition and critical political discourse that might open a response to possibilities for political representation, the abrogation of which is the condition of being made refugee, of statelessness. For the aesthetic procedures by which the image is freed destabilise the visual fields and weaponised aesthetic repertoires that criminalise homelessness, flight and precarity. In this, *Recollection* offers a way of reimagining 'postcolonial life' that deterritorialises the image from its particular setting and history in a gesture of profound and abiding hospitality. Cinematic justice, then, is the opening of a singular image as a universal idea for the not-yet-community of a non-partitioned paradigm that the film makes possible.

NOTES

1. I am thinking here of Ariella Azoulay's *The Civil Contract of Photography* (2008) and her *Civil Imagination: A Political Ontology of Photography* (2011), Gil Hochberg's *Visual Occupations: Violence and Visibility in a Conflict Zone* (2015); T.J. Demos' *The Migrant Image: The Art and Politics of Documentary during Global Crisis* (2014), Gregoire Chamayou's *Drone Theory* (2015) and Eyal Weitzman's *Forensic Architecture: Violence at the Threshold of Detectability* (2017) as most immediately relevant examples.
2. In this regard, Hadas Yaron, Nurit Hashimshony-Yaffe and John Campbell's '"Infiltrators" or Refugees? An Analysis of Israel's Policy Towards African Asylum-Seekers' in *International Migration* (2013) is instructive.
3. Absent presence alludes to the Absentee Property Law of 1952 in which Palestinians who were not in their homes but remained inside the boundaries of the new state at the signing of the armistice in 1949 were defined as Present Absentees. The law allowed the state to seize the properties of Present Absentees and place them under the curatorship of a specially designated office, the office of the Guardian of Absentee Property.
4. See, for example, Amos Elon's *The Israelis: Founders and Sons* (1971).
5. A very brief selection, for example, would include Sammy Smooha, *Israel: Pluralism and Conflict* (1978), Ella Shohat, 'Sephardim in Israel:

Zionism from the Standpoint of Its Jewish Victims' (1988), Sami Chetrit, *Intra-Jewish Conflict in Israel: White Jews, Black Jews* (2009), Smadar Lavie, 'Mizrahi Feminism and the Question of Palestine' (2011), Avi Yalou in conversation with Libby Lenkinski, 'Know your "Enemy"' (2019). Available at https://jewishcurrents.org/know-your-enemy/ and Efrat Yerday, 'Precarious Privilege: An Interview with Efrat Yerday', *Graylit: Liberatory Art and Thought at the Intersection of Palestinian and Jewish Histories*, 1 November 2019. Available at https://graylit.org/blog/2018/12/17/18wpztrlrg0oxiaaluft7sw7s72ayt.

REFERENCES

Atoui, Farah. 'Appropriate, Re-mix, Erase, Zoom-in: The Transformative Power of Film-Making in Kamal Aljafari's Recollection,' *Offscreen* 20, no. 10 (October 2016). Available at https://offscreen.com/view/transformative-power-in-recollection (accessed June 2019).

Azoulay, Ariella. *The Civil Contract of Photography*. New York: Zone Books, 2008.

———. *Civil Imagination: A Political Ontology of Photography*. London: Verso, 2011.

Chamayou, Gregoire. *Drone Theory*. London: Penguin, 2015.

Chetrit, Sami. *Intra-Jewish Conflict in Israel: White Jews, Black Jews*. New York: Routledge, 2009.

Demos, T.J. *The Migrant Image: The Art and Politics of Documentary during Global Crisis*. Durham and London: Duke University Press, 2014.

Elon, Amos. *The Israelis: Founders and Sons*. New York: Bantam, 1971.

Hamid, Dabashi. 'Kamal Aljafari interviewed by Hamid Dabashi', New York, February 2016. Available at http://www.palestine.mei.columbia.edu/cpsevents-spring-2016-events/2016/2/22/recollection (accessed June 2019).

Hochberg, Gil. *Visual Occupations: Violence and Visibility in a Conflict Zone*. Durham and London: Duke University Press, 2015.

———. 'From Cinematic Occupation to Cinematic Justice', *Third Text*, no. 31/4 (2017): 533–547.

Lavie, Smadar. 'Mizrahi Feminism and the Question of Palestine.' *Journal of Middle East Women's Studies* 7 (2011): 56–58.

Libby Lenkinski Avi Yalou in conversation with Libby Lenkinski, 'Know Your "Enemy"', 19 August 2019. Available at https://jewishcurrents.org/know-your-enemy/ (accessed 13 December 2019).

Monterescu, Daniel. *Jaffa Shared and Shattered: Contrived Coexistence in Israel/Palestine*. Bloomington and Indianapolis: Indiana University Press, 2015.

Raz-Krakotzkin, Amnon. *Exile and Binationalism: From Gershom Scholem and Hannah Arendt to Edward Said and Mahmoud Darwish*. Berlin: Wissenschaftskolleg zu Berlin, 2011.

Shohat, Ella. *Israeli Cinema: East/West and the Politics of Representation.* London: I.B. Taurus, [1989]2010.

———. 'Sephardim in Israel: Zionism from the Standpoint of Its Jewish Victims', *Social Text,* no. 19/20 (Autumn 1988): 1–5.

Smooh, Sammy. *Israel: Pluralism and Conflict.* Berkeley: University of California Press, 1978.

Steyerl, Hito. *The Wretched of the Screen.* Berlin: Sternberg Press/e-flux journal, 2012. E-book available at https://www.e-flux.com/books/66675/thewretched- of-the-screen/ (accessed 7 November 2020).

Weitzman, Eyal. *Forensic Architecture: Violence at the Threshold of Detectability.* NYC: MIT/Zone Books, 2017.

Yaron, Hadas, Nurit Hashimshony-Yaffe and John Campbell. '"Infiltrators" or Refugees? An Analysis of Israel's Policy Towards African Asylum-Seekers'. *International Migration* 51, no. 4 (2013): 144–157. Available at https://onlinelibrary.wiley.com/doi/abs/10.1111/imig.12070 (accessed 28 December 2019).

Yerday, Efrat. 'Precarious Privilege: An Interview with Efrat Yerday', *Graylit: Liberatory Art and Thought at the Intersection of Palestinian and Jewish Histories,* 1 November 2019. Available at https://graylit.org/blog/2018/12/17/18wpztrlrg0oxiaaluft7sw7s72ayt (accessed 13 December 2019).

Zraik, Raef Faris. 'Palestine as Exile', *Global Jurist Advances* 3, no. 2 (2003): 1535–1661.

DESCENT

THE HOMOSEXUAL AND HIS FUTURE (CATHER, CLEMENTI AND CRISP)

Taylor Black

PREFACE: NEW YEAR, SAME HANGOVER

New Year is a horrible holiday. While, throughout the rest of the calendar year, I find myself able to keep my mind clear of the anxiety-provoking thoughts about what's happened to me in the past and what's to come in the distant future, there is something about the stretch of time immediately preceding and following 1st January that forces me to take stock of these horrible and abstract notions of time. For starters, the whole month of December is, as is commonly stated, always already a difficult time for those of us who consider ourselves as indigent members of our families and reluctant members of society at large: in just a week's time following Christmas holiday celebrations comes another event that forces the entire world's attention upon itself. With weary, yet hopeful eyes gazing into the distance and the promise of another year, human beings all over the earth take long, hard looks at the mistakes that have made up their pasts and the flaws that constitute their existences in order to make promises. All of the regretful feelings that come up as a result of this are meant to bring forth a flurry of changes and improvements in the new year to come—only like all gambles, the one made with the future comes with odds that are immediately stacked against the large majority of its players: depressives promise they will find happiness; overeaters swear they will overcome their love of food; alcoholics drunkenly decide they will one day reach a state of sobriety; and life's failures pin all of their hopes on the possibility of success.

Much like the feeling of being hungover that manages to mark every single New Year's Day for me each time it comes around, all of the trappings and festivities that go along with preparing for and celebrating this horrible event almost always return the emotional high that is, at a certain moment, associated with the prospect of another year with a state of dizzied, frazzled disappointment and despair. You see, try as we all might to plan our time out and measure out some kind of notion of success in the time to come, any wager made against what we call the future is, at least for most people, already a lost cause.

Further, even though the earth's population is largely comprised of individuals who have at least 'some' chance at winning in the future, there is also a small, awkward minority that not only will lose but who also simply cannot play the game at all. In other words, outside of the winners and the losers of fate, there are also the immediate failures of existence: people who experience life itself as a dead loss.

What really animates my distrust of New Year's festivities is not only the tragic spirit of change and self-determination that overtakes humanity in its prescribed moment of stock-taking and future-planning but also my own intense understanding of the holiday as merely the source of a kind of hangover that, for me, increases and constitutes my experience of being alive. This annual gamble that the world is asked to make against the future and against its own lives is, for those of us who have been dealt a losing hand, the holiday which provides human beings a regular reminder that we just can't win.

The homosexual man is, in the geography of the living, this figure I have been describing. Born with the striking and overwhelming characteristics that constitute him as a mistake of nature, the homosexual steps out of the womb and onto dry land immediately disqualified from the game of success. Life is, then, from this point on not something that can be orchestrated or laid out in any sort of understandable or already-determined fashion. With no chance of winning, the future operates as a kind of insult to the homosexual, who, especially in his earliest stages of development, finds himself constantly threatened with it, by elders and betters who say, each step of the way, that something will have to change in order for happiness and success to come. Knowing full-well from the start that these changes in temperament and gesture that might make life more bearable are, in essence and in repeated practice, not possible, the homosexual has to find a way to operate in daily life without a clear negotiation of what's to come.

Without a certain kind of stoicism of character and strategic cynicism in behaviour, then, the experience of being homosexual can, if performed incorrectly, feel something like a bad hangover. What I would like to do in the rest of this chapter is investigate a few different accounts of homosexuals in their gambles with the future. In order to both historicise the high stakes involved in the development of modern male homosexuals, I will first approach two separate but compellingly resonant examples of lives lost in the fight against the future—Paul from Willa Cather's 'Paul's Case' and Tyler Clementi, the young gay man who became famous for having committed suicide and subsequently being resurrected as an avatar for a media campaign to publicise gay teen suicide. In doing this, I will rely on work done by Eve Kosofsky Sedgwick on the epistemological constructions of homosexual males in the twentieth century as immediately failed figures and a way of being and feeling alive that is, as she says, underscored by a 'very specific association of gay male sexuality with tragic early death' (Sedgwick 1990).

From there, I will look to Quentin Crisp and bring forth my own appropriation of his story and of his life's work to offer a solution beyond the limits of homosexual loss or victory in the game of time: to consider how 'failure', if fully constituted and performed, can be a way out—not as a way of saying or hoping that homosexuals might one day win but that they simply don't have to. The hangover of existence that comes for homosexuals is the product not necessarily of being born a dead loss but of pinning one's hopes in the narratives provided by liberal and positivist constructions of gay identity and epistemology.

Neither a form of optimism nor pessimism, however, failure can provide a strategic and self-sustaining way of remaining on earth and feeling alive: it transforms the wariness of being a hopeless case into a way of refusing the insult of the future. As someone who understood himself to be a failure, and claims to have 'never been legally married to real life', Crisp (1968, 125), nevertheless, dedicated all of his energies to constructing his way of living into 'one, long, tentative flirtation with the world'. Through this ontological approach to feeling and being in the presence of time, Crisp has provided for us an example of how to feel life as pure event. Rather than succumbing to failure as a way of being failed, Crisp developed a method of becoming that was creative and imaginative. For him, failure constituted a kind of conviviality, a life composed by liveliness, non-linearity—an anti-New Years. Rather, his celebration is like throwing a party that cannot finish but keeps circulating, bumping, clinking glasses and forgetting where, why, what and who? The matter of survival—for Crisp—is not about resisting the future but transgressing its limits, accepting it, feeling it.

A SIN AND A LIE: THE LIFE AND TIMES OF THE MODERN HOMOSEXUAL

The stakes are very high for the modern homosexual man. Already having emerged bruised and battered from the nineteenth century, during which time the species found itself detected by western psychological experts and totally pathologised by an entire discourse and culture that surrounded them, the life and times of the homosexual person living after the turn of the twentieth century is one that is immediately marked by a certain kind of challenge: to both overcome and represent the shame of being a failed and tragic figure operating upon the social landscape. The disgrace of effeminacy that homosexuals carry along with them and pronounce with each gilded and willowy gesture, makes the possibility of negotiating a public life a constantly-losing battle. This sad fate, however, not only disrupts the external realities of being a homosexual, but also composes a fragmented inner world, and poses a certain kind of challenge for him to somehow overcome the shame that makes up his emotional state and render some kind of life that is at least partially livable. Tormented and bullied in early life for the extreme nature of both his personality as well as his mannerisms, the adolescent homosexual finds himself, in the early stages of his own gamble at living, under fire and on guard from the word go. The trick is, in this case, either overcoming and hiding that which is shameful and disgusting about himself in hopes of a brighter and more stable future or, as so often becomes the case, succumbing to loss altogether.

The tragic nature of homosexual subjectivity in this case is also, in Sedgwick's terms, marked by a certain kind of sentimentality. Moving from the example of Melville's *Billy Budd* to Oscar Wilde's *Picture of Dorian Gray*, Sedgwick charts this short game-change in the production but also in the very real lives of young homosexual men caught in this period of transition in western culture. While both stories feature characters embodying masculinities that, to the contemporary reader, translate clearly at least as non-normative, if not totally ridden with a certain kind of homosexuality, Sedgwick describes a change in reception that, for homosexuals to come, presents an assortment of new challenges and tragedies. The 'beauty' and 'splendour' that makes Billy Budd so remarkable and which draws not only the attention and love of the characters in the story but also of Melville's reading public becomes, in a post-Wildean universe the cause of sexual stigma and panic:

> For readers fond of the male body, the year 1891 makes an epoch .... For readers who hate the male body, the year 1891 is also an important one. At the end of *Dorian Gray*, a dead, old, 'loathsome' man lying on the floor is the moralizing gloss on the other thing the servants find in Dorian Gray's attic: 'hanging upon the wall, a splendid portrait of their master as they had last seen him, in all the wonder of his exquisite youth and beauty.' (Sedgwick 1990, 131)

All of the characteristics that, in contemporary terms, get recognised as 'camp,' 'gay', or 'queer' about homosexuals became, in this pivotal moment, arbiters of disgust and sources of shame. The masculine beauty that young Billy Budd seems to represent quickly dissolves, as in the example of Dorian Gray, becoming instead something totally suspect and perverse and awful about his personality and personhood. Likewise, the characteristics now associated with the modern and contemporary homosexual man—effeminacy of gesture and excess of emotion—both work to characterise life and make it immediately unliveable. Homosexuality is both a secret to keep and the inspiration for prohibition; a shame to behold for the homosexual person and a source of panic and disorder among the rest of the normal, heterosexual population. The spectacle of the challenge facing homosexuals occurs in the constant attacks made upon them by the glaring eyes and overwhelming anxieties of the people who surround them, marking, in Sedgwick's terms, a strong strain of sentimentality in the telling but also in the experience of living, this story. Staged outside of the grammatical limits of what western culture considers to be acceptable, the life and times of the homosexual is a pity to behold, as he is defined as a living insult:

> These knowing activations of the ambiguities always latent in grammatical person as such, at any rate, point to the range of meanings of sentimentality that identify it, not as thematic or a particular subject matter, but as a structure of relation, typically one involving the author-or-audience-relations of spectacle; most often, where the epithet 'sentimental' itself is brought onto the scene, a discreditable or devalued one—the sentimental as the *insincere*, the *manipulative*, the *vicarious*, the *morbid*, the *knowing*, the *kitschy*, the *arch*. (Sedgwick 1990, 143)

As a matter of performing life, homosexuality is always on the verge of breaking down: it is the spectre of failure itself, hanging in the balance of life as it unfolds and stumbles upon itself across the earth's surface. Marked by the presence of an undeniable perversion, the homosexual performative reality is one, to use terms employed by Sedgwick and Andrew Parker in their introduction to *Performativity and Performance*, disfigured by a constitutive form of illness which makes living life possible only to the extent that it always seems to be going wrong. Citing the presence of the term 'perversion' in J.L. Austin's formative work on performativity and language, *How To Do Things With Words*, they highlight the ways in which it operates in certain kinds of suspect, failed utterances: 'If something goes wrong in the performance of a performative, "the utterance is then, we may say, not indeed false but in general unhappy"' (Parker and Sedgwick 2000, 3). In other words, the impact of homosexuality is not only challenging and shameful on the personal level but also something complicated on an interpersonal level, making a complicated existence for the homosexual man, whose 'secret' is exposed and performed every time he makes a public entrance. The characteristics of the homosexual are both regarded and embodied as insults—something made much worse considering that they are essentially perceived by heterosexual audiences as rude and distasteful acts of unbridled conduct. This 'theatrical' nature is, for Parker and Sedgwick, 'linked with the perverted, the artificial, the unnatural, the abnormal, the decadent, the effete, the diseased . . . inseparable from a normatively homophobic thematic of the "peculiar", "anomalous", "exceptional", "non-serious"'.

TYLER CLEMENTI AND 'PAUL'S CASE': A STUDY IN TEMPERAMENT'

It's no wonder, then, that young homosexual men have such a hard time coping with the challenges and even the very presence of living itself. As promised, I now offer the stories of two men in this stage of development who, like so many between them, played and, ultimately, lost their precarious gambles with the future. One morning in late September 2010, Tyler Clementi threw himself off of the edge of the George Washington Bridge. While known by his friends and family members as a generally happy and contented young man, Clementi's life-ending decision was apparently instigated upon learning that he had been 'outed' by his dormmate at Rutgers University, who secretly broadcast a live feed of Clementi and another man engaging in some kind of physical intercourse (Knickerbocker 2010). While certainly sad and tragic as a personal story, Clementi's case is, unfortunately, not unique—in fact, the now infamous media campaign led by Dan Savage meant to operate as a caution against queer teen suicide, and called It Gets Better, was started just weeks before Clementi's own demise, that itself became the centre of a whole string of incidents like it among young gay men across the United States in the following months. For these deceased people, as well according to the story of homosexual adolescence both preceding and following all of this, the life course is itself a constant source of loss and hopelessness: the future weighs on the stages of development like a hammer, constantly battering any feelings of adequacy or stability.

In this sense, then, Clementi's decision to jump to his own demise off the bridge that morning not only served to prove the point of the It Gets Better campaign and the story of gay suicide it has been telling but also works presently to punctuate the tragic and cautionary tale of adolescent homosexuality itself. The sound and the impact of Clementi's body—dead to the world even before it hit the surface of the cold and unforgiving waters of the Hudson River—is in concert with other young homosexuals before him, reaching back to the beginning of the twentieth century and the formative example of Willa Cather's Paul, who met a similarly horrible collision with his future, when he summoned up the nerve to throw himself in front of a train as it was pulling into Newark's Penn Station. At about the same age and the exact same moment in each young man's development as a homosexual person, both Paul and Clementi realised that they were hopeless cases, and tragically, gave in to the understanding that, as Cather herself puts it, 'was a losing game in the end' (Cather 1983, 120).

Having served his station in life fully sensing his exile from the society of his school and family units in Pittsburg, Paul brought himself to New York City, like Clementi, with a decision weighing on him and held under his breath. Life was, before this moment, also tainted with his distaste for the 'ugliness of the world,' enacting a never-ending sensation of being alone and hungover in the world, set-off by a resounding 'ache in his head' and a 'bitter burning on his tongue' (Cather 1983, 120). Having spent the week preceding his death in New York City, shopping, fucking and theatre-going, Paul packed himself up and left for Newark feeling his life to be complete and sensing his destiny almost too clearly. The synthesis of these two opposing, queer feelings left Paul, in the moments before his death, to radiate with his own failures—or, as Cather would have it, to undergo '*a spasm of realization* ... [burning] like a faggot in a tempest' (Cather 1983, 116).

Paul's love for the theatre and his desires for an effete, resplendent kind of lifestyle, not afforded to him in his hometown, makes for from the start and to his betters an immediately-suspect feature of his personality. His taste and his mannerisms which when fully indulged during his final week's stay in New York, make him feel so fully like himself are interpreted themselves as performative insults in his real life—a disposition he was forced to literally wear upon his chest:

> In one way and another, had made all his teachers, men and women alike, conscious of the same feeling of physical aversion. In one class he habitually sat with his hand shading his eyes; in another he always looked out of the window during the recitation; in another he made a running commentary on the lecture, with humorous intent.... His whole attitude was symbolized by his shrug and flippantly red carnation flower. (Cather 1983, 103)

More than just an act to maintain, though, Paul's case of antisocial behaviour and his homosexual nature is, for him, an embodied reality—something that, like the red carnation he wore upon his lapel, announced to the world exactly what amount of disgust it ought to regard him with. Paul's many and assorted flourishes are both of his doing and the very matters which, in the scheme of things, account for his undoing as a person.

Homosexuality is more than the performance or even the utterance of perversity, it is also the state of embodying and fully sensing total failure and humiliation. To be regarded as sick and impertinent is to realise and become both sick and impertinent yourself: a challenge which adolescent homosexuals are asked and dared to fail at again and again. Both Clementi and Paul made, and in a way, won the gamble they themselves made with the future. By submitting themselves to death, they only used themselves to articulate what they had been clearly instructed, both by the culture that brought them up, as well as the shaky natural state in which they were brought into the world: that life, for homosexuals is a mistake to be made and fate, a game to be lost. While it may be said that Clementi's suicide may be the result of a homophobic culture, it is also true that it was a result of a certain tragic pessimism on his part to his station in life—in other words, his hopelessness for his own future was brought on by his own acceptance of the truth of his homosexuality as well as his overwhelming insecurities about what that meant for him in the future. Paul's more brazen example represents something a bit more outlandish and perhaps even optimistic as an approach to his own failures than in Clementi's case—meaning that, while he soberly accepted his life as ultimately unliveable, he was still able to come to his suicide with at least a brief understanding of what pleasure he was accustomed to feeling. The end of 'Paul's Case' finds our hero suspended in the air above the train tracks, his body waiting for the looming impact of the oncoming train and the all-too-imminent future:

> He felt something strike his chest—his body was being thrown swiftly through the air, on and on, immeasurably far and fast, while his limbs gently relaxed. Then, because the picture making mechanism was crushed, the disturbing visions flashed into black, and Paul dropped back into the immense design of things. (Cather 1983, 121)

With no way out of the game of life, these two characteristic examples prove homosexuality to be a dangerous gamble for those whose very bodies and souls are offered up to the future as a sacrifice.

Even though both Clementi and Paul lost their lives and indeed that they were both born to do so—it is not as if they failed at performing the roles cast for them. As a form of lived and embodied perversity, homosexuality is, as Parker and Sedgwick argue, a very risky kind of performative state for someone to find themselves in—one where the possibility of failure is always as close as your next breath. In this way, the suicides committed by both of these young men should simply be considered an early but not inappropriate curtain call to the tragic drama of their lives on earth. The impact of each violent death is simply the effect of a punch line arriving too early in the insult that each Clementi and Paul surely felt their lives to represent. This is the reality that structures the life of the modern homosexual man, who is forced to act out and predict a truth about themselves that is not actually uttered, whose entire way of being in the world seems to indicate total failure and total humiliation on his part.

This shame that haunts the homosexual man in all of the performances and moments of development of his adolescence, is one that makes him feel the impact of his life like an insult that never ends. *Hungover* in this way then, the sensation of being on earth is akin to be nauseated all the time; in the same way that normal people come to regard flagrant homosexuals with a certain kind of disgust, the homosexual person is, if in touch with his own inner feelings, likewise sickened by the sight of it all. Paul, for instance, answers the continuous accusations of insolence and wickedness brought on by his instructors and family members with his own antagonism against the rest of the world, with his very own performative reproach inflecting each and every move he makes. Here, Cather solves the riddle of Paul's awkward station in life, drawing out the sickening way in which he moved about his existence.

> Perhaps it was because, in Paul's world, the natural nearly always wore the guise of ugliness, that a certain element of artificiality seemed to him necessary in beauty. Perhaps it was because experience of life elsewhere was so full of Sabbath-school picnics, petty economies, wholesome advice as to how to succeed in life, and the unescapable odours of cooking. (Cather 1983, 111)

To escape this feeling, Paul, while in Pittsburg, attends the theatre, under the very glib auspices of an employee of Carnegie Hall. Safe from rude accusations and hidden from the glares of disgust that made up his daily life, Paul finds himself at home in the dark space of the audience. He also is able to access some sense of himself and his pleasures by imagining a fictive elsewhere and other-life that he may have, in different circumstances, been able to live: in the very real presence of his dream of life. Each time, it was coming off this high and re-emerging into the real world that resumed Paul's eternal sickness:

> After a concert was over, Paul was often irritable and wretched until he got to sleep—and tonight he was even more than usually restless. He had the feeling of not being able to let down; of its being impossible to give up this delicious excitement which was the only thing that could be called living at all. (Cather 1983, 106)

Paul's response to the strength of both his fantasy of himself and the disgusting life he finds himself tied down by, while still in Pittsburg, is to change his lot, even if for a fleeting moment of happiness and contentment. As in Clementi's case, Paul tragically understands, even here, that the future is something that won't have him, a prospect he simply can't cope with himself. However, there is a certain optimism present in the clarity of Paul's fantasies that makes his death something more than just sad, unlike Clementi, who seems to have simply given up acting as a normal, heterosexual person at the very moment that the wheels began to come off of his performance. At the heart of the homosexual's dilemma lies, I think, problems and possibilities evident in the very differently-constructed spaces of fantasy each of these boys operated with while on earth. Very much feeling alien in the world, Paul still, in his trips to the theatre and his ultimate sojourn in New York City, is able to understand the unique and even momentarily empowering sense of himself—of his own pleasures, tragic and failed as they may be.

For Clementi, blending into the very drab landscape of Rutgers University became something more than just a temporary profession: it came to constitute the structure of his hopes and dreams, ones he found himself bound to lose. While there is certainly a tragedy to Paul's case of homosexual individuality, Clementi's gamble at getting and getting along undetected makes his story an example of tragic individuality: his homosexual disposition became something he felt he could overcome, until, in the end, he came to feel the weight of his utter helplessness over the matter, crashing into his body like a high-speed train. Having the truth of both his homosexuality and, after that, his decision to commit suicide, all recorded and broadcast on the internet, Clementi left for all of us a disembodied tragedy—one that will keep occurring so long as it is used to back up fantasies of things 'getting better' for homosexuals, of the future being something they should pin their hopes on at all. The trace of Clementi's unhappiness still hangs in the balance, waiting to be connected to other cases of queer suicide and forming a constellation of gay hopes for a happy, but still impossible, future to come.

'YOU DON'T HAVE TO WIN': A HOMOSEXUAL RESOLUTION

As I try and bring this discussion of homosexuality and the challenges presented to it by the future to a close, my mind returns to a comment made by Quentin Crisp each New Year. Never one to miss a chance to give his opinion on any matter or leave any question unturned, when asked, most often by journalists, for his thoughts on the year to come, he would always say: 'It will all get worse.' Like anything he said, this prediction could easily be understood as pert, negative and even bitchy. However, as easy as these kinds of conclusions about Mr Crisp are for other human beings to make, they miss the spirit behind his words and his intentions for them—indeed, about the true worth and effect of the life of this overlooked and misunderstood man.

Looking back, it was, in fact, just after New Year's Day, and almost exactly three years ago to this day, that I had my first 'encounter' with Quentin Crisp. Sometime before I left New York City to visit my family in North Carolina, I received a film in the mail through one of those online rental companies that have become so popular in the United States. Entitled *Resident Alien*, and advertising on the blurb of the sleeve enclosing the disc a brief account of a true iconoclast, of one of the relics of bohemian New York. I packed it in my suitcase and, shamefully, let it sit there until I returned home two weeks later. After almost sending the thing back, I decided, in one of those annual hangover states that seem only to come after New Year's festivities, to pop it in and give Mr Crisp a try. Not even fifteen minutes into the film, my entire life was changed. I had been viewing a montage of scenes of him placed on trial for his inconvenient views and misunderstood presence on earth, one against a gay rights group in New York City and the other as a featured guest on one of the more popular (and trashy) talk shows of the day. In response to a question of whether or not his effeminate and outlandish appearance was a help or a hindrance to the struggle for gay rights and equality, Quentin confirmed what it was that his audience was looking for with a simple 'No.' It was, however, his continued commentary in a follow-up interview to this scene in *Resident Alien* (1991) that floored me, that made me an immediate and dutiful follower of Quentin Crisp and missionary of what he termed *Crisperanto*:

> The worrying thing to me about the gay community is that they are fighting for their rights, and I don't believe anybody has rights. If we all got what we deserved we would starve.

The ultimate usefulness of this comment, much like his New Year's proclamation, is that it is absolutely, staggeringly true. Quentin did not, in his own phrasing, step out of his mother's womb onto dry land in order to say those things about his presence and about the world that it wanted to hear. Born and bred a mistake, Quentin learned to take every step and make every gesture on earth with the full, embodied understanding of himself as totally unique, as completely self-reliant. However, as this montage in *Resident Alien* displays so clearly, as utterly declarative and well-rehearsed his statements and mannerisms became over time, he was, and I would argue, still has never been able to meet an audience worthy of his glory and his wisdom.

Of course, rights discourses are problematic and fictitious, especially for sexual minorities. If Quentin was trained as and understood properly to be an academic or a philosopher, no one would protest his saying this. The effect of his statement to the sceptical crowd of gay community members is not only to protect himself from their attacks upon him and their attempts to place judgement on his life within a political narrative he knew he was not a part of. His 'No' to the question of the convenience of his life and the helpfulness of his words is an answer to all his naysayers—to all those people, whether through homophobic attack or political interpolation, who would like to judge him as anything other than himself, as Quentin Crisp, or as any more or less than Quentin Crisp. For him, prejudice against an identity or a lifestyle was never something he knew, and indeed never a fight he felt the need to dedicate himself to. The problem facing Quentin is and has always been his own and the prejudice the world has had against Quentin Crisp has been for being 'too' like himself, too willing to fix what the world always insisted were ontological wounds. What I find so inspiring about Quentin and his life's work is his insistence upon himself, as well as the very humble and imminently useful ways in which he explains how anyone else might follow his lead in their own professions of being and becoming.

Here on earth, and in the wake of another year moving into the past, homosexuals find themselves again in true need of Quentin's words of eternal wisdom. Following the string of suicides by queer youth, both the gay and mainstream press in the States has started a new campaign to convince homosexuals both young old, nay to 'convince them' that 'It Gets Better'. Unfortunately, the continued presence of homophobic violence and queer suicides, works against the logic of this admittedly optimistic and well-intentioned campaign to change the sexual climate culture. The pressure facing these young people upon the tragic decision to end their lives is the weight of a gamble with the future that narratives of identity and equality and sexuality only work to encourage; understanding themselves as homosexual 'people-to-come', queer suicide victims have decided that this is not a fight they can win.

Survival is, for Quentin, an affective state of becoming open to the future in the present; happiness is, then, not something-to-come or even something to work for—it involves, rather, a concentrated method of feeling absolutely 'in the continuous present from head to foot' (Crisp 1968, 125). Unlike nihilistic forms of living in the present that actively forsake the future, this presentness means being open to, and even experiencing, the future in a whole series of continuous, focused moments. Understanding his past and future in the embodied now, Quentin was able to live full of intensity, without the burden of blame or anxiety. From beyond the grave, he has messages of hope for us trying to live in the future: 'I hope [my example] has inspired you to live your life as carelessly as I have done. I have lived my life in the best way I know how and I regret nothing' (Crisp 2000). While homosexuals, as a political category or epistemological category, may, over time 'win' through measures of political acceptance or cultural equality, actual, living people who find themselves in situations with which they cannot cope in a way they cannot recognise in any human being around them, only need to understand the words that Mr Crisp came on earth, not only to say, but to embody and display, in his own wicked and wonderful way: that you don't have to win.

REFERENCES

Cather, Willa. 'Paul's Case: A Study in Temperament'. In *The Troll Garden*. Lincoln: University of Nebraska Press, 1983.

Crisp, Quentin. *The Naked Civil Servant*. New York: Penguin Books, 1968.

———. 'The Omnibus Afterword.' *Omnibus*, edited by Phillip Ward. New York: Triangle Press, 2000.

Jonathan, Nossiter (director). 1991. *Resident Alien*.

Knickerbocker, Brad. 'Tyler Clementi Suicide: Reaction is Swift and Widespread'. *Christian Science Monitor*, 3 October 2010.

Parker, Andrew and Eve Kosofsky Sedgwick. 'Sexual Politics, Performativity, and Performance.' In *The Routledge Reader in Politics and Performance*, edited by Lizbeth Goodman and Jane de Gay. New York: Routledge, 2000.

Sedgwick, Eve Kosofsky. *Epistemology of the Closet*. Berkeley: University of California Press, 1990.

SAPPHIC LINEAGES: OR, NOTES FOR A QUEER-FEMINIST POETICS

Brinda Bose

> *With my fingers too, rather than with my eyes, I read these poems.*
>
> *Ionic volutes—delicate and ringed—white shells with the inner side of pearl—indented cup with the chiseling as fine as the pattern of the under-leaf lining of the wine itself ... all this—more and much more—and to concentrate my senses, struggling now with faint, exotic perfumes, pungent and stimulating, not quite familiar, with colours, rose and the violet of the rainbow, I close my eyes and with my fingers like one blind would find my way about this poetry.*
>
> —H.D., 'A Poet in the Wilderness: Songs of Anacreon' (2019, 64)

What do animate bodies and the bodies of aesthetic texts have in common, other than in terms of how works of art and literature represent living bodies, their actions and emotions—sensually, intellectually and stylistically? In the representation of bodies in art, we look for signals that tell us how they are, how they look and feel and act; how they are gazed at and acted upon. And we read the bodies of texts for their linguistic, aural, visual and rhetorical effects, their signs and structures. What do we do then, when we bring the two together in our enterprise of reading and meaning-making, when the body of the text fuses with the bodies in and out of the text, bodies real and imagined, living and dead and fantastical? When we are reading poetics through and with the body, we not just read *of* the erotic in texts, but read our texts *erotically*: and the second we do both by engaging with the writing in intimacy, desire, longing, love and pain - and by understanding how the shape and texture of our texts reflect, and expand on, the intimacies of desiring and loss that they are speaking of.

'With my fingers too, rather than with my eyes, I read these poems', says H.D., making the tactile central to the experience of reading, an experience that is imagined through the sensorium, fingers feeling words through tips that trace them on the page, nerve-ends tingling; what if we read with our fingers and eyes both, the type on the page assuming shapes, high-jumping and high-fiving, gambolling and strolling and stopping? What if eyes and fingers are locked and enthralled, no longer knowing where the sensate body ends and the word-print begins? What if these legacies are bequeathed through generations of poet-lovers, lovers of words and of women and men and not-women-not-men, by other women who have been deviantly adventurous, who have looked to write and to love in words and ways that have glanced askance at both love and writing?

Reading a few women poet-philosophers through many centuries that are quite astonishingly interwoven, the ancient Sappho is found to live and breathe in so many of those who followed her through the ages, leaving lineages and lessons for our contemporary times. What is revealed is an echoing that is perpetuated through the idea of the body—and this is not merely the female desiring or loving or suffering body that is strewn across and between poems by Sappho and her sisters through the ages. If we think in tandem, rather, of the female body and of the body of the poem, and certain ways of shaping poetry in extension of the female self that travels beyond Cixous's formulation of '*l'ecriture feminine*' or feminine writing—we are surprised repeatedly by flights of creative and affective imagination that are perhaps not governed by the phallic at all. And if we follow some of these impudent and intrepid queer-feminist aesthetic routes in our reading, meshing the tactile with the intellectual, we could flag a certain method of reading that we call 'queer-feminist' or 'body-poetic'.

In Anne Carson's translation of Sappho's poetic fragments titled *If Not, Winter* (Carson 2003), she distinguishes her interpretation of the remaindered poem by the repeated use of a particular punctuation mark, the single bracket:

]
]
]
]thought
]barefoot
]
]
]
]
—'Fragment' (Carson 2003, 23)

Here are two words and nine symbols (a single closing bracket on each line), walking barefoot down a page, like the thought whose 'bare'-ness this Sapphic fragment conveys. It is sheer serendipity, perhaps, that these two words are all that survive of this fragment that the translator, Anne

Carson, then frames in a vertical series of closing brackets to indicate missing words or lines. So bare the thought, like the foot unshod—and more naked than flesh, the two words here, for being shorn of sentences that are usually crammed with words in neat rows. Deprived of safety in numbers, appearing without comrades on either side, only flanked above and below by a row of lonely single brackets emphasising what was or might have been had the fragment been clothed, un-naked and the foot un-bare.

We can mourn the loss of clothing that covers and completes or we can revel in the words now bared, as Sappho had aspired: 'May I write words more naked than flesh, stronger than bone, more resilient than sinew, sensitive than nerve.' To Sappho, the word was body and flesh, sinew and nerve—and when bared and naked, was strong, resilient and sensitive. Each word crawled and strode through her poetry, more naked than flesh, not for the faint-hearted. A fifth-century *hydria* in the National Museum of Athens that portrays Sappho reading from a papyrus, has become the most abiding image of the Greek lyric poet of the sixth century BC. While it is not known whether Sappho was literate, this image, her translator Anne Carson avers, is an accurate representation of her because the powerful intrigue of word-clusters printed—and missing—on a page has, since, emerged as one of the most fascinating aspects of Sappho's poetic legacy.

Born in 630 BC, this poet of the island of Lesbos is believed to have composed nine books of lyrics, of which only one complete poem and myriad fragments have surfaced; she is known as a poet of fragments as much as the poet after whom lesbian sexual identity has been named. Anne Carson—formidable poet herself, as well as a translator and literary critic—who produced in 2003 the widely-acclaimed translation of Sappho's fragmented lyrics *If Not, Winter*, has upheld the primacy of the eye on a plain sheet by playing with signs and symbols, letters, lines and punctuation scattered with careful intent on each page. With the liberal use of blank spaces and different kinds of brackets, Greek text and English translation facing each other in camaraderie and combat, Carson both recreates Sappho's nearly-illegible etchings on papyri discovered accidentally in an ancient rubbish tip around the start of the twentieth century and seduces attention to the body of the text … that also then becomes, by a peculiar material transformation, the embedded—yet living, and writhing—body in the text.

Between the sixth century BC when she lived and wrote and the present, Sappho has spawned a worthy lineage in poetry, particularly over the last century following the discovery of her poem-fragments on bits of papyrus. It is a lineage, however, that is inadequately traced, concentrating upon the one that legitimises a homosexual identity in women's poetry—'the first lesbian poet from whose birthplace, Lesbos, the term is derived'. What is far more fascinating, however, is an entwined significance of the body in the Sapphic lineage of writing if we take a close look at some of Sappho's poetic fragments and the critical thought and poetic writings of Gertrude Stein, H.D. Anne Carson and Jeanette Winterson. We can imagine each of them, variously, to be in imaginary conversation with Sappho as well as with each other, such is the imprint of the legacy of the almost-lost ancient poet of Lesbos on the twentieth century.

Through our own discrete sets of creative and critical readings of these cross-generational poets—each one an intense thinker and philosopher, as well—we can discover that the sexual (especially female) body and its enactments of desire in this Sapphic lineage is woven with and interrogated by the body poetic in content, language and form: in the images and the materiality of touch that they invoke, in the tactile sensuality of the words themselves as well as in the visual contortions they demand of the eye as printed symbols moving across and down each printed page in unexpected ways, sometimes solid and terse and sometimes liquid and swirling. And that Sappho inspired in these poets/poetic prose writers, who engaged so intimately with her work—its fragmentary presences, its tantalising absences—this conscious experimentation with sensual content, poetic language and poetic form: a constant play as much with the texture and timbre of words as with their shapes and spaces and movements on the page, creating a volatile, sometimes floundering art of poetics as inflammatory and unpredictable as the female body in desire, of desire.

> Eros shook my
> mind like a mountain wind falling on oak trees
> (Carson 2003, Sappho's 'Fragment' 47, 99)

wrote Sappho, and on the printed page 'mind' falls off the line even as Eros begins to shake it: this is a visual a/ffect, not just an e/ffect, a simultaneous internalising and externalising of this emotional and phenomenological falling off. One feels the tremble and tumble as the mind is humbled, even as one sees it visually represented on the page. Eros continually shakes the mind of the poet, for whom the body is relentlessly and unequivocally the site of desire—combining its pain and its pleasures—even as the mind registers it just as relentlessly. Anne Carson, in her study titled *Eros: The Bittersweet* (Carson [1986]1998) describes eros as a state of being in classical philosophy and literature, starting with Sappho, in whom, presumably, all things erotic and romantic begin and sink. And she focuses on the Greek word that is generally the English 'bittersweet'—*glukupikron*—but translates the lines as

> Eros once again the limb-loosener whirls me sweetbitter, impossible to fight off, creature stealing up, saying then: 'Sweetbitter' sounds wrong, and yet our standard English rendering 'bittersweet' inverts the actual.... Should that concern us? If her ordering has a descriptive intention, eros is here being said to bring sweetness, then bitterness in sequence: she is sorting the possibilities chronologically. Many a lover's experience would validate such a chronology, especially in poetry, where most love ends badly. (Carson 1998, 3–4)

Carson's translations are acutely conscious of and make wondrous virtue out of both the accuracy of meaning and the laying out of words on the page. In this case, she inverts the usual English compound word 'bittersweet' into 'sweetbitter', gaining both affect and effect: what we might pass over as commonplace, 'bittersweet', we stop at in surprise, 'sweetbitter'; the shock is deliberate and intellectual at the same time, it wants to surprise but also maintains a chronology for the two elements—first sweet then bitter—that she infers as being more true to lovers' experience of this contradictory affect. It is the state of 'sweetbitter' that causes the 'sensational crises', leading the poet to cry 'I don't know what I should do: two states of mind in me …' (Carson 1998, Sappho's 'Fragment' 51, 8), pushing Carson to conclude, 'Whether apprehended as a dilemma of sensation, action or value, eros prints as the same contradictory fact: love and hate converge within erotic desire. Why?' (Carson 1998, 9).

Many centuries later, 'H.D., Imagiste' as Pound christened her, a New England Modernist strongly influenced by Sappho, was flailing about elegantly within the same contradiction, looking for objective correlatives in language, often, astonishingly, using the same words as Sappho, whose translations were published well after H.D. wrote her poems. H.D.'s 'Oread', said to be the most perfect Imagist poem in six brief lines:

> Whirl up, sea—
> whirl your pointed pines,
> splash your great pines
> on our rocks,
> hurl your green over us,
> cover us with your pools of fir.

echoes Sappho in word and sensuality:

> Eros once again the limb-loosener whirls me
> sweetbitter…

'Whirl' is the graphic, somewhat unusual choice of word that an overwhelming sexuality appears to be riding on, where a limb-loosening Eros in Sappho turns into the splashing, hurling sea in H.D., 'impossible to fight off' in Sappho and invited in to 'cover us…' in H.D.'s troth with the wild waters off the New England coast which mingled fir and water along a rocky coastline. This fraught sexuality, deep desire cohabiting with anxiety, not knowing what to do with the 'creature stealing up', (Sappho), whether to beckon over and embrace such a need—'splash … on our rocks' (H.D. 2019)—or to cry out in frustration.

'I know not what to do, two states of mind in me …' (Carson 1998, Sappho's 'Fragment' 51, 8). H.D. playfully, and seriously attempts a new genre, poetic expansion, when she undertakes a literal completion of this Sapphic fragment, pretending to know what the cause of Sappho's dilemma was or making it her own with a deliberate disregard of what this takeover might mean. In 'Fragment 36', H.D. imaginatively plays upon what Sappho's dilemma might have been, giving it a local habitation and a name:

> I know not what to do—
> My mind is reft.
> Is song's gift best?
> Is love's gift loveliest?
>
> I know not what to do,
> Now sleep has pressed
> Weight on your eyelids.
> Shall I break your rest,
>
> Devouring, eager?
> Is love's gift best?

There are quite a few things happening here. First, there is an intimate appropriation of Sappho and her fragment by H.D., born of a sense of inheritance and belonging, understanding and continuity. Next, there is an eloquent gesture by her, towards a legitimate imaginative flight of poesy inspired by this comfortable intimacy with a lineage of poets and poetry—for Sappho could have been an Imagist, so many centuries before Imagism was conceived as a movement. Further, there is an implication that though Sappho's fragment signals no specific direction for the poetic expansion H.D. undertakes, the younger poet as if naturally assumes it to be about sexual love. The fragment then swells—literally, figuratively, to become a new poem with Sappho's words anchoring it as an epigraph but retains an added dimension for being H.D.'s playful, soulful re/creation of what Sappho's poem may have said. And it is surely not accidental that H.D.'s poem—one that takes the place of Sappho's missing poem, much like a living body occupies the space of a body lost—is both serious and light-hearted, a soliloquy of a lover in the throes of sexual desiring at the bedside of the desired one who is asleep. There is both pathos and bathos in the situation: they reside in the two sexed bodies in the poem as much as these effects play games with each other in the text, mimicking the human bodies lying close and yet so far apart, separated by sleep and waking.

What starts as playful fencing with a sleeping beloved—

> Now sleep has pressed
> Weight on your eyelids.
> Shall I break your rest,
> Devouring, eager …

In contemplation of rousing the sleeping beloved to offer 'love's gift'—her body—the speaker then turns sombre suddenly, fearing coldness and rejection:

> Shall I turn and take
> Comfortless snow within my arms,
> Press lips to lips that answer not,
> Press lips to flesh
> That shudders not nor breaks?
> Is love's gift best?

In tune with much of Sappho's fragments, H.D.'s homage to them is a poem filled with longing and the pain of desire unreciprocated. 'You burn me' says Sappho's fragment 38. (Carson 2003). The divided mind in H.D.'s imaginative expansion wrestles like desiring bodies do, waiting, wanting, uncertain and in an exhilarating extended metaphor, 'two white wrestlers' emerge to represent the moment of the freeze, the still point before action breaks out, the mind at pause before contradiction breaks in:

> As two white wrestlers,
> Standing for a match,

Ready to turn and clutch,
Yet never shake
Muscle or nerve or tendon;
So my mind waits
To grapple with my mind

Like the two bodies in suspended animation, 'ready to turn and clutch', the poem uses the divided mind as a refrain, each return to it also captures H.D.'s desire 'to turn and clutch' at Sappho's troubled image of 'two states of mind' at war within. If one sees the impassioned engagement of later poets with Sappho as a live wire, a dialogue continues. If one recognises that a lineage of Sapphistry has leached through the fabric of centuries into our present, then one would have to disagree with Jeanette Winterson when she said in *Art and Lies: A Piece for Three Voices and a Bawd* of Sappho, 'Her body is an apocrypha. She has become a book of tall stories, none of them written by herself. Her name has passed into history. Her work has not. Her island is known to millions now, her work is not' (Winterson 1995, 69). This has emerged as a hyperbolic complaint on many counts though it is of course true that Sappho's birthplace Lesbos is famed for lending its name to a love that dare not speak it. But it cannot any longer be said that she is not known for her work.

In fact, it seems mundane now to talk of Sappho's legacy as one that has merely 'inspired' others: Winterson herself is proof of how Sappho has not only spawned many poets who are texturally in her thrall but of how she has spread under the skin of prose writers (like Winterson) who could not perhaps have written of the female sexual body in ways they have, without a Sapphic shadow watching over them. In Winterson's musings on eros and artifice fictionalised through three voices, *Art and Lies*, Sappho is one of the three (the others are named Picasso and Handel). She pronounces in the Sappho section, 'There's no such thing as autobiography there's only art and lies' (Winterson, 1995, 69). In this our era of (so-called) post-truth, this may be a truism worth exploring for Sappho and her lineage, especially in the context of Sappho's emergence into light so many centuries after she lived, when the bulk of whatever we have of her work now was discovered on bits and pieces of papyri.

It may be fair to say that Sappho's autobiography is being written on the body and by the body, of other poets' texts; thus, it is a story of her life contaminated by her future, albeit one in which she will be resurrected larger than life in the myths that will whirl up and cover us with her firs—and to that extent, it is not autobiography as we know it, but art and lies in a very Modernist sense. And it is her mythic being, contained in fragmented poems on leaves, that sustains her as a contemporary of women writers since the beginning of the twentieth century, when the Sapphic fragments were discovered and began to be translated.

Winterson writes:

> This is what I saw.
>
> A woman balanced on the edge of a parapet, her arms pulled out in long wings …
>
> Balanced on the primaeval ledge she waits for the gift of tongues. She is a howling belly before the coming of the Word …
>
> The Word calls her. The word that is spirit, the word that is breath, the word that hangs the world on its hook. The word bears her up, translates the incoherent flesh into an airy syntax. The word lifts her off all fours and puts a god in her mouth. She distances up the shrunken world in a single span of her tongue. (Winterson 1995, 73)

Sappho is the Word, and the Word is flesh, a living breathing flying calling thing. Sappho made such a word possible, she birthed it, the 'howling belly before the coming of the Word'.

> And so Sappho said:
>]
>]
>]pity
>]trembling
>]flesh by now old age
>]covers
>]flies in pursuit
>]
>]noble
>]taking
>]sing to us
> the one with violets in her lap
>]mostly
>]goes astray
> (Carson 2003, Sappho's 'Fragment' 21, 39)

To read Sappho in Anne Carson's translation, *If Not, Winter*, is to experience, like a voyeur, the intimacy of a poet translating another whom she both reckons a gift, a legacy and one to quarrel with, be impatient about. Carson is no meek translator in awe of classical

Greek grandeur she can play with because it happens to have come to her in bits and pieces, like remnants of many jigsaw puzzles thrown haphazardly in a bucket together, never to find mates that fit entirely into their nooks and crannies. She, instead, possesses her material and makes it her own and like the best of lovers, discovers new ways of getting under the skin of words she has been offered tantalisingly on papyri fragments, unstrung, like stars in a dark sky.

In her introduction to the volume, Carson explains her ways of seeing and doing:

> When translating texts read from papyri, I have used a single square bracket to give an impression of missing matter, so that] or [indicates destroyed papyrus or the presence of letters not quite legible somewhere in the line. It is not the case that every gap or illegibility is specifically indicated: this would render the page a blizzard of marks and inhibit reading. Brackets are an aesthetic gesture toward the papyrological event rather an accurate account of it.... Brackets are exciting. Even though you are approaching Sappho in translation, that is no reason you should miss the drama of trying to read a papyrus torn in half or riddled with holes or smaller than a postage stamp—brackets imply a free space of imaginal adventure. (Carson 2003, xi)

Carson's excitement breathes through the pores of her plentiful brackets, in which the disappearance of words once spoken by a lover are fair game to be chased and to be marked absent—over and over, such is the poignancy of the single bracket that can never be closed. Each absence is a slim but deep gnash, a wounding, a loss. Each absence is also teeming with possibility, promising a space for the imagination to focus on a bracket and run with it, run riot with it. What the absence further does is turn the spotlight on the word or words that have survived; as in love, what survives through loss is precious as a jewel, both for what it is and what the lost signifies. The words that remain seem to have come through a sieve, they are the essence in which the kernels of meaning reside, the extraneous has loosened like dust from their shoulders. Such a sense of the remaindered that raises itself to glory beyond all imagining is the very lesson of Sappho's fragments. It is also a lesson of modernist women's poetry. This was expedient—if serendipitous.

The lesson that the rather mysterious and angular Modernist Gertrude Stein took from Sappho, one might imagine, is just this: that words must emerge as if from a sieve, those that survive when a poet has run a few sentences through some tiny holes. And thought must come in spurts, fierce and tender, as Stein throws carelessly at us in her long poetic tribute to lesbian sexuality, *Lifting Belly*, written between 1915 and 1917:

> Lifting belly. Are you. Lifting.
> Oh dear I said I was tender, fierce and tender.
> Do it. What a splendid example of carelessness.
> It gives me a great deal of pleasure to say yes.
> Why do I always smile.
> I don't know.
> It pleases me.
> You are easily pleased. (Stein 1989, 3)

It is sometimes said that Stein was a poet before the world was ready for her and this seems true of experiments like *Lifting Belly*, where she writes her lovemaking with Alice B. Toklas into word and truth, though they are also, always, 'art and lies'. Her body and her lovers seep into the pages of her slim book which she fills with reverie and repartee and conversation and rumination, all about her love and their love and their lovemaking her writing their bodies their smell their voices their liquids and solids and her words that flow and stop, stop and flow, even while their bellies lift and fall, fall and lift, fierce and tender.

In 1935, Stein said in the first of the four lectures she delivered to students of the University of Chicago that were published together as *Narration* (Stein 1935), that

> If you live a daily life every minute of the day the description of that daily life every day must be moving, it must fill you with complete emotion and it must at the same time be soothing. It must be completing as emotion and it must be soothing. If you live your daily life every minute of the whole day there must really be very little excitement in the narrative with which you while the time away that is natural enough if you think about it and a great deal of the written narrative in English literature has to do with this thing.... (Stein 1935, 4–5)

It is clear from the ways in which she employs language in her lectures, too, as well as in her poetic prose and poetry, that Stein was intent on breaking narrative moulds and forcing the cadences of the poetic everyday to percolate into the body of every text she produced both visually and aurally, continually changing its shape and form and texture and tone, startling the reader and listener into ever-new intimacies with it.

Rebecca Mark, who in 1989 edited the publication of *Lifting Belly* as a standalone long poem, writes: 'When Gertrude Stein writes "Éclair", she asks us "It is clear?" and she also tells us about the pastry éclair, a pastry in two pieces with cream in the middle. Is it clear? She asks us to think about this.

...

Lifting belly can you see the caesars.

I can see what I kiss.' (Stein 1989, 'Introduction', xxxi)

Can we see Caesar, the nickname for Gertrude Stein? ... Can we see the Caesar, the seizure, the muscle spasm, the orgasm? Mark advises, 'When you listen to this passage, think of Caesar not only as a general, as Gertrude, as a salad, but as cease her, seize her, sees her, and finally as a seizure, a tremor during sex, an orgasm.' (Stein 1989, xxxii)

Stein says in her fourth lecture of 1935,

> One of you brought me poetry to read the other day and I said remember that if you have to use strained words to say what you have to say by strain existing in the words that you are using, what feels to you a rare emotion becomes common-place not ordinary that is alright but just common-place and a common-place thing does not contain feeling. That is what makes a common-place thing a common-place thing, that that it does not contain feeling. (Stein 1935, 46–47)

She experimented with language in her poetry and prose, both, almost entirely as if to avoid this at all cost, this production of a common-place thing—'not ordinary that is alright'—because 'a common-place thing does not contain feeling'. Strained words, Stein said, transforms a rare emotion into a common-place one; Stein's words flow, unstemmed and unstrained, moving forward in little eddies and jet-spurts, making thoughts and utterances loop back on themselves, transforming the ordinary into the rare and shaping a body upon the page that mirrors these liquid shapes and flows. Always conscious of the way words chisel not just meanings but also their own lives and breath upon each page they occupy, Stein juggled with rhymes, synonyms and homonyms in wild, gasping, sexual abandon until 'done'.

> Why am I if I am uncertain reasons may inclose.
> Remain remain propose repose chose.
> I call carelessly that the door is open
> Which if they may refuse to open
> No one can rush to close.
> Let them be mine therefor.

Everybody knows that I chose.
Therefor if therefore before I close.
I will therefore offer therefore I offer this.
Which if I refuse to miss may be miss is mine.
I will be well welcome when I come.
Because I am coming.
Certainly I come having come.
These stanzas are done. ('Stanzas in Meditation: 83')

Queerness reclined across the skin of Stein's life and loves and took fruit in surprising forms in her writing. A close friend of Pablo Picasso's, Stein was also writing what has been called cubist poetry, repeating words and phrases like building blocks that constructed thought and image insistently on bare pages, inspired by cubist art that worked with repetitive lines and angles to pull together, and yet distance, the artist from the art. Stein wrote two memorable, mystifying poems for her friend Picasso, who never read a word of her poetry even as he discussed endlessly with her the intricacies of the modernism they were on the threshold of, and carving into being, everyday. The second of these, 'If I Told Him, A Completed Portrait of Picasso' (1924), uses—like many of Stein's experiments with word-sounds—repetition, to create an overwhelming but blurred sense of meaning, a 'meaning' inlaid with an indulgence of him, an easy, teasing intimacy between long-time friends, a certain affectionate exasperation. A portrait of Picasso inasmuch as it is *her* portrait of him, the one she knows in the way she knows and in the only way she can convey it, through oblique words and sounds. Her focus on the clipped repetition of certain words also deliberately denies the possibility of stringing together sentences that will explicate her thoughts, even while 'A Completed Portrait' in her title mockingly insists on this very impossibility made possible. Together with 'If I Told Him'—the first half of the title, separated by a comma from the second—Stein seems to be saying, with humour and a sharp reality, that what she would tell him would throw back at him a completed portrait of himself, that it could only be in repetitive fragmented phrases, that the cadences from its sounds would hold some hazy, yet deep and 'complete' meaning, as would the frame it built on the page, and that here, finally, was a cubist portrait in a poem: a gift from her in return for the 'complete' portrait that he had painted of her. All this, and so much more—or, less.

He he he he and he and he and and he and he and he and and as and as he and as he and he. He is and as he is, and as he is and he is, he is and as he and he and as he is and he and he and and he and he.

> Can curls rob can curls quote, quotable.
> As presently.
> As exactitude.
> As trains.
> Has trains.
> Has trains.
> As trains.
> As trains.
> Presently.
> Proportions.
> Presently.
> As proportions as presently.
> Farther and whether.
> Was there was there was there what was there was there what was there was there there was there.
> Whether and in there. ('If I Told Him, A Completed Portrait of Picasso')

Georges Perec, in *Species of Spaces and Other Pieces* (1974), conveys evocatively the games one plays with selves, spaces, locations and words, juggling with print and blank on his pages:

> I write. I inhabit my sheet of paper, I invest it, I travel across it.
>
> I incite *blanks*, *spaces* (jumps in the meaning, discontinuities, transitions, changes of key).
>
> I write
in the
margin
>
> I start a new paragraph. I refer to a footnote.
I go to a new sheet of paper.
>
> …
>
> This is how space begins, with words only, signs traced on the blank page. To describe space: to name it, to trace it, like those portolano-makers who saturated the coastlines with the names of harbours, the names of capes, the names of inlets, until in the end the land was only separated from the sea by a continuous ribbon of text. Is the aleph, that place in Borges from which the entire world is visible simultaneously, anything other than an alphabet?' (Perec 1974, 11–13)

In Stein, as in Sappho and in H.D., the body and the page are both travelled upon and travelling, always; the movements uncharted and riotous. In the sexual and the creative, there has been from the beginnings of time a metaphoric obsession with land and its explorers of the new and unknown; queer sexuality and feminist word-making bring an edge to this adventuring that births the possibility of an implosion. They turn the discovering in upon itself. In *Lifting Belly*, as Stein traverses flowers, food, words, memories and her lover's body with equal intensity, she invokes geography almost inevitably:

> Lifting belly naturally celebrates
> We naturally celebrate.
> Connect me in places.
> Lifting belly.
> No no don't say that.
> Lifting belly oh yes.
> Tax this.
> Running behind a mountain.
> I fly to thee. (Stein 1989, 25)

Stein was actually doing in the first quarter of the twentieth century what Jeanette Winterson did at the end of the century, from the 1980s, when writing loves and other relationships into being: allowing the shapes and sounds of words in themselves and on the page to crystallise and melt in prose that could easily merge with the poem laid out like a tall sparse body in print, or the prose-poem spread voluptuously over white spaces that leaves no gaps for breaths to be taken.

In her celebrated long poetic prose rumination, *Written on the Body*, Jeanette Winterson (1992) pays Steinian homage to the lifting of bellies:

> 'Explore me', you said and I collected my ropes, flasks and maps, expecting to be back home soon. I dropped into the mass of you and I cannot find the way out. Sometimes I think I'm free, coughed up like Jonah from the whale, but then I turn a corner and recognise myself again. Myself in your skin, myself lodged in your bones, myself floating in the cavities that decorate every surgeon's wall. That is how I know you. You are what I know. (Winterson 1992, 120)

Experimental poetics that write the lesbian body, the body somersaulting into word, lifting belly as it dances and spins—they are merely making good a long-held lineage, saved on bits of papyrus on the island of Lesbos in sixth century BC. Sappho wrote, 'I would not think to touch the sky with two arms' (Carson 2003, Sappho's 'Fragment', 52) but her fragments have changed the tenor of touch so firmly, and with such fragility, that the poem has become a body of parts, quivering and shivering with shock and delight.

Despite every loss, every longing, every jealousy and dread, Sappho's 'Fragment', 31 is at once wryly affirmative and affirmatively wry:

> whoever he is who opposite you
> sits and listens close
> to your sweet speaking …
>
> for when I look at you, even a moment, no speaking
> is left in me
>
> no: tongue breaks and thin
> fire is racing under skin …
>
> and cold sweat holds me and shaking
> grips me all …

Carson in her translated version retrieves a line that is set apart, and makes up an incomplete last thought, slightly sombre,

> But all is to be dared, because even a person of poverty (Carson 2003, Sappho's 'Fragment' 31, 63)

Carson refutes the common idea that this poem is about jealousy and involves a triangulation of people. She contends:

> Jealousy is beside the point; the normal world of erotic responses is beside the point; praise is beside the point. It is a poem about the lover's mind in the act of constructing desire for itself.... For in this dance the people do not move. Desire moves. Eros is a verb. (Carson 1998, 16–17)

That is indeed what Sappho has been able to inject into all the poetry that remains in intimately sexual conversation with her so many centuries later, the idea that eros is a verb that travels, making word of the body: the body becomes a poem and the poem a body that burns with longing and dances—because for 'even a person of poverty', 'all is to be dared'. This was a lesson that a succession of later queer poets found in Sappho's Fragments and internalised in their making of poems. Carson and Winterson's translations and experimental poetics have borne forward this lesson of daring into the twenty-first century, making contemporary, all over again, that ancient Sapphic art of word and the absence of word together caressing a poem into being—and the artful body that the words form on the page bearing as much significance as the meanings of the words themselves.

It is through this lineage of queer-feminist poetics, validating both the female body and the body of the poem as erotic, that a method for doing the humanities may be emergent, continually focusing on the corporeal texture of lives and loves and words all at the same time and interchangeably. The shape and feel of desire, between women and by women here, and embodied in poetry through its language which is fragmentary and terse but teeming with passionate intensity, this is how we may flag a way to enter and encounter the humanities. The method is in the immersion, the madness, the pursuit of meaning and shape of a single dangling word as a body and the piling up of words in patterns floating and running across pages as bodies. Tracing the movements of letters and words and phrases on a page, marking the ellipses and the spaces and the brackets, savouring the repetitions as though they are lovers' caresses: bodies speak and words reach out to touch each other or turn away. We read their stories by unearthing what is lost as much as what remains, by unlayering, by uncovering, by searching, finding and not finding. Bodies and texts are palimpsests, like Sappho's papyri, like our stories of desiring and losing. We are tantalised by what is missing; we are terrified and yet seduced by the signs and signifiers we discover: we do the humanities like a lover, erotically.

REFERENCES

Carson, Anne. *Eros: The Bittersweet*. Illinois: Dalkey Archive Press, [1986]1998.

———, ed. and trans. *If Not, Winter: Fragments of Sappho*. New York: Random House, 2003.

Doolittle, Hilda (H.D.). 'A Poet in the Wilderness: Songs of Anacreon.' In *Visions and Ecstasies, Selected Essays*. New York: David Zwirner Books, 2019.

Perec, Georges. *Species of Spaces and Other Pieces*. Penguin Classics, 1974.

Stein, Gertrude, ed. Rebecca Mark. *Lifting Belly*. Tallahassee: The Naiad Press, 1989.

———. *Narration*. Illinois: University of Chicago Press, 1935.

Winterson, Jeanette. *Written on the Body*. Vintage International, 1992.

———. *Art and Lies: A Piece for Three Voices and a Bawd*. Canada: Vintage, 1995.

FLUX

TRANSLATION'S DISSIDENCE: MIRAJI BECOMES SAPPHO

Geeta Patel

Wandering from town to house, a wayfarer misplaces
the road that gathers him home. That which was once mine
and your belongings, both foresworn
from memory. Mine and yours no longer known.

Nagarī nagarī phirā musāfir
ghar kā rāstā bhūl gayā,
kyā hai merā, kyā hai terā,
apnā parāyā bhūl gayā.—Mīrājī

Who was Miraji (1912–1949)? Miraji was a resolute re-composer of prose and voluptuously synaesthetic, as well as an exquisitely philosophical poet in Urdu, an avid translator, a voracious essayist and an edgily incisive attuned, empathetic reader, of whom one could, following most appraisals of Miraji's capacious and sometimes startling interventions in both lyric and criticism say, that Miraji augured a new strain of Urdu modernism in the cauldron of anti-colonial politics.[1] Even as Miraji was juggling accolades for lyrical feats, Miraji was also fending off excoriations; widely circulated portrayals of Miraji as an opaque, enigmatic versifier and a supposed sexual pervert. Though many of the questions Miraji fostered sifted through the semantics of solitude, Miraji rarely worked alone—preferring the intellectual camaraderie of those who shared a sense of the times as well as those virulently opposed. Miraji saw them-self always in concert with fellow artists—'*adab nigār*—and singing endlessly towards the infinite finale of a lingering route through the murk, mist or smoke or the *dhundalānā*—of loss.[2]

Dhundalānā, a concept to which Miraji returned in several texts, is a moody nominal adjective that illuminates a stance of being, blended with, melded into or promising an aesthetic politico-philosophical vantage—the animating condition for Miraji's particular registers of modernism (*jadīdiyāt*). In one such place, an essay on new poetry, Miraji teases out *dhundalānā*'s filaments and its nuanced habitations;

here Miraji crafts a mythopoetic, historical genesis for the lyric of the time.

> After this a besieging storm crossed the seven seas and struck. The hurricane of western culture, organization, and education hit. It funneled up dry twigs and leaves, but in its glory also helped new buds sprout. Now, slowly new voices surfaced into hearing....
>
> And the hubbub of all these musical hues stirred up a turbulence, waves seethed out from it that birthed new stages for the journey of life. But whose murkiness/smokiness (*dhundalānā*) was like a maze. The sort of tangle in which only a few could trace the right road and take it.
>
> This was the sensibility of the new poetry in that era. New poets stood at crossroads, a threshold from which many roads ventured outwards—to the right, the left, the front and the back. But poets did not really know which road they had chosen. What value the experiments of the past had for them. For how long they had to stand thus. How long the despairing, violent, agitated sensibility of the present would hang around with them and on which path must they find their way. What desecration the ambience, the quality of their future would pose for them.
>
> New poets slipped away (evaded their circumstances) by using their profound curiosity as their excuse, when truthfully, they were only lost or entombed in the murky/smoky (*dhundalā*) reflection (*aks*) of themselves or their communities. Around them, the old sustenance on the strength of which people could survive or endure everyday (Heimlich) hassles had faded away; they no longer held sway. Poets were now alone and needed to chase support. Sometimes they turned to the wrong things for help. Sometimes even if they reached a place that might provide them with the right sort of assistance/succour they were flummoxed; they didn't even quite know where they had arrived. The major cause of these circumstances was that they didn't know the contemporary foundations of the edifices they had to embellish and which forms had to be drawn up along new templates.
>
> The reasons for this turbulence can be said to be found in the opaque (*mub-ham*)[3] period of 1857, when the old bindings that held the social and political together began to fray to make way for new customs, habits, arrangements and institutions. One can say that a space of a few generations had already been born between new emerging young poets and their elders; those who had seen the intellectual pushes and pulls, quandaries as a pulse.

> If we consider the past of today's poets from a political vantage point, we see that along with our abject state arising from the attenuation of national governance or rule were things that excited or stimulated political life and that these were merely the diminished servilities brought about by adversity. They assumed those political shapes through which our nation while battling the world began to birth new joys and a curiosity and vehement desire for progress and freedom along every path/venue of life. (Jalibi 1988, 523)[4]

These passages make it that clear Miraji envisioned *dhundalānā* as an aesthetic psychic state/circumstance in which poets at the crossroads blundered in a deep bind, a morass of mazes. They idled, skulked, dawdled interminably (pace Arondekar), semi-comatose, enervated, almost unheedingly baffled, swathed in dulled fog, unable (except for a few) to find their route back or to forge a path forward—these were the circumstances in which they were snarled (albeit continuing to draft lyrics) before and after 1857. Politics then, the extant political brutalities and challenges, the estranging potentialities of the time come together with aesthetics to engender *dhundalānā*. Let's call this condition political melancholia, suspended perhaps even toxic depression in the Freudian sense, emanating from a sort of loss where the object, aim (*maqsad*) and thing (*bāt*) had faded away from any chance of being brought to the surface or been so stuffed so deep in one's historical innards (the space of a few generations to which Miraji alludes might call this to mind) so that it was no longer amenable, not even handy to be mourned painstakingly, then released or soaked up in the Freudian sense.[5] David Eng (2019), in his newest take on melancholia with Shinhee Han, quoting Sigmund Freud reminds us that though melancholics might know whom they have lost, they don't know what they have lost. Mourning occurs through time—perhaps fabricates time's flow. Here, however, it is as if even time itself was gummed up; poets didn't even know from whence they had arrived, where they stand, what was portended for them. The past, present and future, all evaded them.

Why do I go to melancholia?[6]

That state of anguish without surcease, grieving without end, which could be said to exemplify melancholia begins with Miraji's predecessor, Altaf Husain Hali, the nineteenth-century poet and critic. Hali composed a *nauhah*, an elegy to the demise of poetry itself, a poem whose sorrow offers up the melancholic palette to which Miraji alludes:

> Poetry has died, it can never be resuscitated ... even the dust, the ashes of death effaced ... I call to the heavens as witness, can anyone be rubbed out more thoroughly than this ... bringing lyric to mind

> over and over uproots my soul, guts it … those whom we lost have given up on us as well … Ghalib and Shefta, Nayyar, Azad and Zauq, time can never unveil these faces for us to gaze upon again. (Patel 2002, 174–175)

Hali does not fall into mourning in the Freudian sense, he does not let grief over who and what has died for him wash him away utterly, and then slowly, excruciatingly grief surfaces again so that he can lose himself in another. Hali grieves interminably and Miraji's *dhundalānā* seems to be its aftermath. Ghalib and Shefta, Nayyar, Azad and Zauq were also poets renowned for their handiness, their *kalā*, their nimble skill, which was love in all its arcane, irritating, soul heaving, searing, minute and epic-making lyrical glory.

Letting this corpus fall somewhat into disuse, Hali re-organised, re-oriented his aesthetic inclinations and his own expertise as a poet away from the tug and pull of love, away from the cast of characters that enacted love's often dire plotted courses, away from the mise-en-scène of gardens, wine haunts, floral cornucopia, the palette that churned feeling; denuding love's resonant metaphoric hues of their succour. The objects and ornate metaphors through which desire, yearning, longing consummated and shaped itself were stripped of their significance. Rather, Hali veered towards other topics and lyrical technae: advocating aesthetic naturalism (one early foray into modernism), *necharal shai'rī* that included poignant descriptions of seasons, alongside a political revitalisation of Muslim history. Many of those metaphors, whiff of breeze, roses wilting to death that stirred love, became the objects of description. Along the way, Hali's lyrics often flattened into literalism; he withdrew his investments in his predecessors, many of whom were his teachers without mourning their demise, dropping metaphorics along the way.[7] Almost as if as he exiled his own past, he jettisoned a self and the tongue he once inhabited.[8]

Hali did this without giving his heart over wholly, without reinvesting himself utterly and unreservedly. Hali withheld a small chunk of what might have washed him away in its torrent, brought him completely to his knees. Hali's melancholic reservation was a profoundly political one as we will go onto see (Cheng 2000; Eng and Han 2019; Munoz 2009). Through two generations of composers, that small piece reserved by Hali fell into disuse perhaps, disappeared through who knows what cracks, no longer available to touch and to eventually release: its effect was the *dhundalānā* of which Miraji speaks. What comprises this loss, what might its enabling conditions have been?

A synoptic, schematic history of the early-to-mid-nineteenth century as a counterpoint to the one Miraji offered which I translated in the opening sequences of this chapter, will provide a leeway into the conditions of possibility I am provoking into presence here. Altaf Hussain Hali's despairing lament was both a requiem to the 1857 revolution and grief over the reverberations of colonial educational policy. Education was one small room in an entire architecture for producing 'benevolence'—the gifts for their welfare bestowed on the colonised—which included hospitals, lunatic asylums, pensions, orphan schools, etc. Hali himself was a recipient and had been funded out of the money that was set aside for education by the colonial state, so he was well-versed in the subtly graphic effects that ensued (Bentinck 1977; Bentinck website; Burke 1884; Dirks 2006; Kerr 1852; Lushington 1824; Minault 1998). Colonial pedagogical projects (Viswanathan) were hegemonic—doing their work by marrying moral fibre to aesthetic forms (Samaddar 2014). Or more simply put, colonial education was vested in transforming the askew moral habits of colonised denizens by inducting them into new ways of making art, of crafting lyric, from verbs to topics to metrical forms (Grant 1813). These were relayed through certain genres of English literature and Greco-Roman literature and law which had been recouped in the late eighteenth and nineteenth-century Britain—all of them translated into Indian languages in order to do what they must. The aesthetic was infected with decadence; love lyric being a preeminent carrier. The cure for dissipation, debauchery, was staunchly proper education that inoculated prose and poetry against iniquity. Money was parcelled off to translation projects. And then to prizes given for newly keyed lyric and prose that would show off, flaunt their debt to translated salutary materials (Pritchett 1994). The result: languages that would speak their art in a colonial tongue, and so, sinew new moralities (Patel 2007, 2016).

As a financial beneficiary of colonial beneficence, Hali fleshed out the necessary paradox, the double bind in which writers who were scrounging around for patrons lived: he took the money and entombed his lyrical forebearers in a litany of accusations, debased their lyrical feats, consigned them to oblivion and handed up a piece of his soul[9] (Patel 2016). In so doing, Hali gave the British a return on their investment but not a complete one. Melancholia, grief without end or surcease, seemed to be the only viable bulwark, a holding station, a last resort against the takeover of everything that might matter (Eng and Han 2019).

And the effects were those of which Miraji speaks—wandering dolefully in the mists—a melancholic's habitations. We might think of *dhundalānā* then as the traces, the scars of maiming (Puar 2017), the upshot of colonial necropolitics (Mdembe 2003) homing in on, targeting and razing aesthetic forms. In the face of this, Hali's melancholia makes sense—but what Miraji speaks of are its intergenerational effects, melancholia's lingering on in the cells of Miraji's compatriots' sentences. Might modernism, then be for Miraji, a possible therapeutic poetics leading through towards and perhaps out of this intergenerationally bequeathed melancholia.

The loss of value in Urdu's literary forbearers under the constant barrage of criticism levelled by colonial commentators against their aesthetic habits was absorbed by Urdu writers in the nineteenth and twentieth centuries and floated to the surface in their judgements *(ma'yyār)* on beauty and pleasure, in their accounts of what failed and what succeeded. This, after all, is the work of hegemony in the Gramscian sense, it shows up in the ways in which taste is given or is on the tongue. To reanimate, in a certain fashion, what had been scrapped on the way and through it engender the circumstances that might bestow life to their voice and idioms, poets in the twentieth century such as Miraji tried their hand at translation.

To speak to this, I turn to Miraji's essay on Sappho. In this closing section, I will focus more closely on it while bringing in fragments and titbits from other writings. I have chosen this essay because it, in particular, forges responses that speak to the narrowest fissures through which violence comes to reside in the ordinary. In other words, this essay on Sappho performs its tasks by taking on ideologies that planted their tentacles deep into the political grammar, desires and into each word crafted by Miraji's compatriots. The essay's plotting and grammar of the evocations of desire, love, anguish, joy, gender, history and governmentality incite *indirect* commentaries on the processes of governance that left Urdu poets in a coma. Indirection was, paradoxically and ineluctably, the only direct way to intervene in the cellular (in hegemonies) and through it funnel into what had been displaced from immediate view. Here, one might want to drift slightly away from the Freudian psyche to bring a medicalised analytic to bear on melancholia—the Unani/Greek lexicon of humours.[10,11] Melancholia's scourge was black bile, seated in the liver.[12] Livers are the organs/channels where love's potency finds its place for Urdu and Unani medicine, where love's blood is stored. Medicinal revitalisation of those suffering from melancholia's doldrums, its dolorous, lugubrious, enervating effects might well be through galvanising the hot, humid jolt into one's senses that love demands—Sappho, the poet of love, was an ideal instrument or medium.

As I will go on to show, Miraji's impetus was double-edged and fraught with the double-bind of that time. The work or the *'amal*, the *kām*, that Miraji performed dug in deep, pulled out the guts of everyday phrasing, tugged and tussled with the tacit as well as baldly stated addressees of (those who were asked to listen to) the rhetorical gesticulations and genuflections of political lyric, a lyric which had been hewn for their putative edification. Miraji guided everything and wrote towards those who held tightly onto the value of their place as addressors. Since, Miraji's aim, or *maqsad*, was nothing less than the unravelling of hegemonies in their minutest capillary flows, Miraji rhetoric steered towards the most potent and virulent of their effects. This was the incubation of realism (the anti-love-lyric lyric), the literary form that was believed by fellow writers to be the most efficacious political aesthetic for the only robust indictment of colonialism: *haqīqat parastī*, the twentieth-century rendition of Hali's naturalism (*necaral*) or mimesis—much of it magnetising around the place of and the status of women.[13] To target the literalism of mimesis, Miraji had to evade or slide past the crudely literal, veering instead to an arsenal of rhetorical gestures of indirection and possibility, from allegory to metaphorics, slyly insinuating through them other venues for gazing, for intellectual labour, for fancy—*takhayyul*, a word that fused thinking with dreaming, both of which were terms essential to Miraji's repertoire. In bringing a Perso-Arabic and Sanskrit lyrical glossary, methodically withheld from and straying away from parsimonious realism to augment Miraji's theoretical vocabulary, Miraji also implicitly advocated a literary path that swerved away from an exclusively English one (while refusing to give up on it entirely).

When I look at Miraji's entire corpus of essays on poets that came from other places and other times, taken along with the translations of those lyricists for Miraji's own time, I see something more sinuous in them than I had when I first wrote on them in my book, where I portrayed them as an alterior archive, one that broke with the conventional English curriculum that had been installed for the edification of the colonised (Patel 2018; Viswanathan 2014) and that brokered other lineages in their stead. Looking closely and incisively at one essay helps me understand each such essay as a quest, whose project is sometimes baldly stated but more often insinuated into the flow of its plotting.

Miraji's essay on Baudelaire for example stakes its narrative impetus explicitly at its outset—on the fetishised figurations, the centrepieces of the pedantic political poetics of Miraji's time: women, workers and the poor. Baudelaire furnishes another iconography and pedigree for them than one garnished from colonised South Asia—so the gauntlet is also thrown at Europe's feet, to its ghouls tucked away in its own dark corners (Miraji 161–190). Sappho, on the other hand, does her dirty, so to speak, through constant subtle reminders, a mnemonic code, as it were, to a webbing of allusions which scroll backwards to the education policies that engendered the forgetting entailed in melancholia. In so doing, the reminders clarify, *izahār*, a path through the labyrinths, into a truth sedimented in them. Foucault might call alethurgy, glossed in Urdu as *izahār*, of which he says,

> the set of possible verbal or non-verbal procedures by which one brings to light what is laid down as true as opposed to false, hidden, inexpressible, unforeseeable, or forgotten, and say that there is no exercise of power without something like alethurgy … hegemony cannot be exercised without something like alethurgy. (Foucault 2010, 7)

Miraji, in this essay on Sappho, revisits alethurgy, as *izahār*, clarity several times. So, Foucault's appeal to alethurgy, perhaps as a device to speak to what Miraji is attempting to massage, *dhundalānā* the state in which even the possibility of finding one's way to *izahār* fails, might be particularly apposite.

Alethurgy had to be claimed by Miraji in another key. Hegemony, to paraphrase Foucault was about conduct—Miraji's *maqsad*, then, was directed at conduct, its potentialities, its foreclosures and its miscarriages. And given the Greek textual history that Foucault makes his base in the lectures on the government of the living, where he explores the lineaments of alethurgy, in a peculiarly apposite fashion, Miraji turns to Sappho. Here, in Miraji's essay, *izahār* or disclosure, or bringing to light, hurtles headlong into the possibilities of its constant, consistent and necessary failure. Miraji exploits many of these possibilities in the grammar of sentences, in the plotted flow of narrative, in the miniscule twists of rhetorical play, the call of images, the folding of their own voice into others, in melancholia.

Sappho is an ideal muse for Miraji, partly because she herself had been brought to life so many times as herself, in translation. In the essay on her, Miraji talks about the ebb and flow of translation as tolling the tales of Sappho's demise and rebirth from the crypt of forgetting each time a translator found her again, most notably in the hands of the nineteenth-century decadents and more recently with translations based on new poem fragments. Sappho died—in the hands of her interlocutors, the quarry, Miraji explains, of Christian pogroms against immorality. And Sappho's chronicle is told via Miraji's charting of the loves she had, dying a little death, each time she lost one love and finding her being again as she hitched her feelings onto another. A poet whose biography, as narrated by Miraji, began in exile and ended with a chase, away from her own land, her *vatan*, to pursue a boatman she loved that led to her spectacularised suicide, Sappho's own life required her to find her place over and over every time she lost it (Nagy 1990).[14] Sappho's life becomes the melancholic's object lesson—a how to lyrical manual for mourning.[15]

But, more significantly perhaps, the deepest rapport that Miraji as a poet and translator had with Sappho, one where Miraji begins to fold into her, was her love for another woman, Atthis. Here Miraji hails readers, asking them to feel for her—as *hamdard*—in a kind of acutely shared listening, through which a reader comes to experience Sappho's joy and love and to suffer her grief. It is through Sappho's queer loves and her wandering life, the genres through which she unearths possibility that we might see the genesis of pathways through melancholia. The history of Urdu poetics in the nineteenth and early twentieth centuries was love lost—love was forsaken as a lyrical device and those who sang love vanished from view—and translation was its vehicle. Love's metaphors furnish the arsenal for the language of grief, even if the same object gets re-instated when it is found again. In the final analysis, in Miraji's hands Sappho becomes, as she does for so many others who have spoken in her voice in translation, the poetess best known for love lyric and lyric attuned particularly to Sapphic desire.

But I'd like to pause here for a moment and turn for a small hiatus to the idea of the quest in Miraji's work that might provide an augmenting mise-en-scène for the essay on Sappho. Miraji wrote a number of poems I have termed journey-*jātrī*-poems—each meandered, almost in dreaming, along the chancy, magical path towards creativity—*takhalikiyāt*. Creativity was the soul of much of Miraji's corpus, its raison d'etre, the search for it, where, how and what consumed Miraji. And it had to—given what Miraji believed was true, alethurgy, about that time—that poets were grasping about, blundering in a blanketing morass of loss, with a denuded sense of their past and with only murky avenues towards a thin tenuous future. Creativity, metaphors that hummed with potency, the craft of the voice, required feeling, *ehsās*, coupled with intellect, *zahan*. Without each, the other was hollow, did not invigorate, provided no fodder for the pen, fired no pleasure in listeners; words flattened out into literalist tedium. Sappho, then, comes along as the ideal muse for this quest. The essay on Sappho can be seen as a journey poem, on a quest towards creativity, the craft of the voice invigorated through feeling, *ehsās*, coupled with intellect, *zahan*; but more importantly it is a gendered and sexualised lyrical tongue.

So, what does Miraji do in the essay? Miraji opens the essay on Sappho with *dhundalānā*—the state in which Miraji says Greek lyric lies, from which the pathways to Sappho, the voice that enfleshes creativity, must be tracked. Sappho then is one possible route through *dhundalānā*, not in some undemanding sense, but one that is thorny and discomfiting, as barbed and meandering as the slow course of mourning. Miraji's *maqsad* is to bring Urdu's creativity to life, in the face of its floundering in and under the aegis of great loss, from the bits and bobs that he can scrounge from wherever he finds them.[16] Sappho is peculiarly apposite for Miraji's orchestration of a world out of the fissures and crumbs that have been left behind as a legacy of Miraji's own past—after all, she herself is compiled out of the muddied melodies from ancient Greece.

As I have indicated, colonial education policies and projects and their governance of the living were often underwritten by substantiating claims garnered from or fashioned through classical authors translated (literally and figuratively). Miraji's journey into alethurgy via Sappho begins with them. Calling Plato, Socrates and Athens the purported fount of European civilization Miraji fleshes Sappho through phrases and quotes taken from this archive: most notably, dotting the essay with Socrates' invocation to her as 'beautiful Sappho' (321). Miraji then goes onto Catullus and Horace, who 'profit' from her writings and Homer, by whom she was so revered that she could be justly named a 'poet' (322). Here, we see Miraji's use of the word *duniya* or world as a something that organises a canon both in its successes and shortfalls, its culling of materials for profit. It is the world that British officials commanded into being.

When Miraji brings Sappho to presence via the annals of classical authors, something askance is birthed; classical enchantment loses its gloss somewhat. First, because Sappho is the very embodiment of depravity. Then, though Miraji launches his essay with giving both Greece and Rome their due, Miraji very quickly turns that around on its head, with a searing exposé of the dire state of gendered subjects in Greece—an indictment of Greek democracy that failed some of its most vulnerable denizens.

This line of exploratory historiography is suggestive of what the essay poetically plays out, the provenance of conduct and history in the most capacious sense possible. The essay meanders. In doing so, as *jātrī* nazms did to similar effect, Miraji's essay could be said then to be a lyrical paean to, a series of byways to conduct: the stances poets take, history as a reservoir for comportment, what poetics can evoke for us as a guideline to our own demeanour, the legacies of composition that seed the mannerisms of analysis we usher in.

Miraji composes the essay through reiterations of the vocabulary associated with surmise: *andāzah* (estimation), *ho saktā hai* (it might have been), *mumkin hai* (it's possible), *hu'ā hogā* (it might have happened), *lāzmī* (what must be). In closing this chapter, I will offer possibly the most salient features of what Miraji might have hoped to achieve with 'Saffo'. One is tucked into the word '*shāyad*' perhaps, conjecture and surmise.

Perhaps it is the signature of prophecy and the essay is a recital, an inventory of the syntax of surmise, of what might be in the guise of what might have been or must have been. History is conjectural but not merely so, the possibilities it brings to bear Miraji seems to say, bear the heft of futures which are thrown from it. The past, then, is as prophetic as the future, the present lying in their wake (suspended between *abad* and *azal*, between eternity and time without an ending). Perhaps this is Walter Benjamin's angel of history, facing the past? Almost everything that has the texture of historical truth about Sappho, described with meticulous tender care so that it comes across as a vivacious present—beginning with Sappho's mother's rush across the sharply scented pine forests of Lesbos to Mythilene with her young children, following upon her father's death, her library of contemporary resources, her staunch political stances, the spirited conclave of poets who composed in concert—is hedged in by surmise, perhaps this was so. All these are prophetic futures by which Sappho's voice would live in the time given by Miraji to fellow sojourners (Miraji, 324–328). And because we are speaking of Greece, the heartland of the classical, whose registers ground colonial claims for themselves and the prophetic future they propose, for those who they have colonised, the grammar of surmise gently deflects the censuring surety of their pens. Even as Sappho's past unravels the labyrinth in which Urdu found itself and its lost past is unobtrusively smoothed away in surmise and what is possible.

Here, I'd like to return to the lexicography of surmise, lodged not in the more predictably historical but in the poetry that Miraji's translated, in Miraji own inimitable style as something that expands the sparseness of Sappho's fragments into lyrical, dreaming history. Fidelity is not Miraji's stance, recomposition is—in tuning Sappho's voice to Miraji own lyrical one, Miraji calls her back, resurrects her for Urdu (Apter 2014). In her rebirth Sappho marries, loves both men and women. And love, after all, is all about surmise. Who hasn't turned to guesswork when they hurtle into love: from potential to possible? Is it true, can it be true, how certain am I, does she or doesn't she, am I imagining it: are all such familiar phrases when love hails one, overtake one's senses, turns one into a bumbling bubbling fool. Her marriage is entirely coded in surmise; and not one with which Sappho is enchanted. And even Phaon, Sappho's last great love, assumes gloriously inspired shape through surmise:

> It's possible that this astonishingly graceful young man might have been hired by Sappho to row her in his river barge. And perhaps when, on the water's surface lit up by the full moon, under the stars' shadows, the flat bottom barge flowed towards her, Phaon

> standing by his oar, his beauty and grace turned to flesh, this poet, so overflowing with feeling may have arrived at love. (276–277)

Women, however, are never given the grammar of surmise, the may-have-been, the possible. For them, Miraji uses only certainty. And, more than in any other place, Miraji's portrayals of desire emanate directly out of the poetry. It's as though Miraji's voice takes over from Sappho's, flowing easily into enjambment from the verse. Miraji is born again, as Sappho sings, whether in ecstasy or deep mourning, jealousy or joy. In love's fervour, melancholia loosens its tenacious grip. And here is where Miraji asks readers and for the poets that belong to *jadīdiyāt* for *hamdardī*—asks them to follow in those footsteps and become one with Sappho. Bring *takhayyul* to *takhlīq* in *ikhlāq*. The embers of envy ignited Sappho's heart because by now her passion had turned stormy.

> Like the gods I've come to see what is before me/ the one who sits facing me/I look upon your face/ attend your voice/your sexy style shakes my heart/Ah! Longing for sacrifice stuns me so/my voice faded to nothing/were I to glimpse you/my tongue would hitch to silence/words empty in my mouth/fire mortify my flesh/I am blind when I turn to look/monstrous noise fill my ears/but 'no' is scripted into sorrow's fate/my life cannot deliver me/I endure grief as I wait/I cannot see my death even when I search for it far and wide/my death refuses to reveal when it will show up/.

And in 'Prison of love':

> Passion shackled me/rebellious terror brought me to my knees/ In bitterness is also the clarity of milk/where tyranny there also kindness/I've come to understand love's respite in a heart's ordeal/ my life burned to nothing/Atthis has left me/she's bound her soul to a stranger. (Miraji, 274–276)

Atthis' loss is death withheld, held out but not given, Sappho's love for her deeply paradoxical, flesh mortified and tantalised, tender and pitiless. With Phaon's bad faith, however, Sappho takes her death into her own hands, leaping into the sea in Sicily the place to which she had earlier been exiled. Once Sappho had died, Miraji was free to release the prophetic poet and bring to life 'Prophecy from another time', the first lyrical fragment Miraji translated in the essay on the poet. Rather than finishing off Sappho's life with her historical death, Miraji restores her in the closing section of this essay. Sappho, Miraji says, tells us that love makes even a brute a lyricist. 'In a world of sorrow dusted with agony/I live, survive in a sort of loss, as though the wind's lament sends my tale of love on/that mischief though brutal/leaves not a trace' (Miraji 281). But it does change something profound for Miraji and Sappho's sorrow traces possibilities that are more than mere surmise. For after these lines, written ostensibly for Phaon and his faithlessness, Miraji commences a conversation with/as Sappho—a *guftagu* in which Sappho goes back and forth exchanging verses with Indian poets who lived in Miraji's present and then back to the past. First, Akhtar Sheerani, the leading romantic poet from Miraji's time, who inspired Miraji and then Mirabai the medieval mystic in whose voice Miraji also sang, and finally, further back Bhratṛhari, who Miraji also translated. They become Sappho's conclave, it is to them she speaks in verse and they respond in kind.

But the converse between poets is not absentminded, not haphazard. Poets are pulled towards each other through metaphor. It's as though metaphors were alive, vibrant, thrumming, voluptuous, prickly and gutting.[17] They throw out resonances, create moods and speak to one another. The bulbul calls out to the nightingale, the flushed earth summons the earth garlanded in colour and willy-nilly drags Mirabai towards Sappho. Mirabai trades with, senses with, Sappho through metaphor. Metaphors have claims on people and people have claims on metaphor—the result is an ambience which the two partake. Metaphors as doing—not just being—they do something to lift melancholia's doldrums?

What then can we take away for ourselves from the lead up to Miraji's finale? Logos is embodied in a lexicon that provokes the question of value, scattered as though artlessly throughout the entire text: measure, profit, accrue, assay of money and pressing for claim. But Miraji was nothing if not a meticulous wordsmith. And Miraji braces Sappho against claims that siphon value away from her, even as her craft calls her worth into being.

We might begin with what it means to speak as a woman who loved women—something Miraji did and something that was snatched away from women whose proxies staked claims on their behalf (both the British who acted for their so-called protection and the Progressive writers who wrote in their stead). 'Only women can compose' says Miraji in an essay on poetics. Here, Sappho does not compose in her own solitude. Rather her *mahfil* composes her and this *mahfil* encompasses Miraji's—making poetry is not a solitary craft, lyric is deeply social, the fraught convivialities from which Urdu modernism was shaped. And what Miraji shows us is that these composite compositions do not mirror a world, they are not mimetic in any simple sense, and in this way, they will not accede to British installed proprieties for poetics so assiduously followed by both Hali and the Progressives. Rather, lyrical compositions could be thought of as a series of washes in painting, where what was freshly observed was tuned into lament and euphoria, politics and hope. Metaphor tugs and calls and poetry reassembles worlds but not in the architectural blueprints of convention that format solace; more especially, if those lyrics called to speak anew are love's fragments composed by a woman for a woman.

It is in the absence of returning, as though guilelessly, to truth value that those who have to live the legacy of violence can find their hopes might bear something more than the brutal. Colonial education stripped legacies away, stripped communities bare of their putative histories (whether valued or cheapened). So, also with Sappho as pedagogical figuration. But what Miraji translating Sappho and translating as Sappho directs us to attend to is that history as fidelity stalls within the boundaries of literalness—histories waylaid or abraded away cannot be recouped through restoring their exactness. Neither repair, nor reparation, nor restoration, nor compensation alleviates melancholy into mourning. Only when the historical is released into someone else's surmise, history as dream fragments of another's exilic lives and desires (flowing with delight, caught up in deep despair), can something that is not inimical to metaphoric creativities burgeon. Translation held tightly to impropriety, becomes both composition and analytic. Lyric may be the only place where, Miraji suggests through Miraji's translations of Sappho, fusing with her queer loves and softening ourselves to metaphors that are alive and lively and troublesome and awkward, we might escape. Seeing flourishing where endless death or marring lived, where creativities' runaway possibilities might find their voices and melancholia, whether its lineaments are Unani or Freudian, might surcease. But these are also places where betrayals are still one arbiter of possible futures: here, in all of them, is a possible genesis for modernism.

The two poems with which Miraji concludes speak to these measures:

> When nights hours have slipped away, morning's flame about to dawn
> when fickle sleep tests one's eyes, a god brings dreaming
> these words so grim, how can my heart bear
> the sorrow and calamity that fills it
> how can I let my soul's hope persist unfinished
> exultation lifts my mind, I won't let grief overwhelm me
> the sky's tender joy will engulf, soak my heart
> when I was young, guileless, my mother offered me play things
> I opened my hands to accept them, it wasn't as though I could refuse
> the heavens bestow rapture to those who chance hope, and the hymns and sacrifices
> in my songs
> shed their disquiet and my melodies dance, bloom, flower. (Miraji 355)

And the final one, which is Miraji's culminating paragraph, '[t]hose who have beauty are worthy, whether a beautiful statue or a charmed one/But the one who does not please in this way, is instead worthy, truly exquisite' (Miraji 356) is his conclusion. *Ma'yyār*: the measure of worth. And it is Sappho's own character that measures up: perhaps a measure for Miraji's compatriots, whose tongues are held silent or voice only what has been given them as the proper arbiters of political speech. Therein lies their melancholia—with Sappho's voice the gift that might release their *jadīd* melodies into song.

NOTES

1. Many lineages and forebearers have been suggested for Urdu modernism or *jadīdīyāt*. One such finds its inception in the poet Altaf Husain Hali and his turn to lyrical naturalism which I will speak to later in this chapter. See Ahmed (2008) for another assortment of engagements that fall under the auspices of modernism, Ahmed's lineage building exercises focus on transformations sited primarily in the formal features of lyric. Most conventional histories of twentieth-century Urdu poetry are routed through three well-known lyricists—Miraji, N.M. Rashid and Faiz Ahmed Faiz.
2. Because Miraji was a putative man who took the name of a woman (either a bhakti poet or a woman with whom Miraji was infatuated). I am trying to not use the masculine or feminine when I speak about Miraji.
3. I contrast *dhundalā* to *mubham*—both are concepts for Miraji—in fact Miraji thinks of *mubham* in relation to *tasavvur* as idea or concept/imagination. *Mubham* comes closer to the notion of undecidable, even ineffable (the first perhaps almost Derridean in its scope), uncertainty, ambivalence, where ordinary categories of analysis or genre conventions cannot reach or even do their work. It opens up possibilities for reading—here in this prose snippet it probably comes closer to uncertain, or even a time where things haven't been settled or causes can't be determinate (Patel 2002, 269–277). Against this is *dhundalā*—closer to something murky, a morass even, more a state of being than a stance for an analytic.
4. All translations from Indian languages in this chapter are mine.
5. Given Miraji's avid perusal of Freud or Freudian readings of writers such as Charles Baudelaire—turning to Freud to think about a term Miraji coins seems particularly apt.
6. Swift schematic takes on the work of an abbreviated posse of scholars might offer some foreshortened guidelines. Many of them turn to melancholia as a genre of being that comes into presence for black or Asian or Latinx or Jewish or Cypriot communities lingering under legacies of colonial or racialised or ethnic brutality, or histories of violent dispossession that underwrote political ascendancy by communities such as the British. Even if these situations that have either fallen way from the repertoire of those

who were responsible for them or been repudiated by the stolen habitation of places and objects that were handed over to people who had also paid a steep price as was the case in Cyprus. Each scholar opens some of their forays into exploring the somatic-political conditions that underwrote melancholia through Sigmund Freud's early essay 'Mourning and Melancholia' (1959), often routing their interrogations through Frantz Fanon. Many of these theorists of melancholia give its energy different nomenclatures, postcolonial or critical melancholia being two instances.

7. I am playing with demetaphorisation and literalisation that are considered symptoms of and the linguistic grammar of melancholia; when melancholia was enfleshed in and through language. See both Khanna (2003) and Abraham and Torok (1994) from whom Khanna draws. In the cases I delineate language is the target, its forms desecrated, so it is not just the symptom but also that which must be reoriented—and that rupture is not just an effect of but constitutes the causal circumstances for melancholia. In South Asia, this metaphor bore the brunt of colonial razing. This is true also for indigenous communities whose tongues were literally shredded by policies of settler colonialism.
8. Bhaskar Sarkar's (2009) wonderfully enunciated, careful parsing of melancholia in his book on partition cinematics provides me a route to also envision this dropping away of self and the moral features that are activated in that loss; here Abraham and Torok (1994) can also be considered alongside Sarkar's invocations. Hali works well with Sarkar's schema: loss of an object that is not set apart from one's self but necessary to how one envisions and lives, reflecting as Sarkar suggests, one's self worth. As Sarkar points out, turning to Freud to elaborate what he is exploring, melancholia is central to the make-up of the ego itself—the lost object or ideal substituted for, preserved by and as the ego. In other words—herein lies the dilemma that melancholia brings. And that might be carried over into the *dhundhalānā* that Miraji presages for their own compatriots—a multigenerational melancholia, mourned as Sarkar intimates as 'chimera'. Sarkar is also productive in the ways in which he speaks of the 'contingent, traumatic event that remains largely inaccessible' about which communities encounter difficulties in understanding the experience, placing it in a meaningful account, so that it is rendered opaque with only fuzzy symptoms left over or persisting beyond the realm of language—this may well be alluded to as Miraji's *dhundhalānā*.
9. Most writers on melancholia would term this ambivalence (Khanna and Bhabha). I prefer double bind (Patel 2016) because it articulates the conundrum (I kill off my ancestors to revitalise myself but in the process, I also destroy myself) in a starker more unambiguous fashion.
10. Freud was clearly aware of the humoral theory of medicine, but as many commentators have suggested, his melancholia did something slightly different than the usual understanding of melancholia as a humour. Unani medicine that was akin to the Galenic system, could be considered the translation of it used by physicians in a later period. See Ahmad (1999); Ayush website; Azmi (2001).

11. and 12. See Yael Navaro's (2012) invocation of *maraz* or illness that her Turkish-Cypriot interlocutors used to describe what they were; the Urdu for patient is *marīz*. One might then want to put these two together to grapple with melancholia's effects as somatic-psychic.
13. See also Bhaskar Sarkar (2009).
14. Mackail (1910) gives Miraji some of his information on Sappho. For alternative translations, see Carson (2002) and also https://digitalsappho.org/bibliography/.
15. The curious synergy between Sappho returning from exile, her capacity for love coming back and her living again over and over through translation provides us a much more polygonal, packed calibration for the lifting of melancholia into grief that just what we could see through one transit bereft of all the others.
16. Donald Winnicott the psychoanalyst speaks in *Playing and Reality* (1971, 67) about creativity as the antithesis of what he seems to describe as melancholia (where a person does not care where they are alive or dead engendered in what he terms compliance). He poses the enchantment of creativity as venue through which life becomes possible and viable. I think that Miraji turns to creativity in the same fashion to enable similar pathways of possibility. Sappho might be what Winnicott calls a transitional environment or phenomenon—through which something can be worked through.
17. See Navaro on metaphor—which helped me craft my own analysis. She meticulously works through the allegiances enabled through thinkers who might be set off against one another—to bridge the separation between psyche and thing, between human and not. Metaphors for her do—they are active, they generate. Here she builds on the work of Teresa Brennan, taking off where Brennan leaves us slightly stranded. Navaro also speaks about metaphor creating a mood or state, objects, things, detritus producing more generalised affects, not more personal feelings. Indic (Perso-Sanskrit) *rasa-dhvanī-bhāva*—aesthetic theory might be more viable as a way of feeling through the nuances of what Navaro suggests. (Patel 2007) Partly because mood—perhaps the Urdu *kaifiyat*—is only made possible, only comes to be through objects, through nature—objects and nature produce moods (more generalised ones that are mobilised through many mood shifts). And mood is akin to an ambience in a room, shared across everyone in each other's presence.

REFERENCES

Abraham, Nicolas and Maria Torok. *The Shell and the Kernel: Renewals of Psychoanalysis*. Translated by Nicholas T. Rand. Chicago: University of Chicago Press, 1994.

Ahmad, J. and A. Qadeer. *Unani: The Science of Greeco-Arabic Medicine*, 9–19. New Delhi: Lustre Press/Roli Books, 1999.

Ahmed, Sheikh Aquil. 'Experiments in Form in Urdu Poetry.' *Indian Literature* 52, no. 2 (244, March–April 2008): 111–126.

Apter, Emily S. *Against World Literature: On the Politics of Untranslatability*. New York: Verso Books, 2014.

Ayush Website: indian medicine.nic.in/html/unani.htm.

Azmi, A.A. 'Impact of Arabian Medicine on the Western World in the Middle Ages.' *Studies in History of Medicine & Science* 17, no. 1–2 (2001): 1–12.

Bentinck, William. *The Correspondence of Lord William Cavendish Bentinck*. 2 vols. Edited by C.H. Phillips. Oxford: Oxford University Press, 1977.

———. Available at https://archive.org/stream/lordwilliamben00boul/lordwilliamben00boul_djvu.txt (accessed 11 September 2017).

Burke, Edmund. *The Works of the Right Honorable Edmund Burke*. Boston: Little, Brown, 1884.

Carson, Anne. *If not, Winter: Fragments of Sappho*, 244. New York: Vintage Books, 2002).

Cheng, Ann Anlin. *The Melancholy of Race*. New York: Oxford University Press, 2000.

Dirks, Nicholas. *The Scandal of Empire: India and the Creation of Imperial Britain*. Cambridge, MA: Harvard University Press, 2006.

Eng, David and Shinhee Han. *Racial Melancholia, Racial Disassociation: On the Social and Psychic Lives of Asian Americans*. Durham: Duke University Press, 2019.

Foucault, Michel. *On the Government of the Living: Lectures at the College de France, 1979–1980*. New York: Picador, 2010.

Freud, Sigmund. 'Mourning and Melancholia.' In *Collected Papers, Volume IV*, 152–170. New York: Basic Books, 1959.

Grant, Charles. *Observations on the State of Society among the Asiatic Subjects of Great Britain, Particularly with Respect to Morals; and on the Means of Improving it—Written Chiefly in the Year 1792*. London: House of Commons, 1813.

Jalibi, Jamil, ed. *Kulliyāt-i Mīrājī* [The Complete Works of Miraji]. London: Urdu Markaz, 1988.

Kerr, James. *A Review of Public Instruction in the Bengal Presidency from 1835–1852*. Calcutta: J. Thomas, Baptist Mission Press, 1852.

Khanna, Ranjana. *Dark Continents: Psychoanalysis and Colonialism*. Durham: Duke University Press, 2003.

Lushington, Charles. *The History, Design, And Present State of The Religious, Benevolent and Charitable Institutions, Founded By The British In Calcutta And Its Vicinity*. Calcutta: Hindostanee Press, 1824.

Mackail, J.W. *Lectures on Greek Poetry*. London, New York, Bombay and Calcutta: Longmans, Green and Co., 1910.

Mdembe, Achille. 'Necropolitics.' *Public Culture* 15, no. 1 (2003): 11–40.

Minault, Gail. *Secluded Scholars: Women's Education and Muslim Social Reform in Colonial India*. New Delhi: Oxford University Press, 1998.

Miraji. *Mashriq o Maghrib ke Nagmen* (Songs from the East and the West). Lahore: Punjab Academy, 1958.

Munoz, Jose. *Cruising Utopia.* Durham: Duke University, 2009.

Nagy, Gregory. 'Phaethon, Sappho's Paon, and the White Rock of Leukas', 'Reading the Symbols of Greek Lyric. In *Greek Mythology and Poetics.* Ithaca: Cornell University Press, 1990.

Navaro, Yael. *The Make-Believe Space: Affective Geography in a Postwar Polity.* Durham: Duke University Press, 2012.

Patel, Geeta. *Lyrical Movements, Historical Hauntings: On Gender, Colonialism and Desire in Miraji's Urdu Poetry.* Palo Alto: Stanford University Press, 2002.

———. 'The Rasa of Unimaginable Grief.' *Parasher—Partition and Beyond.* London and Berlin: Indian Council for Cultural Relations, 2007.

———. 'Vernacular Missing: Miraji on Sappho, Gender, Governance.' *Comparative Literature* 70, no. 2 (2018): 132–144.

———. *Risky Bodies & Techno-Intimacy.* New Delhi: Women Unlimited, 2016.

Pritchett, Frances. 'Poetry and Morality.' In *Nets of Awareness: Urdu Poetry and its Critics,* 169–83. Berkeley: University of California Press, 1994.

Puar, Jasbir. *The Right to Maim: Debility, Capacity, Disability.* Durham: Duke University Press, 2017.

Samaddar, Ranabir and Suhit K. Sen. *New Subjects and New Governance in India.* New Delhi: Routledge, 2014.

Sarkar, Bhaskar. *Mourning the Nation: Indian Cinema in the Wake of Partition.* Durham: Duke University Press, 2009.

Viswanathan, Gauri. *Masks of Conquest: Literary Study and British Rule in India.* New York: Columbia University Press, 2014.

Winnicott, Donald W. *Playing and Reality.* London: Tavistock Publications, 1971.

IS THERE A HOMOSEXUAL IN THE TEXT?

Rahul Sen

> Moon in Cancer, Pisces rising. Sign of the exile and the poet. Wealth is spurned. Success at thirty-six. Early death. Eccentricity lessens with age. Literary success, world travels, pilgrimages, a house by the sea. A twenty-year Venusian proficiency in the arts; aesthetics and the sexual. Conventionally speaking a bad-charactered person but devoted to the learned, friend to society's rejects, sacrificing, attaining wisdom after repentance at Eros. Last years in decline. Friends are progeny. Beloved of women. Disappearance of an aged woman. Moon and Jupiter cushioning against poverty. Great faith in mankind.
>
> —Hoshang Merchant, *The Man Who Would Be Queen* (2011)

To read these lines of Hoshang Merchant's autobiographical fiction is to witness a torrent of scattered words, discontinuous phrases, sparse images and lone ruminations, spread on the page like Sapphic fragments, glaringly staring back at the readers with a rage and pathos that perhaps only sequestered marginality can uphold. One can manoeuvre through the disjointed distributions of words and non-linear placements of isolated images, awaiting the arrival of an interpretative serendipity that would cause an explosion, detonating the unflinching truth underneath words that seem more naked than flesh. But it is only an illusion of explosion, one realises, a non-arrival of serendipitous truth that obscures meaning and thwarts any easy attempt at a poetic exegesis. The words brim with prurient energy and through the evocation of 'Eros' and 'aesthetics', 'friend' and 'beloved', paint the canvas with a literary transgressiveness that resists singularity of meaning and proves counterintuitive not only in terms of content but also form—generically betraying the autobiographical narrative.

Hoshang Merchant's autobiography, *The Man Who Would Be Queen*, which he intriguingly calls 'autobiographical fictions', was published in 2011. Arguably, the first gay autobiography in the English language, published in India, 'the book took almost thirty years to be completed and published,' says Hoshang in a personal interview. In the text which is divided into four sections—tracing the narrator's childhood days in a conflicted family, to his education, experiences and sexual encounters abroad in the United States, Palestine, Jerusalem, to his days as a professor of literature in India—one can witness the juxtaposition of two uncoupled, or perhaps not, ideas which shape its meaning and possibilities of reading—that of the growth of a poet's mind and/or the sexual philandering of a gay person at home and the world. The text's resistance to any easy generic qualifier is borne out by the contradictory description of being 'autobiographical fictions' on the cover page to 'a collection of lyric essays' on the end page. In between these two lurks a panorama of sentiments from love, rage, hatred, jealousy, heartbreak, joy, pain, orgasm, ecstasy and all the complexities and contradictions that permeate the narrator's personhood.

Hoshang Merchant's narrative uncovers the multiple tongues or 'polyglossia', as Mikhail Bakhtin[1] (1934) would term it, of the queer individual. It is this splinteredness within, and fragmentation without, that materialises a queer aesthetics and politics of which Merchant is an exemplary exponent. It is perhaps significant to note that 'the literary' not only serves as a referential axis in the text—lines ranging from Anaïs Nin to Proust, Plato to Lorca, Borges to Auden, Shakespeare to Rumi, Sufi poetry to his own poems—but becomes sites of identification for the narrator who anchors his queerness not only to categories of identities such as 'gay', 'homosexual' or 'queer' but on to the transient malleability of the literary which prides itself on contingency, infinitude, borderlessness, felicity and jouissance. The 'literary', however, is never taken or received on its face value; the subversive turning around of the title of Rudyard Kipling's novella, *The Man Who Would Be King* to the seductive and titillating *The Man Who Would Be Queen*, not only bears testimony to the appropriation or affirmative sabotage of canonical literary texts but also punctures the masculinist common sense that sustains the canon. This, accompanied by the image of Merchant that adorns the book cover, turning his back to the readers, looking contemplatively on his side and holding a hand-fan with long hair flowing alongside his bodily curves, perhaps, resembling a naked geisha or mermaid[2]—not only underscores the queer aesthetics of the text but brings back the body in conversation with notions of writing gender and sexuality, literature and politics, femininity and queerness.

THE AUTHOR IN CONVERSATION

March 2017: Hoshang Merchant was staying in Jawaharlal Nehru University for a week as a 'writer in residence', conducting workshops, delivering public lectures and holding poetry reading sessions. I decided to speak to him about his book and his understanding of queerness, writing, politics, poetry and aesthetics.[3] Merchant was everything that I had imagined; the image conjured by those hauntingly lyrical words was coming alive. Walking with the support of a stick, maintaining his usual queer idiosyncrasy, there was an air of joy, loneliness, jubilance, passion, sexiness, longing, pathos, sadness, ecstasy and bereavement about him. With affectation and whimsicality, he responded to my questions as if a yesteryear queer is speaking to his progeny! Hoshang Merchant unequivocally admits that women's autobiographies were an inspiration for him behind writing this book 'since, there were no homosexual autobiographies from India at that time', he says. With a playful and affective tone he mentions, that, 'I grew up imitating the women, took inspiration from them to write my autobiography. Now the women imitate me, I am the queen.' He ends the sentence with impeccable hijra[4] claps, a sardonic grin and poetry in his eyes. Merchant prides himself on claiming the 'beginning' on many grounds—his edited anthology, *Yaarana: Gay Writing from India*, was published in 1999,[5] one year before the publication of Ruth Vanita and Saleem Kidwai's *Same-Sex Love in India: A Literary History*. It is regarded as the first gay anthology from India, apart from his autobiographical fictions which is the first queer autobiography written in the English language in this country. 'I am the alpha and omega', says Hoshang with a campy flamboyance, claps again and adds, 'I am beyond "gay" and "queer". I am the fairy, the queen. I am the empress *chakki*.' Hoshang loved and lived in the pre-queer theory days; he frontally positions this temporality in our conversation—'in those days "queer" was not in vogue. I was a faggot, a campy, limp-wristed homosexual who took the penis of all those straight men out there, inside me'—then breaks out in a laughter that holds dissidence and pride in a high-pitched feminine voice.

I realised the difficulty of interviewing a person like Hoshang Merchant, most of whose replies were circumlocutory and erratic, always substituting the apparent with metaphors, analogies and anecdotes that demand interpretation. Even in the most mundane and dreariest of conversations, he seems to be at his lyrical best, turning the ordinary into poetry with his prodigious wit. It was much later that I realised, it was part of a larger queer practice that Merchant seems to embody—of frolicking and playing around with words that hold multiple meanings and double entendre, oftentimes, bordering on the sexual, erotic and risqué overtones. 'Language made me gay', says Merchant, emphatically, who believes the self to be nothing more than a literary construction. On being asked, why did he prefer to choose 'autobiographical fictions' over autobiography, Merchant revealed that he sees the self as a fictive imagination; a construction from selected dominoes of memory. 'The subject first constructs itself, then constructs his autobiography'—this idea seems to run all along his book and it is this imaginative impulse that comes alive in pages after pages, paragraphs after paragraphs. In a self-referential tone, he writes:

> He said my autobiography was 'made sublime,' that I wanted to present myself in a good light. To one's beloved one shows the potential self, the beautiful self, though I do not care for public opinion. Autobiographical art is suspect. All art is falseness not only in the sense that it is a moulding, a retelling but also in the sense that art is the hand-making of one's life; it is a made universe. Even autobiography is fiction. (Merchant 2011, 68–69)

Merchant gives a literary, almost poetic explication to what Judith Butler writes in her second preface to *Gender Trouble*. She opines, 'the difficulty of the "I" to express itself through the language that is available to it. For this "I" that you read is in part a consequence of the grammar that governs the availability of persons in language' (Butler 2007, xxvi). While acknowledging the inability of a complete escape from the limits of linguistic availability, Merchant's queer project seems to be one that withstands the masculinist deployment of grammar, by turning words on their heads that obscures easy intelligibility within the available frameworks of knowledge-production.

It is interesting to observe that Merchant's verbal rage and aggression do not get translated into his writings: all the cuss words and slurs that animate his speech, sublimate on the page, get substituted by an aesthetic serenity that one may witness in Sufi poetry. One realises that this performative contradiction marks Merchant's queer aesthetics and reveals that behind words are other words of varied significations; it also creates the political in ways that are contingent, not easily readable as transparent moments in the text. His latest book of poetry—*My Sunset Marriage*—which was to be released on the following day, embedded the performative contradiction at the level of textuality by combining felicity and farewell in two words. In the subsequent part of the chapter, I will further engage with these contradictions in his writings and explore the possibilities that they open in terms of queer politics and aesthetics.

WRITING GAY

In the introductory chapter of her third book, *Tendencies*, published in 1993, Eve Kosofsky Sedgwick wrote a deeply personal and autobiographical response to the current state of queer studies in the United States. The chapter, titled 'Queer and Now', not only expositions Sedgwick's engagement with gay and lesbian suicides, the AIDS epidemic crisis, her own struggle with cancer, but also exhibits, stylistically, how the autobiographical/personal can serve theoretical purposes. Merchant's text too can be considered as meta-autobiographical—in the penultimate section of the book, he gives an account of 'How I write' and 'Why I write'. The text, therefore, not only remains 'autobiographical fictions' but offers a theory of autobiography, commenting upon itself in a self-referential gesture. He asks: 'how do you write gayness when there is no gay culture? How you create a gay aesthetic for urban India?' (Merchant 2011, 168). I would like to hold on to the idea of 'writing gayness' and 'gay aesthetic' in the subsequent part of my chapter and explore the limits and openings of these concepts as explicated by Hoshang and other practitioners.

'What do you mean by writing gayness', I had asked Merchant right at the moment he was about to put a fresh chikoo inside his mouth. After a few seconds of silence, that is needed to chew and gulp the succulent fruit, he retorted with an actressy flamboyance: '*doctor sahib, maine kaccha chikoo kha liya. Mere pet mein chikoo ka bachcha toh nahi ayenge na?*' which approximately stands in the English translation as: '*Oh doctor, I just ate a raw chikoo. Will I get pregnant by its seeds?*' Hoshang had already responded to my query with a counter-question and explained a complex theoretical speculation using an easy analogy and farcical light-heartedness. His response reeked of a textual queerness and bore the evidence of what he means by 'writing gayness', playing around with intelligibility and resisting the easy readability of signs and words, their meanings and significations. Let us consider the following passage for a better understanding of the concept that I am trying to tease out:

> I stumbled upon Priscilla of the Desert. S/he hadn't been reincarnated yet on Hollywood celluloid. But here was the living type. If only I knew! Thinking him to be an Adonis I was soon tossed up into his hot embraces, enjoying his kisses. But this was Venus with a penis. S/he turned and slept on her stomach. I slipped manfully into her manhole. Coming took some doing for lack of friction. I persisted a full half hour under the desert sun only to have my performance applauded by a group of gay voyeurs on a sand-bluff above us! (Merchant 2011, 117)

On the surface, this is an act of passionate intercourse and searing romance from foreplay to orgasm. By means of a reference—Stephan

Elliott's film, *The Adventures of Priscilla, Queen of the Desert* which deals with the lives of two drag queens and a transgender woman—Merchant textualises his lovemaking with a person whose gender identity seems indeterminate. At the level of plot, the embodied queerness of these lines is unequivocally evoked and is easily identifiable, readable and rendered transparent. The presence of the intertextual sign of 'Priscilla' affirms the motif of non-normative desires and gender variance that embellish the paragraph. What is interesting, however, is the achievement of this gender-variance at the level of language. Through a careful or playful selection and deployment of words, the author interrupts the ennui of specificity—in this case, of gender. Not only is the pronoun of the other person split open as 's/he' but phrases such as 'Venus with a penis' and 'manfully into *her* manhole' lay bare the non-finality of meaning in the text, inscribing an uncertainty in the register of linguistic legibility that denote a 'doubleness' not only in the identitarian sense—of the actors involved—but also in terms of writing itself. If queerness is indeed 'the open mesh of possibilities, gaps, overlaps, dissonances and resonances, lapses and excesses of meaning when the constituent elements of anyone's gender, of anyone's sexuality aren't made (or can't be made) to signify monolithically' as Sedgwick argues (2003, 8), the previous passage, perhaps, provides a literary explication to her observation. If the title of the autobiography is *The Man Who Would Be Queen*, then the sentence—'I slipped manfully into *her* manhole'—brims with ramifications and possibilities that push the frontiers of our literary imagination, thereby, affecting and altering our epistemological performance. A 'man', who is a 'woman' (queen) penetrates a 'woman' who is a 'man'—a deconstruction would perhaps yield a convoluted and syntactically serpentine result: the man is not a man is a woman is not a man is not a woman. Intelligibility is rendered precarious by the author, its limits and internal contradictions exposed vis-à-vis sex, gender, desire and bodies. The contradictions do not, however, limit readability; rather, enable the readers to re-imagine gender and sexual possibilities outside the available grammatical/syntactical frameworks of binary mundaneness. Merchant's text, therefore, offers us a lesson in imaginative reading or aesthetic education. Speaking in favour of literature and the literary in the training of our imagination, Gayatri Chakravorty Spivak writes:

> ... we who learn from fiction must think a borderless world of unconditional hospitality.... In this activation, a literary education can be a great help, because the teacher engages directly with the imagination. The teacher of literature has nothing else to teach.... And engaging with the imagination in the simplest way makes us

> suspend our own interests into the language that is happening in the text, the text of another traced voice, the voice of the presumed producer of the text. I use these words 'trace', 'text', 'voice' because the utility of the imagination is not confined to what we recognize as 'literature' today. The element that we might call the 'literary', that trains the imagination to step out of self-interest, exists in many shapes and forms in the pasts of all civilizations. In the thinking of a borderless world today, we have to use the imagination through literary training in the broadest sense, including the filmic, the videographic, the hypertextual, learning to read in the broadest sense. (Spivak 2014, 3–4)

Towards the beginning of the chapter, I had contended that the author anchors his queerness, oftentimes, to the literary and works of literature. In this regard, his text offers a lesson in the training of our imagination, impelling us to think the unthinkable, read the unreadable. 'Writing gayness' then also becomes an exercise in envisioning a 'borderless world', as Spivak would argue, where a tapestry of words holds revolutionary possibilities of social justice and rearranging human desires.

I will stay with the idea of 'writing gayness' and look closely at two other sections from the text for further explication. While recounting his days in Palestine, Merchant writes:

> Power cuts can be fun. They can be tragic too. The newspapers reported a mother lacing her bride-to-be daughter's school sandwich in the dark at dawn with rat-poison, thinking it to be black pepper. The high school girl merrily ate it: her last sandwich as a carefree lass. She was brought home from school, dead. A scene of rejoicing became a scene of mourning. Palestinians are used to that. (Merchant 2011, 111–112)

On another occasion, he writes with a digressive tone: 'it is all a matter of concentration: if you concentrate on wealth, you become a rich man, if on love, a prostitute, if on beauty, a poet, if on god, a saint.' (Merchant 2011, 74). However, a little later in the same chapter, in a letter written to Behzad, he writes: 'I have become an ordinary human being, no longer poet, prostitute or saint...' (Merchant 2011, 80). It is interesting to note the strain of doubleness in Merchant's writing—of contradictions, anomalies, metalepses and messy misalignments—that informs and interrupts the text from within. By challenging the violence of meaningful singularity and textual totalitarianism, Merchant embeds in his writing, stylistically, an ambivalence or dissimulation that causes substitutability of signification. His writing, like queer desires, is displacing, fissured and contrarian—marked by a textual excess that overdetermine strategies of reading and meaning making. From the lines mentioned earlier that I chose for discussion and several other lines and passages in the text, it can be discerned that objects and metaphors lack fixity, they are floating signifiers that at once mark the particular and its lexical opposite, oftentimes, rendering redundant their textual reverseness. In Merchant's textual economy, therefore, 'fun' is always 'tragic', 'rejoicing' is always already 'mourning', prostitution is inevitably contained in sainthood—through laying bare the inseparability of polar opposites and the substitutability of words, Merchant writes gayness that opens a mode of transaction between writing and desire, gender and literature, politics and philosophy, wrapping expressions around boisterous erotic energies. One can read queerness in the text, not only in non-normative sex acts but in the texture of the alphabets, the positioning of the words, (dis)placements of symbols and metaphors that constitute meaning by continually thwarting, deferring and dispersing it. Borrowing Barthes' (2012) terminology of 'readerly' and 'writerly' texts, it can be said that *The Man Who Would Be Queen* is both a readerly and writerly text and is neither a readerly nor a writerly work.[6] It is this idea, of *both is and is not* that renders Merchant's writing queer, affirming the textual doubleness that is spread across chapters. In this regard, the entire text seems to be in drag, suggesting and implying a literary/theoretical cross-dressing, bringing into question the epistemic and ontological regimes of writing and the written, effecting and affecting a spilling over of meanings and categories.

There are several things that 'writing gayness' may mean, or be made to mean, in the context of literature, art and aesthetics. Hoshang Merchant is certainly a prominent expositor in this genre but not without artistic antecedents; two literary giants—Shakespeare and Tagore—made their venture into this artistic form years before 'gay' became a political category of identification. Both Shakespeare and Tagore seemed to forge a queer aesthetics, oftentimes through the deployment of language that serves as a literary and theoretical blueprint for scholars of posterity. In an untranslated essay titled 'Banglar Lingo Prakriti O Rabindranath' ('The Nature of Gender in the Bengali Language and Rabindranath'), Sibaji Bandyopadhyay (2011) explores the gender-neutral nature of the Bengali language, exploited and appropriated by Tagore in most of his works to equivocate the gender-identity of other persons, characters and referents. Through the usage of the third person gender neutral pronoun, *shey*, Bandyopadhyay discloses the techniques and strategies used by Tagore to supplant the limits of masculinist signifying economy, facilitated by the Bengali language that is not circumscribed by the institutions of phallogocentrism. Consequently, he traces 'desire' in the oeuvre of Tagore by articulating how, not only pronouns but even nouns and adjectives can be made to signify gender neutral subjects, as these seem to be used habitually rather than controlled by grammatical conventions. *Shey* in the Tagorean oeuvre and in the Bengali language in general can, therefore, mean both masculine and feminine and neither masculine nor feminine. In his celebrated play, *Chintrangada*, Tagore does not delineate an easy transition of gender from 'man' to 'woman', *kurupa* to *surupa* but frisks, frolics and foreplays with the gendered possibilities and fluidity of the Bengali language—he uses *kurup*, the gender-neutral form, to obfuscate an easy readability of his protagonist's gender identity pre and post transition. It is also significant to note, that, in the English translation of the play—*Chitra*—Madan, one of the major characters become Eros. While Eros is the Greek god of sexual attraction, it can simultaneously be read as the life force or will to live in the Freudian sense. While the English language proscribes Tagore to revel in a linguistic fluidity, it unbolts other possibilities—from an individual god, Madan gets translated into an erotic principle, thereby, refusing to get interpellated into the constraints of a masculinist signifying economy. Tagore's words, like Merchant's, defer and dupe the impediments of the linguistic registers, fulminating with contingency vis-à-vis gender, sexuality and desire.

In this game of language, power and displacement, Tagore is joined by William Shakespeare, who despite writing within the English linguistic register conjures words, phrasings, images and metaphors that (dis)locate identities, confound intelligibility and romp with meanings and signs. Malvolio's famous description of Viola/Cesario to a mourning Olivia, in *Twelfth Night*, who having rejected the advances of all amorous men, is ardently overwhelmed by his words and hastily allows him/her inside her chamber:

> OLIVIA: Of what personage and years is he?
> MALVOLIO: Not yet old enough for a man, nor young enough for a boy; as a squash is before 'tis a peascod, or a cooling when 'tis almost an apple: 'tis with him in standing water, between boy and man. He is very well-favoured and he speaks very shrewishly; one would think his mother's milk was scarce out of him.
> OLIVIA: Let him approach: call in my gentlewoman. (Shakespeare 1993, 54)

Overlapping of pronouns, riddles of images and symbols, violent juxtaposition of opposing ideas mark the lines that open myriad interpretative possibilities and imaginings, resisting a singularity of thought and identity. Shakespeare plays with the established conventions of grammar and lexical rigidity which restricts the gender and sexuality of persons in language. This is perhaps expressed more beautifully, in two other instances in *Romeo and Juliet*, whose wanton-word-play precludes all heteronormative readings of the drama, presenting a linguistic queerness that seems sweeter than honey, fiercer than maenads. When Romeo attempts to kill himself, after being banished by the Prince, for he cannot reconcile with his separation from Juliet, Friar Lawrence reprimands him:

> Hold thy desperate hand!
> Art thou a man? Thy form cries out thou art.
> Thy tears are womanish; thy acts |denote|
> The unreasonable fury of a beast.
> Unseemly woman in a seeming man,
> And ill-beseeming beast in seeming both! (Shakespeare 2011, 149)

If language produces the 'subject' and renders it available within the matrix of intelligibility; if the grammatical norms of language naturalise gender then the most elemental way to challenge gender norms and their comprehensibility would be to contest the grammatical conventions of the language within which gender is given. Sara Ahmed has argued that words can have 'orientations' too—sexual or otherwise—Shakespeare maximises the orienting powers of words to (dis)orient and muddle their signifying practices. 'Unseemly woman in a seeming man'—one fails to distinguish the 'original' from the 'imitation', the 'real' from the 'unreal', dismantling our notion of an essential identity.

There is another way in which *Romeo and Juliet* may spark the imagination of the queer theorist. The kind of 'doubleness' that one witnesses in the writing of Merchant, can be discerned in the lines of Shakespeare too. Hoshang Merchant, being a reader and teacher of Shakespeare was certainly influenced by the bard's queer practices. One finds lines of Shakespeare being quoted in his autobiography. Towards the beginning of the play, Shakespeare deploys this textual doubleness in at least two instances. After her first meeting with Romeo, and knowing his identity, Juliet tells her nurse: 'If he be married/My grave is like to be my wedding bed' (Shakespeare 2011, 61). Upon knowing that Romeo is a Montague, belonging to the enemy clan, Juliet contemplates:

> My only love sprung from my only hate!
> Too early seen unknown, and known too late!
> Prodigious birth of love it is to me
> That I must love a loathed enemy. (Shakespeare 2011, 61)

Opposite words and phrases spelled out in the same breath, crisscrossing meanings and truths in an irretrievable fashion and creating ontic confusions at the textual level. Not only does one fail to distinguish between the wedding bed and the death bed, but 'love' and 'hate', 'beloved' and 'enemy' are uttered with a queer synonymity. Similar to Hoshang's narrative, here too, we have interchangeability of words and substitutability of meanings; a spilling over of ideas where 'love' is always already 'hate', the beloved is inevitably the 'enemy'. Instead of being heralded as the archetypal heterosexual love story or romance, *Romeo and Juliet* might as well qualify as the greatest hate-story ever written if one aligns with Juliet's passionate uttering.[7] Shakespeare's queer aesthetics, like Merchant's, can be witnessed at the textual level, stylistically and formalistically—in his word-plays, metrical arrangements and drag techniques of a literary crossdressing—not simply at the level of content and plot.

In an essay titled 'Paranoid Reading and Reparative Reading', Eve Kosofsky Sedgwick (2003) argued for a shift in the practice of critical reading from a paranoid position to a reparative position—the former predicated on a 'hermeneutics of suspicion' and examining the liberatory or oppressive/homophobic status of texts; while the latter is pleasure-centric, emphasises on feeling/affect and how texts might heal/help us to think alternatively and feel better. Taking the theoretical cue from Melanie Klein, Sedgwick encourages the readers to adopt a 'depressive' position rather than a 'paranoid-schizoid' position. If the paranoid critic's task is to expose the strengths and weaknesses of texts, the depressive/reparative reader's relationship with texts is more complex where one fails to see the inseparability of strength and weakness, engages with the surprises, resources and pleasures that texts have in offer. In reading the instances of 'writing gayness' in the three texts, that, I discussed earlier, adopting a depressive/reparative reading position might allow us to shift the critical attention away from queer desires to a more queer focus on techniques, strategies, modes of reading and writing and thinking queerly about and with the form of the text.

NOTES TOWARD WRITING QUEERNESS

> ... woman does not bring about the same regionalization which serves the couple head/genitals and which is inscribed only within boundaries. Her libido is cosmic, just as her unconscious is worldwide. Her writing can only keep going, without ever inscribing or discerning contours, daring to make these vertiginous crossings

> of the other(s) ephemeral and passionate sojourns in him, her, them, whom she inhabits long enough to look at from the point closest to their unconscious from the moment they awaken, to love them at the point closest to their drives; and then further, impregnated through and through with these brief, identificatory embraces, she goes and passes into infinity. She alone dares and wishes to know from within, where she, the outcast, has never ceased to hear the resonance of fore-language. She lets the other language speak—the language of 1000 tongues which knows neither enclosure nor death. To life she refuses nothing. Her language does not contain, it carries; it does not hold back, it makes possible. (Cixous 1976, 889)

Hélène Cixous in her canonical essay 'The Laugh of Medusa', published in 1976, argued that the only means through which women can liberate or reclaim their sexuality, bodies and voices is through putting herself 'into the text' by effecting a mode/practice of writing that is distinctively and markedly 'feminine'. Écriture feminine or 'feminine writing' works towards inscribing the femininity, female body and female sexual difference into language and came to influence French feminists such as Monique Wittig and Luce Irigaray. In Cixous' words, the two aims of this kind of writing is 'to break up, to destroy' the masculinist signifying economy of phallogocentrism and 'to foresee the unforeseeable, to project' a future that is unequivocally feminine (Cixous 1976, 875). It is important to note that Cixous places the female body as the site of this kind of writing—as both that makes the writing possible and itself gets written in the process. Cixous' project apparently seems to be an identitarian one where lines, words, phrases, images and symbols of subversion, sensuousness, longing, insurgency, love, militancy and desire flow out of a female-identified body. However, like all great poems and literary art, one soon begins to witness the contradictions and fissures in Cixous' arguments. 'Which works, then, might be called feminine?' she asks and replies that 'the only inscriptions of femininity that I have seen were by Colette, Marguerite Duras … and Jean Genêt' (Cixous 1976, 878–879). It is riveting and queer to see Jean Genêt being invoked in the same sentence along with two other female artists; despite not inhabiting a female body, Genêt is capable of producing 'feminine writing' or a feminine aesthetics that transgresses masculinist conventions. A little later, Cixous hails Molly Bloom's soliloquy in James Joyce's *Ulysses* as being capable of transgressing and transcending the masculinist discursive practices and setting an exemplary example of what she theorises as 'feminine writing'. Does Merchant's idea of 'writing gayness' serve as an analogous standpoint to Cixous' notion of écriture *feminine*? Would Cixous have validated Hoshang Merchant's writing as an example of 'feminine writing'? Would Hoshang like to see his writings function under the rubric of écriture *feminine* or is there a possibility of a homologous bracketing of écriture *queer*? I would leave these at the level of speculation, for the answers would entail both affirmation and negation, and would touch us, caress us, lick us with 'the language of 1000 tongues'—that Cixous alludes to—which knows no finality of meaning.

Almost nineteen years after the publication of 'The Laugh of Medusa', Lee Edelman (1994) in his path-breaking work, *Homographesis*, further complicated the relationship between textuality and sexuality, writing and the body, identity politics and critical practice. If Cixous' insistence was on a differential writing that is markedly 'feminine', Edelman's engagement borders around the idea of the 'mark'—what renders it legible and intelligible? Under what condition does this 'mark' make its entry into the system of writing and language? What political ramifications might this 'mark' entail? Towards the end of his autobiography, Hoshang writes: 'As everyone knows by now, I'm homosexual. To write this sentence and to speak it publicly, which is a great liberation, is why I write' (Merchant 2011, 154). Hoshang's writings, therefore, admittedly bear the 'mark' of the homosexual. I would hold on to this 'mark' for a brief while and see what purpose it serves! What are its limitations and possibilities? In the opening chapter to his book, Edelman writes:

> I want to call attention to the formation of a category of homosexual person whose very condition of possibility is his relation to writing or textuality, his articulation, in particular, of a 'sexual' difference internal to male identity that generates the necessity of reading certain bodies as *visibly* homosexual. This inscription of 'the homosexual' within a tropology that produces him in a determining relation to inscription itself is the first of the things that I intend the term 'homographesis' to denote. (Edelman 1994, 9)

In the light of Edelman's argument, who views the existence of the homosexual person in 'relation to writing or textuality', it is difficult to comprehend in the case of Hoshang's statement, that, if it is the homosexual person who writes or conversely, does writing produce his homosexuality? In other words, does identity precede writing or writing produces a legible identity? When he says—'how did I write my first poem? I was beaten up while cruising the streets of a small university town in Michigan, one summer in the early 1970s' (Merchant 2011, 154)—one feels as though Merchant's text is in conversation with Edelman's where he refers back to the 'body' as a homograph, a site of sexual difference but also that which 'demands to be read … a body on which his "sexuality" is always already inscribed' (Edelman 1994, 10). Throughout the text of Merchant's narrative, the body is diffused through words that bear its pain, longing, ecstasy, desire, beauty, sensation and the myriad nameable and unnameable feelings that the body is capable of repertoiring. Featuring the body becomes a major trope of what Hoshang calls 'writing gayness'—it is not simply an act of writing about the body but simultaneously, with the body, through the body, on the body. One can discern the reverberations of Cixous, who too had urged women to write 'through their bodies'. However, Edelman's theory of 'homographesis' performs a double-bind; taking the theoretical cue from Derrida, Edelman writes:

> Writing, therefore, though it marks or describes those differences upon which the specification of identity depends, works simultaneously … to 'de-scribe,' efface, or undo identity by framing difference as the misrecognition of a 'différance' whose negativity, whose purely relational articulation, calls into question the possibility of any positive presence of discrete identity. (Edelman 1994, 10)

In other words, although, Merchant proclaimingly writes as 'a homosexual', the inscription of his sexuality into writing postpones and defers the production of its meaning. This difference and deference of meaning, instead of reifying and consolidating his identity, adjourn it. It no longer remains a stable, comprehensible and differential identity but becomes a confusion, an error, a trouble, a Derridean différance that shifts legibility and intelligibility. Edelman is cognizant of this double-bind of homographesis when he writes:

> Like writing, then, homographesis would name a double operation: one serving the ideological purposes of a conservative social order intent on codifying identities in its labor of disciplinary inscription, and the other resistant to that categorization, intent on *de*-scribing the identities that order has so oppressively *in*scribed. That these two operations, pointing as they do in opposite directions, should inhabit a single signifier, must make for a degree of confusion, but the confusion that results when difference collapses into identity and identity unfolds into différance is, as I will suggest ... central to the problematic of homographesis. (Edelman 1994, 10)

It is difficult, almost impossible, to pin down the 'mark' of difference to a specificity; and therefore, while 'writing gayness' may flow out of homosexual bodies, it liberates the body from the aegis of writing and renders it illegible. The 'single signifier' performing the twin tasks of inscribing and *de*-scribing identities, thus, is not simply the 'problematic of homographesis' alone; it informs Hoshang's project of 'writing gayness' as well as Cixous' postulations on écriture *feminine*—in either instance, the writing can both be traced back to homosexual and female bodies respectably and not be followed back to the identitarian bodies as points of derivation. Who owns the queer aesthetic then, one may ask? What political imagination works behind the framing of such an interrogation? If post-structuralist criticism has taught us anything, it is the *fiction* of identities and their foundationalism—hetero, homo or otherwise. If one is to believe that gay writing can only emanate from gay bodies, then the logic of heteronormativity appears to be an immutable absolute, insulated from transgression and border-crossings.

'Is there a gay art?' asked Bersani in 2010. Taking a series of artists and authors from Da Vinci to Caravaggio, Mallarmé to Beckett, he opens with the provocative lines:

> In speaking of gay film—or, more generally, gay art today—we tend to mean films or novels with gay topics, more often made or written by gay or lesbian filmmakers or novelists. That is, for all the anti-identitarian rhetoric of current queer theory, what we mean by gay and lesbian art would seem to be inseparable from notions of gay authorship, gay audiences and gay subjects. I want to propose a notion of gay art—more exactly, a homo-esthetic—to which homosexual desire is essential, but which, precisely and paradoxically because of this, can dispense with the concept of homosexual identity. (Bersani 2010, 31)

Nothing, perhaps, teaches this better than *The Man Who Would Be Queen* which through a series of contradictions and self-cancellings demonstrates itself to be an anti-identitarian document. (Dis)embodying a queer aesthetics that reeks through every word and page, images and utterances, the text simultaneously discloses everything and nothing about the narrator, rendering the autobiography as mere fiction. Through means of writing gayness or queerness, Merchant's testimony closes with an anti-autobiographical remark: 'When Laura Riding, poet, had uninvited visitors she would yell out of an upstairs window: "I am not in." Anaïs Nin too does not live here anymore. Nor does "Hoshang Merchant"' (Merchant 2011, 200). The narrator has already disappeared by now, sublimated into the ecstatic excess of his text; he is nothing more than third-person at this moment. Do not go and search for him in vain, you will find him in the silhouette of every word of the book, in the intricate patterns and designs that he has carved out of his desires. He has learned to live in negation, cross borders—internal and external—with his libidinal heaves, and conjure lines, emotions, words, alphabets and poetry that bring political imagination to life.

NOTES

1. For an explanation of heteroglossia or polyglossia refer to the chapter, 'Discourse in the Novel' in *The Dialogic Imagination* (1981).
2. I am referring to the Penguin edition of the book. For further details, check citations.
3. He spoke in a combination of Hindi and English. For institutional reasons, I have translated the Hindi words and phrases into English. Much has been lost in translation but I have tried to remain as close to the original as possible. Also, the interview was much longer; I have used only the sections that are relevant for discussion here.
4. The word '*hijra*' is a local variant of the anglophonic 'transgender'.
5. He spoke a lot on the publication history of *Yaraana*. I have deliberately not ventured into that discussion for primarily two reasons: one, much has already been said and written about it; second, it demands a much broader and elaborate space and cannot be achieved within the limited scope of this chapter. For a detailed discussion on the politics of selection and publication of this anthology see the fifth chapter of Akhil Katyal's book *The Doubleness of Sexuality*.
6. In *The Pleasure of the Text*, Roland Barthes (2012) articulates the distinction between 'readerly' and 'writerly' texts. The former has a more coherent narrative, stable meanings and status-quoist; the latter has no fixed meanings, constituted by non-linear meta-narratives that demand active readers for meaning production.
7. I am indebted to Professor Madhavi Menon for this idea. This came up during a private conversation in 2017.

REFERENCES

Bakhtin, Mikhail. 'Discourse in the Novel'. In *The Dialogic Imagination*, 1934, 549–868. USA: University of Texas Press, 1981.

Bandyopadhyay, Sibaji. 'Banglar Lingo Prakriti O Rabindranath.' In *Rabindranath, Bakpati, Bishwamana*, 63–111. Kolkata: Calcutta University, 2011.

Barthes, Roland. *The Pleasure of the Text*. Notting Hill Editions, 2012.

Bersani, Leo. 'Is There a Gay Art?'. In *Is the Rectum a Grave? and Other Essays*. USA: University of Chicago Press, 2010.

Butler, Judith. *Gender Trouble: Feminism and the Subversion of Identity*. New York and London: Routledge, 2007.

Cixous, Hélène. 'The Laugh of Medusa.' *Signs* 1, no. 4 (Summer 1976): 875–893.
Edelman, Lee. *Homographesis*. London and New York: Routledge, 1994.
Katyal, Akhil. *The Doubleness of Sexuality: Idioms of Same-sex Desire in Modern India*. India: New Text, 2016.
Sedgwick, Eve Kosofsky. *Tendencies*. Durham: Duke University Press, 1993.
Merchant, Hoshang. *The Man Who Would Be Queen: Autobiographical Fictions*. New Delhi: Penguin, 2011.
Sedgwick, Eve Kosofsky. 'Paranoid Reading and Reparative Reading, Or, You're So Paranoid, You Probably Think This Essay Is About You.' In *Touching Feeling: Affect, Pedagogy, Performativity*, 123–151. United States: Duke University Press, 2003.
Shakespeare, William. *Twelfth Night, Or, What You Will*. United States of America: The Folger Shakespeare Library, 1993.
———. *Romeo and Juliet*. United States of America: The Folger Shakespeare Library, 2011.
Spivak, Gayatri Chakravorty. *Readings*. Kolkata: Seagull, 2014.

FLESH

THIS CITY, 'STINKING CORPSE': ADONIS'S POETICS OF MODERNITY AND DEATH

Al-Khoder Al-Khalifa

The crisis of poetry arises in the presence of human loss, yet it is in this moment that poetry effectuates its promise of establishing its own world. The coming of an apocalyptic state, with all its grimness and destruction, makes poets question the futility of writing in the presence of a catastrophe: what is it that poetry can do when, finally, the unthinkable and the unspeakable become reality? Martin Heidegger, in his reading of the nature of Rilke's poetry and the metaphysical aspects of poetry in general, starts his essay with an excerpt from Holderlin's poem 'Bread and Wine' that goes as '... and what are poets for in a destitute time?' (1971, 89). For Heidegger, what defines the poet's position in this 'destitute time' is that the poet should delve into this abyss to unveil Being. The destituteness of time is constituted not only by 'the God's failure to arrive' but also by how '[m]ortals have not yet come into ownership of their own nature. Death withdraws into the enigmatic. The mystery of pain remains veiled' (Heidegger 1971, 94). It is this creation of the void by the destitute time that brings the poet into achieving the impossible task: 'To be a poet in a destitute time means: to attend, singing, to the trace of the fugitive gods.' The poet, then, by experiencing and enduring the abyss, 'utters the holy' even when time is that of devastation that sanctions utter silence (Heidegger 1971, 92).

Similarly, in his elegy poem 'Tibaq', translated as 'Edward Said: A Contrapuntal Reading' and written on the occasion of the death of Edward Said, Mahmoud Darwīsh physically and intellectually invokes a dialogue with Said thirty years ago. Darwīsh shows the thinker's take on questions like identity, home, exile, loss and death. But more effectively, one matter seems to be of paramount concern to Said, that is, the impossibility, yet the necessity of writing. This necessity emerges out of the dire need and the hopeful task of questioning, 'What can poetry say in a time of catastrophe?', when bloodletting becomes the main scene as 'blood' covers not only humans, but taints 'the almond flower', 'the banana skin,/in the baby's milk, in light and shadow,/in the grain of wheat, in salt' (Darwīsh and Anis 2007, 180–181). This scene of death proliferates where the land of Palestine becomes 'smaller than the blood of its children/standing on the threshold of doomsday like/sacrificial offerings. Is this land truly/blessed, or is it baptized/in blood/and blood/and blood'. In this scene of death, the world appears 'without a sky, the earth becomes an abyss' where 'prayer', 'sand' the 'Sacred Book' fail to arrive. Therefore, Said's will after his own death is for Darwīsh to fulfil the impossible task of writing, because it is only poetry that can sing amongst the wreckage and become 'a consolation, an attribute/of the wind, southern or northern' (Darwīsh and Anis 2007, 181).

To confront the atrocities caused by constant bewildering events is a process of poetic experimentation. The poet, facing unprecedented destruction, piles of corpses, and hence, the nebulousness of tomorrow, comes into a moment of befuddlement. What follows might be a questioning of the validity and even the possibility of writing poetry in a similar assessment to Adorno's dictum that 'to write poetry after Auschwitz is barbaric. And this corrodes even the knowledge of why it has become impossible to write poetry today' (Adorno 1967, 34). However, if such a time of carnage instils silence, it is this very time that necessitates revolutionising poetry so as to bring a hopeful change to our reality. The poet's role, as Heidegger would think, is to substitute the gods who fled the place and sing in the void created by the destituteness of time, and, as Darwīsh tells us, '[poets] invent a hope for speech,/ invent a direction, a mirage to extend hope./And sing, for the aesthetic is freedom' (Darwīsh and Anis 2007, 181–182).

This need for revolutionising poetry should not be understood as a result of an external catastrophe occasioned due to events such as war. Revolutionising poetry can also be a part of a superior project of modernity as the poet feels that the catastrophe is a consequence of certain maladies intrinsically structured from within that have long been incapacitating the progress of culture into dynamicity, and thus leading into chaos. This can be inferred from the various writings of many poets from the Middle East since mid-twentieth century till the present day who have put in mind the need for a more transformative poetry regardless of the issue as internal or external. Reading Adonis's poetics of modernity and poetry helps understand this. This chapter studies the poetics and poetry of one of the most influential, yet controversial, contemporary Arab writers: Adonis. The attempt is to read his poetics on Arab modernity so as to understand the deeper structure of the limitations and the need for revolutionary poetry which, in a Rancièrean sense, disrupts, reconfigures and, hence, transforms the formal norms of Arab culture. Therefore, the study covers some of Adonis's theoretical writing on Arab poetics, modernity and language and their relation to the death of Arab intellectualism. Also, to see how

Adonis performs his modernist tendency in poetry, a close reading of the long poem *This is My Name* is conducted.

At the age of 18 in 1948, Ali Ahmed Said Esber decided to take on the name Adonis, equivalent to the Levantine and Mesopotamian deity Tammuz. The choice that was made by a *hadatha* (modernity) poet like Adonis at the time when the mainstream was favouring *al-turath* (traditionalism), marks his early transformative nature manifested in the rejection to belong to any fixed and inherited identity in favour of something more universally dynamic. This dissenting act was addressed in the 1980s by Jacques Derrida[1] who asserted that the Syrian poet 'carried an infinity of names within him', that such an act is manifested in his eagerness to 'step outside of himself'. Now, Adonis can 'tear his given names from the soil, thereby detaching from the identitarian borderlines of place', transcending into a new poetic identity, 'a cultural passport', to achieve universality (Rapaport 2013, 109). More importantly, it stands for the poet's chutzpah and attitudes towards the current state of the Arab culture, it is the cornerstone of Adonis's project of modernity.

Adonis's understanding of modern Arabic poetry has four major issues and concerns he presents in his article '*muhawala fi ta'rif al-shi'r al-hadith*' ('An Attempt to Define Modern Poetry'). First, he believes that modern poetry is an intellectual and spiritual vision that goes beyond, if not discards, the long-established principles. It is a rejection of the old poetic methods and forms and a reconfiguration of its attitudes and techniques of representing realism without causing a change:

> [Poetry of realism] discusses *a priori* ideas, opinions and feelings already existing in the minds in which its role is to sing them—sorting and presenting them as rhythms. The essence of modern poetry is based on reversing the values of 'realism', substituting the hormone of 'reality' with 'creativity', and finding a unique truth beyond the reality of the world. (My translation; Adonis 1959, 80–81)

Second, Adonis argues that because modern poetry is a vision of discovery, mysteriousness and irrationality, it should discard 'the fixed form', adopting a more open and free one. It is forever escaping from the 'imprisonment ... of specific meters or rhythms'. Third, in traditional Arabic poetry, the role of language is to 'express' reality without changing it, while the language of modern poetry is that of 'creativity' that transcends apparent meaning, unearths ulterior truth and leads to unfamiliar visions (Adonis 1959, 85). The poet now produces 'magic' and is no more under the subordinate of language (Adonis 1959, 86).

Ambiguity, finally, completes, yet is influenced by, the first three issues. Poetry that exceeds the norms in its vision, whose form never rests and whose language explodes, belongs to the logic of strangeness in its attempt to 'reach the depths of reality, beyond appearances and surfaces, and towards the marvelous and the transcendental' (Adonis 1959, 88).

Throughout his oeuvre—an effort presented in thirteen criticism volumes and more than twenty volumes of poetry—Adonis extensively discusses the social, political and theological hindrances to innovation and modernity in the Arab culture, its catastrophic consequences, the necessity of a transformative language as a method to renew this culture through reconfiguring its very long-established values. The year 1957 witnessed what Adonis would call his intellectual birth as he joined the poet Yusuf al-Khal in Lebanon in editing the avant-garde journal *Shi'r* (Poetry).[2] Through *Shi'r*, Adonis, along with Muhammad al-Maghut and Unsi al-Hajj, introduced his first modernist poetic tendency manifested in the emergence of the Arab prose poem. The form was at first disdained even by the most progressive writers of the time as being a strange and threatening innovation to the traditional *buhur al-shi'r al-arabi* (metre of Arabic poetry). For Adonis, labelling the prose poem as such is not surprising and comes as part of a bigger debate between the dominating ideology of literalism and modernity.

In *fatiha li nihayat al-qarn* (An Overture to the Century's Endings, 1980), Adonis finds that the essential problem preventing the progress of the modernity project and limiting individual creativity and imagination is the subjugation of reason to orthodox theological authorities imposed by *usul* (traditions) and *al-harfiah* (literalism). This literalism is effective due to the dominating traditional belief that regards history and the sacred text as the only reference of truth which fixates on the staticity of Arab cultural identity to which all descendants should conform. For Adonis, this monistic view of truth has taken Arab culture into the verge of decline:

> the space of freedom has shrunk, and the repression has increased … we have today less religiosity and less tolerance and more confessionalism and more fanaticism. We are more enclosed and enwrapped in darkness … and what we call homeland is becoming a military barrack, a confessional hamlet, a tribal camp. (quoted in Kassab 2010, 129)

This traditional tendency in the current Arab culture runs deep in the region's history since the caliphate era. During the Islamic Golden Age, all what was called "the people of innovation' (*ahl al-ihdath*)' were pejoratively indicted for heresy, 'a rebellion against religion' for their criticism of the caliphate.[3] In poetry the use of '*ihdath* (innovation) and *muhdath* (modern, new)' as terms characterising writing that violates 'the ancient poetic principles' have religious origin:

> The modern in poetry appeared to the ruling establishment as a political or intellectual attack on the culture of the regime and rejection of the idealized standards of the ancient, and how, therefore, in Arab life the poetic has always been mixed up with the political and the religious, and indeed *continues to be so* … [This] is indicative of a general cultural crisis, which is in some sense a crisis of identity. (Adonis 1990, 76)

During the Arab *Nahda* (renaissance) the question of modernity was adopted to the extreme by two different tendencies: 'the traditionalist/conformist (*usuli*) tendency, which considered religion and the Arab linguistic sciences as its main base; and the transgressing/non-conformist (*tajawuzi*) tendency, which saw its base, by contrast, as lying in European secularism.' What prevailed was the *usuli* with its vision that 'the ancient … is the ideal of true and definitive knowledge'; only within this vision the future is imagined (Adonis 1990, 77). The effect, Adonis elucidates, is felt in the artistic production of the *Nahda* period that retuned to 'the values of pre-Islamic orality', revived the 'forms of expression' of the past to talk about the problems of the present, and, therefore, established these forms as 'absolute inviolable principles'. Arab identity seems to be 'a bundle of self-delusion, and Arab time to stand outside time' (Adonis 1990, 79–80).

Although modernity for Adonis and other *Shi'r* poets stands for 'the rupture or the discontinuity' that distinguishes it from the conventional and classical Arabic verse, this 'discontinuity' does not mean to be in isolation from the past and cultural heritage (Haydar 1981, 51). Modernity, for Adonis, is a rejectionist vision of the sacredness and absolutism of institutionalised interpretation of a text as a source of truth and knowledge. What is favoured now is the individual's freedom, the celebration of plurality and multiplicity of readings. In a Bakhtinian sense, this vision denounces the fixed, closed and monophonic cultural identity and necessitates an ever dynamic, open and heteroglossic interpretation. It 'travels towards the other and its profound essence', establishing a heterogeneous culture in a constant process of becoming 'the most perfect presence'[4] (Adonis 2005a, Part 1, Ch. 5.16).

The impact of the inviolability of the *usuli* ideology in the present Arab literary scene is, however, more unrelentingly effective more than any time before. In his book *al-muhit al-aswad* ('The Black Ocean'), Adonis approaches questions of religiosity of politics, the hegemonic authority of censorship, the crisis of writing and innovation and the current scenario of the more disturbed Arab culture after, and during, wars and invasions. Creative language is seen as both a tool for expression and 'an act of liberation' in man's 'constant journey towards the unknown and search for truth'. However, under the unshaken authority of orthodoxy, the 'word … is essentially a "security" question', where culture functions as a tool for underscoring political and securitarian hegemony:

> What is the secret behind this Arab political obsessiveness to strengthen the hegemonizeation and subjugation over the ways of using the word? What is the source of this vision of politicizing language in this way? When politics transforms language from being the power of man's self-expression and freedom into the domain of creating censorship, ban, repression, and subjugation, it 'produces' … a home which has no place but for humiliation and slavery. (My translation; Adonis 2005b, 229–230)

The liberating function of the creative language is inspirational for creating poetry that challenges this cultural death with disruption of the norms. For Adonis, transforming Arab culture into a culture that radically revises its own old inherited values is possible when more power and freedom is given to language: when the word becomes 'a force for creativity and change', it places its culture in an 'atmosphere of investigation, questioning and inquiry'. The result is emptying the old language from 'the prevailing traditional meaning', and, therefore, the word becomes 'a mass radiating with unfamiliar associations' (Adonis and Elmessiri 1987, 115). This word is an explosive 'fire that burns only in the depths of humans filled with the sun': an innovative writer does not exist without living in and writing about that moment of the quake, the moment when the role of the free word is the 'deconstruction of traditional time' (Adonis and Elmessiri 1987, 118).

This word of change is uniquely practiced by the avant-garde Adonis. His antipathy towards fixed and inherited identity granted him an impenetrable modern idiom of change. He started first with his poetic self, with his *given* name, and, therefore, he *chose* a name, a word that detached him from belonging to place or time, embracing an ever-dynamic identity. This emigration outside one's self invokes an abstention from using both the poet's original language and even a foreign language. This establishes, in a Derridean sense, a unique idiom of the poet that others 'cannot appropriate and that performatively suspends, decides and … yields a certain unreadability or untranslatability' which 'instantiates the instability of meanings across borderlines' (Rapaport 2013, 111–113). This rejection to be easily grasped is Adonis's invocation of a poetic revolutionary strategy to criticise the static norms and values and to attain pluralism and inclusiveness through the dynamism of a word. Indeed, Adonis writes 'literature [that] "does" politics as literature' (Rancière 2010, 152). In doing so, he vigorously spares no effort to aesthetically reimagine a space of equality that establishes a new world whose founder is finally the long unnoticed voice. Interestingly, the relevance of the concepts of the political aesthetics and equality of the French historian and theorist Jacques Rancière are clearly echoed in Adonis's dissenting poetics.

Rancière explores the inseparability between the two 'forms of the distribution of the sensible', art and politics that are 'two strands of the same originary configuration'. Their main concern is liberation and equality as 'politics consists in reconfiguring the distribution of the sensible which defines the common of a community, to introduce into it new subjects and objects, to render visible what had not been' (Rancière 2009, 25). In order to understand the relation, or rather relations, between politics and aesthetics, it is necessary to examine the functionality of both forms. Aesthetics 'is the system of *a priori* forms determining what presents itself to sense experience. It is a delimitation of spaces and times, of the visible and the invisible, of speech and noise, that simultaneously determines the place and the stakes of politics as a form of experience' (Rancière 2004, 9). Accordingly, aesthetics not only precedes but determines politics in which the later appropriates 'the modes of presentation or the means of establishing explanatory sequences produced by artistic practices' (Rancière 2004, 60). Besides, 'the distribution of the sensible' is that system which constitutes the limits of 'sense perception' and, therefore, decides who can participate within the boundaries it creates (Rancière 2004, 7). Within this biased system there are others who are prevented from participating and stay outside these established boundaries. This is the moment of aesthetic politics: through dissensus, art 'redistributes' and reconfigures 'the given perceptual forms' (Rancière 2004, 59). This aesthetic politics produces 'a sensorium that had been outside and elsewhere in relation to the common and given its disruptive appearance, makes for an interruption and reconfiguration of the network of the distribution of the sensible'. By 'changing sensible perception itself' it changes the framework 'of what constitutes political experience and possibility' (Fisher 2013, 164).

When the dominating politics and ideologies of a culture establish boundaries around its own past and strictly structure life within it as per inherited traditions, it does not instigate equality as it leaves no hope for creativity and innovation. For Adonis, these powerful authorities turn their culture into the culture of death, or what he calls, 'theatre of nothingness', which is full of 'corpses, shrapnel, funerals, graves, and ruins'. A writer who radically 'registers his agitation against this policy is regarded as irrational' because 'the death of the other, whether this other is a friend or an enemy, is necessary' for the existence of the orthodox ideologies (my translation; Adonis 2005b, 243–244). The structured death of intellectualism, language and imagination is a provocative occasion for a dissenting writer such as Adonis who deliberately chooses irrationalism as a method to voice out against conservatism and the limitation of dominant discourses and to grant egalitarianism and inclusiveness to all the voices that were otherwise denied before. This artistic act of equality affects the nuances of a culture where the construction of both 'the enunciating "I" and the self of the subject' and 'poetic and fictional texts' now demonstrate 'signs of fragmentation'. This 'rich, though fundamentally different modes of writing and cultural creation' is characterised by being inclusive of 'a multiplicity of voices' and 'a language of possibilities, uncertainty, alternatives and contradictions', while discarding the credibility of 'the notion of unity' (Abu Deeb 2000, 339–340).

This Is My Name is Adonis's eloquent and radical critique of this declining culture for its blind attachment to live within the borderlines of the past.[5] Through this 'secret manifesto' he reaches the pinnacle in prophesying a revolutionary and transformative poetic practice that erases with fire to transcend this world into a new sublime reconfiguration. The poem came during a period of defeatism—after the six-day war in 1967 and the decline of Arabness—but it is not a direct response to it. War is part of a bigger cultural apocalypse Adonis has always warned of. Arabs are not in crisis because a culture in crisis means to be in the in-betweenness of either survival or death as this culture 'has a vision and a project of adventurously improving to a better state'. All the external factors—catastrophes, invasions, constant wars, slaughters—besides the repression and censorship practiced by the dominating absolutist ideologies over creativity and pluralism are all indications of 'a slave society' that is culturally dying and 'declining' (my translation; Adonis 2005b, 239). The poem begins with an act of erasing to write some new realities:

> Erasing all wisdom this is my fire
> No sign has remained—My blood is the sign
> This is my beginning (Adonis 2010, 107)

There are indications of a forthcoming revolution: 'erasing', 'my fire', 'my blood' and 'my beginning'. It is the 'fire' and 'flame' of creativity and innovation the speaker intends to perform that forces 'the footstep of life' to end 'at the door of a book ... erased with [his] questions' (Adonis 2010, 108). Thereafter, the speaker's determinist vision regarding the ravaging reality created by the prevailing totalitarians power: obsolete norms should be eradicated through nebulous questioning to reconstruct an ever-evolving world of endless possibilities.

Adonis forms a complex metric construction throughout the poem to challenge the metric unity of traditional Arabic poetry. The poem confusingly uses familiar Arabic metres but its open form simultaneously disrupts its familiar musical unity as it never clearly shows when that metric unity of (a) certain line(s) comes to an end and when another meter starts. Also, the poet abruptly shifts from this disruption of the metres into inserting a more revolutionary poetic form he is famous for, that is, the prose poem. With full awareness of the long-established poetic rules that have been dictating the writing of poetry since the eighth century, Adonis performs a modernist act of reconfiguring these rules.[6] The critic Khalida Said comments that the poem performs poetic dynamism and declares its own principle of change by destroying 'the principles of the poetic inviolability, stability and classicism' that hostilely oppose poetic newness and fossilise life itself. This poem 'transcends all the previous achievements of poetry and that includes even that of the poet' as it shows 'no relaxation, no finale, and no final form, but rather a constantly ever-renewing creativity, adventure and beginning' (my translation; Said 1970, 254). Adonis uses paradox as another modernist technique which intensifies the poem's mysteriousness in targeting the Arab self and identity. The speaker strikes us with the paradoxical images of 'country', which is static, and 'river', which is dynamic, when he says, 'My country runs behind me like a river of blood' (Adonis 2010, 113). This paradox expresses the geography of death in Arab culture: it is as long as a 'river' but instead of water, that stands for life, it carries 'blood' that covers all of its geography. This is followed by another opaque paradox: 'The *forehead* of civilization is a *floor* slathered with algae' (Adonis 2010, 113; emphasis added). After the 'river of blood' covers the 'country' with the red colour, it continues its progress and now reaches 'the forehead of civilization' and history itself that needs a transformation of its obsolescent conventions.

Throughout the poem's open form, Adonis repeatedly uses a word that represents a line on its own surrounded by white spaces of silence. This modernist technique dismantles the traditional Arabic rhythm that depends on the unity of the poem's metre and the rhyme and the length of the lines. In this example, 'as its flag' appears in Arabic as one word in one line, *rayah*: This country/raised its thighs/as its flag (Adonis 2010, 109). And then in another occasion he says:

> No place for me, no use in death   This is the dizziness of a man who sees the corpse of the ages on his face and falls No motion (Adonis 2010, 115)

This 'rhythmic event' which makes out of 'a single word a line of poetry' is a Mallarméan impact on Adonis and never existed in previous traditional Arabic verse. These isolated words do not take the word-rhyme role as they vary in their positions and their role becomes more complex with the surrounding white spaces. They both generate a unique rhythm that 'makes silence speak, and turns space among words into another writing in which the essence is erasing that intensifies the rhythm of both the seen-written and erased-written' (my translation; Bennis 2001, 152). What is manifested in Adonis's poetry is the collapse of ordinary experience that dominated the classical literary text and the rise of a new unfathomable discourse which as he says, 'I walk on the ice of my pleasures/I walk between miracle and confusion/I walk inside a rose' (Adonis 2010, 113). The poet no more cares about traditional rhythm and rhyme or the sacredness of language so 'breaks the crutches of song and roots out the/alphabet' (Adonis 2010, 112).

These disruptive techniques are clear markers of the poem's impenetrability which is one major characteristic of contemporary Arabic poetry. This deliberate act 'occurs within a quest to secularize Arabic poetry and society', in which a rejectionist poet like Adonis 'enacts a secular self, which takes the religious as its other'[7] (Furani 2012, 238). This is manifested through the dialogic nature of the poem's speaker that nebulously questions, critically contrasts and vehemently expunges and negates the dominating religious discourse. For example, the voice announcing, 'This is my name' has the decisive authority of no one but God who tells Moses in Exodus 3:15: 'this [is] my name for ever, and this [is] my memorial unto all generations'. Also, in Islamic tradition one of the names of God is The Wise, like in 2. 45: 'They said, 'Exalted are You; we have no knowledge except what You have taught us. Indeed, it is You who is the Knowing, the Wise." Here, the quest for wisdom from no authority but the Absolute is a central issue of faith conveyed through the established interpretations of the sacred text. Then, when the speaker says, 'this is my beginning', it coheres with 'this is my fire' for the 'erasing [of] all wisdom' is negated through this very 'fire' of questioning and rejection. This results in the speaker's self-discovery of death and life at the same time which is his new genesis: 'No sign has remained—My blood is the sign'.[8] For Adonis, 'erasing' the discourse of death by 'fire' has 'the authority of naming through negating' where poetry finally has the power, unlike before, to be 'a language that names' (my translation; Bennis 2001, 227–228).

What seems central here is the debatable question of interpretation of the authoritative sacred text. In *Sufism and Surrealism*, while examining the resemblance between the aesthetics of the Sufi and surrealist visions, Adonis explains that both produce 'unorthodox forms of writing'.

They extensively use figurative language that does not lend itself to any 'conclusive answers' but rather 'raises more questions', and, therefore, disturbs knowledge. In religion 'interpretation, i.e. figurative language' of the religious text is either rejected for the sake of literalism or accepted only when 'any answer that conflicts with the orthodox view is outlawed'. As such, interpretation, functioning as an analytical work, confirms what 'conforms with the … literal meaning of the text' rather than *al-tasa'ul* (questioning) it. In poetry, Adonis adds, the power of the figurative language resides in its innovative nature:

> [It] renews man in that it renews thought and language and relations to things. It is a movement that denies a present existence in its search for another existence … just as the language it uses transcends itself, so too does the reality that it is explaining transcend itself. Thus figurative language links us to another dimension of things—its invisible dimension. (Adonis 2005a, Part 1, Ch. 5.5)

The poem's modernist disrupt-to-reconfigure strategy of questioning, erasing and then naming marks a complete shift from a long history of *al-naqil* (conveyance) into *al-aqil* (reason), performed through the creative language of *al-inkaar* (negation), *al-hadm* (subversion), *tajawz* (transgression) and *al-taghyir* (transformation). The poem bewilders its reader with highly symbolic imagery, devastating moments and events of death as a reference to the decline of the Arab culture. The naming that Adonis articulates is secularism that protests against the state of being culturally stagnant, and, therefore, declining, if not entirely dead. It is a protesting voice calling for a civil society to abolish absolute authorities like the 'sultan', the 'caliph', whose 'word is a crown studded with human eyes', and 'mosque and church' that determine politics, life and death 'as two executioners and the earth is a rose'. For the poet, these institutions, and even the seemingly progressive thinkers who dignify Arab *Nahda* and its traditionalist tendency, repressively force 'histories [of] swarms of locusts' and '[t]he dust of the legends' to structure 'the bones' of our present, turning their lands into a 'stable on the moon,/the sultan's staff, the prophet's prayer rug'. Therefore, the speaker decides to 'name this city "stinking corpse"' whose people are 'absence', 'a river without sound' and 'foam spewing from a river of words/Rust in the sky and its planets,/rust in life'. The sceptic Arab intellectual now is in 'dizziness' and 'falls no motion' after realising the futility of seeking 'shelter' or even to escape to 'death' as 'the corpse of the ages' sheds its light, if not darkness, on the present and feeds it like 'a nipple for infants' (Adonis 2010, 109–116). Later in the poem, the image of the 'Dajjal' shows the deceptive nature of these institutions:

> Dajjal[9] buried a people in his eyes
> Dajjal excavated a people from his eyes
> and we heard him praying above them
> and we saw how he made them kneel
> and we saw
> how the people were like water cupped in his palms and
> we saw
> how water became a windmill (Adonis 2010, 119–120)

Interestingly, these dissenting rhythms of secularisation are strategically structured on this very trope of death for this culture, like the phoenix should burn to die and resurrect, returning to life from its own ashes.[10] Adonis's deliberate repetition of war-like images such as 'fire that weeps', 'fire to conquer', 'flames', 'ashes', 'erase', 'flood is coming' and 'river of blood' are a reminder that his erasing revolution of the past is, on the one hand, full of 'sorrows' and 'turns the green branches into snakes and the sun into a black lover'. On the other hand, it is brought about by and is meant 'for the people of flame' and 'fire to conquer' and 'bear ashes for all the sultans' of the old time (Adonis 2010, 107–108). Those 'people of flame' are Arab poets, of past and present, presented in the poem as the libertines who question absolutism via subversive language and new visions of life. In the poem, Adonis illustrates how the modernist poets have always been suffering because of their fervour to challenge the institutionalised 'word':

> I see a word—
> All of us around it are mirage and mud Imruulqais could not shake it away, al-Ma'ari was
> its child, Junaid crouched under it, al-Hallaj and al-Niffari too
> Al-Mutannabi said it was the voice and its echo 'You are a slave, and it is your angel master' The nation is tucked deep within it like a seed
> Go back to your cave (Adonis 2010, 116)

The speaker adds that banishment or death are the expected punishments these iconoclasts have always been facing. In his book *muqaddimah li al-shi'r al-arabi* (Introduction to Arabic Poetry) and while discussing the daring poetry of Abu Nuwas, one of the prominent poets of the Abbasid period, Adonis figures out that poetry is all about living the danger of questioning, rejecting and transcending any dogmatic form of power. Because this poetry grants its people 'the will and the choice' that compensate for the downfall in the future, 'the poet is never afraid of punishment, instead he willingly does what leads him into punishment' for the sake of his people who are 'disturbingly shattered by the winds of death':

> When the poet evokes the strange death and resurrects and lives in its presence, he then hybridizes and familiarizes it, emptying it from the terror of menace and downfall. The poet faces death with a determination and not as a surrender, and lives to see its end instead of staying burdened by its perpetual threats. (my translation; Adonis 1971, 48)

The speaker relates the suffering, death and rebirth of Ali, nobody but Adonis himself. The character of Ali here echoes the koranic story of the prophet Joseph. It simultaneously embodies the miserable, yet creative, stories of the Arab freethinker's rise from underneath the rubbles. 'This is the time of death, but/in each death there is an Arab death' (Adonis 2010, 112), where the Arab intellectual, like the prophet Joseph, is thrown 'into a well and covered … with straw', preventing him from radiating enlightenment upon the public. However, an idea never dies and disruptively, like a quake, resurrects from its own death to deconstruct the static norm of life and move into the dynamism of constant reconfigurations, where avant-garde 'light find[s] its way to Ali's land' (Adonis 2010, 109). For Adonis, revolutionary language is a 'fire that burns only in the depths of humans filled with the sun', a fire that is capable of renewing even itself, an act which has a futuristic appeal inherent in itself (Adonis and Elmessiri 1987, 118). Therefore, the speaker is granted with a new 'voice' of freedom and fragmentation like 'the ravings of a warrior as he breaks the crutches of song and roots out the alphabet' (Adonis 2010, 112). Hence the deceleration: 'I can transform: Landmine of civilization—This is my name' (Adonis 2010, 108). To create a new present, the speaker first becomes 'a flame/a magician that burns in all waters—/storming he rages, invades all books and soils/He sweeps away history and blots out the day with his wings' (Adonis 2010, 112). After this storm that erases all forms of traditionalism, the speaker moves into naming: 'This broken earthen jug/is a defeated nation This space/is ash These eyes/are holes/I will see a craw's face/in the features of my country I will name this book/"shroud."/I will name this city "stinking corpse"'. A new civil form of life, like 'a flower or song' can 'grow out of [this] naming', where nature 'and the earth may waken and return/as a child, or a child's dream' (Adonis 2010, 114–115).

This poem, and many of Adonis's poems, can be read as examples of a modernist variation of a subgenre well-known in Arabic poetry, *ritha' al-mudun* (city elegy). Robyn Creswell (2019) argues that this 'modulation', of which Adonis is a precursor, is not strewn with gestures of a nostalgia to 'a happy and prosperous past before lamenting the fallen present', and it also rejects to express verbally that sense of 'affective solidarity' with those suffering within a city as is the case with *ritha' al-mudun*.[11] Instead, Adonis, through the use of series of questions in the poem without getting answers, registers an exilic idiomaticity of being in a state of aphasic 'solitude', archives 'melancholy' and establishes a remarkable topography that shows 'the interior wastes and the seacoasts of exile' (Creswell 2019, 176). As '[n]othing but madness remains' (Adonis 2010, 121), the speaker's city turns into cul-de-sac, mounting 'disaffection', and the poem becomes an 'invective' written 'document of disaffiliation'[12] (Creswell 2019, 177). Therefore, Adonis's elegiac genre functions within the parameters of his modernist project. It reconfigures the relation between literature and politics so as to extricate poetry from the 'mobilising power of the state' and, thus, this facilitates and frees the process of cultural transformation from politics (Creswell 2019, 179). This Adonisian subgenre of elegy is extraordinarily similar to Mallarme's *tombeaux*.[13] Although these poems are about other poets in pain but they do not eulogise or celebrate the harmony between these poets and the collective. Rather, Adonis's poem does not mourn but revises things, producing 'a countertradition' as we feel a 'common exclusion' and 'painful species of exile' shared between him and the other revolutionary figures from the history of the Arab culture. The appearance of these figures, mostly poets, is, on the one hand, to witness and comment on a dystopic present, not very different from its past, and, on the other hand, to show how these poets have 'an unsponsored legitimacy' and 'freedom' of being autonomous 'from the workings of power' which enables them to revise and transform (Creswell 2019, 184).

NOTES

1. The seminar is referred to in Rapaport (2013).
2. Arguably one of the earliest modernist literary journals in the Arab World, *Shi'r* was established when modernity began preoccupying Arab culture. It showed an association with this by pursuing poetic change and innovation (Haidar 2008, 73). Over its forty-four issues, *Shi'r* introduced new forms into Arabic literature such as the prose poem and manifestoes and was open to non-Arabic literature. What distinguished the *Shi'r* poets from their contemporaries is the awareness of the necessity to reconfigure poetry through redefining *al-turath* (tradition) (Creswell 2019, 1–5).
3. Among the 'people of innovation' who tremendously influenced Adonis are Abu Tammam, Abu Nuwas, al-Ma'arri, al-Mutanabbi, al-niffari and al-Hallaj.

4. Reference is being made here to 'Epic and Novel: Towards a Methodology for the Study of the Novel' that appears in Bakhtin (1981).
5. Adonis first published this long poem in *Mawaqif* journal. Then he reintroduced it in 1971 in a volume that contained two other long poems: *An Introduction* to the *History of the Petty Kings* and *A Grave for New York*.
6. The traditional Arabic metre of poetry was founded by Al-Khalil Al-Farahidi during the Islamic Golden Age in the eighth century. Before that, prosodic rules where incoherent and did not work within a system. Changing this way of writing poetry into a strict prosodic system, Al-Khalil established the sixteen metres of poetry that determine whether a poem can be written and accepted. Any poetic attempt to write beyond these metric rules was simply unacceptable. The musical unity of the poem is created through the stability of the poem's form itself. In this sense, every metre of these sixteen commands the length of the line, which sustains its stability all over the poem and this line has two balanced hemistichs, called *al-sadr* and *al-'ajuz*, which give the musical unity of the poem. This unity comes from the equal division of these lines into certain numbers of accents and syllables, where *al-taf'ilah* (poetic foot) is created through the repetitions of these syllables and accents. The unity also comes from the rhyme of the poem that is also unvaried. This unity of the form determines even the meaning of the poem itself as the poet has to choose a certain metre that suits the theme of the poem. For example, if the poet's theme is pride, praising or reciting events and news, then they would clearly choose *al-bahr al-tawil* (the long metre).
7. The term 'rejectionist poet' is used here to refer to the fact that Adonis labelled himself and was labelled, along with other prose poets who adopted radical transformation as a strategy, as *al-shu'ara al-rafdiyyun* (rejectionist poets), for his tendency to reject not only the interference of religion in politics but the tendency of other poets of his time to return blindly to traditions.
8. In the Arabic text, the poet uses the word *ayah* (verse), but the English translation prefers the word 'sign', one of the senses of the word *ayah*.
9. *Dajjal* (the deceitful) is 'the one-eyed giant' eschatological figure that appears in Islamic tradition. Known also as *al-Masih al-Dajjal* (pseudo-Christ), he calls himself God and many people follow him, ruling over 'the earth for forty days … before being slain by Jesus son of Mary' (Halperin 1976, 213).
10. Adonis extensively uses mythological and legendry figures of death and finitude in his poetry for they grant him 'timeless perspective from which to view the human condition and strengthened [his] feeling of being … a constant present' (Adonis 1990, 95).
11. A traditional Arabic poetry genre that was occasioned and developed by the decline of al-Andalus during the Abbasid Caliphate. It responded to the catastrophic fall of the premodern Islamic city and talked about longing, displacement and collective recuperation. Among the known poets of this subgenre are abu al-baqa' al-rundi and Ibn Zaydun. For further reading on city elegy, see Elinson (2009) and Basha (2003).

12. This invectiveness is close to a form of elegy known in Arabic literature as *hija' al-mudun,* which is the opposite of *rith' al-mudun*. See Fakhreddine and Orfali (2018).
13. As much as Adonis was influenced by Arab libertines in poetry, he was also 'captivated by Western culture', especially French, where reading Baudelaire revealed [Abu Nuwas's] particular poetical quality and modernity and 'Mallarme's' writing explained 'the mysteries of Abu Tammam's poetic language and [its] modern dimension' and that through 'Rimbaud, Nerval and Breton' he discovered 'the poetry of the mystic writers in all its uniqueness and splendour' (Adonis 1990, 80–81).

REFERENCES

Abu Deeb, Kamal. 'The Collapse of Totalizing Discourse and the Rise of Marginalized/Minority Discourses'. In *Tradition, Modernity and Postmodernity in Arabic Literature: Essays in Honor of Professor Issa J. Boullata*, edited by Kamal Abdel-Malek and Wael Hallaq, 335–366. Leiden: Koninklijke Brill, 2000.

Adonis. '*muhawala fi ta'rif al-shi'r al-hadith*' (An Attempt to Define Modern Poetry), *Shi'r*, 11(1959): 79–90. Available at http://archive.alsharekh.org/newPreview.aspx?PID=2386150&ISSUEID=838&AID=52732.

———. *muqaddimah li al-shi'r al-arabi* (An Introduction to Arabic Poetry). Beirut: Dar al-A'wda, 1971.

———. *Fatiha Li Nihayat al-Qarn: Bayanat Min Ajl Thaqafa Arabia Jadida* (Overture to the Century's Endings: Manifestos for a New Arab Culture). Beirut: Dar al-A'wda, 1980.

———. *An Introduction to Arab Poetics*. Translated by Catherine Cobban. London: Saqi, 1990.

———. *Sufism and Surrealism*. Translated by Judith Cumberbatch. London: Saqi, 2005a. Accessed in Kindle format.

———. *al-muhit al-aswad* (The Black Ocean). Beirut: Dar al-Saqi, 2005b.

———. *Adonis Selected Poems*. Translated by Khaled Mattawa. London: Yale University Press, 2010.

Adonis, Nancy Berg and Nur Elmessiri. 'Adonis: Language, Culture and Reality/أدونيس : اللغة ، الثقافة ، الواقع'. *Alif: Journal of Comparative Poetics*, 7 (1987): 112–120. Available at http://www.jstor.org/stable/521857 (accessed 7 November 2020).

Adorno, Theodor W. *Prisms*. Translated by Samuel and Shierry Webber. Massachusetts: MIT Press, 1967.

Bakhtin, M.M. *The Dialogic Imagination: Four Essays*. Edited by Michael Holquist. Translated by Caryl Emerson and Michael Holquist. Austin: University of Texas Press, 1981.

Basha, Muja Amin. *ritha' al-mudun wa-al-mamalik fi al-shi'r al-Andalusi* (City and Kingdom Elegy in the Andalusian Poetry). Damascus: Shira' li-l-Dirasat wa-al-Nashr, 2003.

Bennis, Mohammed. *al-shi'r al-arabi al-hadith bunyatahu wa ebdalataha: al-shi'r al-mu'aser* (Modern Arabic Poetry: The Structure and Changes in Contemporary Poetry). Casablanca: Tobqal Publishing House, 2001.

Creswell, Robyn. *City of Beginning: Poetic Modernism in Beirut*. Princeton: Princeton University Press, 2019.

Darwīsh, M. and M. Anis. 'Edward Said: A Contrapuntal Reading.' *Cultural Critique* 67 (2007): 175–182. Available at the Project MUSE database: https://doi.org/10.1353/cul.2007.0026.

Elinson, Alexander E. *Looking Back at al-Andalaus: The Poetics of Loss and Nostalgia in Medieval Arabic and Hebrew Literature*. Leiden: Brill, 2009.

Fakhreddine, Huda and Bilal Orfali. 'Against Cities: On Hija' al-Mudun in Arabic Poetry'. In *The City in Arabic Literature: Classical and Modern Perspectives*, edited by Nizar F. Hermes and Gretchen Head. Edinburgh: Edinburgh University Press, 2018.

Fisher, Tom. 'Making Sense: Jacques Rancière and the Language Poets', *Journal of Literature* 36, no. 2 (2013): 156–174. Available at https://www.jstor.org/stable/10.2979/jmodelite.36.2.156.

Furani, Khaled. *Silencing the Sea: Secular Rhythms in Palestinian Poetry*. California: Stanford University Press, 2012.

Haidar, Otared. *The Prose Poem and the Journal Shi'r: A Comparative Study of Literature, Literary Theory and Journalism*. Reading: Ithaca, 2008.

Halperin, David J. 'The Ibn Sayyād Traditions and the Legend of al-Dajjāj'. *Journal of the American Oriental Society* 96, no. 2 (1976): 213–225. Available at www.jstor.org/stable/599824 (accessed 7 November 2020).

Haydar, Adanan. 'What Is Modern About Modern Arabic Poetry?', *Al-'Arabiyya* 14, no. ½ (1981): 51–58. Available at http://www.jstor.org/stable/43195490 (accessed 7 November 2020).

Heidegger, Martin. *Poetry, Language, Thought*, translated by Albert Hofstadter. New York: HarperCollins Publishers, 1971.

Kassab, Elizabeth Suzanne. *Contemporary Arab Thought: Cultural Critique in Comparative Perspective*. New York: Columbia University Press, 2010.

Rancière, Jacques. *The Politics of Aesthetics: The Distribution of the Sensible*. Edited and translated by Gabriel Rockhil. London: Bloomsbury, 2004.

———. *Aesthetics and Its Discontents*. Translated by Steven Corcoran. New York: Polity Press, 2009.

———. *Dissensus: On Politics and Aesthetics*. Edited and translated by Steven Corcoran. New York: Continuum International Publishing Group, 2010.

Rapaport, Herman. 'Performativity as Ek-Scription: Adonis After Derrida'. In *Performatives After Deconstruction*, edited by Mauro Senatro, 109–130. London: Bloomsbury, 2013.

Said, Khalida. 'hawla qasidat 'Hhhatha hwa esmi': iqa'a al-shaoq wa al-tajathub' ('On the Poem "This is My Name": The Rhythm of Longing and Gravitation'). *Mawaqif* 7 (1970): 250–271. Available at http://archive.alsharekh.org/newPreview.aspx?PID=1878673&ISSUEID=15725&AID=350715.

EATING DISSIDENCE OF ANTONIN ARTAUD: TOWARDS A POOR AESTHETICS

Soumyabrata Choudhury

I am hungry. I have no appetite.

—Antonin Artaud

1

Unlike Kafka in 'A Hunger Artist', Antonin Artaud—on the verge of physical collapse, body ravaged by cancer, towards the end of his life—actually feels hungry. Artaud can be imagined to go on a lunch date with his friend and, eventually, legatee to the rights of his works, Paule Thévenin, just a few days before his death and at Thévenin's door make this extraordinary assertion: 'I am hungry. I have no appetite.'[1]

In this respect, he is indeed unlike Kafka's hunger artiste. The latter, mostly silent during his forty-day fast, has no need to express any particular thoughts towards his acts because he is rigorously and silently dedicated to the performance of his fasting in the same way that one does not need to express any thoughts about performing any ritual. The hunger artist is only concerned about the fact that he could better his performance if given a chance but for ritual reasons again the impresario stops his fast every time on the fortieth day. For the hunger artiste, the medical reason for doing so by the impresario is no different from ritual reasons because, every time, the last day arrives as a repetitive occasion that both ends his performance and frustrates his confident ambition to break his own record. Indeed, the rigorous and endless repetition of the ritual sequence of fasting makes it, in the exact sense, a performance that is an encoded and expert action with no vacillation or interruption by thought. The hunger artiste, in other words, is a professional.[2]

2

Antonin Artaud experiences his relationship with food as real. His illness prevents him from assimilating food with the normal efficiency and periodicity of a healthy person—which results in a body partially starved and emaciated. At the same time, this very physical deprivation causes in him great surges of hunger. And, as in any state of hunger, food transmutes from being merely an object of assimilation and excretion to an *idea*. It is as an idea that food becomes a scintillating and interruptive thought for Artaud. His hungry body is as if addressed by a kind of beatific aura of food, a greater horizon of satisfaction that both pulls him forward and uplifts his spirit—hence, we can imagine him nearly traipsing through the streets of Paris to Paule Thévenin's house for lunch, and simultaneously, he can be pictured as being repulsed by the *presence* of food in both the ritual setting of a social occasion like lunch and an alimentary setting of the substance called 'food'. So, at the precise point of intersection between the flight of the idea and the assault by food, Artaud can be thought to produce his singular and shattering act of speech: 'I am hungry. I have no appetite.'

Unlike the hunger Artiste's continuous and ritually encoded performance of fasting, Artaud is confronted with real negativity that knots together food and thought. No ritual form or medical prescription quite suffices to untie this knot and free Artaud's life from a kind of alimentary thinking that he both thinks and suffers, suffers and speaks. At this crossroad, the reality of thought interrupts the great chains of ritual that encircle a society of performance but at the point of this slight chink that opens the great ritual grids of the world—we are not at all greeted by any triumphal cry of either new thought or new art. Antonin Artaud experiences this chink or opening within the discipline of the world, that is meant to churn out endless forms and sequences of performance and crystallise into society as a performance machine, as an opening and aperture of his own being. In so far as Artaud belongs to the same performance society that the hunger artiste does, he must either fulfil his obligations as a professional artist—which could mean in his case, an actor, a poet, a painter—or he must retire from his professional status. This is what Antonin Artaud either refuses to do or his so-called illness comes as too quick an interruption, like a lightning flash, for him to discern the very elements of a situation so as to enable himself to take a measured and rational decision on his life and work. So instead of simply being counted as one of those enormously talented individuals who professionally could not realise their promise, that is being counted as a 'failed artist', Artaud's is a life of art interrupted by life itself. There are two dimensions to this interruption: the first is the interruption produced by Artaud's illness and the second is that produced by his thought—*and insofar as they are the same*, we might call this an interruptive and 'poor' thought.

3

In a letter Artaud wrote to Jacque Rivière, he invented a strange French word created by nothing less than an impulse of the negative—*impouvoir*. The two alternative English translations for this word are 'un-power' and 'im-power' (in this context, see Blanchot 2004, 109–115). Both translations indicate a strange operation of negation or opposition that does not come from any term or force that is outside the object being negated or opposed. So, if Artaud, as he writes to Rivière, admits to feeling an *impouvoir* gripping his thinking then it is not that he is hampered or deprived of thinking properly by some agent or force that is blocking him like an enemy or adversary outside himself. To that extent, it would seem that the question of illness is too historical and empirical an instance to account for Artaud's 'poor thought'. Yet, at no point, can Artaud be thought to think outside the sufferings of his body. This is the real enigma of the singular experience that the eating paradox and the alimentary utterance of Artaud's life must be traced along their itineraries as experiences of thinking.

Artaud himself indicates to Rivière a kind of symptomatology of this thinking. He says that thought slips in such a way that he can't quite find himself or grip himself in the act of thinking. Hence, the signification attached to such neo-words as 'impower' or 'unpower' is to somehow grasp this slipping beneath the forms of the thinking given in and to the world that provide the grid for the world as thinkable and knowable. Surely, one part of this thinkable and knowable world is the artistic one and one great form of the world thinkable as and through art is the form of ritual. In that sense, ritual is not merely the content of the performances that take place in the world in the common way we understand a religious ritual or a social ritual. It is the other way round: ritual is the very form of the world as performance. So, it is not a question of this ritual performance, or that; it is rather, that ritual is the general logic of a world that is guaranteed in its performances, and in that sense, a 'performance world'. It is this guarantee of the world, through both a techno-ritualistic procedure and a metaphysical one, that the enigmatic experience enclosed within the hollow of Artaud's *impouvoir* hollows out. In the very movement of this hollowing out, the ritual richness of the world as performance is denuded and the poverty that resultantly grips the world strangely becomes an affirmation of thought.

4

'Poor thought' as we have called it, is neither a pure inward activity of the subject nor a new objective knowledge that can be added to the world's encyclopaedias. In this respect, 'poor thought' is not an affair of the *power* that forever entwines itself with knowledge. Then the question follows that what does such thought have to do with the strange provenance of neo-words like *impouvoir* or impotential/impower? One has to clarify here that the affirmation of poor thought is neither an affirmation of power nor an affirmation against it. It is rather, an affirmation of the constitutive *weakness* of power, its exposure to a fragment of contingency that hollows its political and professional mastery from within. But even 'within' is too interiorising a spatial expression; the 'within' here is similar to the status of 'food' for Artaud's eating paradox. In both cases, the impulse or the assault arrives from without as either an object of hunger or revulsion but simultaneously, the object seems to enclose within itself the very essence of an experience that has lost both its subjective identity and its objective locus. This is the reason why Artaud needs to resort to some sort of a language of weakness when writing to Rivière that speaks of his thought slipping away from or slipping beneath the capacity to symbolise his own experience. Exactly at this point, the logic of ritual performance and its technical as well as metaphysical guarantees are echoed in the general logic of discursive expression and symbolic competence. Artaud is the most singular thinker of an experience of weakness or poverty that befalls him but insofar as it *is* a weak, poor and denuded thought, it only testifies to the tortures of techno-ritually speaking, an 'incompetent' thinker.

However, such incompetence is the rare creation of a thought that refuses to yield to the ritual and professional temptation of *performance*. Artaud's incompetent or unperforming creation of thought is precisely that—thought as a dissident creation against the world as performance. It is in this context that one must re-read some of Artaud's most well-known and lacerated texts to realise that what is affirmed against the regime of performance is a word or idea as old as the performance itself and yet sought to be wrenched free from it—the word 'theatre'.

5

Antonin Artaud's texts and scenarios for what he called the Theatre of Cruelty are often seen as prophetic announcements for a future of performance freed from bourgeois proscenium-staging of psychological drama and redirected towards a future of the *total ritual* or *Total Theatre as Ritual* (1994).[3] This hyper-performative appropriation of Artaud, in fact, departs more and more from the *thought* of theatre, which is incipient in the word 'cruelty'. This appropriation seeks to tempt us with ritually sanctified and institutionally legitimated images of what could be called merely cruel performances from the world of theatre arts, performance art, video art, installation art and so on. We are not saying that this rich historical corpus of performance works or ritual successes is to be disparaged in any way; we are only asking whether this contemporary, as well as archival, wealth responds to the test of Artaud's thought of 'cruelty', when Artaud said that 'cruelty is necessity'.[4] In this sense, we are asking a frankly counter-intuitive question: whether performance is *necessary* for the thought of theatre. In fact, we can exacerbate the question even further: we can ask whether theatre was not always a thought of *exit* from performance insofar as the latter's success was already guaranteed by the ritual technology of the world while the former was, in its very birth, meant to be a gesture of the *real*. It is on the question of the real that the thought of theatre as a necessary exit from the great enclosure of performance and food as the mere alimentary object of physical satisfaction must be thought together. In both cases, the real is the opposite of anything that is otherworldly and metaphysical; it is the interruption that is felt in the body as a weakness, as an insistent hunger but only weakly oriented towards the exact food destined to satisfy it. The idea of theatre and the idea of food are similar in that they are a betweenness flanked by the professionally incompetent body and the intellectually illegitimate act of thinking. In other words, hunger and thought are the respective madnesses of the body and the mind, insofar as both refuse to be satisfied by any ritual foods, whether of the body or the mind, that are offered as a recompense for the professional labours of the great performers of the world including the performer of hunger.

6

So it is a matter of some interest that Kafka's 'A Hunger Artist' does not actually end with the reconfirmation of the web of the world as a web of ritual performances. The hunger artist at the fag end of his dimming career as well as dimming life admits to the overseer that he would never have undertaken the fast had he found the food that he liked. 'I couldn't find the food I liked. If I had found it believe me I should have made no fuss and stuffed myself like you or anyone else.'[5] Thus, the hunger artist no longer speaks of food as ritual food, something to be ritually assimilated or in the same fashion rejected within the professional act of fasting but as the *real* co-relate of desire. The very last words of his life reveal the professional performer to be a forever deprived being, deprived of the real of his desire. At this point, the tale moves into a strange metaphoric luminosity. Once the hunger artist is dead and buried, his cage is now occupied by a panther who strides that confined space with such luminous energy that the crowds are back and everyone is transfixed to this magnetic site in sharp contrast to the last failing days of the hunger artist performance when most of the people would pass by his cage to the ones hosting the fabulous and dangerous animals of the circus. Now that the hunger artist has gone, the cage is re-occupied by one such animal who re-incites great spectatorial interest in the world as performance. However, exactly as part of this performance, the panther is brought food to eat—*real* food, that sets the panther's shining throat and jaws in motion and seems to generate a light that captures one and all. So, exactly at the loss of ritual efficacy of one artist, and one sequence of performance, another is instituted and this time it is the institutionalisation and ritualisation of that very animal reality—real food—which was the locus of a fabulous and disciplined deprivation ritually practised by the genius of the hunger artist. At this point, the Great Form that is performance, the encoding of repetition within a ritual and the luminous assimilation of reality by the body of the performer, the shiny throat and jaws of the panther cannot be distinguished anymore.

What Kafka localises in the dying and disciplined body of the hunger artist—the discipline of dying/fasting—and equally, delocalises and discloses to be a fragment of reality perpetually lost or yet to come—the reality of a food that the hunger artist would like and never did find—Antonin Artaud re-insinuates in his own vital and historical being and body. For Kafka's hunger artist, everything was set off because he could never find the food he liked; for Artaud, he could never satisfy his great hunger for food because his *body* did not like the food he liked. To that measure, what Artaud never ceases to declare is that he is captured and tortured by a body that is nothing but a history of errors, bad organs and bad combinations of organs, a series of bad localisations. So, instead of merely announcing the deprivation of his being by the absence of the real of food, the food that he would 'like', Artaud rages at the deprivation of his being by the error of his body and in that cry of repudiation, he strangely affirms a new theatre of the real. It is a theatre which cannot conceivably be performed within any historico-ritualistic form because the fundamental pre-supposition of that performance, which is the body of the performer, is constitutively repudiated by Artaud. So, for Artaud the real to come is a new body, a body whose localisation is still too dim, too weak, too enveloped in a kind of 'impouvoir', impower/unpower to produce itself as historically and ritually verifiable body. It is in this sense of a real to come which will not be subjected to either the historical contingency or the ritual binding of that contingency, both of which one calls 'performance', that Artaud articulates with the word cruelty in his manifesto Theatre of Cruelty and identifies cruelty with 'necessity'.

7

Let us take a brief detour to trace an episodic journey on different meanings and connotations of something like 'necessary food' across different contexts. For instance. in fifth century BC, in Ancient Athens, we find an interesting bifurcation proceeding from the status of food, or rather, food grain in society. While grain is the basic subsistence material for human life, and any human being, whether free man or slave must eat to survive, we find in Athens at this time (which is the time of Periclean democracy in 450 BC) a strange privilege or value attached to the act of *citizens eating*. Pericles seems to have instituted a state fund called *theoric* which was meant to be disbursed as a direct payment or dole to the citizens, rich and poor alike, who were meant to utilise these funds to undertake certain civic activities including buying of grains and, among other things, theatre attendance. So, paradoxically, while a citizen is meant to make a minimal payment made available by a state fund, effectively both subsidising food as well as making it mandatory too for the citizen, other sections of society including slaves and women are not privy to this state fund. This means that the latter can both be imagined to not be given a state subsidy but also to be given free grain or allowed free entry into the theatre depending on specific circumstances. In other words, the citizens' act of eating is rendered by this uniform prism of civic funding, a *significant* eating (Choudhury 2013).

The significance mentioned earlier displaces the meaning of necessity from one that is based on subsistence and minimal reproduction of the species to a new type of civic necessity. By this second logic of necessity, even food serves a symbolically constitutive function and mere nutrition now functions as a refraction of the citizens' civic constitution rather than the natural constitution of any living body whether the citizens' or the slaves'. Hence, from natural necessity, we move to a political semiotic necessity where food is both the substance of the sign citizenship as well as its signifying enactment. In ancient Athens, this second logic of necessity corresponds to what could be called a *liturgical* logic that was founded on a certain system of public services. By the common and natural logic of the necessary nutritive reproduction of species, the act of eating is simultaneously individual and species-centric. The human-animal eats to preserve its particular self but its particular self is inseparable from the general reproduction of the species. The liturgical logic of the Athenian city, in significant contrast, *chooses* to grant necessity to only a civic act of eating. Of course, in physical terms, the animal and the civic acts (of eating) cannot be distinguished from each other. What is effectuated is internal bifurcation within the act between a symbolically constituted a significant part and a naturally given nonsignificant part. And the mechanism of this effectuating Athenian state fund, that is provided only to the citizens who are properly liturgical subjects and in eating (just as in attending the theatre), they perform a public service to themselves on behalf of themselves. By this civic-nutritive mobilisation of the liturgical logic, the citizens distinguish themselves from women, slaves and foreigners, in that the latter, whether in the act of eating or that of attending the theatre, remain confined to the automatism of natural necessity.

Another historical site of symbolic mobilisation of food and its sublimation into a necessity higher than a mere natural one, is accomplished in the ritual appropriation of eating (and drinking) during the catholic Eucharist. As part of the Eucharistic celebration of the memory of the Last Supper, bread and wine serve as both physical substances to be 'tasted'[6] as well as signs to be transformed into the Body and Blood of Christ. What, in terms of natural necessity, can only be received as a divine miracle of transubstantiation, defying the natural law of unexchangable substances (bread/body, wine/blood), in terms of symbolical constitution within the logic of religion can be understood as a re-semiotisation of food into a new regime of necessary *signs*. As signs, bread and wine surpass their capture by 'taste' and instead, make taste an aesthetic prism to refract the real ritual activity of barely touching the little wafer of bread and the drop of wine with the tongue so as to ensure that this minimal sensation or *aesthesis* is only a material platform to launch the work of the ritual code. This code *prescribes* in a necessitarian move the transformation of a natural substance into ritual-symbolical value, bread and wine into Body and Blood. Once this ritual efficacy is secured, the contingency of taste is sublimated into both ritual rigour and theological dogma—the two necessitarian masks flanking the merely 'natural' face and function of the human-animal.

It is interesting that, in the nineteenth century, Marx locates the crux of surplus values in the difference between what the labour produces as value and what is its own value. The later value is what

Marx calls the reproduction of living labour—that is the value of labour expressed in terms of what is necessary to reproduce itself as an exchangeable commodity, in other words, its price on the market.[7] This simply means, when labour has produced the value of *labour power*, it has secured its value of reproduction. So, while labour produces surplus value, it is exchanged as a commodity only as labour power. The exchange value of labour power is nothing more or less than its necessary natural value of being reproducible as the substance of living labour, which is to say, all the nutritive and other substances that are required to reproduce labour power. But Marx's theory of value is precisely that value is *not* natural; it is socially-necessary value that is determined by the logic of exchange of commodities. Value is the co-creation of a society of commodities. In this, Marx goes beyond Adam Smith who would still understand something like poverty as an equivocal experience confronted with natural necessity and defined by socially necessary parameters. For Marx there is only socially-necessary determination of value which is measurable and expressible only by the meaning of exchange value. In this respect, Marx grasps labour as both a living substance and as a structure of the exploitation of value without, in any way, making an organic and historical gradation between these two dimensions, insofar as for Marx, the human species is constitutively labour. The specific social formation that is a capitalist society capitalises or invests all of human animality into a social process of the extraction of surplus values. Hence, with Marx's analysis there is no remainder that survives the circuit of commodity exchange whether, that remainder be a normal human-animal seen as purely nutritive or even socially-equivocal straddling the line between society and nature as Adam Smith imagines as a 'poor'.

While it is true that Marx did not resort to any residual logic of natural necessity and attempted to rigorously demonstrate a social capture of all so called natural values, he did produce a *political imagination* of the worker as a subject-imprisoned to a socially-determined natural level of existence. To that extent, the poor and the immiserated classes partake of a social misery whose analogy still lies in natural necessity.[8] Precisely because the subject of labour, that is the worker, is locked to the level of socially-determined parameter of his or her natural reproduction, the worker, politically speaking, confronts the class enemy—the bourgeoisie, with images of a kind of *surplus experience*. Conforming to such an image, Antonin Artaud in the twentieth century accuses this *surplus experience*, whether in a poem, in a letter or in unfinished theatre-scenario, 'you eat too much! You petty bourgeois initiates ... you smell of garlic mayonnaise ...'[9] To the extent that these words express a rebellion against decadent capitalist consumption, whether nutritive or cultural, Artaud stands at the threshold of a modern western culture saturated by late capitalist hedonistic promise of sensuous aesthetic and material 'surplus pleasure'.[10] But this threshold is intrinsically unstable because all surplus is already a movement beyond the necessitarian logic that forms the social infrastructure of the experience itself. It is this contradiction that in Artaud's life and work, occupies the threshold to eventually displace it towards a strange solution to the contradiction. The solution either prophecies something like an absolutely new ritual regime and a surplus-culture that exceeds its own infrastructure so overwhelmingly that its codes and ceremonies, its exchanges and values are rendered completely unrecognisable to its own ideological mirror—or it returns to a strictly necessitarian threshold so rigorous and so exact that it becomes infra-social whose secret measure is nothing less than cultic.[11] This is the critical and tremulous threshold Artaud occupies at the beginning of the twentieth century—a position from where the thought of theatre is launched towards multiple futures.

8

Antonin Artaud and Simone Weil, apart from being near contemporaries, are also philosophically united in one respect: both were dissatisfied with the mere social or organic determinations of necessity. While Artaud gave the name 'cruelty' to the thought of necessity, Weil joined necessity to a force or power that she called 'super natural'. Again, the logic of a surplus beyond an economic doctrine of surplus is at stake. For Weil, such a pure surplus-necessity could be found, for instance, in the Hindu text of the *Bhagwad Gita*, in which the idea of duty according to Weil is performed not along the lines of interests or even egoistic power but as a form of pure obedience. So strangely, in this interpretation, the relation of obedience to command is not a motivated by submission to power but a determination of power or force without any of the predicates or properties of power that we associate with what is conventionally called 'social power' or 'political power'. Hence, with Simone Weil, we encounter a speculative experience, which the contemporary Italian philosopher Roberto Esposito (2015, 120–155) calls 'the sovereignty of sovereignty'.

This extraordinary coincidence of pure necessity and pure surplus is to be found in both Artaud and Weil, though both use very different measures to measure and express their definitions of 'necessity'. For Weil, the example of the Hindu text of *Gita* is illustrative of her desire to interpret this canonical text in a fundamentally anti-ritualistic way. If the *Gita* were to be interpreted as an ideological document, presenting a philosophy of duty determined as *ritual performance*, then Weil's interpretation of pure impredicative power contained in the text's meaning would fall apart.[12] Without entering into these specific historico-philosophical debates, one can pay attention to Weil's *analogical* passion when it comes to measuring and expressing ideas according to new improvised philosophical measures. For instance, she refers to Gandhi and his pronouncements of non-violence, in a specific historical context, to propose the following analogical test: Weil suggests that true Gandhian thinking on non-violence should test non-violence on the grounds whether it contains in its very core, in its self-activity, the same *tensile* and 'muscular' force that violence contains (Esposito 2015, 137). According to Weil, only if non-violence possesses the same muscular force as violence, does it reach the status of true thought or a true principle. In proposing this tensile and 'muscular' test for the idea of non-violence, Weil almost replicates the last paragraph of Kafka's 'A Hunger Artist' in so far as the magnetic and shiny rhythm of the panther's mouth with the food caught between its jaws renders this food 'necessary', rather than food being merely a natural necessity. Similarly, for Weil, non-violence can be made necessary by its self-activity, its very own shiny jaws, its own 'necessary food' rather than it being either a theatrical or a political ritual merely being practiced as a hunger fast in tactically-chosen periods of self-deprivation of nutrition. At the same time, Weil's test should not be misunderstood as an aesthetic one. The panther is not putting up a performance in the same way as the Hunger Artiste does; its rhythm is the rhythm of the real. Even better, the real is only verifiable in a kind of experience and analytics of rhythm. All ritualising is only retrospective and to that extent, unnecessary. Simone Weil also calls this ritual technology 'idolatrous' (Esposito 2015). To this extent, she includes even Marx among thinkers who render the 'super natural' force of necessity—a force without force, articulated with the im-power of sovereignty—into the force of the social and the measure of the animal. Instead of this reductive field of social and political philosophies of power, Weil proposes a thought of 'action', where the action and the thought cannot be disaggregated into subject and object. To this extent, the thesis is clear: necessity is thought. And this is a thesis intensely shared by Weil and Artaud, albeit in drastically heterogeneous sights and ways.

Simone Weil expresses this thesis again in an analogical pursuit of the most vivid and elusive measure. She says that necessity is not determination of this or that; necessity is the very real of determination as such. That there is determination is what solicits the thought of necessity. Weil says that 'determination' (or one could alternatively say, the 'real') is without any substance yet harder than any diamond

(Esposito 2015, 154). Antonin Artaud's thought of cruelty seems to pursue a similar analogy. Cruelty is determination, not of this or that, but of its own necessity. In this respect, cruelty is indeed expressed by the old Greek word for both necessity and fate—*ananke.*

The only question that still remains somewhat unaddressed is: what does the thought of cruelty have to do with the thought of theatre? Again, to grasp this relationship one might take recourse to Simone Weil's precise philosophical thesis that determination is actually the point—insubstantial yet harder than any diamond—at which all forms and predicates of power that underlie a political philosophy give way to an experience of impower or as Esposito calls it, of impolitics. Similarly, for Artaud, cruelty is that point at which all ritual codes and ceremonies lose their encoded efficacies and are immanently exposed to their own being-ritual or even, to the gesture of such ritual-being. In being self-exposed, Artaud seems to be saying that ritual necessity is rendered contingent but the contingency of the *event* of ritual itself becomes a 'necessary' thought of what he calls a Theatre of Cruelty. This is the most one can travel with Antonin Artaud and Simone Weil, as themselves co-travellers on a brief but singular journey.

9

The limits of comparison between Artaud and Weil impinge on both sides of the comparison. If, for Weil, the exit from the socio-vital ideology of modern politics lies in a certain existential, and even physical, experiment with 'super natural' necessity, in the case of Artaud the very exposure of ritual to its gestural contingency confines this critical self-reflection to the space of fundamental equation: theatre = ritual. For Weil, as well as for Artaud, the limits are broken in disparate, if not incommensurable, ways such that analogical comparisons must be abandoned from this point onwards. We will not speak of Weil further, apart from indicating that her conclusive and *dying* experiments with starvation both embodied a certain supernatural distance from natural assimilation of food, as well as converted the determination of the world as affliction or suffering in the very element of personal existence (Weil 2002, 80–84). Of course, one cannot leave this trail without clarifying that the determination of the world as an affliction, for Weil, is the very passage of exit from the world as it exists. For Artaud, the Theatre of Cruelty is a self-confessed manifesto without any models or examples. To that extent, it must have neither an archive nor a future. It must be what it is—the breakout of the contingent thought of necessity as cruelty. However, a certain chapter does open up in the accidental future of Artaud's crypt and one figure who attempts to 'read' the cryptic language he presumes to inherit from Artaud is the Polish director Jerzy Grotowski. In a short essay, called 'He wasn't entirely himself', Grotowski suggests Artaud's crypt contains a prophesy or a vision but the actual work of theatre must find a method suitable to realise this cryptic agenda for the future (Grotowski 2004, 59–64). Indeed, Grotowski undertakes such a rational search for a true theatre of cruelty appropriate to Artaud's vision. More than that, in his own work and corpus of writing, Grotowski names such a rational-historical theatre a 'poor theatre'.

For Grotowski the meaning of poverty is not privative; rather, it is subtractive. The actor is both a rational and vital unit, who must subtractively discover her 'truth' which, in turn, must be 'revealed' as a *necessary* gesture of this very poverty. But the gesture that must be arrived at through this rational revelatory subtractive method—a method flanked clearly both by science and religion—cannot but be both historical and be necessarily reinserted into ritual web of the world as performance. Despite his pioneering and daunting initiative Grotowski, in the history of theatre, exemplifies a peculiar contradiction. On the one hand, his subtractive or minimising method subtracts from all predicates including communitarian and cultural ones but the more he minimises his self-relation as *western* theatre director, the more he multiplies in his work signs of other than western cultures and cultural predicates. This eventually leads to a generalised communitarian project alternatively called Theatre of the Roots or Cross Cultural Theatre. The second contradiction that follows from this one is that while Grotowski concentrates the experience of the actor's revelation within her own 'truth process'[13] and to that extent, she frees herself from the empirical reality of the spectator, the more her truth demands a kind of confessional and anonymous other who, instead of being the public spectator, would now exude the authority of the master, or the guru, that is Grotowski himself.

Given this somewhat futile, and yet collaterally fertile, search that Grotowski undertook—guided by what he called Artaud's prophesy—is there a possibility of finding a philosophically-truer relationship of Artaud's notion of cruelty in Theatre of Cruelty neither with the history of philosophy, nor with that of theatre, but with *events* that are able to produce certain undecidability between these identified regimes of history? Let's conclude with one rather random example of such an event from the French Revolution. In the very early stages of the revolution, between 1789 and 1790, when the first festivals of the revolution were created by the different revolutionary groups as well as the new government, one striking festival was called the Festival of Misery.

This was a peculiar, if not absurd, festival in which poverty and misery were celebrated. What rational meaning can be given to such a celebration unless the entire exercise is imagined to be a massive act of collective masochism? However, when one examines the actual historical unfolding of the event, it reveals something quiet unprecedented and extraordinary. The Festival of Misery is a celebration of misery, poverty, even hunger—neither as religio-social virtues bordering on martyrdom, nor as wilful embodiments of impotential or impower but as the real of history that manifests poor, miserable and hungry people insofar as they *exist*. And insofar as they exist, they already testify to a necessity that goes beyond the mere contingent fact that even if they are hungry today, potentially they can eat not just well in the future but, who knows, they could also become those decadent petty bourgeoisies who an Antonin Artaud could turn and accuse of eating too much and smelling of garlic mayonnaise. Surely neither Marx nor any other egalitarian thinker would deny such an optimistic and dismal possibility but this very contingent possibility is what the festival of misery, at a specific historical moment, superseded by affirming the existence of a real people in their real material conditions. And insofar as such a reality is affirmed and celebrated in the festival it frees the fact of poverty and hunger from both the empirical causality of nutritive and other deprivations and from the entrepreneurial ontology of potential that sees every deprivation as a future opportunity, an aspiration and self-enrichment. Insofar as both these evaluations dominate the imagination of poverty, the poor are necessarily *not thought* (Castel 2003, 159–167).

It is this deprivation not so much from the food, as from thought, that the festival of misery enthusiastically, and revolutionarily, corrects. It also produces a certain social discourse of law and duty which provides a kind of ideological emblem for the festival of misery. The festival announces that, henceforth, society owes a 'sacred debt' to the poor. This is obviously a counter-intuitive idea of debt because society from now on owes a debt to those people who, by definition, are not credit-worthy. This counter-intuitive logic is the essential logic of a new necessity—the necessity of generic equality—or the equality that binds a generic humanity. In this respect, the festival of misery invents a language, as well as a gesture, for the thought of the real which neither submits to the model of natural necessity (necessary food), nor to that of socio-liturgical necessity (significant food). And insofar as the festival celebrates and affirms an experience whose reality cannot be encoded or incorporated into a limited ritual form the festival of misery is not a ritual festival. It is, even within the sequence of festivals of the French Revolution from 1789 to 1794, an exceptional festival to the extent that its performance is indiscernible from the historical reality of the *revolution itself*. The exceptional event that the festival celebrates is part of the festival itself. And so, at this insubstantial point in history, harder than any diamond, the thought strikes like a new and necessary lightning flash, and instead of being stupefied by this event, speaks in Artaud's imagined voice—a voice so cruel and so frail as to be beyond any imagination, 'What is a revolution if not a festival, what is a festival if not a revolution?' (Derrida 2002, 290–316).

NOTES

1. This essay creates a series of scenarios, partly imagined and partly citing from documents from Artaud's life particularly after his release from Rodez asylum in 1946 up to his death in March 1948. The documents themselves are mostly incomplete and fragmented hence the imagined supplementation is almost constitutive of the nature of these documents. Some of these scenarios/documents are 'Letter to Peter Watson', 'Tete-a-Tete with Antonin Artaud', 'To put an end to the judgement of God', 'Last letters to Paule Thévenin'. Antonin Artaud left the rights to his works for Paule Thévenin who among the several works that she authored, co-authored the book *The Secret art of Antonin Artaud*. See Jacques Derrida and Paule Thévenin (1998, 1976). Also see Antonin Artaud 'To put an end to the judgement of God' in *Selected Works*. It might also be mentioned here that the author of this essay has written a play based on these very fragments and documents called 'Tete-a-tete with Antonin Artaud'. Though unpublished the play has been performed as a solo-piece since 1998 by the author more than 25 times.
2. See Kafka (1998, 243–256). As for the founding of the space and status for acting as a profession *and* ceremony in modernity we have to probably go back to Denis Diderot as the first philosopher of acting as a profession. For the key Diderot text on this, see Diderot's *Paradox of Acting*.
3. In addition to this, one could read some of his 'scenarios' including 'The conquest of Mexico'.
4. Among several valuable commentaries on Artaud's identification of cruelty with necessity, two specific texts that stand out are Jacques Derrida (2002, 290–316); Andre Green (2011).
5. Kafka (1998, 255).
6. See Agamben's reference to Campenella in the short text *Taste* by Giorgio Agamben (2017, 24).
7. See Karl Marx 'The Labour-Process and the Process of Producing Surplus-Value' in *Capital*, vol. I, translated by Samuel Moore and Edward Aveling (with a Preface by Frederick Engels). Noida: Maple Press.

   In particular Marx says '... the capitalist incorporates labour as a living ferment with the lifeless constituents of the product. From his point of view the labour process is nothing more than the consumption of the commodity purchased i.e. of labour power' (p. 172). It is interesting to note that in contrast to Marx's total socialisation of the 'living ferment' that is labour, Adam Smith's measure of poverty or the 'poor' has the following equivocation: The poor is someone who feels 'shame' while living in society in so far as he is a being who has to expose his existence to that very society as 'poor', meaning he lives a degraded life. In Smith's subjective measure the 'shame' the poor feels is co-related to an objective condition of a life spent 'without breaches'. 'Breaches' or boots signify both the objective measure of a civic and solvent existence but a life without 'breeches/boots' or a life of 'shame' is precisely a life exposed and degraded to a condition of 'natural' necessity. In this connection, also see Sen (1999).

8. In this context see the analysis of primitive accumulation in *Capital*. Ibid. 771–831.
9. See Antonin Artaud 'letter to Peter Watson'. Available online at https://my-blackout.com/2019/03/28/antonin-artaud-letter-to-peter-watson/.
10. The coinage of 'surplus pleasure' refers to the ambiguous meaning of the French word *jouissance* which both indicates, the simple sense of pleasure as well as something unassimilated or even traumatic in that very experience.
11. This division between a prophetic Artaud and a performative Artaud is actualised in the twentieth as well as the twenty-first century by the alternative trends of myriad cultural performances and rituals, particularly subtended by the sign 'oriental' and a certain Artaud style whose performativity is interestingly seen more in cultic poetry, performance art even visual arts rather than in the space of legitimate theatre.
12. For an interpretation of the *Gita* in the light of caste and ritual action and ritual obedience, see Ambedkar (1987).
13. This is a conceptual invention that Alain Badiou, the contemporary French philosopher has made in his work. Whether there is any structural or subjective similarity between Grotowski's performance system and Badiou's philosophical system is a matter for the reader to decide.

REFERENCES

Agamben, Giorgio. *Taste*, translated by Cooper Francis. Kolkata: Seagull Publications, 2017.

Ambedkar, B.R. 'Krishna and his *Gita*: Philosophical Justification of Counterrevolution.' In *Writings and Speeches*, vol. 3, edited by Vasant Moon, 357–380. Bombay: Education Department, Government of Maharashtra, 1987.

Antonin Artaud. 'To put an end to the judgement of God.' In *Selected Works*, edited by Susan Sontag. Farrar, New York: Straus and Giroux.

Artaud, Antonin. *Theatre and its Double*, translated by Mary Caroline Richards. New York: Grove Press, 1994.

Blanchot, Maurice. 'Artaud'. In *Antonin Artaud: A Critical Reader*, edited by Edward Scheer. London and New York: Routledge, 2004.

Castel, Robert. *From Manual Workers to Wage Laborers: Transformation of the Social Question*, translated and edited by Richard Boyd. New Brunswick and London: Transaction Publishers, 2003.

Choudhury, Soumyabrata. *Theater Number Event: Three Studies on the Relationship between Sovereignity, Power and Truth*. Shimla: IIAS Publication, 2013.

Derrida, Jacques. 'Theater of Cruelty and the Closure of Representation.' In *Writing and Difference*, translated by Alan Bass, 290–316. London and New York: Routledge, 2002.

Derrida, Jacques and Paule Thévenin. *The Secret Art of Antonin Artaud*, translated by Mary Ann Caws. Cambridge: MIT Press, 1998, 1976.

Diderot, Denis. *Paradox of Acting*, translated by Walter Herries Pollock. Piccadilly: Chatto & Windus, 1883.

Esposito, Roberto. 'A Politics of Ascesis.' In *Categories of the Impolitical*, translated by Connal Parsley. New York: Fordham University Press, 2015.

Green, Andre. *The Tragic Effect: The Oedipus Complex in Tragedy*, translated by Alan Sheridan. Cambridge: Cambridge University Press, 2011.

Grotowski, Jerzy. 'He wasn't Entirely Himself.' In *Antonin Artaud: A Critical Reader*, edited by Edward Scheer. London and New York: Routledge, 2004.

Kafka, Franz. 'A Hunger Artist.' In *Selected Short Stories: Franz Kafka*, translated by Willa and Edwin Muir. New Delhi: Srishti Publishers, 1998.

Marx, Karl. 'The Labour-Process and the Process of Producing Surplus-Value.' In *Capital*, vol. I, translated by Samuel Moore and Edward Aveling (with a Preface by Frederick Engels). Noida: Maple Press, 2014.

Sen, Amartya. *Social Exclusion: Concept, Application, and Security*. New Delhi: Critical Quest, 1999.

Weil, Simone. 'Affliction.' In *Gravity and Grace*, translated by Emma Crawford and Mario von der Ruhr. London and New York: Routledge, 2002.

EPHEMERA

NOCTURNALS (A REMINISCENCE)

Anil Yadav, translated from the Hindi by Chinmaya Lal Thakur

It must have been an ordinary winter morning in Nakhlau. I was going to the 'reporters-meeting' at my office that took place every day at 11:00 am. As one approached the glare of the vehicles caught in traffic, one felt that a fire that one had seen in a dream had broken into millions of pieces and was lying scattered on the road. The usually-boring traffic lights at Hazratganj crossing appeared welcoming and generous, for they saved me from the cold winds. The sunlight felt soothing. The beggars perched on the veranda of the dilapidated Coffee House building were dozing off. An urgent frenzy was running through the kids who cleaned the car-glasses as they wanted a little something to eat. Their hands moved under the force of some insipid inspiration drawn from pity. In such a state, one inevitably looks up at the tower-clock of the general post office which hasn't worked for a while and at the eagles that keep flying in circles above it. With them, I must have, at that moment, been lost in seeing time swim comfortably in the river of sunlight. Suddenly, at very close quarters, I felt the powerful odour that rises from the bodies of madmen who live on the road. Someone knelt close to my ear and said, 'Sir, please, will you give me two rupees for a smoke!'

'Hunh ... What?'

Disinterestedly, I looked away from the pleasures of the winter morning. That man, wrapped in a filthy and torn blanket, leaned gently while standing. He held a *beedi* within the tender grasp of his fingers. His eyes, burdened with insufficient sleep, had a watery glint that made it appear as if he had known me for ages. There was a prominent smile between his thick, ash-coloured beard and moustache, further accentuated by his broken incisor. His incredibly lush hair diverted my attention; despite my best attempts, my own hairline kept receding and here was this man who had such cascading hair that it made up a crown for him!

I could not stop smiling and kept looking at him. He was happier and more attentive than I was, for it seemed as if he had crossed paths with an old acquaintance after a long, long time. Suddenly, the traffic-lights turned red and the noise of the engines reached a crescendo. I blurted, 'Come and sit at the back.'

Without hesitation, he sat pillion as if we had indeed decided that we would meet today. Unexpectedly, at that moment, I became worried about the wallet in my back-pocket for I could not feel it despite several attempts. Finally, despite the shame that he would realise what I was doing, I ascertained that my wallet was intact.

I made him sit on a chair at the reception. Before I went to the meeting, I asked the peon to get him some tea and a bundle of *beedi*s. The peon, in order to garner support for his mocking surprise, looked towards the office. The office looked at me and said, 'You got him for an interview?'

'I know him, thought he could have tea here.'

By the time I returned, he had gulped down two cups of tea and run through 10–12 *beedi*s. The latter had been put down on the centre-table, though, and not in the ash-tray. They had been lined-up on the table's boundary so that they could be lit up again. He picked up the cup, gave it a gentle shake and said, 'The tea was *beautiful*.'

'The winters must be agonising?'

He guffawed and said, 'The summers will always be hot and the winters will always be cold.'

The peon complained, 'Sir, there is such a terrible smell here. Lice have spread through the entire office because of him and none but you all will suffer as a result.'

He would push his long fingers through his hair from the back of his head and give it a scrub as if he was searching for something. Then, whatever was found would be thrown on the floor. Dirt and grease spots marked his fingers. The yellowed nails had begun to wilt under their own weight and turned inward.

I asked, 'Do you have lice in your head?'

Looking across, he laughed silently for a while. As if what I had said made no sense at all. He then went on to explain, even as he kept searching the roots of his thick hair,

> I was a small kid when I was going to my grandma's place. My mother was with me. In a train. I looked out of the window every once in a while. My mother tried to dissuade me but I did not bother to listen to her. Some charcoal fell into my eyes. I cried, shrieked, and howled, but it could not be taken out. Medical treatment also did not help. Now, that coal has entered my brain and has become larger.... It keeps breaking into pieces and comes out intermittently.

'So, there is a colliery within?'

'Who knows what is inside!'

Since that day, I kept searching for men like him among the mad people, the beggars and the addicts, so that I could hear more of such incredible stories. Often, in the mornings, I would find him and take him to the office so that he could get some tea. In his presence, the office became an anxious space, a space that couldn't carry the weight of his presence. The peon would deliberately cause a delay in providing his tea. The unit-manager would desperately want him to leave and keep asking, with fake laughter, 'Have the sages themselves come down from the Himalayas?'. My colleagues would say,

> Such people should be given 10–20 rupees outside the office itself so that they don't come in. The newspaper office is getting corporatised and even we are being expected to get rid of our burly moustaches and report to work every day in sharp ties. Someday, this mad fellow will make you lose your job and then you will understand.

Apparently unaware of all of this, he would sit cuddled under the blanket, sip tea and say, 'Sir, it is a cold day. Let us bask in the sun.'

I would feel a great respite as I took him to the terrace. The terrace was occupied by newspapers, rusty typewriters, coolers, tyres and unidentifiable glut that had rotted due to exposure to rainwater. These articles competed among themselves to outlive each other and continue flourishing on the terrace. A *peepal* tree had broken its way through the wall so that it could inspire the competitors. It seemed as if it said to them, 'My children! Stay on! For, one day, life will burst from within each of you.' One fine day, while watching paper-kites swishing in the sky, after having had a plate of *khasta-kachori*s from Rattilal's shop, he said, 'Sir, hand me some paper. I want to write something.'

'Will you need a computer or will it be handwritten?'

'I will be comfortable if I write with my own hands.'

I felt a great sense of urgent inevitability running through me—as if the purpose behind our meeting was going to be fulfilled soon. Indeed, something so great and truthful and yet so simple was going to emerge, it would be that even the best of writers was incapable of producing such. They would commit suicide in the disappointment that they were not able to say what this man was surely going to present to the world soon. I took him to my corner desk at the office. I unlocked the windows and offered him my seat. I left him with two pens, two bundles of *beedi*s, a thick sheath of paper attached to a clipboard and a glass of water.

At that moment, I was anxious and restless like a child who buries a coin into the earth and wishes to harvest a treasure. I knew, though, that everything could be spoilt if he came to know that I was waiting for him to produce the masterpiece. So, I did not disturb him.

He was gone by the time I returned in the evening. Multiple sheets of paper lay scattered on the table. The floor, too, was littered with bits of crumpled paper. He had also left his smell at the corner, the powerful smell that reminded me of smoke, filth and fear. I went through the papers. Not even a scribble was to be found on them. They were as blank as they were when I had left them with him. I did not find anything even when I unfolded all the crumpled balls of paper that lay on the floor. A few lines had been scratched on some, though. And from those, one could tell that his grip on the pen wasn't at all stable. His hands would have shaken horribly or the pen itself would have run away, afraid of colliding with some mountain-like rough and uneven mass.

The bureau-chief Shivshankar Goswami was trying his best to suppress his giggle. Amused at my anxiousness, he said, 'Do you know who he is?'

'No, not at all.'

'He is Mr Ajay Kumar from Allahabad. He used to work at the desk for the *Northern India Patrika* (NIP). I also used to work at Allahabad then, for *Amrit Prabhat*, NIP's Hindi edition. I could recognise him somehow, with great difficulty.'

'How did he come to such a state?'

'Got into bad business with girls! We had heard that he was beaten black and blue by the girl's relatives. Lost his mind as a result. He has a big house in Tagore town but boys from the university have taken it over.'

'Did you speak with him?!'

'How can you talk to someone who has lost his senses?'

The next day, I found the stairs leading to the office smelling of the extra dose of phenyl with which they had been wiped. The manager himself had ensured that the entire office be given a 'hygienic' scrub. The two chairs and the centre-table that adorned the reception had disappeared. Only the sofa remained. The peon had been instructed that he should not leave his work to make tea for one-two random persons who might enter the office. I kept looking for him on the streets only to be disappointed. He himself found the right place to meet me though and began coming to the Pioneer Square every day.

The Pioneer Square is not a Square, actually. It used to house the offices of *The Pioneer* in the past. It faces the busiest road of Nakhlau, that is, the Ashoka Road that traverses the Charbagh Railway Station, Vidhan Sabha and Nishatganj. Every night, the 100-metre footpath along the road transforms into the largest depot for newspapers published in the city. At 2:00 am, trucks drop bundles of newspapers there which are attended to by agents and sleepy newspaper hawkers who ride bicycles with large carriers attached. The air at the Square is burdened and lightened at the same time—with the smell of printing ink and with the surprise that marks those who take a quick glance at the fresh headlines printed in the newspapers, respectively. An atmosphere of rejoicing and gaiety prevails there, generated by the scrambling in which the hawkers indulge and by the choicest abuses that they hurl at each other. By 5 am, pushing down on the pedals with the greatest force they possess, the hawkers leave the Square like darting arrows. The Square attracts all kinds of nocturnals. Two-three tea-stalls, a *dhaba* and a couple of *khokha*s selling betel-nut and cigarettes cater to them till their own lightbulbs grow tired, dim and ultimately, fade out.

The boundary of *The Pioneer*'s office is marked by a dried-out drain. The concrete at the drain's bank has caused an old *sharifa* tree to become diseased and grow only to dwarf size. As if to console the tree, a *gul chandni* shrub has grown to lean on it and it blooms every night. Just below the *gul chandni* is a neglected stone that symbolises some god or deity. A stone plinth bounds the *sharifa* tree and it must have served as a shanty-like tea stall at one point of time. Behind the tree and the shrub are numerous mango and *ashoka* trees, with leaves the colour of dirt and ash. These trees hardly allow any light to pass through them and reach till the plinth. The little light that gets to the plinth is the same as the light that is left in the Elephant's life. This must be the reason why he searched for the moon from within the space between the leaves as he sat there at the plinth alone, gulping rum. It is only later that others also began to gather there.

One night, to get rid of his loneliness, he drained his alcohol on the small stone and decorated it with four *chandni* flowers that he picked up from the ground. The mound thus became a shrine to Shiva and he called the place *Madireshwar Mahadev*, meaning *where wine and drinks are offered to the greatest of the Gods, Shiva*. The city already had temples dedicated to *Koneshwar*, *Lodheshwar*, *Bhanvareshwar* and *Gardeneshwar Mahadev*. So, this name came to act as the parody of the parody of the tradition of giving context-specific names to shrines.

The Elephant hardly had any eyebrows. He had heavy-set, wrinkle-ridden cheeks that housed small eyes with a narrow gaze. Hence, hidden among the trees, he seemed an elephant to the world. He was a journalist of good repute. His reports were most ordinary but were marked with his desire to say something of his own. As a result, the sequinned stars in his writing often became visible. But he could not work at one place for too long a time. He was his own master, a man of his own heart. So, he was either thrown out of work or he would himself resign from his position, and thus, cut the very branch on which he was perched.

He was a misfit. At the Press Club, often he would get into fistfights with others. So, he started to sit here, near the Square. The more scared he became, the lonelier and more aggressive he turned.

The Elephant, armoured with at least a quarter of rum, came to the Square by 15 minutes to 9 pm or so. Very soon, with the arrival of the duo of Sudhanshu Trivedi and Siddhartha Kalhans from the university, a bench picked up from Bhagauti's *dhaba* would be set up in front of the plinth. Siddhartha was a journalist who was unemployed ever since he had returned from Delhi. The sheer disappointment and boredom that he felt at the ordinariness of life made him eager to enliven it by telling some or other fanciful tale. If he felt that there was something that could force the listener to pay attention to what he was saying, he indeed possessed the power to make his narrative sound realistic and believable. Everyone thought that he suffered from some strange disease that forced him to tell lies but his genius was such that he could fit a rocket's engine in a three-wheeled *tempo* and make it fly. Sudhanshu, unemployed since he finished his studies, had the talent to express flippant moral statements on the 'decline' of those around him. He could also mimic others, often with great accuracy.

Alok Trivedi from Hussainganj followed Sudhanshu and Siddhartha to the Square, with his own followers Mamma and Manna. The latter had been to Japan on a work visa and had proved to be useful in some factory there. Having learnt from Japanese foremen, Alok would make a strange whistle-sound with his teeth and tongue: 'Eessh ... Eessh'. He would then order Mamma and Manna to follow suit and what inevitably followed were glasses, water, cigarettes and everything else.

From Dar-ul-shafa appeared Bhau Raghvendra Dubey and Ravindra Ojha who, according to popular opinion, constituted the pair of Chacha Chaudhary and Sabu. Despite having worked in Nakhlau for decades together, Bhau has never rented a house for himself to live in. Often, at the MLA quarters, he would just pull the curtains in any of the rooms and sleep on the *durrie*. Ojha, who hailed from Baliya, had undertaken an intense study of pulp literature for five years. His mouth was always full of chewing tobacco and he had again found a job with a newspaper. Once, when he went to the village, his wife had insisted that she, too, would like to return to Nakhlau with him. When Ojha did not agree, and she had realised that she would not have her way, she had made sure that their six-year-old daughter had accompanied her father back. Because there was no one to take care of her, Ojha began to bring her along even to press conferences. On one occasion, I ran into the father-daughter duo while returning from Chief Minister Mayawati's press conference. The anxious, irritated and helpless Ojha shouted and said to me, 'Hey Anil, this spoilt girl has bothered the hell out of me! She has had so much of cashew that her tummy just won't stop running. What should I do now?'

By the time the night shift would come to an end at the newspaper offices, others would also arrive at the Square—Ramesh Pant, Mausiya, Divya Prakash, Yashwant, Pradeep Mishra, Kunwar ji Anjum, Vinay

Shreekar, Anil Upadhyay, Rajeev Deekshit from the Department of Information, (newspaper) agent Haider.... This would bring about a huge pile of scooters and motorcycles in circles right in front of the *sharifa* tree. As more people would arrive, the circles would only become larger and larger. Seat cushions would be lifted off from rickshaws till the arrival of their passengers.

Just at this moment, the actor Siddhartha Pakrasi from Sitapur would come, carrying a tiny suitcase in his hands. His gait was so clumsy and he would give himself such a shake while walking that it looked as if he was unable to balance himself while being caught in some storm that was approaching the Square. Though we never asked, it was believed that he was an officer at the Excise Department. He would present the suitcase filled with pouches of country liquor to the Elephant and say, 'Dear child, here, take this and drink as much as you like.' Then, he would recline on the plinth and make himself adequately comfortable.

Once the pouches had been emptied into the bucket brought from Bhagauti's *dhaba*, all kinds of *addha*s and *pauwa*s—halves and quarters—were poured into the mixture. A mug was used as the stirrer and, with the addition of water, the resultant fluid-like substance would begin to glisten. With respect and adoration, it was called *Halahal*, after the poisonous liquid that Shiva himself had gulped down. Just two pegs of *Halahal* of the size of tea-glasses were enough to send any person into a world that he had never known before. During the conversation at the Square, if a reference was made to some artist, actor or actress who worked at the theatre after he had lain down on the table for a while, Pakrasi Dada would suddenly become alert and get up. His eyes would narrow as a result of the anger, hurt and pride he felt. At such moments, he would roar, 'I was the one who made him what he is, here, in Nakhlau itself. I gave birth to him.'

I had always thought that he reacted in such a manner because he had to give up on his theatre work for the sake of his family and household. The truth, apparently, was otherwise. Actually, dark-humour was an indelible part of his personality and it could not be controlled, no matter how hard one tried. Between his roar and dialogue, he would thus be found giving birth, on the footpaths of Nakhlau, to all the self-made abbots and braggart art-gurus of his time. The theatre in Nakhlau used to enjoy great repute in the past. Once, someone was speaking about the actor Anupam Kher, who had studied at the Bhartendu Natya Akademi in Nakhlau. Some students had beaten him up, after which he had left the city for Mumbai. Having heard this, at once, Pakrasi Dada got up and said, 'He was indeed a big one, monkey!'

Past midnight, there would arrive at the Square, *hijra*s who had been refused payment for their services by the soldiers of the Central

Command at the Cantonment. They were beaten up and forced to flee after the sex and would thus come to the Square tearfully abusing the soldiers. They said that the government can only give food to the soldiers but can't provide for what *they* could do. 'Man' does not understand this fact actually but acts, for a brief while, as if he gets it. Till the 'work' is not done, he perceives the *hijra* as a desirable woman. As soon as there is the inevitable 'release' following the sex, the *hijra*s, for him, become the laughable, dirty, middling-substance that he uses and let's go. There would also come to the Square young boys who would sniff petrol stolen from scooters. They told horrible tales of the great lusts of the greats in the society. There would also come students enamoured of seeing the sights of the city during the stunned night for they just could not hide their surprise at the fact that something that looked so ordinary and accessible during the day could transform into something so wonderful at night. Rani, the *duggi*, would come at any time. She wore anklets that produced a ringing sound with every step she took. She would bring out a glass from under the bright and loose *lehenga* that she wore and request, 'Dear, make a peg for me as well.'

Women who are in the business of selling their own bodies on the streets of Nakhlau, without letting any discretion or fear impede their way, are called *duggi*s. The customer has to work hard to gain access to the costlier prostitutes—*ekki*s, *begum*s and *dahla*s—but he himself is easily spotted by *duggi*s and *chakka*s. Rani lived with her mother under the stairs of the Coffee House's verandah. She would get pregnant every year. When the bulge in her belly couldn't be concealed any longer and became easily noticeable, she would disappear for a while. After a month or two, the foetus would either itself give way or someone would take away the newborn from her. She would then return and resume her trade. The Elephant got her a job of selling newspapers in the afternoon on multiple occasions but she just could not sustain it beyond a brief period of time. The resultant losses had to be borne by the Elephant himself. Rani was squint-eyed and had chipped two of her incisors. The latter had created a gaping hole which made it appear as if she was smiling all the time. Every day, two or four young men got enticed by that smile. She felt a great sense of victory, a great satisfaction whenever she would catch someone superior to herself in her trap. Perhaps this is why she never gave up on this business and picked another trade. Drunk, she would either get lost in herself or begin to complain, 'Those two boys sitting at the garbage collection place are not paying me the money they owe.'

Once she realised that the mood at the gathering was gloomy, Rani would orchestrate a stratagem whose conclusion would be known to us already. Around the Square are three places where MLAs can stay—Dar-ul-shafa, Royal Hotel and OCR. After getting off from trains at night, most of those who come to stay at these places also come to the Square for some refreshment, usually, betel nut and cigarettes. Rani, having already reached the Square, would eye travellers in safari suits carrying briefcases or those wearing starched, white kurtas and tell the Elephant, 'Dear, do keep an eye. I am going now.' She would then start moving and walking around the target who, typically tired after having endured a long train-journey, wanted to sleep but couldn't. The sound from her anklets would generally form the backdrop in which the target and she spoke with each other, wordlessly. Her drama began only when the target started to negotiate the price and bargain. She would then start shouting as if she were completely helpless, 'You scoundrel! Rascal! You with the charred face! Don't you have a mother and sisters at home? My brothers, please come and see! He is creating such trouble for me. Please come.' Shocked and horrified at this sudden turn of events, the target would usually run away or be beaten black and blue by the two-three young boys who kept waiting for opportunities like this one to arise.

This trick, this plan that Rani employs could easily be called 'morality', which our society has been using since times immemorial. Once unachievable and impossible moral expectations are attached to someone, the easy-to-acquire skill to trap and hunt him has been developed to such an extent now that all of us have come to distinguish between right and wrong according to our own convenience and choice. Ajay Bhaiya, for instance, did not enjoy drinking and he was always looking for some dry accompaniment to go with it. He believed that morality provides sustenance and security. Much like animals change their colour, mimic the sound of others, act as if they are dead and produce poison and electricity within themselves to acquire these two things, the humans too forego their original character and seek to mingle with the grass, leaves and environment of society by acquiring behavioural traits that aren't at all their own. Indeed, morality is actually an invention of the animals and we have merely adopted it for ourselves.

The Elephant, at first, tried to control this unruly gathering by using a candle but was unsuccessful. Then, he adopted another ploy. Through the day, he would read poems, *ghazal*s and *nazm*s published in books and magazines and then copy the appropriate ones that could be used at night. Then, with the performers reclining on the plinth, the chosen verses were recited and discussed under the light of *shamaa*s which were hung as if a *mushaira* or some grand function was underway at the Square. Without showing any regard for the recital to reach its intended crescendo, Rajeev Deekshit would start singing and playing *tabla* with his hands on the bench. As this singing programme that paid great heed to the requests of all of its listeners moved ahead, embarrassed new singers would keep cropping up and join Rajeev. If Rajeev could not remember a song, he would inevitably find someone who sang one or two lines. Ajay Bhaiya could sing almost any song that had been picturised on Dev Anand. The problem, though, with poets and *shayar*s was that someone's hero and beloved was another's stupid fool. There was a wide gap between what he had written and how he had lived. As one stared into this hole pulled by the weight of one's relations and likes and dislikes, quite often, there was a chance that people could start hurling abuses at each other or come to blows.

On the other side of the Square, at the deck of Baba's tea-stall, 'devotional hymns' kept playing. By virtue of their sheer power and intensity, they could keep the nocturnals awake throughout the night. The Elephant had got Baba a tape cassette whose first song was '*Sarkai lyo khatiya, jara lage*' ('Move your cot closer to mine, oh darling! Come to me, for I feel so cold!'). When the deep-seated fantasies and lusts of the nocturnals, mixed with the waves of *Halahal*, escaped the underground and came to be expressed openly, then each one of them danced their hearts out. They swayed to the rhythm of Baba's songs played at full-volume and yet somehow stayed within a huge circle of benches that covered the entire road. They stopped only once they were bathed in sweat. If the dancing wasn't satisfying enough, they played a football-like game with empty beer cans or bottles of Coke.

On one of many such bacchanal nights, the Elephant winked while pointing towards Ajay Bhaiya and said, 'Let's test him tonight'.

Whenever the Square got a visitor who wasn't really the type who could frequent the place, he was, at the very outset, subjected to a madness test. But our kind consideration had caused considerable delay in Ajay Bhaiya's case. A motorcycle race in which the 'subject' would be sitting pillion, held at the empty Ring Road outside the city, was the chosen method for the madness test. If the man was happy at a speed greater than ninety kilometres an hour, then he would be accepted as mad. Otherwise, declared a fake, a poser, he would be taken by the scruff of his neck and forced out of the scene. There was a great disagreement though over this method of testing madness. I felt that when a man is subjected to great risk and danger, we can surely estimate his bravado but cannot say anything about his madness. Most people, on account of some fear or the other, fall prey to mental imbalance. As no one gave two hoots about my argument that there is no point in subjecting an already scared man to greater fear and risk, it became clear that the thrill for speed held sway over logic at the Square.

One night, on the race, I took Ajay Bhaiya to Chinhat, an area twenty kilometres away. Once we reached the place, with great concern and pity, he said to me, 'You controlled the motorcycle so well. Kindly accept my gratitude.'

He had passed the test and was accepted by the nocturnals at the Square.

We had adopted an absolutely despicable and cheap method to test him. This became known when he went with me to get alcohol for the first time. The weight in our pockets usually determined our access to liquor once the shops had closed. If we had money, we went to Lakdi Mohal or Subhash Mohal at the Cantonment. There, some retired soldiers had collected a stock of rum by controlling the quota meant for some serving soldiers. They would sell from this stock to make a profit for themselves. Sometimes, we would also meet some large-hearted fellow who would serve us a couple of pegs without charging a single penny, in exchange for some quality conversation and talk. When money was scarce, we would knock on the doors of stores that sold country-liquor. If there was an even greater scarcity, we would go to the by-lanes of Old Nakhlau where raw alcohol, brewed illegally on the sandy banks of the Ganga at Unnao, would be sold in empty bottles of English liquor.

It wasn't money that made liquor available at country-shops, it was actually something else. Within their dark windows used to be a small skylight which when knocked upon continuously for about ten minutes would evoke a sleepy but wry and heavy response from the inside, 'Bloody hell! How much do you want that you have been rustling your bangles so hard?'

'Five, white.'

'Get the change out.'

Having taken the money, he would throw the pouches out and say, 'You mother's dick! Bloody drunkards! Don't even let me sleep and just come whenever they like.'

Once this happened, the window would never open again, no matter how hard one tried knocking or doing anything else.

On one occasion when it was raining, the entire house went to drag the foul-mouth out of his tiny hole. With the help of a jack-and-wrench borrowed from the workers who were laying underground wiring-lines by cutting across the road, the shutter was broken down. Tired from the effort and breathing heavily, by the time we reached inside, he had not only escaped through some unknown route but also carried away the quota that was meant to be cleared during the night. Around filthy and dilapidated benches, we saw that there lay empty pouches, bottles, rotting leftover food, sputum and a rush of frothing urine. The picture these presented to the eyes was truly horrifying. We all stared at each other with blank gazes for a while and then returned.

One night, Ajay Bhaiya and I were returning successfully from our expedition. We had asked fellow nocturnals for the way to a derelict country liquor stall situated behind the muddy pothole that lay beside the trucks lined up near Charbagh Railway Station. It must have been around 2:30 or 3:00 am. A group of excited teens and kids was passing through from the other side of the road, beside the Udayganj drain. The boys held sticks and batons in their swaying arms. To our surprise, we noticed that some of them were holding a man with their arms and legs. He was clinging on, somehow and he didn't have a single piece of clothing on himself. He spotted us and broke the silence that the night had cast by pleading loudly, 'Oh my lords! Please save me! They are going to kill me!'

The voice was recognisable. I stopped. He ran a *dhaba* in front of the Charbagh Station. His face was swollen, an eye was battered and closed and he was bleeding from his mouth. One could easily observe the beating-marks that had appeared on his back and thighs. The boys had thrashed him thoroughly. He tried to fold his hands that seemed to hang loosely in the air and said, 'Save me, brother! I will close my hotel and leave for my village.'

Even before we could ask anything, the boys dragged out a nine-year-old from within their group and presented him to us. They said, 'Look at what the scoundrel has done! The boy's cheek has been bitten so hard that it bleeds! This man abuses those who work at the hotel. We will kill him tonight and throw the body into the drain!'

The boy, wearing a tattered vest, hid his cheek with his palm and stared at all of us. He was clearly bewildered. I tried to persuade them, 'If he dies, all of you will go to jail. Let us all go and let the police take care of him.'

The leader laughed and said, 'That would be even better as we would become the mafia once we are in jail. Then this bastard will pay taxes to us.'

'Take him back. I will send the police after you.'

'He feeds them for free, brother. I swear the police will do nothing.'

After much pleading, coaxing and cajoling, the boys relented on the condition that they would kill him if he did not close the hotel immediately and leave for his village on that very day. As soon as they placed him on the ground, he, in his stark-naked state, ran up to the drain's slope.

On the way back, Ajay Bhaiya said, 'This happens because all of you have eroticised everything, filled everything with sex. So, everything has a gender—the sun, the earth, water, air, pillar and the door. "Man" is only exploiting the sex that is hidden in everything.' One day, a reporter at the office informed me, 'That mad fellow who used to come here earlier has met with an accident. He is seriously injured and is lying at the crossing. The police crime-bulletin telecast last night also mentioned the incident and there his full name was reported as 'Ajay Kumar Srivastava'.

I rushed to the spot along with a friend. He was lying on the road at Akbari Gate, among the beggars who were attempting to fight the winter by sitting around a small bonfire. Some heavy vehicle must have hit him for he had broken his head. Skin from his foot had also grated off. He had lost two-three teeth and could not lift one of his hands. While anti-tetanus injections were being administered to him at a nearby clinic, a thought crossed my mind. I wondered how this man could traverse two worlds—one, within society and the other, outside it—with so much ease? I reasoned that, perhaps, the desire to return to a place still persisted in him.

He was admitted to the general ward of the Civil Hospital after his arm had been plastered and feet strung together. Compared with the other patients there, he was taken care of more earnestly, for the reporters who looked after the medical beat often arranged food, medicines, blanket and check-ups for him in consultation with the doctors. He received greater attention also because he spoke with the doctors in English.

I wanted his wounds to heal only gradually so that he could survive the remainder of the winter with the regular food and heater's warmth provided by the hospital. But he was recovering with disappointing alacrity. About ten days had passed since he had been admitted. Saved from the exposure to ash, dust and filth, the lines on his face had begun to be visible. His palms, as yellow as ripe maize from the sustained exposure to small flaming fires, had started to pale in colour. With his clean *kurta-pyjama* and with some glow restored in his eyes, he had now come to resemble the other patients in the ward. And, just at that time, he gave us the slip at night. Intensive and detailed searches yielded no result. Everyone at the Pioneer Square, including Rani, was asked to keep an eye out for him but he wasn't found anywhere.

Meanwhile, a man named Sateesh Ranjan began to call and ask about him. He wanted to meet him. I wondered why. Ranjan responded, 'Ajay was my classmate.'

Ranjan was an industrialist, the brother of the Home Secretary Rajeev Ranjan Shah. Some journalist or policeman had told him that Ajay Kumar was in touch with me. He came in a big car along with his son. The search for the absconder then became organised and systematic. There was no news on the first night. On the second night, he was found clad in the red hospital blanket, enjoying the warmth from a small bonfire on Cantonment Road. The plaster on his arm had turned the colour of his skin.

'How are you, Ajay?', shouted Sateesh Ranjan but his voice got crushed under the weight of his own emotions.

'... My son! ... He is your uncle! Come on, greet him. Say "*Namaste*".'

The boy, alarmed by the appearance of this man, tried to hide behind the driver. He put his hands into the pockets of his shorts and said, '*Naste*'.

If one looked at Ajay Bhaiya's face, one felt that he was used to meeting his friend Sateesh Ranjan almost every day. It was as if, while crossing the road, they had met again and had decided to enjoy the warmth of the bonfire. Meanwhile, Sateesh Ranjan reined his emotions, thanked me and left along with him in his car.

He was kept in the guest room of a bungalow in Aliganj. Before he began to enjoy the soft, white bed, the spotless, white pillows and curtains and the warmth from the sharply coloured quilt, a servant ruled over his nails. A barber was called to shave his beard and thick hair. To rid him of germs, a couple of servants bathed him thrice in warm water mixed with a skin cleanser. A doctor came and gave him a thorough check-up. Everything, he reported, was normal but Sateesh Ranjan felt that compared with the situation in Allahabad when Ajay and he were friends, everything was now anything but normal.

It is supposed that the great cleansing and scrubbing that he went through after so many years would have had a powerful impact on him. He must have shrunk a little for some energy would have escaped from his body pores that would have been unlocked after a long time. The mouth of the colliery within his head, usually hidden under the thick mass of his hair, would have been opened. The entry of fresh air, light and other waves and currents into his body would have allowed him to resume contact with the entire universe. Nonetheless, the result was that he dozed off even before he could have dinner and continued to sleep for four days. The doctor continued to report that everything was normal and alright.

After he woke up, he made someone call me and got it conveyed that he was doing absolutely fine and that I should visit him at the earliest. I was thoroughly engaged at the Pioneer, though, and couldn't go.

Presently, the season altered, and one began to feel the warmth of the summer wind behind one's ears. One fine day in the month of March, I was on my way to the office. Sunlight was skimming the waters of the Gomti river. The seriousness that marks the winters had disappeared and the westerly gave an abrupt shake to everything that it encountered in its way. From a distance, I could see a man looking for something on the banks of the river. The grass and the weed reached up to his knees. Dogs were barking at him. The outline seemed vaguely familiar. It is him, I realised suddenly. After parking my bike at the bank, I waded into the grass. It was him, engrossed with something.

He smiled at my sudden appearance. Then he laughed as he put his hand on my shoulder and said, 'You, my friend ….'

I asked, 'You ran away from the bungalow too! Why?'

He stared into my eyes and vigorously moved his hands up and down as if to indicate that I should never even broach that subject. 'Why …'

'What happened?'

He turned his palm towards the grass and it glistened in the sunlight being reflected from the river water. He exclaimed, 'Hunh! … *This* pleasure, the pleasure *here* cannot be found anywhere else, my friend.'

At that moment, the fresh green grass on the bank was laughing like madmen do. It was to disappear in a few days though, bound to be burnt down by the summer heat, and be extinguished.

ABOUT THE EDITOR AND CONTRIBUTORS

Editor

Brinda Bose teaches at the Centre for English Studies at Jawaharlal Nehru University, New Delhi. Her research interests are in modernisms, gender/sexuality studies, feminist and queer theory, cinema and humanities studies. She co-founded/co-steered *MargHumanities*, a platform for conversations on the arts and literature, in and outside the university (2011–2016). Her book, *The Audacity of Pleasure: Sexualities, Literature and Cinema in India*, was published in 2017. She is the editor of *Translating Desire* (2002) and *Gender and Censorship* (2006) and the co-editor of *Interventions: Feminist Dialogues on Third World Women's Literature and Film* (1998) and *The Phobic and The Erotic: The Politics of Sexualities in Contemporary India* (2003). She has done critical editions of Woolf's *Mrs Dalloway*, Conrad's *Heart of Darkness* and Carroll's *Through the Looking-Glass,* and a critical anthology on the early novels of Amitav Ghosh. Her chapbook, *Calcutta, Crow and Other Fragments*, was published in 2020. She is currently working on the politics and erotics of avant-garde modernisms, and editing an anthology on the avant-garde in India.

Contributors

Al-Khoder Al-Khalifa is a Syrian researcher and currently a doctoral scholar at the Centre for English Studies at Jawaharlal Nehru University, New Delhi. In 2016 he completed his Masters in English from the University of Delhi on a scholarship from the Indian Council for Cultural Relations (ICCR). After completing his BA degree in English in Syria, Khalifa worked there as a Teaching Assistant at the Department of English, Furat University, from 2010 to 2014, where his research interests included modern American literature, Arab writers in the diaspora, Arab modernism and translation. Currently, his focus is on un/translated contemporary literature from the Arab *Mashriq*, war literature, avant-gardism, political aesthetics, death and bare life. In his current PhD work, Khalifa is studying the political aesthetics of death and bare life in the context of the Arab *Mashriq* by engaging with contemporary texts emerging from the long-disturbed areas of Iraq, Syria, Lebanon and Palestine.

Anil Yadav is a senior journalist with the online Hindi edition of BBC. He is the author of *Woh Bhi Koi Des Hai, Maharaj!* (translated into English by Anurag Basnet as *Is That Even a Country, Sir!*, 2012), *Nagarvadhuwen Akhbar Nahi Padhti* (City Brides Don't Read the Papers) and a collection of essays *Sonam Gupta Bewafa Nahi Hai* (Sonam Gupta Is Not Unfaithful). He lives in Lucknow and New Delhi, India.

Aveek Sen is a writer, teacher and collaborator in the arts. He was associate editor (editorial pages) at *The Telegraph* and lecturer in English at St Hilda's College, Oxford. He read English literature at Jadavpur University, Calcutta and University College, Oxford, where he took a First as a Rhodes Scholar. He won the 2009 Infinity Award for writing on photography given by the International Center for Photography, New York. He has collaborated as a writer with Dayanita Singh, Roni Horn, On Kawara, Dominique Gonzalez-Foerster, Moyra Davey, Bharti Kher and Subodh Gupta.

Charles Russell is Professor Emeritus of English and American Studies at Rutgers University, where he was Director of American Studies and Associate Director of the Institute on Ethnicity, Culture, and the Modern Experience. He also served as the Rutgers, Newark Associate Provost for Academic Affairs. He received his PhD in Comparative Literature from Cornell University. Among the eight books he has published are *Groundwaters: A Century of Art by Self-Taught and Outsider Artists* (2011); *Self-Taught Art: The Culture and Aesthetics of American Vernacular Art* (2001); *Poets, Prophets, and Revolutionaries: The Literary Avant-Garde from Rimbaud through Postmodernism* (1985); *The Avant-Garde Today: An International Anthology* (1981) and, co-edited with Professor Carol Crown, *Sacred and Profane: Personal Voice and Vision in Southern Self-Taught* Art (2007). He is currently at work on a book-length manuscript on the visual aesthetic.

Chinmaya Lal Thakur is a doctoral researcher in the Department of Creative Arts and English at La Trobe University, Melbourne. His work concerns the limits of subjectivity as inscribed in the novels of David Malouf. Postcolonial studies, Continental philosophy, novel-theory and modernist literatures constitute his research interests.

He holds an MPhil from the Centre of English Studies, Jawaharlal Nehru University for the dissertation, 'The Novel and Epistemological Critique: Reading Franz Kafka'. His essays and critical reviews have been published in several edited volumes and journals including *Journal of Postcolonial Writing*, *The Charles River Journal*, *South Asia Research*, and *Contemporary South Asia*. In 2018, he edited the anthology *Literary Criticism: An Introductory Reader* for Worldview Publications.

Eyal Amiran is Professor of Comparative Literature at UC Irvine and Editor of the journal *Postmodern Culture* (Johns Hopkins). He has published *Wandering and Home: Beckett's Metaphysical Narrative* (Penn State) and *Modernism and the Materiality of Texts* (Cambridge) and co-edited the collection *Essays in Postmodern Culture* (Oxford). His essays on the relation between contemporary literature and electronic culture have appeared in *Cultural Critique* (on 'pornocracy' in popular media), *Discourse* (on utopian digital architecture), *TDR* (on Stelarc), *Ex-position* (on 'the open' in the age of Big Data), *parallax* (on digital ontology and the echosphere) and elsewhere. He is working on a book on psychological ideas of politics in modern comics.

Geeta Patel is a Professor at the University of Virginia, Charlottesville, with three degrees in science and a doctorate from Columbia University, New York, in inter-disciplinary South Asian Studies (in Sanskrit and Urdu). She has published widely in both academic and popular venues and translated lyric and prose from Sanskrit, Urdu, Hindi and Braj. Her first monograph, *Lyrical Movements, Historical Hauntings: On Gender, Colonialism and Desire in Miraji's Urdu Poetry*, writes the history of Indian literary modernism through its harbinger Miraji. Her second book, *Risky Bodies & Techno-Intimacy: Reflections on Sexuality, Media, Science, Finance*, uses techno-intimacy as the locus for interrogating capital, science, media and desire. She is completing several other projects: a manuscript on the Muslim woman writer Ismat Chughtai; a manuscript on fantasies embedded in advertising titles *Billboard Fantasies*; a series of small books on the poetics of historical pensions, insurance, credit and debt. Her current research is on the ways in which the history of bacteriology and our relationship to our own bacterial life gives rise to our everyday violence. She and Meghan Hartman are also compiling a monograph of their new translations of Miraji's poetry. And she has recently started composing her own lyrics under the lockdown in India.

Heidi Grunebaum is a writer, scholar and poet. She is director of the Centre for Humanities Research at the University of the Western Cape where she convened a research platform on Aesthetics and Politics. Grunebaum's work focuses on aesthetic and social responses to war and mass violence, the politics of memory in South Africa, Palestine/ Israel and Germany. She is author of *Memorializing the Past: Everyday Life in South Africa after the Truth and Reconciliation Commission* (2011), co-editor of *Uncontained: Opening the Community Arts Project Archive* (2012), *Athlone in Mind* (2017) and the poetry chapbook *Book of the Missing* (2019). With Mark J. Kaplan, she made the documentary film, *The Village Under the Forest* (2013). She is currently working on a collection of essays on nonpartitioned aesthetics and a film on the politics of race, racism and Jewish memory in contemporary Germany.

Laura Piippo completed her doctoral thesis on the poetics and affects of a prominent Finnish experimental novel *Neuromaani* (2012) by Jaakko Yli-Juonikas, at the University of Jyväskylä, Finland. This study and her other projects focus mainly on experimental and avant-garde literature, the concept of assemblage and theories of transtextuality on different literary platforms, both analogue and digital. Her peer-reviewed articles, edited volumes and special issues on these topics have been published (or are forthcoming) both in English and in Finnish. Currently, Piippo works as a University Lecturer at the Department of Music, Art and Culture Studies in the University of Jyväskylä, where she has been teaching literature and literary theory since 2012. Previously she has also worked as a researcher in the consortium *The Literary in Life: Exploring the Boundaries between Literature and the Everyday* (Academy of Finland, 2015–2019) and as a visiting early career researcher at the University of Amsterdam in 2016.

Michael Levenson is William B. Christian Professor of English at the University of Virginia and author of *A Genealogy of Modernism* (Cambridge University Press, 1984), *Modernism and the Fate of Individuality* (Cambridge University Press, 1990), *The Spectacle of Intimacy* (Princeton University Press, co-author Karen Chase, 2000), *Modernism* from Yale University Press (2011) and editor of the *Cambridge Companion to Modernism* (2000, 2nd edition 2011). His more recent book is *The Humanities and Everyday Life* (Oxford, 2018). He has published essays in such journals as *ELH*, *Novel*, *Modernism/Modernity*, *The New Republic*, *Wilson Quarterly*, *Raritan*; among his public lectures are those at Harvard, Yale, University of Chicago, Johns Hopkins, Berkeley, Delhi University and Oxford University. At the University of Virginia, Professor Levenson has been chair of the English Department and is the founding director of the Institute of the Humanities and Global Cultures, where he built partnerships with institutes in Nanjing, Shanghai, Delhi, Oxford and London.

Moinak Biswas is Professor of Film Studies at Jadavpur University, Kolkata. He is also a Coordinator at the Media Lab, a centre for experiments in digital forms, at Jadavpur. His books include *Apu and After: Revisiting*

Ray's Cinema (2005) and *Ujan gang baiya* (1990). He edits the *Journal of the Moving Image*, and was one of the founding editors of *BioScope, South Asian Screen Studies*. Apart from having written and co-directed the award-winning Bengali film *Sthaniya Sambaad* (2010), he created the installation *Across the Burning Track*, which was commissioned for the 11th Shanghai Biennale in 2016.

Rahul Sen taught courses on critical writing, feminism, queer theory and literature at Ashoka University for four years. He has joined the English Department at Tufts University, Boston, from Fall 2020 as a graduate student for doctoral research. His areas of interest revolve around literary theory, sexuality studies, and cinema. Rahul mostly revels in the kitsch and the camp; his secret fantasy is being Clarissa Dalloway, who throws successful evening parties for his friends. Not only will he buy the flowers himself, but also cook—which is the other art that he has begun to master.

Rajarshi Dasgupta teaches at the Centre for Political Studies, Jawaharlal Nehru University, New Delhi. Formerly a Fellow at the Centre for Studies in Social Sciences Calcutta, he did his BA from Presidency University, Kolkata, MA and MPhil from Jawaharlal Nehru University and his DPhil from Oxford University. Dasgupta mainly teaches courses on Marxism, biopolitics and political theory. His research and publications address the history of Indian radicalism, the relations of culture and politics and the distinctive features of urbanisation in South Asia. Some of his publications include 'Ethics and Politics' in P.K. Datta and S. Palshikar eds, *Indian Political Thought*, 'Rhyming Revolution: Marxism and Culture in Colonial Bengal' in *Studies in History* and 'The Ascetic Modality: A Critique of Communist Self-fashioning' in Menon, Nigam and Palshikar eds, *Critical Studies in Politics*. His latest publications are 'Frontier Urbanism: Urbanisation beyond Cities in South Asia' in *Economic & Political Weekly*, 'The Consolidation of BJP: Analysing Lok Sabha Elections 2019' in *Socialist Perspective* and 'Capital in Bangla: Postcolonial Translation of Marx' in Chakrabarty et al. eds, *Capital in the East: Reflections on Marx*.

Sophie Seita is an artist and academic working with text, sound and translation on the page, in performance and in other media. She is the author, most recently, of *My Little Enlightenment* (Pamenar, 2020) and *Provisional Avant-Gardes: Little Magazines from Dada to Digital* (Stanford University Press, 2019); the translator of Uljana Wolf's *Subsisters: Selected Poems* (Belladonna, 2017), and the editor of *The Blind Man* (Ugly Duckling Presse, 2017), named one of the Best

Art Books of 2017 by *The New York Times*. She works internationally on various projects and has performed at La MaMa Galleria, Bold Tendencies, the Royal Academy, the Arnolfini, Kunsthalle Darmstadt, Jawaharlal Nehru University (New Delhi), Raven Row, Parasol Unit, the Drawing School, Art Night London, and elsewhere. In 2019, she had a solo exhibition of text, videos, and performance props at [SPACE] Gallery London. Following her Junior Research Fellowship at Queens' College Cambridge, she is currently an Assistant Professor at Boston University and co-organises the Sound/Text seminar at Harvard. She is working on a number of projects: a book of lyric essays called *Lessons of Decal*; an academic trade book titled *Literary Live Art*, and a practice-based and speculative collaboration with musician Naomi Woo in the form of *The Minutes of the Hildegard von Bingen Society for Gardening Companions*.

Soumyabrata Choudhury currently teaches at the School of Arts and Aesthetics, Jawaharlal Nehru University, New Delhi. He has previously taught at CSSSC, Kolkata, and has been a fellow at the Centre for Studies in Developing Societies (CSDS), Delhi, and the Indian Institute of Advanced Studies (IIAS), Shimla. His book *Theatre, Number, Event: Three Studies on the Relationship of Sovereignty, Power and Truth* was published by IIAS, Shimla in 2013. His new book *Ambedkar and Other Immortals: An Untouchable Research Programme* came out in 2018.

Taylor Black is Assistant Professor of English at Duke University. He has published on twentieth-century American literature, popular music, gender and sexuality studies, queer theory, ontology and theories of becoming and, above all, the subject and practices of style in *Women's Studies Quarterly*, *American Quarterly*, *Discourse* and the *Journal of Popular Music Studies*. Black is the co-editor of the Spring 2016 issue of *WSQ*, 'Survival', with Frances Bartkowski and Elena Glasberg.

INDEX

M

N

O

P

W

Y

Z